PCI	a process capability index, p. 126
P_p	a process performance ratio, p. 134
P_{pk}	a centered performance ratio, p. 134
R	the range of a set of data, p. 24
$\bar{R}$	the Average Range, p. 44
$\tilde{R}$	the Median Range, p. 47, 228
s	the Standard Deviation for a set of data, p. 26
$\bar{s}$	the Average Standard Deviation, p. 57
s_n	the Root Mean Square Deviation of a set of data, p. 24
$s_{\bar{x}}$	the Standard Deviation of the Subgroup Averages, p. 59
SD(X) or σ	the standard deviation parameter for a theoretical distribution, p. 322
σ^2	the variance parameter of a theoretical probability distribution, p. 146
σ_θ	a generic dispersion parameter used by Shewhart, p. 60
$Sigma(X)$	a measure of dispersion for Individual Values, pp. 111, 244, 393
$Sigma(\bar{X})$	a measure of dispersion for Subgroup Averages, pp. 93, 244, 393
$Sigma(R)$	a measure of dispersion for Subgroup Ranges, pp. 93, 244, 393
t	Shewhart's multiplier for control chart limits, p. 60
τ	the Target value for a product quality characteristic, p. 143
$\bar{\theta}$	a generic location parameter used by Shewhart, p. 60
u_i	the Poisson Rate for the ith sample, p. 275
$\bar{u}$	the average rate of nonconformities per unit area of opportunity, p. 275
UCL	Upper Control Limit for a control chart, p. 44
UNPL	Upper Natural Process Limit, p. 46
USL	Upper Specification Limit, p.142
$\bar{X}$	the average of a set of data, p. 22
$\bar{\bar{X}}$	the Grand Average, the average of the Subgroup Averages, p. 44
$\bar{\tilde{X}}$	the average of a collection of subgroup medians, p. 232
X or X_i	a single measurement, p. 26
$\tilde{X}$	a median for a set of data, p. 22
x_{scrap}	the product dimension at which an item is scrapped, p. 147
XmR	symbol for Individual and Moving Range chart, p. 49
Y_i	a Binomial Count, p. 260
Z_L	the standardized distance between the Grand Average and the Lower Specification Limit, p. 123
Z_U	the standardized distance between the Grand Average and the Upper Specification Limit, p. 123

Understanding
Statistical
Process
Control

Second Edition

David S. Chambers
1917–1989

Emeritus Professor of Statistics
University of Tennessee, Knoxville

Close associate and Friend of Dr. W. Edwards Deming, David Chambers was a world renowned consultant and instructor in statistical process control. A Fellow of the American Society for Quality Control, he was also a past President, and past Board Chairman for that organization. He was a recipient of the Eugene L. Grant Award for his educational activities, and was an Academician in the International Academy for Quality. A list of his associates and former students would read like a who's who of the quality industry.

David Chambers was born in Clarksville Texas, and received his bachelor's and master's degrees from the University of Texas. He taught there from 1941 to 1947, and in 1947 became an Associate Professor of Statistics at the University of Tennessee. He was Professor of Statistics there from 1958 to 1981, when he retired in order to devote more time to teaching in industry.

In the words of Dr. Deming, "his loss is irreparable."

To the memory of David S. Chambers:

Mentor and Friend to so many who
understand statistical process control.

Understanding
Statistical
Process
Control

Second Edition

Donald J. Wheeler

David S. Chambers

SPC Press

Knoxville, Tennessee

SPC Press, Inc.
5908 Toole Drive
Knoxville, Tennessee 37919
(615) 584–5005
Fax (615) 588–9440

ISBN 0–945320–13–2

5 6 7 8 9 0

Contents

Contents

Contents

W. Edwards Deming

Photo © Helaine Messer

Foreword

by W. Edwards Deming

It is an honour to have the privilege to write a foreword for this book by my friend Dr. Donald J. Wheeler. The reader may wish to remember that Dr. Shewhart perceived two kinds of variation.

1. Variation from constant causes, the same causes from hour to hour, lot to lot, worker to worker. Dr. Shewhart's term was chance causes.

2. Variation from a special cause.

How did the problem arise? The management of the Western Electric Company, the Hawthorne Plant, Chicago, sought to achieve uniformity, so that a telephone company that bought their product could depend upon it. The aim was noble. Their methods, though, were folly. They took action, made some kind of a change at every sign of departure from uniformity. They were smart enough and honest enough to observe that their actions only made this worse. They sought help. The problem went to Dr. Shewhart in the Bell Telephone Laboratories, 463 West Street, New York, newly formed.

There are obviously two kinds of mistake to make in efforts to achieve uniformity.

Mistake 1. Attribute an outcome to a special cause of variation when actually it came from common causes of variation.

Mistake 2. Attribute an outcome to common causes of variation when actually it came from a special cause.

Both mistakes are costly. Anyone may set for himself a perfect record from this hour henceforth, never to make Mistake 1. Simple: attribute any outcome to common causes. In doing this, though, he will maximize his loss from Mistake 2. Likewise, anyone may set for himself a perfect record from this hour henceforth, never to make Mistake 2. Simple: attribute any outcome to a special cause. In doing this, though, he will maximize his loss from Mistake 1.

It would be good never to make Mistake 1 and never to make Mistake 2. This unfortunately is impossible.

Dr. Shewhart settled on a different aim: make Mistake 1 now and then. Make mistake 2 now and then, but regulate the frequencies of the two mistakes to achieve minimum economic loss from both mistakes. To this end, he gave to the world the control chart, with 3-sigma limits. The control chart does a marvelous job under a wealth of applications. It works.

Statistical control may be achieved by hunting down and identifying each special cause as a point goes outside the control limits, and taking appropriate action.

I need not emphasize here the advantage of having a process in statistical control. Costs are predictable with a high degree of belief. Limits of variation are predictable.

In closing, it is fitting to add my deep appreciation for the mathematical achievements of Dr. Wheeler. His understanding of theory, and his application, are guided by mathematical knowledge. It has been my privilege to learn from him.

W. Edwards Deming

Washington
8 June 1992

Preface to Second Edition

Statistical Process Control is, first and foremost, a way of thinking which happens to have some tools attached. By this I mean that there is a framework of ideas which make the statistical ideas relevant, understandable, and useful. Without this framework the tools and techniques simply cannot be used to full effectiveness. The aim of SPC is action to improve the underlying (causal) process, and this requires both an understanding of the process and an understanding of the way to use the tools and techniques of SPC for continual improvement of the system. We have attempted to illustrate these fundamental aspects of SPC in this text.

Inevitably, one never quite says all that one wants to say in a book. As both David Chambers and I taught out of the first edition we became aware of certain gaps and other things which we wished to revise at some point in the future. Therefore, we began to plan for this edition in 1987. Lists of topics were drawn up, and outlines of the proposed changes were drafted. This activity went on in the same informal manner that characterized our whole working relationship. Phone calls would be exchanged, and a consensus would develop as both of us used these tools and talked with others who used them. Thus, even though David Chambers did not participate in the actual drafting of this second edition, he did help to lay the foundation and set many of the priorities for the revisions herein.

I must also acknowledge the invaluable suggestions of Dr. Deming. These came both in the form of his comments on the first edition, and in his astute observations on the nature of statistical practice and the statistical method. Many of the significant improvements in this edition had their origin in these suggestions and observations.

Chapter One incorporates new material regarding Dr. Deming's contribution. This material includes some excerpts from his lectures in Japan in the 1950's, and some early forms of some of his famous graphics.

Chapters Three and Four have been totally reorganized. Chapter Three now introduces the computation of control chart limits for both Average and Range Charts and XmR Charts while Chapter Four covers the fundamental concepts behind Shewhart's charts. Among the topics in Chapter Four one will find the right and wrong ways of computing control chart limits, a discussion of why three-sigma limits are action limits, the effect of non-normality upon control charts, myths about control charts, and the four foundations of Shewhart's charts.

Chapter Five has had the section on rational subgrouping expanded. Not only does this chapter now include the rest of the story for the subgrouping example, but it also includes a new list of questions regarding the data and a discussion of the principles of rational subgrouping.

Chapter Six has been considerably revised and expanded. In addition to new material about the common numerical capability summaries this edition includes a graphic technique for displaying process capability. The fallacy of converting capability numbers into fractions nonconforming is explained, and a new section on World Class Quality explains both the Taguchi Loss Function and its implications for a manufacturing operation.

Chapter Eight includes a new technique for setting the process aim. This technique is based upon an *XmR* Chart, and is useful in those situations where one cannot obtain more than one value at a time.

Chapter Nine has been greatly expanded. In addition to the topics previously included, this chapter also covers the right and wrong ways of computing control limits for Charts for Individual Values, the construction of Moving Average charts, and guidelines for when to use the different charts for measurement data. Two new sections discuss the revision of control chart limits and updating limits. Finally, the last section of Chapter Nine explains the control chart constants in terms of basic quantities, and shows what these basic quantities are.

Chapter Ten has a new example of count data used with an *XmR* Chart, an expanded discussion of the limitations of the Binomial Probability Model, and a new flowchart for choosing which chart to use.

Chapter Twelve has had new material on Flowcharts and Pareto Charts inserted, along with new examples.

Chapter Thirteen was added to include several topics that will be of interest to the advanced student. These topics include interpreting skewness and kurtosis, the effect of variation upon a balanced system, and the last topic on which David Chambers and I collaborated: the characterization of batches of product. A brief discussion of Enumerative and Analytic Studies is included, along with some thoughts on the transformation of data.

In addition, new, and hopefully more instructive, exercises have been included throughout the book as appropriate. Complete answers for these exercises are included in the Appendix.

Finally, I must acknowledge the help which I have received in the preparation of this edition. Specifically, graphic and editorial help were provided by David Wheeler, Sheila Poling, and Frances Wheeler. Rough drafts were reviewed by Dr. Deming, Dr. Andrew Palm, Ray Phillips, and Kay Gordner. Their suggestions have made many improvements possible.

Donald J. Wheeler
16 January 1992

Preface to First Edition

Each of us has been engaged in teaching the concepts and techniques of statistical process control throughout the whole of our professional careers. Out of this experience, we have long felt the need for a book that explained both the use of the tools and the motivation behind the tools. This book is our attempt to fill this need.

We have tried to produce a book that will be understandable by the industrial practitioner who may have had little or no formal training in statistical techniques. To this end, we have relied upon graphs, examples and case histories. The graphs and examples are provided to facilitate the explanations of how the techniques work, and the case histories are provided to show how the techniques are used in context.

The emphasis upon the concepts that motivate and underlie the techniques is one of the unique aspects of this book. As many have observed, the techniques themselves are very simple. There is no great complexity about their structure or their use. Yet, in spite of this, many have had a difficult time using the techniques effectively. In our experience, these problems of implementation have centered around the conceptual basis for the techniques. Therefore, it is this conceptual basis that we have attempted to explain and reinforce.

This brings us to state the way the reader should approach this book. The examples and case histories are used to convey the complex issues involved in using control charts. Thus they form a very important part of the book, and should be studied carefully. We hope that the reader will endeavor to go beyond the specific information in each example to grasp the principles of the approach used. For it is only by grasping these principles that the reader can become equipped to handle various situations.

Finally, this book is incomplete. Many other things could (and probably should) be said, but an end must be made somewhere. We simply hope that what has been included will prove to be beneficial to those engaged in the struggle to increase quality and productivity.

David S. Chambers
Donald J. Wheeler
15 December 1985

Donald J. Wheeler

Donald J. Wheeler is a consulting statistician who had the great good fortune to have been an associate of David S. Chambers from 1970 to 1989. He has been teaching statistical process control since 1971, first at the University of Tennessee, and then in industry around the world. He has been actively engaged in consultation since the mid 1970's. Dr. Wheeler had the privilege of first hearing Dr. Deming's lectures in 1974, and has been a student of Dr. Deming's ever since. Periodically, from 1981 to the present, Dr. Wheeler has assisted Dr. Deming with his four-day seminars, and his own philosophy of process improvement rests firmly upon that of Dr. Deming. He is author or co-author of 6 books and over 60 articles. He has worked with all types of industries world-wide, and is in demand as a speaker both in the U.S. and abroad.

Dr. Wheeler graduated from the University of Texas, Austin, with a Bachelor's Degree in Physics and Mathematics, and holds M.S. and Ph.D. Degrees in Statistics from Southern Methodist University. From 1970 to 1982 he taught in the Statistics Department at the University of Tennessee. In 1982 he resigned from the university in order to spend more time teaching and consulting in business and industry. He currently lives in Knoxville, Tennessee.

Donald J. Wheeler

Walter A. Shewhart

In September 1960, a new definition of World-Class Quality was quietly introduced...

"On-Target with Minimum Variance."

Operating "On-Target" requires a different way of thinking about our processes.

*Operating with "Minimum Variance" is achieved only when
a process displays a reasonable degree of statistical control.*

Both of these concepts are revolutionary.

There are people who are afraid of clarity

because they fear that it may not seem profound.

Elton Trueblood

Chapter One

Two Approaches to Variation

One axiom has been apparent from the beginning of man's efforts to make things.

NO TWO THINGS ARE ALIKE.

Anyone who has ever tried to work with supposedly identical items will eventually come to this discovery, and that is why manufacturers generally appreciate this axiom. Yet recognition of variation is not enough. Something must be done about variation if parts are to fit together properly. Exactly what can and should be done is the topic of this book. If the managers of a company work together to implement the philosophy of operation outlined herein, the twin goals of increased productivity and virtually uniform product can be attained with today's technology and today's workforce.

1.1 The Engineering Concept of Variation

Prior to the Industrial Revolution manufacturing consisted of making things by hand. Each part was custom made to fit in with the other parts in each assembly. Of course, this made every product unique and expensive.

As early as 1793, Eli Whitney had the idea of the interchangeability of parts. While this idea was revolutionary, it was also hard to implement. The problem was how to make the parts interchangeable. Try as one might, the parts would not turn out to be identical. Therefore, manufacturers had to be content with making them similar. If the parts were similar enough, they would fit (most of the time) and the product would work (more or less). Since the economic benefits of this approach were so great for both the producer and the consumer, it became a way of life in the industrialized world. Specifications were developed in order to define how similar the parts had to be in order to "fit," and all variation was classified into one of two groups:

PERMISSIBLE: MEETING ENGINEERING REQUIREMENTS

EXCESSIVE: OUTSIDE OF ENGINEERING REQUIREMENTS

The object of this engineering concept of variation was clear. It was an attempt to define those parts that could successfully be used to build a functioning assembly. It was an effort to make the distinction between a "good part" and a "bad part." This concept did not help the producer make parts that met the requirements, nor did it help him discover why nonconforming product was produced. All that could be done with this concept of variation was to use it at the end of the production line to sort the "good parts" from the "bad parts." As a result, the typical manufacturing operation became one of fabrication, inspection, and rework.

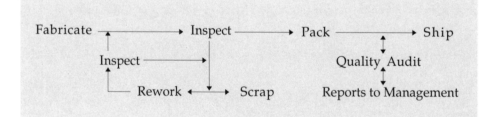

Figure 1.1: A Typical Western Manufacturing Process

The natural consequence of the engineering concept of variation was added complexity for the manufacturer. While manufacturers understood that this added complexity hurt productivity, they had no way to do anything about it. It was a way of life. Industry after industry had become accustomed to the process of making, inspecting, sorting and assembling "good parts." "Bad parts" were scrapped or reworked, and those that were reworked were inspected once again. As a result, manufacturing became an attempt to meet production requirements by using the sorting process. If enough "good" units were not produced, then marginal units would be used in order to meet the shipping schedule.

From this, the next step was the acceptance of "deviations" from the engineering requirements. This happened because it was often necessary to use all, or nearly all, of the parts produced in order to meet the production schedule. Thus, instead of using the specifications to ensure that all parts met requirements, manufacturers tried to change the specifications in order to use as many parts as possible. This was inevitable because the producer could not use the specifications to find out why nonconforming parts were produced. He was operating in the dark. All he could do was hope for the best, and when he failed, the consumer had to suffer the consequences.

Out of this conflict came a perpetual argument about how good parts had to be. Manufacturers always sought relaxed specifications. Customers demanded tighter specifications. Engineers were caught in the middle.

This conflict obscured the original and fundamental issue—how to manufacture parts with as little variation as possible. Manufacturers lost sight of the fact that if dimensions were virtually identical there would be no need to worry about "good" and "bad" pieces. There would be no need for sorting, for a scrap budget, or for rework. All the parts would fit together and work properly without the added expense and extra handling. This original objective was forgotten in the scramble to meet yesterday's production quotas with today's scrap and rework.

With processes that produce virtually uniform product, this scramble is no longer necessary. The whole production process looks different.

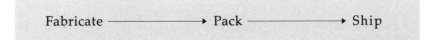

Figure 1.2: A Manufacturing Process Making Virtually Uniform Product

A state of virtually uniform product can be achieved only through the careful study of the sources of variation in a process, and through action by the management to reduce, or eliminate entirely, sources of extraneous or excessive variation.

This idea is a completely new dimension in both management and manufacturing. Management's daily task must be to learn as much as possible about the sources of variation affecting the product, and then to take the necessary steps to reduce the variation.

Unless this is done the old method of inspect and sort, rework and resort, will guarantee a lack of progress, low productivity, and an increasingly noncompetitive position.

In this new pursuit of process improvement through reduced variation, the concepts and techniques created by Walter Shewhart, and expanded by W. Edwards Deming, are the most effective and powerful means for making the changes that are necessary for survival.

Dr. Shewhart originated the concept of "control" as applied to variation, and he developed a simple way to classify process variability. This classification is the first step on the road to reducing the variation in the product.

1.2 The Shewhart Concept of Variation

Based on his work at Bell Laboratories in the early 1920's, Dr. Shewhart looked at variability as being either within the limits set by chance, or outside those limits. If it was outside, he believed that the source of variability could be identified. This viewpoint had its basis in his studies of the laws of variation in nature. In these studies Dr. Shewhart used statistics to describe the way that variation affected sample outcomes. When he tried to apply the same principles to manufacturing data, he found that such data did not always behave the same way that natural data did. Out of this inconsistency he formulated a distinction which can be phrased as follows:

While every process displays variation,
some processes display controlled variation,
while others display uncontrolled variation.

Controlled Variation is characterized by a stable and consistent pattern of variation over time. Dr. Shewhart attributed such variation to "Chance" Causes.

Uncontrolled Variation is characterized by a pattern of variation that changes over time. Dr. Shewhart attributed these changes in the pattern of variation to "Assignable" Causes.

Consider a manufacturing process making a series of discrete parts, each with a measurable dimension or characteristic. Some of these parts are periodically selected and measured. These measurements vary because the materials, machines, operators and methods all interact to produce variation. Such "chance" variation is relatively consistent over time because it is the result of many contributing factors. Dr. Shewhart called these factors "Chance Causes," and thought of the resulting variation as "controlled variation." An idealized drawing of controlled variation is shown in Figure 1.3.

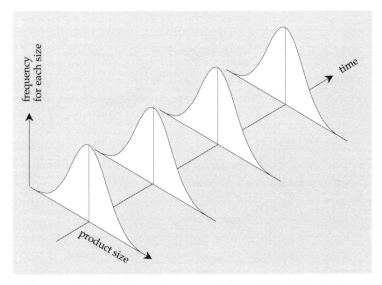

Figure 1.3 Idealized Concept of Controlled Variation

In addition to the multitude of Chance Causes, occasionally there are special factors that have a large impact on the product measurement. These factors might be machines out of adjustment, materials that are slightly different, methods that may be slightly altered, differences between workers, or differences in the environment created by inconsistency on the part of management. Shewhart argued that such factors were identifiable and that the impact of such "Assignable Causes" would be sufficient to create a marked change in the pattern of variation. A characterization of uncontrolled variation is shown in Figure 1.4.

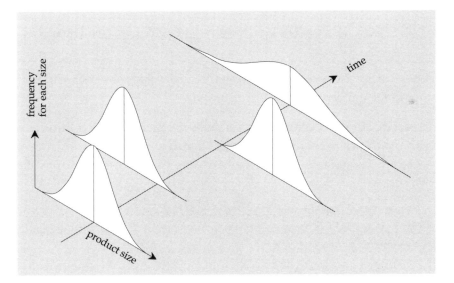

Figure 1.4: Characterization of Uncontrolled Variation

Not only would these Assignable Causes have a marked impact upon the variation of the data, but, according to Shewhart, they would also undermine predictability. On page 6 of *Economic Control of Quality of Manufactured Product* he noted:

> *"A phenomenon will be said to be controlled when, through the use of past experience, we can predict, at least within limits, how the phenomenon may be expected to vary in the future."*

So, while the essence of statistical control is predictability, the converse is implicit in this statement. A process which does not display statistical control will be unpredictable. Although the known inputs for such a process may remain unchanged, the output(s) for an unstable process will change in an unpredictable manner over time. While some correctly observe that such inconsistency of output argues that the process is not well-defined (and thus hardly deserves to be dignified by being called a "process") we shall for convenience continue to speak of a "process which displays a lack of control." When this is done nothing special is intended or implied by the use of the word "process."

All data streams may be viewed as the output of some process. If the data stream displays a reasonable degree of controlled variation over an extended period of time, then one can predict, within limits, how the data stream is likely to behave in the future. Planning, production, and management are all made easier by such predictability. On the other hand, when the data stream displays uncontrolled variation, then it is essentially impossible to predict what will occur in the future. Planning, production, and management will be filled with uncertainty. This is why Shewhart's distinction is essential for any interpretation of real world data.

1.3 Two Ways to Improve a Production Process

A consequence of Shewhart's classification is that there are two different ways to improve any production process.

When a process displays controlled variation, it should be thought of as stable and consistent. The variation present in the process consists only of that which is inherent in the process itself. Therefore, to reduce the variation, the process itself must be changed. Or, as Shewhart said:

> *"This state of control appears to be, in general, a kind of limit to which we may expect to go economically in finding and removing causes of variability without changing a major portion of the . . . process."* [1]

---

[1] *Economic Control of Quality of Manufactured Product*, p.25

On the other hand, if a process displays uncontrolled variation, it is changing from time to time. It is both inconsistent and unstable. This instability creates excessive variation that has nothing to do with the way the process was intended to operate. Therefore, the first step in improving the behavior of the process output is the identification of the Assignable Causes of excessive variation. If the Assignable Cause is detrimental, remove it. If the Assignable Cause results in a beneficial change, then try to make it part of the process. Shewhart gives several examples of how the removal of detrimental Assignable Causes leads to substantial improvement in the behavior of the process.[2]

Notice that these two approaches to process improvement are fundamentally different. One looks for ways to modify a process which is consistent and well-defined, while the other seeks to create a consistent process as an identifiable entity. The approach to use depends upon the type of variation displayed by the process. Thus, as a first step in any attempt to improve a process, the producer must determine whether or not the process displays uncontrolled variation. And the tool for the detection of uncontrolled variation is Shewhart's control chart.

Shewhart's control charts were based on a combination of probability theory and practical experience, and are effective at detecting the presence of uncontrolled variation in any process. Shewhart published his first control chart in 1924. By 1931, he had written *Economic Control of Quality of Manufactured Product.*

Unfortunately, Shewhart's ideas were not widely known or used in industry. While many in the Bell System knew of his work, few managers and engineers had any training in statistics. Therefore, the methods were mostly regarded as technical. They might be used in a special case, or to help in the solution of a difficult engineering problem, but industrial personnel had no overall view of how to use them throughout the plant, and managers had no idea how to use them to run the business. W. Edwards Deming was the exception.

1.4 Dr. W. Edwards Deming

Dr. Deming had worked with Walter Shewhart at Western Electric, and quickly realized the power of Shewhart's techniques. He began to talk of the need for American industries to make greater use of control charts in their manufacturing processes. In 1938, he arranged for Dr. Shewhart to give a series of lectures at the graduate school of the U.S. Department of Agriculture. These lectures were then edited by Deming and published in 1939 under the title *Statistical Method from the Viewpoint of Quality Control.*

The entry of the United States into World War II presented an opportunity for Dr.

---

[2] *Economic Control of Quality of Manufactured Product,* pp.18, 21, 29

Deming to push for the use of statistical methods in the manufacture of war materials. He helped organize and teach short courses for defense contractors at Stanford University. These courses spread to other centers, and by 1945 over 30,000 engineers and technicians had been given elementary training. Out of this nucleus of people the American Society for Quality Control was founded in February 1946.

However, in spite of the extensive nature of this training, and in spite of the spectacular reductions in both scrap and rework made possible by Shewhart's techniques, there was still no sense of how to use them to run the business. As Dr. Deming later said, "the courses were well received by the engineers, but management paid no attention to them."

Following the war, Dr. Deming periodically travelled to Japan to assist the Department of War in conducting surveys and studies. During these visits, he became close friends with several Japanese statisticians and scientists. During this same period when Deming was working in Japan the Union of Japanese Scientists and Engineers (JUSE) was formed and began to look for ways to help in the reconstruction of Japan. Dr. Nishibori, recalling Dr. Deming's encouragement, steered JUSE towards the use of statistical methods in the reconstruction effort. Thus, in late 1949 the managing director of JUSE, Mr. Koyanagi, invited Dr. Deming to come to Japan to teach statistical methods. Dr. Deming went in June, 1950. The class in Tokyo had 230 students. The class in Fukuoka had 110. Yet Dr. Deming felt a sense of despair. In his journal he wrote:

"They were wonderful students, but on the first day of the lectures a horrible thought came to me. 'Nothing will happen in Japan; my efforts will come to naught unless I talk to top management.' By that time I had some idea of what top management must do. There are many tasks that only the top people can perform ... I knew that I must reach top management. Otherwise it would just be another flop as it had been in the United States."

By asking friends, Dr. Deming was finally placed in contact with Mr. Ichiro Ishikawa, the founder of the Kei-dan-ran, an association of Japanese executives. Following three sessions with Dr. Deming, Mr. Ishikawa summoned 45 of these industrialists to meet with Dr. Deming. In this meeting and the follow-up sessions Dr. Deming was able to convince these leaders that they needed to try these new techniques for running their businesses. When Deming returned to Japan in the following years, these same executives were able to show him many notable successes. In fact, several of these executives were personally involved in the work. As Dr. Deming continued to work with these executives they developed a broad understanding of the need to continually redesign and refine their processes and products. The methodology of these efforts for continual improvement was embodied in what the Japanese call the "Deming Cycle." Thus by combining this cycle with Shewhart's categorical description of variation, the Japanese turned Deming's road to continual improvement into a reality.

The lectures given by Dr. Deming during these visits to Japan contained several themes that are still found in his lectures today. Among these basic themes is the "Production Viewed as a System" concept. The following excerpt from the introduction to one of his Japanese lectures shows this concept in its early form.[3]

"Now let me tell you what I mean by statistical techniques applied in all stages of production. In any manufacturing plant, raw materials come in, and product flows out. ... There will be a chain of production, and to make the problem simple enough for me to deal with in one lecture, I shall draw a diagram (Fig. 1).

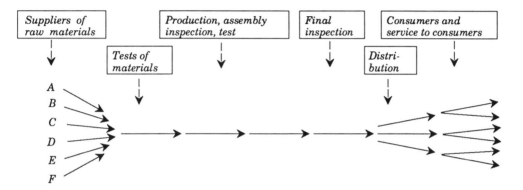

Figure 1.5: Dr. Deming's Figure 1

"By statistical quality control, I mean statistical work in all these stages of production."

Another of these basic themes is what Dr. Deming calls the Shewhart Cycle. While the concept expressed below was implicit in Dr. Shewhart's 1938 lectures,[4] Dr. Deming has popularized it to the extent that it is more widely known as the Deming Cycle. The following excerpt from the introduction to one of his Japanese lectures shows that this idea was fully formed over 40 years ago!

THE OLD WAY

"Manufacturers used to think of manufacturing in three steps, as shown in Fig. 2. Success depended on guess-work—guessing what type and design of product would sell, how much of it to make. In the old way, the three steps of Fig. 2 are completely independent.

---

[3] Material on pp.9-10 from Cecelia Kilian, *The World of W. Edwards Deming, Second Edition*, 1992.
[4] *Statistical Method from the Viewpoint of Quality Control*, p.45.

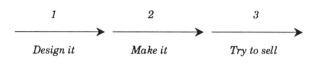

Figure 1.6: Dr. Deming's Figure 2

THE NEW WAY

"In the new way, management introduces, through consumer research, a 4th step, and runs through the four steps in a cycle, over and over as in Fig. 3, and not in the line of Fig. 2.

1. Design the product (with appropriate tests)

2. Make it, test it in the production line and in the laboratory

3. Put it on the market

4. Test it in service, through market research, find out what the user thinks of it, and why the non-user has not bought it

5. Re-design the product, in the light of consumer reactions to quality and price
Continue around and around the cycle....

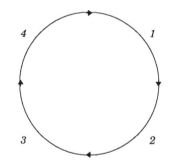

Figure 1.7: Dr. Deming's Figure 3

"A still better way is to begin the manufacturing and marketing of a product on a pilot scale, and to build up its production on a sound economic basis, only as fast as market conditions indicate, re-designing the product from time to time in the light of consumer needs and reactions."

Those who have attended any of Dr. Deming's lectures in the 1990's will immediately notice how up-to-date these excerpts are. These concepts are a key part of the message. They are basic to the control chart approach. Statistical Process Control has always been, first and foremost, a way of thinking which happened to have some techniques attached. Without the right concepts—without an understanding of "Production Viewed as a System," and without an understanding of how to use the Deming Cycle for continual improvement—the techniques are of little use.

Dr. Deming later characterized the theme of these Japanese lectures as follows: "It is good management to reduce the variation of any quality characteristic (say thickness, or measure of performance), whether this characteristic be in a state of control or not, and even when few or no defectives are being produced."[5]

"Zero defects" is not good enough. Industry must do more than merely meet specifications. Management must learn to study the process. Products should be constantly improved by searching out the sources of variation and eliminating them. The charts should be used as a guide to pinpointing these sources. As the variation in the process is reduced, the parts will be more nearly alike, and the products will work better. This is the message Dr. Deming took to Japan in 1950. The Japanese understood the message, and have been successfully implementing it ever since.

1.5 The Two Alternatives

As philosophical guides for manufacturing the engineering concept of variation and Shewhart's concept of variation have nothing in common. They have different objectives and different results. The engineering concept of variation has the object of meeting specifications. This naturally results in products that vary as much as possible, because anything within "specs" is considered "good enough." In contrast, the object of Shewhart's concept is process consistency, and this naturally results in products that are as consistent as possible. Therefore, it makes no sense to try to reconcile these two concepts of variation. Management must adopt one or the other as a guiding principle: mere conformance to specifications, or continual process improvement.

Management has been trying the first alternative since the beginning of the industrial revolution. After almost 200 years, the goal has not been met. The legacy of focusing solely upon conformance to specifications has been a lack of progress. There is no reason to believe it will be different in the future.[6]

On the other hand, the Japanese experience has proven the effectiveness of continual improvement of processes. By applying Shewhart's concepts, Japanese manufacturers have relentlessly improved their quality and increased their productivity. As a result, conformance to specifications has become no more than a benchmark on the path of continual improvement.

Thus we come to the paradox. As long as management has the conformance to specifications as its goal, it will be unable to reach that goal. If the actions of management signal

---

[5] W.E. Deming, *Interfaces*, 1975, Vol. 5, No.4.

[6] Larry Sullivan of Ford Motor Company observed that in a study of 4583 processes, half of the processes were not able to meet specifications, and 42 percent displayed evidence of a lack of statistical control. "Reducing Variability: A New Approach to Quality," *Quality Progress*, July, 1984.

that meeting specifications is satisfactory, the product will invariably fall short. Total conformance to specifications comes only by focusing on the continual improvement of processes. Thus, it is only when management supports, in both word and deed, the goal of continual improvement, that it will begin to see increases in both quality and productivity.

1.6 The Necessity of Control Charts

If continual process improvement is the goal, how is progress to be measured? The production of 100% conforming product is one benchmark. Achieving a state of statistical control for the process is another. Neither of these achievements is permanent. Both are subject to reversal. Taken together these process characteristics identify four possible states. Each and every production process may be characterized as falling in one of these four states.

The Ideal State

The first of these four possibilities is the Ideal State. A process in this state is in statistical control and is producing 100 percent conforming product. This complete conformity to specifications implies that all of the product is suitable for its intended purpose. Being in statistical control means that the variation present in the product stream is consistent over time. Such a process will continue to produce nothing but good product hour after hour, day after day, week after week, as long as it remains "in control." Clearly this would be an ideal state for any process.

How does a process get to be in this Ideal State? Only by satisfying four conditions:

1. The process must be inherently stable over time.

2. The manufacturer must operate the process in a stable and consistent manner. The operating conditions cannot be selected or changed arbitrarily.

3. The process average must be set and maintained at the proper level.

4. The natural process spread must be less than the specified tolerance for the product.

When a process satisfies these four conditions, the manufacturer can be confident that nothing but conforming product is being shipped. Whenever one of these conditions is not satisfied, the possibility of shipping nonconforming product exists. For reasons that will be explained below, the only way that a manufacturer can know that these four conditions apply to his process, and the only way that he can maintain these conditions day after day, is by the use of process control charts.

Therefore, if a manufacturer has a process that is operating in the Ideal State, and if he wants it to continue to operate in that state, he will be using control charts to become aware of problems before they are severe enough to result in nonconforming product.

Moreover, once a process is in the Ideal State, the continued use of control charts will naturally result in continuing process improvement. This will lead to ever more uniform product, which will yield lower costs and greater productivity. Examples of just how the control charts make this possible are given in Chapter Seven.

The Threshold State

The second of these four categories is the Threshold State. A process in this state will display a reasonable degree of statistical control, but it will be producing some nonconforming product. As before, the fact that the process displays statistical control means that the variation in the product stream is consistent over time. Hour after hour a consistent pattern of variation is present in the output of the process, and this consistency will continue as long as the process remains "in control." When such consistency is seen in a process that is producing some nonconforming product, the producer can count on producing the same amount of nonconforming product day after day until he finds a way to change the process or to change the specifications.

The traditional solution of 100% inspection is not satisfactory because it is always imperfect. As long as any nonconforming product is produced, some will be shipped. Screening only reduces the amount of nonconforming product shipped. It cannot eliminate it entirely. The real solution is to stop making the nonconforming product. To do this with a process that is in the Threshold State, the producer will have to modify the process *because the process is already operating as consistently as possible!*

If the nonconformity occurs because the manufacturer is unable to set the process average properly, then a relatively simple procedure may be all that is needed (see Chapter Eight).

On the other hand, if the nonconformity occurs because the natural variation in the process exceeds the specified tolerance, the producer must either change the specifications or change the process variation. If he decides to change the specifications, he will have to get the customer to agree to the change. Most customers are reluctant to agree unless they can be convinced that the producer does indeed have a stable and consistent process. Thus, the control charts are the key to any success in getting the specifications relaxed.

If the producer decides to try to reduce the process variation, he will have to modify the process itself. Moreover, different modifications will have different effects, so the producer will need to evaluate these effects. Once again control charts will provide the necessary information. Therefore, process control charts not only help the producer achieve a stable and consistent process, but they also help in moving the process from the Threshold State to the Ideal State.

The Brink of Chaos

The third state is the Brink of Chaos. Processes in this state are out of statistical control even though they are producing 100% conforming product.

Many people find this combination hard to imagine because they are accustomed to thinking that any process which makes 100% conforming product is okay. In one sense they are right. As long as the process is producing 100% conforming product there will be no problem with rejected shipments. But this happy circumstance is not likely to last indefinitely, for the fact that the process is out of control means that the pattern of variation in the product stream is inconsistent over time. The process is unstable, and this instability will continually change the product characteristics.

The problem with any process that is out of control is that it is subject to the effects of Assignable Causes. These effects can best be thought of as changes in the process that apparently occur at random intervals. So while the conformity to specifications may lull the producer into thinking all is well, the Assignable Causes will continue to change the process until it will eventually produce some nonconforming product. The producer will suddenly discover that he is in trouble, yet he will have no idea of how he got there, and no idea of how to get out.

These sudden panics occur because, despite appearances to the contrary, a process on the Brink of Chaos is not under the control of the manufacturer. The Assignable Causes "control" what the process will produce by determining when the process average or process dispersion will change. Thus, there is no way to predict what such a process will yield tomorrow, or next week, or even in the next hour. The change from 100% conforming product to some nonconforming product can come at any time, without the slightest warning. When this change occurs the process will be in the State of Chaos.

The only way to move out of the Brink of Chaos is to first eliminate the Assignable Causes. This will require the use control charts.

The State of Chaos

The State of Chaos exists when a process is out of control and is producing some nonconforming product. The lack of control means that the producer is confronted with a changing level of nonconformity in the product stream. So even though he may know that he is making nonconforming product, he is likely to find that he cannot reliably predict the percentage nonconforming from hour to hour.

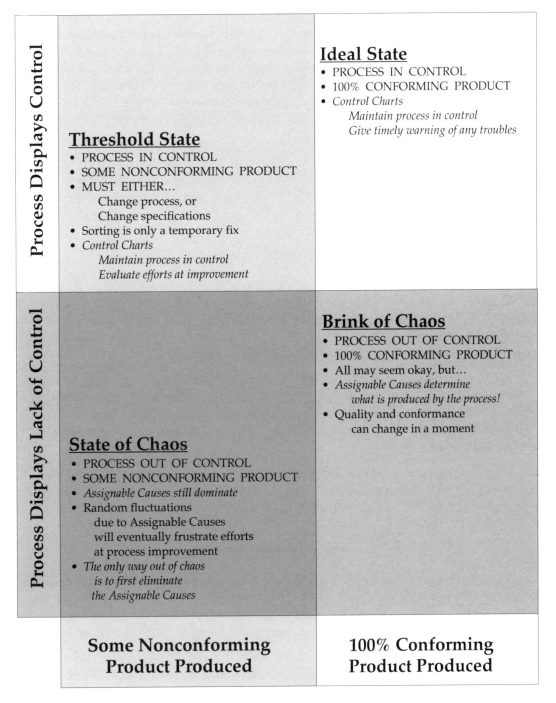

Figure 1.8: The Four Possibilities for Any Process

A manufacturer whose process is in the State of Chaos knows that he has a problem, but usually does not know what to do to correct it. Moreover, his efforts to correct the problem are ultimately frustrated by the random changes in the process, which result from the presence of the Assignable Causes. When he makes a needed modification to the process, the effect will be short-lived because the Assignable Causes continue to change the process. When he makes an unnecessary modification, a fortuitous shift by the Assignable Causes may mislead him. No matter what he tries, nothing works for long, because the process is always changing. As a result, he finally despairs of ever operating his process rationally, and begins to speak in terms of "magic" and "art."

The only way to make any progress in moving a process out of the State of Chaos is to first eliminate the Assignable Causes. This will require the use of control charts. As long as Assignable Causes are present, the manufacturer will find his efforts to be like walking in quicksand. The harder he tries to get free, the more deeply mired he becomes.

The Effect of Entropy

All processes belong to one of these four states. But processes do not always remain in one state. It is possible for a process to move from one state to another. In fact there is a universal force acting on every process that will cause it to move in a certain direction. That force is entropy. It continually acts upon all processes to cause deterioration and decay, wear and tear, breakdowns and failures.

Entropy is relentless. Every process will naturally and inevitably migrate toward the State of Chaos. The only way this migration can be overcome is by continually repairing the effects of entropy. Of course this means that the effects for a given process must be known before they can be repaired. With such knowledge, the repairs are generally fairly easy to make.

On the other hand, it is very difficult to repair something when one is unaware of it. But if the effects of entropy are not repaired, it will come to dominate the process, and force it inexorably toward the State of Chaos.

The Cycle of Despair

Since everybody knows that they are in trouble when their processes are in the State of Chaos they inevitably appoint Chaos Managers whose job is to drag the process up from the State of Chaos. With luck, these Chaos Managers can get the process back to the Brink of Chaos—a state which is erroneously considered to be "out-of-trouble" in most operations.

Once they get the process back to the Brink of Chaos the Chaos Manager is sent off to work on another problem. As soon as his back is turned, the process begins to move down the entropy slide toward the State of Chaos.

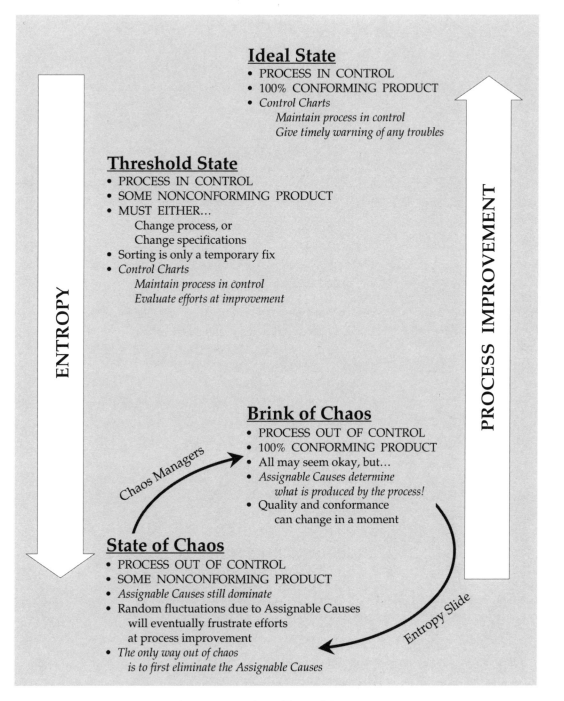

Figure 1.9: The Effect of Entropy

New technologies, process upgrades, and all the other "magic bullets" which may be tried can never overcome this Cycle of Despair. One may change technologies—often a case of jumping out of the frying pan and into the fire—but the benign neglect which inevitably occurs when the process is on the Brink of Chaos will allow Entropy to drag the process back down to the Brink of Chaos. Thus, focusing solely upon conformance to specifications will condemn one to forever cycle between the State of Chaos and the Brink of Chaos.

The Only Way Out

There is only one way out of this Cycle of Despair. There is only one way to move a process up to the Threshold State or the Ideal State—the effective use of Shewhart's control charts.

Every manufacturer is confronted with a dual problem. He has to identify both the effects of Entropy and the presence of Assignable Causes. Entropy places a process in the Cycle of Despair. Assignable Causes doom it to stay there.

The only way a manufacturer can ever meet the dual objectives of overcoming the barrier created by the Assignable Causes and counteracting the effects of Entropy is by the use of process control charts. No other tool will consistently and reliably provide the necessary information in a clear and understandable form.

Therefore, any process operated without the benefit of process control charts is ultimately doomed to operate in the State of Chaos.

The best that Chaos Managers can hope to achieve is to get their process to operate in the Brink of Chaos for at least a short period of time.

Control charts are the only way to break out of the Cycle of Despair.

1.7 The Uses of Shewhart's Charts

The many different ways of using control charts in both service and manufacturing applications may be summarized under five major headings. These five categories are arranged in order of sophistication below.

The first of these is that of *Report Card Charts*. Report Card Charts are charts kept for the files. They may be occasionally used for information about how things are going, or for verification that something has or has not occurred, but they are not used in real time for operating or improving the processes and systems present. This is a valid but weak usage of control charts.

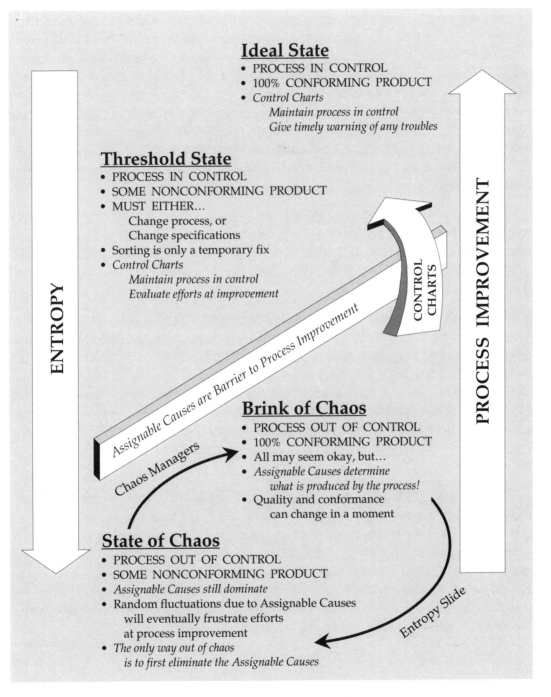

Figure 1.10: The Only Way Out

The next category consists of *Process Adjustment Charts.* Some product characteristic may be plotted on a control chart and used in a feedback loop for making process adjustments, or some input characteristic may be tracked and used in a feed-forward loop for the same purpose. In many cases these Process Adjustment Charts will result in substantially more consistent operations than was the case prior to the use of control charts. (This assumes that one will know how to properly adjust the process. In some cases such knowledge can only be gained by some of the following uses of control charts.) However, once this initial improvement has been achieved, Process Adjustment Charts simply strive to preserve the new *status quo.* The potential for dynamic and continual improvement is missing from this usage of the charts. Unfortunately, this seems to be the only usage considered in most of the articles recently published in the theoretical journals.

The third category consists of *Process Trial Charts.* These are charts used to analyze the data from simple experiments performed using production equipment. This short-term usage of control charts is a simple and easy to understand alternative to the use of ANOVA and other statistical techniques. This usage is often found in conjunction with the next category.

The fourth category consists of *Extended Monitoring Charts.* Extended monitoring is the use of multiple control charts to simultaneously track several related characteristics in order to discover just which charts provide the best predictors of process or product performance. This usage will generally involve a project team with a specific mission, and is one of the preliminary steps for both the effective utilization of control charts and the effective use of process experiments. Without the constancy of purpose evidenced by extended monitoring, and without the process stability obtained by getting the process into statistical control, it is doubtful that designed experiments will be of any long term benefit.

The fifth category is the use of Control Charts for *Continual Improvement.* It is only by means of the constancy of purpose required for extended monitoring and process trials that one can progress to this last category. The control chart becomes a powerful tool for continual improvement only as those involved with the process learn how to use the chart to identify and remove Assignable Causes of uncontrolled variation. Every out-of-control point is an opportunity. But these opportunities can be utilized only by those who have prepared themselves in advance. SPC is ultimately a way of thinking with the charts acting as a catalyst for this thought process.

Chapter Two

Summarizing Data

Statistical Process Control is a way of thinking with some techniques attached. The way of thinking was featured in the first chapter, and will be explained more fully throughout the rest of this book. Our discussion of the techniques of SPC will begin with a review of the ways of summarizing data.

How to summarize data is rather like the problem presented by the busy man who said, "I haven't got time to read the whole story. Just give me the unabridged, condensed version." Presumably the unabridged version would have all the interesting bits left in, while the condensation would remove all the dull stuff. Since tables of data are intrinsically dull, the challenge of summarizing data is how to extract all of the interesting bits while removing the uninteresting details. In this quest there are several techniques which are especially useful.

While Shewhart carefully and rigorously considered many different ways of presenting data,[1] we shall only review a few of these techniques in this book. In this chapter the common measures of location and dispersion are defined, and some of the more powerful graphic tools are illustrated.

---

[1] *Economic Control of Quality of Manufactured Product,* pp.55-120.

2.1 Measures of Location

The Average

The average is the most common measure of location for a set of numbers. The average identifies the center of mass for the values in the data set. It is the balance point. Thus, it intuitively locates the "center" of the data. If the values in the data set are denoted by the symbol X, then the average will be denoted by

$$\overline{X}$$

The calculation of the average is not complicated. It is the sum of all the values divided by the number of values. (To minimize round-off error, the average should be calculated to two or three more digits than are in the original measurements.)

EXAMPLE 2.1:   *Finding the Average:*

Consider a simple data set with eight values:

(3, 10, 16, 1, 5, 14, 11, 6)

The average is the sum of these eight values, divided by 8.

$$3 + 10 + 16 + 1 + 5 + 14 + 11 + 6 = 66$$

$$\overline{X} = \frac{66}{8} = 8.25$$

This value is the balance point for these data.

A Median

A median is another measure of location for a data set. This statistic identifies a 50th percentile of the data. At least half the data will be greater than, or equal to, a median, and at least half the data will be less than, or equal to, a median. Thus, while the average describes the balance point, a median splits the data into halves. Median values will usually be close to the average, except when the data are dramatically skewed, or lopsided.

In the calculation of a median, the first step is to arrange the data in numerical order. This is essential. The second step is to find the middle value of this ordered data set. If there is an odd number of values, then there will be one middle value, and the median is defined to be equal to this middle value. If there is an even number of values, then there will be two middle values, and a median may be defined to be the average of these two middle values. A median of the X values will be denoted by the symbol

$$\tilde{X}$$

EXAMPLE 2.2:   *Finding a Median:*

Consider the same data set used in Example 2.1:

$$(3, 10, 16, 1, 5, 14, 11, 6)$$

A median is found in three steps.

(i) Arrange the data in numerical order:

$$(1, 3, 5, 6, 10, 11, 14, 16)$$

(ii) Since there is an even number of values (n = 8),
find the two middle values:

$$6 \text{ and } 10$$

(iii) Average these two middle values to get a median:

$$\tilde{X} = \frac{6+10}{2} = 8$$

Half of the data are greater than, or equal to, 8,
and half of the data are less than, or equal to, 8.

EXAMPLE 2.3:   *Finding the Average and a Median:*

Consider a data set with fifteen values:

$$(44, 50, 80, 72, 97, 12, 93, 10, 25, 26, 32, 44, 56, 63, 70)$$

The balance point for these data is the average:

$$\bar{X} = \frac{774}{15} = 51.60$$

To find a median, arrange the data in numerical order

$$(10, 12, 25, 26, 32, 44, 44, 50, 56, 63, 70, 72, 80, 93, 97)$$

Since there is an odd number of values, the median is the one middle value:

$$\tilde{X} = 50$$

At least half the data (8 out of 15) are less than, or equal to 50,
and at least half of the data (8 out of 15) are greater than or equal to 50.

2.2 Measures of Dispersion

The Range

The range is the simplest measure of the dispersion for a data set. This statistic is defined to be the maximum minus the minimum. Denote the range by the symbol R.

EXAMPLE 2.4:   *Finding Ranges:*

Consider the data of Example 2.1:

$$(3, 10, 16, 1, 5, 14, 11, 6)$$

The range is $R = Maximum - Minimum = 16 - 1 = 15$

For the data of Example 2.3:

$$(44, 50, 80, 72, 97, 12, 93, 10, 25, 26, 32, 44, 56, 63, 70)$$

The range is $R = Max - Min = 97 - 10 = 87$

Since the range depends only on two values, it is very easy to compute. This ease of computation makes it the preferred dispersion statistic for practical applications involving small data sets. Unfortunately, since the range is based upon the maximum and the minimum, it does not explicitly use the "middle values" in the data. This makes it somewhat inefficient for very large collections of data. Therefore, the range is generally used only with small data sets ($n < 15$). However, since the techniques of process control emphasize small sets of numbers, the range will be used throughout the remainder of this book. The following subsections describe two other measures of dispersion. They are included here for completeness, and may be skipped at the reader's discretion.

The Root Mean Square Deviation

The Root Mean Square Deviation, s_n, utilizes all of the information regarding dispersion which is in the data. Exactly what this statistic measures, and how it is calculated, is best introduced by means of an example.

EXAMPLE 2.5:   *Finding the Root Mean Square Deviation:*

Consider the data from Example 2.1:

$$(3, 10, 16, 1, 5, 14, 11, 6)$$

The Root Mean Square Deviation is calculated in four steps:

Step 1: *Find the deviation of each value about the average. (Do this by subtracting the average from each value.)*

3.0	10.0	16.0	1.0	5.0	14.0	11.0	6.0
-8.25	-8.25	-8.25	-8.25	-8.25	-8.25	-8.25	-8.25
-5.25	1.75	7.75	-7.25	-3.25	5.75	2.75	-2.25

These deviations describe the displacement of each value relative to the average. They contain 100% of the information about dispersion that is in the data. The next step is to summarize this information in one number. The average of these deviations will always be zero since the positive deviations will always cancel out the negative deviations. Thus, these deviations must be modified before they can be summarized.

Step 2: *Modify these deviations by squaring them.*

27.5625   3.0625   60.0625   52.5625   10.5625   33.0625   7.5625   5.0625

Step 3: *Average these squared deviations. The sum is:*

(27.5625 + 3.0625 + 60.0625 + 52.5625 + 10.5625 + 33.0625 + 7.5625 + 5.0625) = 199.5

So the average squared deviation is $\dfrac{199.5}{8} = 24.9375$

Step 4: *To get a number that has the same units of measurement as the original numbers, take the square root of the average of the squared deviations.*

$$s_n = \sqrt{24.9375} = 4.9937$$

The Root Mean Square Deviation uses all of the information about dispersion which is contained in the data. This makes it a "most efficient" dispersion statistic. Thus, the Root Mean Square Deviation is recommended for use in summarizing the dispersion of large amounts of *homogeneous* data.[2]

The steps in the calculation of the Root Mean Square Deviation can be easily remembered if the name is read backwards, from right to left. The first step is to find the DEVIATIONS. The second step is to SQUARE the deviations. The third step is to find the

---

[2] Data collected, in the same way, from a process which is *known to display statistical control* can be said to be homogeneous. The homogeneity of all real-world data is suspect. This will severely limit the usefulness of this dispersion statistic with large data sets.

MEAN (or average) of these squared deviations, and the fourth step is to find the square ROOT. Thus, with a little practice, one can compute the Root Mean Square Deviation, s_n, without reference to a formula. However, for those who prefer to have a formula, the formula for the Root Mean Square Deviation, s_n, for a set of n values, can be expressed as:

$$s_n = \sqrt{\frac{\sum_{i=1}^{i=n} (X_i - \bar{X})^2}{n}}$$

Of course, modern calculators often have the capability of calculating the Root Mean Square Deviation with the push of a button. However, the reader should check the operator's manual to see exactly what summary statistic is provided by the calculator. The reason for this caution will become clear below.

The Standard Deviation

A third statistic for summarizing the dispersion of a data set is the Standard Deviation, denoted by the symbol s. For a set of n values, the Standard Deviation, s, can be expressed as:

$$s = \sqrt{\frac{\sum_{i=1}^{i=n} (X_i - \bar{X})^2}{n-1}}$$

The only difference between the formula for s_n and the formula for s is the divisor. Therefore, s_n and s will yield similar, but different, values when computed for the same data. With the data from Example 2.5, the values for s_n and s are:

$$s_n = \sqrt{\frac{199.5}{8}} = 4.9937 \quad \text{while} \quad s = \sqrt{\frac{199.5}{7}} = 5.3385.$$

Both s_n and s contain the same information, yet the fact that they yield different values can lead to confusion. Especially since neither the names nor the symbols used for these statistics are consistent from book to book, calculator to calculator, or computer program to computer program. This means that the user must be careful to determine which statistic is intended in each application. (Many students find this to be a compelling argument in favor of the range statistic!)

One other caution is appropriate here. In spite of what several textbooks say about s applying to samples and s_n applying to "populations," both s and s_n are statistics. They are both purely arithmetic functions of the data.

2.3 Histograms

In addition to the numerical summaries described above, there are graphic ways of summarizing data. Perhaps the simplest of these is the histogram. A histogram is a plot of the data which has possible values on one axis and frequencies for those values on the other axis. The frequency is traditionally placed on the vertical axis, so that the observations accumulate in a pile at each value.

EXAMPLE 2.6:   *Histograms for Camshaft Bearing Diameters:*

Consider the data given in Table 2.1. Each value represents the diameter of a camshaft bearing (in inches). When looking at a table of numbers, such as Table 2.1, the details are often overwhelming. A histogram is an effective way to suppress the unwanted detail while highlighting the relevant information.

Table 2.1: Camshaft Bearing Diameters

Bearing One			Bearing Two			Bearing Three		
1.3749	1.3751	1.3751	1.3750	1.3750	1.3752	1.3750	1.3746	1.3752
1.3752	1.3756	1.3752	1.3749	1.3752	1.3749	1.3751	1.3742	1.3750
1.3751	1.3752	1.3750	1.3749	1.3750	1.3748	1.37505	1.3744	1.3748
1.37495	1.3751	1.3752	1.3748	1.3749	1.3748	1.3749	1.3743	1.37495
1.3753	1.3752	1.3751	1.3750	1.3749	1.3749	1.3750	1.3746	1.3749
1.3751	1.3755	1.3751	1.3751	1.3751	1.3752	1.3743	1.3742	1.3745
1.37505	1.3749	1.3751	1.3750	1.3750	1.3748	1.3742	1.3743	1.3743
1.3751	1.37525	1.3750	1.3749	1.3750	1.3750	1.3745	1.3742	1.3746
1.3750	1.3750	1.3753	1.3748	1.3750	1.3747	1.3747	1.3745	1.3742
1.3752	1.3750	1.3753	1.3748	1.3749	1.3748	1.3749	1.3749	1.3752
1.3752	1.3752	1.37515	1.3752	1.3752	1.3753	1.3746	1.3750	1.3751
1.3751	1.37495	1.3752	1.3753	1.3751	1.3751	1.3750	1.3751	1.3750
1.3751	1.37515	1.3751	1.37515	1.3749	1.37545	1.3752	1.3752	1.3754
1.3751	1.3750	1.37505	1.3750	1.3748	1.3750	1.37525	1.3754	1.3751
1.3751	1.3751	1.3751	1.3747	1.3749	1.3749	1.3751	1.3751	1.37495
1.3756	1.3750	1.3750	1.3748	1.3750	1.3752	1.3752	1.3749	1.3749
1.37525	1.3757		1.3748	1.3748		1.3750	1.3750	

The histograms for these three bearing diameters are shown in Figure 2.1 on the following page. They were constructed by representing each possible value on the horizontal axis, and then adding a box to the appropriate stack for each individual value in the data set. These histograms show that there is a marked difference between the three data sets. One would have to study the data for a long time to discover the information made instantaneously obvious by the histograms.

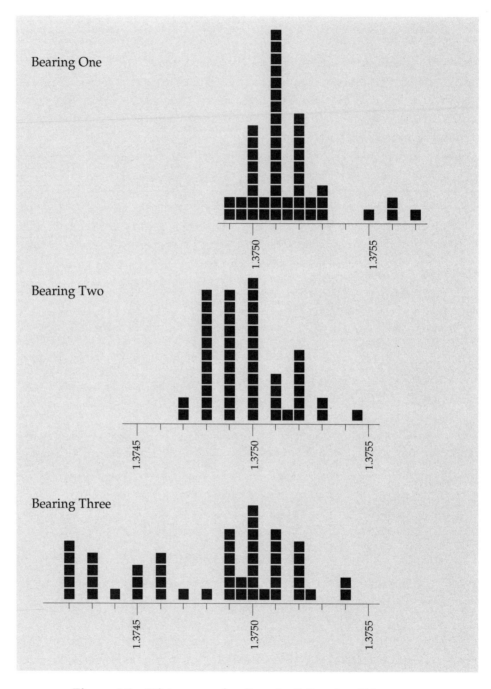

Figure 2.1: Histograms for Camshaft Bearing Diameters

If one computed the summary statistics for each Camshaft Bearing separately, the shifts in location and dispersion between the three bearings could be seen in the numbers.

$$Bearing\ One:\quad n = 50\quad \bar{X} = 1.375146\quad s = 0.000168$$

$$Bearing\ Two:\quad n = 50\quad \bar{X} = 1.374978\quad s = 0.000168$$

$$Bearing\ Three:\quad n = 50\quad \bar{X} = 1.374820\quad s = 0.000354$$

As one goes from Bearing One to Bearing Two and on to Bearing Three, one can see the average dropping. Moreover, Bearing Three has a Standard Deviation that is twice as large as those of the other two bearings. In spite of these numerical differences, the histograms provide a much more powerful summary.

Graphs have always constituted the most powerful and effective way of communicating the information contained in a data set. *Numerical summaries may complement histograms and running records, but they can never replace them.*

Virtually any plot of frequencies versus values may be called a histogram. Even a simple tally sheet is a type of histogram.

Occasionally the data are so spread out that a simple plot of frequency versus value will be virtually flat. When this happens, the traditional remedy is to group the data values into intervals, and plot the frequency for each interval.

When organizing such grouped data into a histogram, there are three general guidelines which are useful:

(1) use equal sized intervals; [3]

(2) choose end points that are easy to use, and choose them in such a way that there is no uncertainty about where a borderline value belongs;

(3) use ten to fifteen intervals, more or less, as appropriate.

A grouped frequency histogram is shown in Figure 2.2.

---

[3] There are cases where unequal sized intervals are appropriate. See Lloyd Nelson, "Technical Aids," *Journal of Quality Technology*, v.20, October, 1988, pages 273–274.

EXAMPLE 2.7:   *A Histogram for the Shipment Weight Data:*

Thirty-six shipment weights are given in Table 2.2. The Average is 911.53 and the Root Mean Square Deviation is 18.73. A grouped-data histogram is shown in Figure 2.2.

Table 2.2: Thirty-Six Shipment Weights

950	895	950	902	919	895
901	908	877	883	904	912
884	908	950	892	921	950
908	921	908	903	916	900
925	915	907	916	908	898
902	909	950	920	899	909

The minimum value is 877, and the maximum value is 950. Fifteen or sixteen intervals that are five units wide should span this difference. Use intervals of 875 to 879, 880 to 884, 885 to 889, 890 to 894, 895 to 899. . . 945 to 949, and 950 to 954. This choice of end points yields 16 intervals.

The frequency with which the data falls into each of these sixteen intervals is represented by the height of a bar on the histogram. Each bar is centered over the interval to which it refers.

Once again, the histogram reveals what the details in the table obscured. Notice that in this case, the numerical summaries did not reveal the most interesting aspect of the data: the spike at 950.

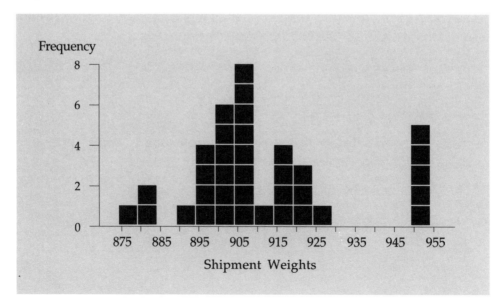

Figure 2.2 : Histogram for Shipment Weight Data

2.4 Stem and Leaf Plots

A stem and leaf plot is another form of a grouped data histogram. It not only presents a graphical representation of the data, but also preserves the actual values.

The idea of the stem and leaf plot is to write the data in parts. The most significant portion (the digits to the left) will form the stem, and the least significant portion (the digits to the right) will form the leaves of a stylized branch. The following example uses the data given in Table 2.2.

EXAMPLE 2.8:   *A Stem and Leaf Plot for the Shipment Weights:*

Since the data in Table 2.2 are three digit numbers, begin with the hundreds position as the stem values. Since every number begins with an 8 or a 9, there would only be two values on the stem. Therefore, include the tens position values in the stem. The resulting stem values are written in a column:

85
86
87
88
etc.

The last digits are added as leaves on this stem. Take each value in the data set, and write the last digit opposite the pair of digits that correspond to that value. Thus, the first value of 950 is represented by a 0, following 95. Likewise, the value of 901 is represented by a 1, following 90. Having done this for all 36 values, the result is the stem and leaf plot shown in Figure 2.3.

```
87 | 7
88 | 3 4
89 | 5 5 2 8 9
90 | 2 1 8 4 8 8 8 3 0 7 8 2 9 9
91 | 9 2 6 5 6
92 | 1 1 5 0
93 |
94 |
95 | 0 0 0 0
96 |
97 |
```

Figure 2.3:   A Stem and Leaf Plot for the Shipment Weight Data

Once again, the graph reveals what the table obscured. This stem and leaf plot shows the same interesting feature that was seen in the histogram in Figure 2.2. This plot has fewer intervals than the histogram, but the essence of the graph is unchanged.

The stem and leaf plot is possibly one of the quickest ways to summarize a data set graphically without losing any of the details. It is especially well suited for preliminary examinations of data. This technique is described more fully in John Tukey's book.[4]

2.5 Running Records

One aspect of the data that is not preserved by any of the foregoing techniques is the time-order sequence in which the values occur. Since the time-order sequence is very important in many situations, a graphical summary that will preserve this information is often needed. The running record is just such a graph.

A running record can be described as a plot in which the values are shown on one axis (usually the vertical axis), and the time-order sequence is shown on the other.

EXAMPLE 2.9:   *A Running Record for Camshaft Bearing Three:*

Consider the data for bearing three in Table 2.3:

Table 2.3: Diameters for Camshaft Bearing Number Three

1.3750	1.3743	1.3746	1.3752	1.3752	1.3746	1.3742	1.3750	1.3749	1.3752
1.3751	1.3742	1.3750	1.3750	1.3746	1.3742	1.3743	1.3751	1.3750	1.3750
1.37505	1.3745	1.3752	1.3749	1.3742	1.3744	1.3742	1.3752	1.37495	1.3748
1.3749	1.3747	1.37525	1.3754	1.3743	1.3743	1.3745	1.3754	1.3751	1.37495
1.3750	1.3749	1.3751	1.3751	1.3745	1.3746	1.3749	1.3751	1.3750	1.3749

The data in the first column were collected before the data in the second column, etc. Within columns, the time-order corresponds to movement down the column. The running record consists of the following points:

$$(1, 1.3750), \ (2, 1.3751), \ (3, 1.37505), \ . \ . \ . \ (50, 1.3749)$$

where the first coordinate is the time-order sequence value, and the second coordinate is the measurement value. This running record is shown in Figure 2.4.

The running record allows a process to be tracked through a period of time. If dramatic changes occur at particular points in time, the running record will make those changes visible. Thus, the running record and the histogram can be thought of as com-

---

[4] John W. Tukey, *Exploratory Data Analysis*, Addison-Wesley, 1977.

plementary to each other. While the histogram collapses all the data, showing its overall shape, the running record stretches out the data, showing the sequential information that is obscured by the histogram.

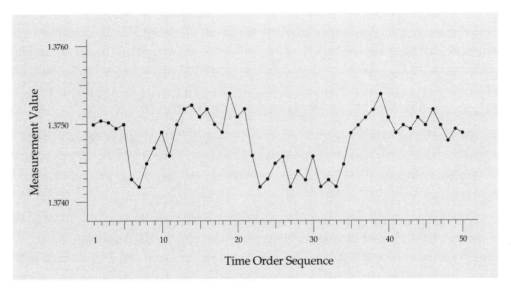

Figure 2.4 : Running Record for Camshaft Bearing Three

Both of these graphic summaries are powerful ways of portraying data. Either one is immensely better than a tabular presentation, even when the numerical summary statistics are included with the tabular data.

2.6 Summary

The techniques of descriptive statistics summarize the information in a data set in a way that can easily be understood. For most data sets, extraneous details must be removed, while the important information must be extracted in a coherent manner.

The numerical summary statistics remove the extraneous detail by expressing, in numerical form, specific characteristics of the data. Each statistic is specific to a certain characteristic. For example, a median and the average focus on different characteristics, even though they are both measuring the location of the "center" of the data. This narrow and specific interpretation of the numerical statistics is what makes them useful in comparing different sets of data. However, it also makes them capable of missing some unusual features of the data. Numerical summary statistics do not provide the whole story, because they do not attempt to answer all possible questions.

The graphic summaries remove the fine detail, expressing in geometric form the overall relationship between the data points. These graphs are much less specific than the numerical summaries, making them much better at revealing interesting and unusual features. Even if they reveal an absence of interesting and unusual features, this in itself is useful information not provided by the numerical summaries.

Thus, the graphic summaries and the numerical summaries are complementary to each other. Both are needed in any careful study of a data set. When used collectively, the techniques in this chapter will reveal most of the structure in those data sets encountered in practice.

Finally, it might be well to remember Shewhart's two rules for the presentation of data: *Rule 1: Original data should be presented in a way that will preserve the evidence in the original data for all the predictions assumed to be useful.* Among other things, this means that one should always interpret data in its original context.

Rule 2: Any summary of a distribution of numbers in terms of symmetric functions [such as averages, ranges, histograms, etc.] should not give an objective degree of belief in any one of the inferences or predictions to be made [from these data] that would cause human action significantly different from what this action would be if the original [data] had been taken as a basis for evidence. In short, do not, by omission or commission, lie with statistics.

Exercise 2.1:

The thickness of 4 parts is measured to the nearest thousandth of an inch. The values recorded are the number of thousandths by which each part exceeds the minimum specification value of 0.300 inches. The value for the four parts are [3, 7, 5, 5].

(a) Verify that the average for these data is 5.00.

(b) Verify that the range for these data is 4.

(c) Verify that a median for these data is 5.

(d) Verify that the Root Mean Square Deviation for these data is 1.414.

(e) Verify that the Standard Deviation for these data is 1.633.

Exercise 2.2:

Eight additional parts are measured in the same way as those in Exercise 2.1. The values are   [4, 5, 9, 2, 7, 5, 6, 5].

(a)   Verify that the average for these data is 5.375.

(b)   Verify that the range for these data is 7.

(c)   Verify that a median for these data is 5.

(d)   Verify that the Root Mean Square Deviation for these data is 1.9325.

(e)   Verify that the Standard Deviation for these data is 2.0659.

Exercise 2.3:

The weights of 100 rubber parts are shown below. These 100 parts were consecutively produced by one machine. The values recorded are the deviations from the nominal weight, in grams.

3	-3	-2	2	-4	-6	-2	-5	-2	5	5	3	2	6	2	4	7	11	6	3
3	-2	3	-1	-3	4	-1	-2	2	3	-4	-11	-5	-7	-5	-6	15	-5	-1	-1
1	3	7	-6	2	-1	-5	1	2	1	2	2	-1	-8	-7	5	3	6	13	1
-2	-2	4	9	1	6	7	1	3	2	5	2	9	5	-3	-3	-5	-1	-2	-1
3	-1	-1	1	-2	-3	2	-7	-9	-1	-3	-2	-6	-2	-6	-8	-2	4	-1	-1

(a)   Plot a histogram of these 100 values.

(b)   What unusual characteristic of these data is shown by this histogram?

(c)   The values are arranged in time order by rows, 20 values per row. Reading each row in sequence, plot these 100 values in a running record.

Exercise 2.4:

144	150	180	193	210	225	235	233	228	198	190	178	168	137	121
116	85	65	88	111	120	138	160	179	200	245	248	211	201	155
145	102	83	80	101	106	95	90	107	127	142	159	167	178	199
181	173	163	158	147	134	128	113	104	113	122	108	135	145	158
133	125	112	105	95	63	72	97	112	126	132	144	156	163	170
181	180	202	250	205	175	157	148	140	157	139	121	131	125	111
118	115	92	99	79	111	127	135	130						

(a) Find the stem and leaf plot for these 99 values. Let the tens and hundreds values define the stem, and let the single digits define the leaves.

(b) The values are arranged in time order by rows, 15 values per row. Reading each row in sequence, plot these 99 values in a running record.

(c) What does the running record reveal about these data that the stem and leaf plot does not show?

Exercise 2.5:

Hot metal is transported from the Blast Furnace to the Steel Furnace by rail. The Transit Times (in minutes) for 140 consecutive taps of the Blast Furnace are given below, 20 values per row:

40	45	125	100	40	40	100	65	55	40	125	65	40	45	95	105	45	110	40	50
120	45	65	105	35	70	55	25	50	55	50	40	40	45	55	50	45	125	55	100
40	70	40	40	110	55	50	30	50	105	45	45	55	50	25	65	60	60	55	70
55	45	100	60	45	145	45	50	65	180	60	45	35	35	55	55	55	50	120	35
45	35	45	55	50	70	45	75	60	45	60	40	60	40	50	60	65	95	65	60
50	25	25	100	50	60	45	35	40	30	180	50	30	30	30	65	130	80	20	45
65	65	45	40	50	25	120	115	50	85	40	35	40	40	30	55	50	25	75	55

(a) Plot a histogram or a stem and leaf plot for these data.

(b) What does this plot show about these data?

Chapter Three

Shewhart's Control Charts

Having made the distinction between controlled variation and uncontrolled variation, Shewhart created the control chart in order to detect the presence of uncontrolled variation. Thus, with one stroke, he provided both a simple but effective vehicle for the presentation of data and an operational definition of when a process is in trouble. This chapter will introduce the two basic control charts.

3.1 The Logic of Control Charts

The question that is addressed by control charts is somewhat different from the questions which are commonly considered by statistical procedures: instead of seeking a theoretical model for data obtained from some well-defined phenomenon, the control chart seeks to determine if a sequence of data may be used for predictions of what will occur in the future. While most statistical procedures are deductive in nature, the control chart is essentially a technique for inductive inference.

A deductive procedure involves a logical progression from general principles to specific and unavoidable conclusions. No extrapolation is necessary. Everything is nice and neat.

An inductive procedure involves the extrapolation from specific observations back to general principles. This progression from specifics to generalities is never cut and dried. It will always involve some degree of uncertainty.

Deductive arguments use interpolation, while inductive arguments use extrapolation. So while students everywhere are warned about the dangers of extrapolation, they soon discover that real-world operations always involve prediction, and that prediction always requires extrapolation.

Control charts are tools for the inductive problems of the real world. When prediction is feasible and appropriate, they will provide the basis for the predictions. When prediction is not feasible or inappropriate due to uncontrolled variation, the control charts will warn of this instability. Recall Shewhart's definition of statistical control: *"A phenomenon will be said to be controlled when, through the use of past experience, we can predict, at least within limits, how the phenomenon may be expected to behave in the future."* The essence of statistical control is predictability. A process is predictable when it is in a state of statistical control, and it is unpredictable when it is not in a state of statistical control. Since the decision is to be based upon past experience, it follows that one will need to begin with data generated by the phenomenon in question. When a reasonable amount of these data have been accumulated they are used to calculate appropriate limits. If the historical data fall within these limits, and if data collected after the limits have been calculated also stay within these historical limits, then it becomes reasonable to make a prediction regarding future observations.

If, on the other hand, the historical data do not fall within the limits (calculated from those data), there is little or no reason to expect that future observations will fall within the limits, and there is no basis for predictions regarding future observations.

Thus, the control chart is not ultimately concerned with probabilities, or questions concerning which probability model best fits the data. It is instead concerned with helping people understand when they can make predictions concerning future observations, and when they cannot safely do so. In order to achieve this objective, Shewhart created a simple, robust, and yet sophisticated tool which we call the control chart. In order to use this tool to full effect one will need to appreciate some of the sophistication behind the charts, and to respect the fundamental principles which are the foundations for the charts.

The logic behind Shewhart's control charts is shown as a flowchart in Figure 3.1. The initial assumption is that the process is stable over the period of time represented by a set of subgroups. This assumption justifies the use of the Grand Average and the Average Range in finding the control limits.

Next, based on the values obtained for the Grand Average and the Average Range, a prediction is made concerning how the process should behave. In particular, this prediction comes in the form of calculated limits for the amount of variation that is expected for the Subgroup Averages and the Subgroup Ranges.

Finally, the observed Subgroup Averages and Subgroup Ranges are compared with the predicted limits. There are two possible outcomes of this comparison:

(1) If the observations are consistent with the predictions, the process may be stable. At least there is no solid evidence to contradict the assumption of stability for the process. Continued operation of the process within the calculated limits is the ultimate "proof" of a stable process.

(2) If the observations are inconsistent with the predictions, the process is unstable. This is due to the nature of the way the control limits were computed. The inconsistency between the observations and the predictions is almost surely due to an incorrect assumption of stability rather than a violation of the principles behind the calculation of the limits.

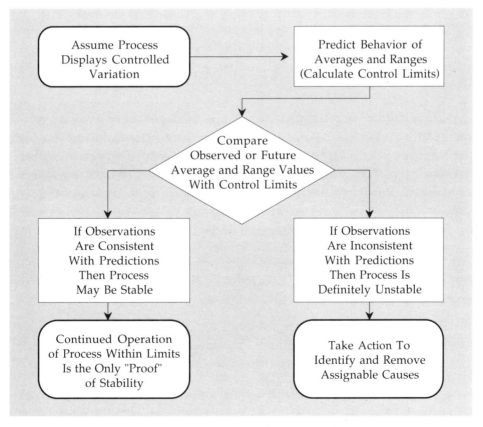

Figure 3.1: The Logic Behind Control Charts

Thus, evidence of a lack of control is strong evidence, and can be safely used as the basis for action. The absence of such evidence is not as conclusive, but since no action is required, the process should be left alone until the control charts indicate that it has changed.

It will always be a mistake to take action prior to detecting a change in a process. No matter how eloquent the explanation, action taken in the absence of a detectable signal from the data is essentially based upon nothing more than wishes and hopes. This is why it is imperative to learn how to separate potential signals from probable noise. Shewhart's control charts are the primary tool for filtering out the probable noise which is present in every data set.

Notice that there is no requirement regarding the number of subgroups needed before an out-of-control point can be interpreted as an indication of uncontrolled variation. The logic outlined above shows why this is the case. Any evidence that is strong enough to create an inconsistency is, almost certainly, due to an Assignable Cause. Thus, even if there are only two or three subgroups, any out-of-control point can be interpreted as evidence of uncontrolled variation. For an example of this, see Example 8.1, p.192.

3.2 Using Subgroups to Monitor the Process

Given some phenomenon from which a stream of numerical values may be obtained, how can the stream of values be used to draw inductive conclusions about the underlying phenomenon? Shewhart's answer was to organize the data in a rational manner which will allow one to monitor both the location and the dispersion of the values generated by the phenomenon. This is easily done by the use of periodically obtained subgroups. At a given point in time, several measurements will be obtained, and these values will then be grouped together and treated as a separate set of data.

If the subgroups display consistent behavior, then it is reasonable to assume that the process is not changing over time If the subgroups display inconsistent behavior, then the process is said to display uncontrolled variation.

Consider the following illustration. Assume that a process is stable over time (in statistical control). Let the curves in Figure 3.2 represent the total output of the process each hour. Since this process is stable, these curves are all the same, hour after hour.

If a subgroup of four pieces is selected each hour, and these four pieces are measured, different measurements will be found in different subgroups. Let the X's represent these measurements. Each subgroup is summarized by the calculation of a Subgroup Average and a Subgroup Range. These summary statistics are then plotted on a control chart, such as in Figure 3.3. These control charts are simply running records with limits attached. The way to find the limits will be given later in this chapter.

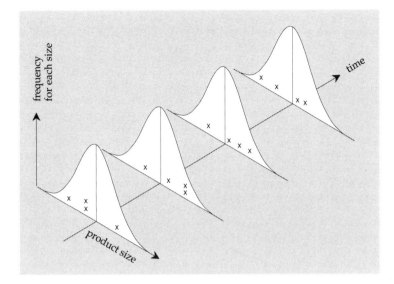

Figure 3.2: Four Subgroups Selected from an Idealized Stable Process

As long as the process remains stable and unchanging, the Subgroup Averages and the Subgroup Ranges will move around within the control limits in an erratic and random manner. While this happens, it can be said that no uncontrolled variation is detected, and it is plausible that the underlying phenomenon has remained unchanged during the interval represented by the data.

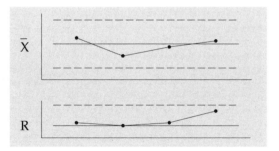

Figure 3.3: The Average and Range Chart for a Stable Process

Now consider what happens when the process itself is changing from hour to hour. Let the curves in Figure 3.4 represent the output of the process hour by hour. The X's beneath these curves will represent the subgroup measurements obtained each hour. Once again, the subgroups are summarized by finding the Subgroup Average and the Subgroup Range, and these statistics are plotted on their respective control charts.

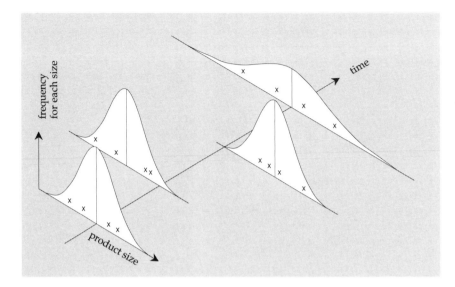

Figure 3.4: Four Subgroups Selected from an Unstable Process

At the second hour, the process average increased, and the Subgroup Average for that hour moved above the upper control limit.

At the third hour, the process average dropped dramatically, and the Subgroup Average for that hour moved below the lower control limit.

During the first three hours, the process dispersion did not change, and the Subgroup Ranges all remained within the control limits.

At the fourth hour, the process dispersion increased, and the process average moved back to its initial value. The subgroup obtained during this hour has a range that falls above the upper control limit, and an average that falls within the control limits. Thus, by monitoring the subgroups with a control chart, changes in the process can be detected in a timely manner.

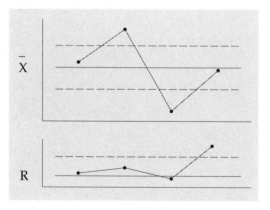
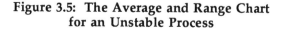

Figure 3.5: The Average and Range Chart for an Unstable Process

3.3 Average and Range Charts

Notice that with Shewhart's use of periodic subgroups, two additional variables were introduced: the Subgroup Average, and the Subgroup Range. In fact, it is these additional variables that are actually used to monitor the process. The Individual Measurements are primarily used to get values for the Subgroup Average and the Subgroup Range. The following example illustrates the behavior of these new variables, and how they are related to the measurements when the process is stable.

EXAMPLE 3.1:   *80 Thickness Measurements:*

The measurements shown in Table 3.1 represent the thickness of a certain part. The numbers recorded are the amount by which the part exceeded 0.300 inches, in units of one-thousandth of an inch. Figure 3.6 shows three histograms based on these data: one histogram for the 80 measurements, one histogram for the 20 subgroup averages, and one histogram for the 20 subgroup ranges.

Table 3.1: Data for Example 3.1

Subgroup	Values				Average	Range
1	1	4	6	4	3.75	5
2	3	7	5	5	5.00	4
3	4	5	5	7	5.25	3
4	6	2	4	5	4.25	4
5	1	6	7	3	4.25	6
6	8	3	6	4	5.25	5
7	7	5	6	6	6.00	2
8	5	3	4	6	4.50	3
9	4	5	9	2	5.00	7
10	7	5	6	5	5.75	2
11	4	5	6	5	5.00	2
12	6	7	8	5	6.50	3
13	3	3	7	3	4.00	4
14	6	3	2	9	5.00	7
15	7	3	4	3	4.25	4
16	6	4	6	5	5.25	2
17	5	5	0	5	3.75	5
18	6	4	6	3	4.75	3
19	6	4	4	0	3.50	6
20	6	2	5	4	4.25	4

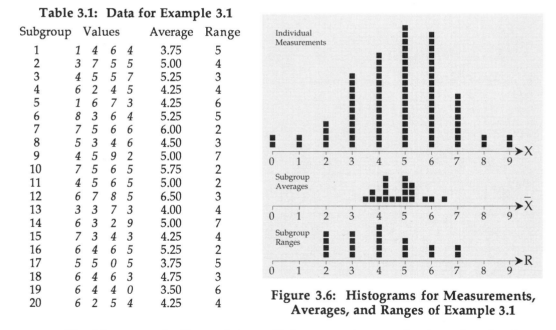

Figure 3.6: Histograms for Measurements, Averages, and Ranges of Example 3.1

The histograms in Figure 3.6 are all drawn to the same horizontal scale. In considering these three histograms, one fact should be immediately obvious: the histograms for these three variables are completely different; they have different shapes and different dispersions. Therefore, it is essential to distinguish among these three variables. This is especially true with respect to the difference between the Individual Measurements and the Subgroup Averages. The histogram for Subgroup Averages will always be narrower than the histogram for Individual Values.

Control limits for subgrouped data are calculated in the following manner: given k subgroups, where each subgroup consists of n observations,

1. Compute the average and range for each of the k subgroups.

2. Compute the Grand Average, $\bar{\bar{X}}$, by averaging each of the k Subgroup Averages.

3. Compute the Average Range, $\bar{R}$, by averaging each of the k Subgroup Ranges.

4. The Central Line for $\bar{X}$-chart is $\bar{\bar{X}}$.

   The Central Line for R chart is $\bar{R}$.

5. Find the values for A_2, D_3 and D_4, which correspond to the subgroup size n.

6. Multiply $\bar{R}$ by $A_2 = A_2 \bar{R}$

Table 3.2
Constants for
Average and Range Charts
Based on the Average Range

n	A_2	D_3	D_4
2	1.880	--	3.268
3	1.023	--	2.574
4	0.729	--	2.282
5	0.577	--	2.114
6	0.483	--	2.004
7	0.419	0.076	1.924
8	0.373	0.136	1.864
9	0.337	0.184	1.816
10	0.308	0.223	1.777

7. Add the quantity from step 6 to the Grand Average to get the Upper Control Limit for the $\bar{X}$ Chart: $\quad UCL_{\bar{X}} = \bar{\bar{X}} + A_2 \bar{R}$

8. Subtract the quantity from step 6 from the Grand Average to get the Lower Control Limit for $\bar{X}$ Chart: $\quad LCL_{\bar{X}} = \bar{\bar{X}} - A_2 \bar{R}$

9. Multiply $\bar{R}$ by D_4 to get the Upper Control Limit for the R Chart: $UCL_R = D_4 \bar{R}$

10. Multiply $\bar{R}$ by D_3 to get the Lower Control Limit for the R Chart: $LCL_R = D_3 \bar{R}$

EXAMPLE 3.2:   *Calculating Control Limits for the Thickness Data:*

The control limits for the data in Example 3.1 are found as follows:

From the Data: *The Grand Average is* $\bar{\bar{X}} = 4.7625$

       The Average Range is $\bar{R} = 4.05$

       And the subgroup size is $n = 4$

From Table 3.2: $A_2 = 0.729, \ D_3 = 0, \ and \ D_4 = 2.282.$

So the Formulas give:

$$UCL_{\bar{X}} = \bar{\bar{X}} + A_2 \bar{R} = 4.763 + 0.729 \, (4.05) = 7.715$$

$$CL_{\bar{X}} = \bar{\bar{X}} = 4.763$$

$$LCL_{\bar{X}} = \bar{\bar{X}} - A_2 \bar{R} = 4.763 - 0.729 \, (4.05) = 1.811$$

$$UCL_R = D_4 \bar{R} = 2.282 \, (4.05) = 9.24$$

$$CL_R = \bar{R} = 4.05.$$

$$LCL_R = D_3 \bar{R} = \textit{(does not exist for } n = 4)$$

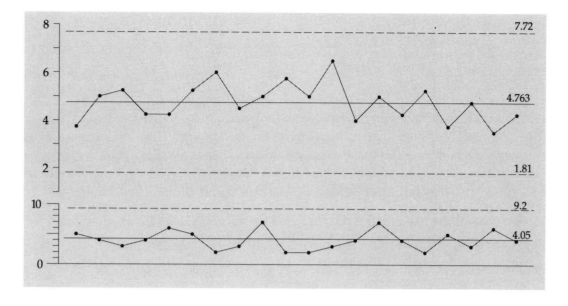

Figure 3.7: Average and Range Chart for the Thickness Data

The limits need to be computed to enough digits to provide a watershed. In the preceding example the Subgroup Averages are multiples of 0.25, so two or three decimal places will be sufficient for the limits on the Average Chart. The Subgroup Ranges above are integer valued, so one decimal place will be sufficient for the control limits for the Range Chart. However, since all computations are based upon the Grand Average and the Average Range, these values should not be rounded-off to any appreciable extent until after the limits have been computed.

When the data can be obtained quickly it is common to wait until there are 20 to 30 subgroups available before calculating control limits. The reason for this is the insurance it provides against one or two extreme values having an undue influence upon the computed limits. However, when limited amounts of data are available, or when the data are obtained slowly one may calculate control limits with whatever data are available.

When a small amount of data is used, any out-of-control points on the chart are definitely out-of-control, and therefore the only risk one takes by computing limits with a small amount of data is the risk of missing a signal. Since this is exactly the same risk that one incurs by waiting for more data before computing limits, there is really no penalty for computing control chart limits with small amounts of data. If and when additional data become available, one may appropriately update the limits. The revision of control limits is discussed more fully on pages 226 to 230.

3.4 Limits for Individual Values

While one does not usually compute control limits for the Individual Values, it is possible to do so. Such limits are called Natural Process Limits. This change in nomenclature serves two purposes. It emphasizes the difference between these limits for X and the Control Limits for the Subgroup Averages, and it correctly describes the predictive role these limits play when the data display a reasonable degree of statistical control.

The Natural Process Limits for X are found by using the same summary statistics used to compute the control limits. The computations are:

11. Find the value for d_2 which corresponds to the subgroup size, n. (Table 3.3 or Table A.1 in the Appendix)

Table 3.3	
n	d_2
2	1.128
3	1.693
4	2.059
5	2.326
6	2.534
7	2.704
8	2.847
9	2.970
10	3.078

12. Divide the Average Range by d_2 to get[1] $Sigma(X) = \dfrac{\bar{R}}{d_2}$

13. Multiply this quantity by 3 to get $3\, Sigma(X) = \dfrac{3\,\bar{R}}{d_2}$

14. Using the Grand Average as the Central Line, Add and Subtract the value in Step 13 to get the Upper and Lower Natural Process Limits for X:

$$\text{UNPL}_X = \bar{\bar{X}} + \frac{3\,\bar{R}}{d_2}$$

$$\text{LNPL}_X = \bar{\bar{X}} - \frac{3\,\bar{R}}{d_2}$$

These Natural Process Limits can be used on a histogram of Individual Values, they can be plotted as control limits on a running record of the Individual Values, and, when the process appears to display a reasonable degree of statistical control, these limits can be used to *predict* what the process is likely to produce in the future. Thus, these limits may be used as a criterion for judging if a set of data appears to display statistical control, and, occasionally, as a prediction of what might be expected in the future.

---

[1] The symbol *Sigma(X)* will define any one of a set of measures of dispersion for X. See Appendix Table A.1.

EXAMPLE 3.3:   *Natural Process Limits for the Thickness Data:*

From the Data:
The Grand Average is 4.763,
the Average Range is 4.05,
and the subgroup size is 4.
From the Formulas:
11. $n = 4$ *gives* $d_2 = 2.059$

12.

$$\frac{\bar{R}}{d_2} = \frac{4.05}{2.059} = 1.967$$

13.

$$\frac{3\,\bar{R}}{d_2} = 5.901$$

14.

$$UNPL_X = \bar{\bar{X}} + \frac{3\,\bar{R}}{d_2} = 10.664$$

$$LNPL_X = \bar{\bar{X}} - \frac{3\,\bar{R}}{d_2} = -1.138$$

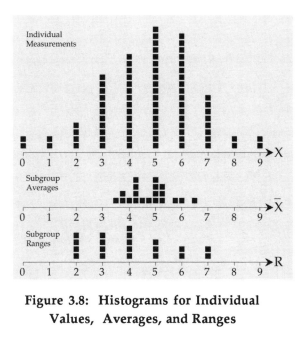

Figure 3.8: Histograms for Individual Values, Averages, and Ranges

All 80 Individual Values fall within these limits, just as the 20 Subgroup Averages fell within their limits and the 20 Subgroup Ranges fell within their limits.

3.5 Other Charts for Subgrouped Data

Instead of using Subgroup Ranges, some prefer to use other dispersion statistics, such as the standard deviation, s, or the root mean square deviation, s_n. These substitutions are perfectly acceptable as long as they are done in the correct manner: namely, a separate dispersion statistic is computed for each subgroup. Appendix Tables A.4 and A.5 give the appropriate formulas and factors for computing the appropriate limits for these charts.

Some prefer to use a Median of the Subgroup Ranges, $\tilde{R}$, instead of the Average Range in computing the control limits. This practice is valid, but it has two drawbacks: first, many people who already know how to compute an average do not know how to find a median. Second, control limits based upon a Median Range are effectively computed using only two-thirds of the data. So while there are situations where a Median Range is appropriate, it is not the best statistic for general usage.

Appendix Tables A.3 and A.7 give the appropriate factors for using a Median Range.

Finally, some instances occur where a Subgroup Median is used instead of the Subgroup Average. This technique is discussed in Section 9.8, p.231.

3.6 Control Charts With Subgroup Size One

There are several situations where the logical subgroup size is $n = 1$. This might happen when each measurement represents one batch, or when the measurements are widely spaced in time, or when each measurement needs to be used to evaluate the process.

With only one measurement per subgroup there is no way to calculate Subgroup Ranges. Since this makes the regular formulas inapplicable, it is necessary to return to the basic concepts to develop a way to find appropriate control limits.

The Average and Range Chart bases the control limits on the average variation within each of the subgroups. Since each subgroup is defined in such a way as to minimize this variation, the regular control chart is, in effect, using short-term variation to define the long-term limits for process variation. This same principle can be applied to Individual Measurements, but it must be done in a slightly different manner.

The short-term variation for a sequence of Individual Values will be represented by the variation from one point to the next. The long-term variation will be represented by a long sequence of such values. The estimate of the short-term variation will be the average of a Moving Range that is based on the successive differences between the Individual Values. This estimate can then be used to establish three-sigma limits for both the Individual Values and the Moving Ranges according to the formulas:

$$\text{UNPL}_X = \bar{X} + 2.660\, \overline{mR}$$
$$\text{CL}_X = \bar{X}$$
$$\text{LNPL}_X = \bar{X} - 2.660\, \overline{mR}$$
$$\text{UCL}_R = 3.268\, \overline{mR}$$
$$\text{CL}_R = \overline{mR}$$

where 2.660 is the multiplier of 3.0 divided by 1.128. This value of 1.128 is the appropriate value of d_2 for use with ranges based upon subgroups of size $n = 2$. The multiplier 3.268 is the value of D_4 for subgroups of size $n = 2$.

A manufacturer uses one rail car load of a certain chemical each month. Each car-load comes with its own certificate of analysis. The user tracks the key ingredients in each car-load on separate control charts in order to avoid unnecessary adjustments in the manufacturing process. Since the question of interest here is whether or not the new shipment is consistent with the previous shipments, it does not make sense to subgroup these values. For one key ingredient the Individual Values from the past 12 shipments and the associated Moving Ranges are:

X	39	41	41	41	43	44	41	42	40	41	44	40
mR		2	0	0	2	1	3	1	2	1	3	4

The Average is 41.42.
The Average Moving Range is 1.73.

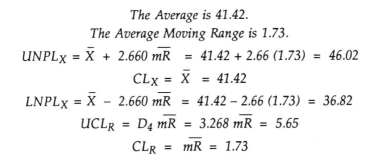

$$UNPL_X = \bar{X} + 2.660\,\overline{mR} = 41.42 + 2.66\,(1.73) = 46.02$$

$$CL_X = \bar{X} = 41.42$$

$$LNPL_X = \bar{X} - 2.660\,\overline{mR} = 41.42 - 2.66\,(1.73) = 36.82$$

$$UCL_R = D_4\,\overline{mR} = 3.268\,\overline{mR} = 5.65$$

$$CL_R = \overline{mR} = 1.73$$

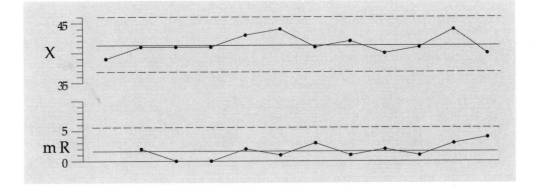

Figure 3.9: *XmR* Chart for Rail Car Data

The Moving Ranges are treated as if they came from subgroups of size $n = 2$. Any Moving Range which falls above the UCL_R value will indicate a sudden shift in the time series. Such a shift should be attributed to the presence of an Assignable Cause, and, as always, one should endeavor to identify and remove this Assignable Cause. It should also be noted that it is possible for a Moving Range to be out-of-control even when the two Individual Values used to compute that Moving Range fall within the Natural Process Limits. This is why one should always examine the Moving Ranges. While most of the signals will be visible on the chart for Individual Values, some signals will only show up on the Moving Range chart.

3.7 Choice of Scale for Control Charts

How should one pick a scale for plotting control charts? The easiest way to answer this question is to wait until a small amount of data is available and then to compute "trial limits." Such trial limits may be used to pick scales for Individual Charts, Average Charts, and Range Charts.

The vertical scale for the Average Chart will need to be about twice as large as the spread between the control limits. That is, if the difference between the Upper Control Limit and the Lower Control Limit is 12 units, then the vertical scale on the graph should show about 24 or 25 units. To obtain such a scale one could use the following procedure: collect a few subgroups, compute "trial control limits for Averages," and pick a "nice" value near the "trial" Grand Average as the midpoint for the scale. Next consider making each tick on the graph equal to "one" unit (*i.e.* 100, or 10, or 1.0, or 0.1, or 0.001, or 0.0001, *etc.*). If this choice will result in "trial control limits" that fall about halfway between the mid-point and the edge of the graph paper, then use this scale. If this scale doesn't work, then try using "two" units per tick mark (*i.e.* 200, or 20, or 2.0, or 0.2, or 0.02, *etc.*). If neither the "one" unit scale nor the "two" unit scale work, then try using "five" units per tick mark (*i.e.* 500, or 50, or 5.0, or 0.5, or 0.05, *etc.*). When the trial control limits fall in the middle half of the plot, the scale will usually be satisfactory. If the trial control limits are too wide, try letting each tick mark represent a larger value. If the trial control limits are too narrow, try letting each tick mark represent a smaller value.

The scale for the Range Chart will need to begin at zero and continue to a value that is roughly twice as large as the trial upper control limit for the Ranges. Since Ranges will always have the same discreteness as the original data, begin by letting each tick mark equal one measurement unit. Again, adjust this scale to make the space available on the graph paper cover the values between 0 and twice the trial control limit.

The scale for an Individual Chart is adjusted in the same way as that for an Average Chart. Trial Natural Process Limits may be computed using a small amount of data, and the scale chosen to cover about twice the range of values indicated by these limits.

In every case, the control charts will be easier to plot, easier to read, and easier to use if the scale is a "nice" scale with each tick mark equal to one, two, or five units. Every fifth or tenth tick mark should be labelled.

For example, the first subgroup of Table 3.1 has an Average of 3.75, so center the Average Chart near 4.0. The first Range is 5, so trial control limits are 3.75 ± 0.73 (5) = 0.1 to 7.4. A scale that is twice this size would go from about –3 to 11. Choose divisions on the graph paper to accommodate this range of values. Likewise, the trial upper control limit for Ranges would be 2.3 (5) = 11.5, so a scale of 0 to 20 should suffice for the Range Chart.

When one person routinely uses several different charts which track the same measurement (e.g. viscosity) it will be easier to keep the charts if *all* of the charts have the same scale, that is, if the tick marks represent the same increment on every chart.

3.8 What is a Reasonable Degree of Statistical Control?

While the control chart is intended to detect a lack of control when it exists, the logic shown in Figure 3.1 also indicates that continued operation within the limits will be an indication of statistical control. If we, like Shewhart, consider a state of statistical control to be an ideal which can only be approximated in practice, then we will need a criterion for deciding when a process is reasonably close to the ideal. Shewhart provided a minimal criterion for an Average and Range Chart with subgroups of size $n = 4$: if such a chart has at least 25 consecutive subgroups which do not indicate any lack of control, then the process may be said to display a reasonable degree of statistical control.[2] In his next sentence Shewhart interprets this minimal criterion in terms of the total number of observations present, therefore this minimal condition could be adapted to become: whenever at least 100 consecutive observations fail to indicate a lack of control the process may be said to display a reasonable degree of statistical control.

In giving this minimal criterion Shewhart noted that there is a fundamental difference between a failure to display a lack of control and the inference that a process is operating in a state of statistical control. The failure to display a lack of control may be a consequence of the time period covered by the chart. Assignable causes will come and go, and a short period of observation will not necessarily show any points to fall outside the control limits. However, as more and more data accumulate without giving evidence of Assignable Causes, one will naturally feel more confident about the inductive inference that the process is operating in a state of statistical control. Shewhart also noted that in circumstances where one may want near certainty regarding this inference it may be desirable to wait until a 1000 observations, instead of 100, fail to display a lack of control.

---

[2] *Statistical Method from the Viewpoint of Quality Control*, p.37.

3.9 Summary

A manual control chart for Averages and Ranges is a simple and effective way to present data for use as a basis for action. The original data are preserved, in time order, with the contextual information needed to understand the data. At the same time the Average and the Range Charts provide powerful summaries which separate the routine variation from that which is likely to be due to Assignable Causes. The reader is referred to Chapter 7 for an especially good example of these features.

A process is in trouble when it is not operating as consistently as possible, and the control chart provides an operational definition for the presence of this type of trouble. It is up to the user to take the appropriate action—to look for the Assignable Cause and take steps to make things better based on this knowledge.

Exercise 3.1:

The weights of 100 consecutively produced rubber parts were given in Exercise 2.3. These 100 parts are arranged in 20 subgroups of size 5 and listed along with the Subgroup Averages and Subgroup Ranges below.

subgroup	values					$\bar{X}$	R	subgroup	values					$\bar{X}$	R
1	3	-3	-2	2	-4	-0.8	7	11	2	2	-1	-8	-7	-2.4	10
2	-6	-2	-5	-2	5	-2.0	11	12	5	3	6	13	1	5.6	12
3	5	3	2	6	2	3.6	4	13	-2	-2	4	9	1	2.0	11
4	4	7	11	6	3	6.2	8	14	6	7	1	3	2	3.8	6
5	3	-2	3	-1	-3	0.0	6	15	5	2	9	5	-3	3.6	12
6	4	-1	-2	2	3	1.2	6	16	-3	-5	-1	-2	-1	-2.4	4
7	-4	-11	-5	-7	-5	-6.4	7	17	3	-1	-1	1	-2	0.0	5
8	-6	15	-5	-1	-1	0.4	21	18	-3	2	-7	-9	-1	-3.6	11
9	1	3	7	-6	2	1.4	13	19	-3	-2	-6	-2	-6	-3.8	4
10	-1	-5	1	2	1	-0.4	7	20	-8	-2	4	-1	-1	-1.6	12

(a) Verify that the average of subgroup 20 is -1.6.

(b) Verify that the range of subgroup 20 is 12.

(c) Construct an Average and Range Chart for these data.

(d) Compare the Average Chart with the Running Record of the 100 Individual Values from Exercise 2.3 (c).

Exercise 3.2:

The pressure of the cooling water for a particular process is continuously monitored and recorded on a circular graph. Periodically the circular graph paper is changed and the old record is filed away. (No one knew what else to do with these data.) Having taken a course in SPC, one engineer decided to place these data on a control chart.

date	pressures					$\bar{X}$	R	date	pressures					$\bar{X}$	R
12/1	60	59	54	57	58	57.6	6	12/17	55	55	55	52	58	55.0	6
12/2	60	59	56	63	59	59.4	7	12/18	58	66	60	62	61	61.4	8
12/3	61	55	56	61	58	58.2	6	12/21	70	69	70	70	70	69.8	1
12/4	63	60	57	59	61	60.0	6	12/22	70	70	70	61	71	68.4	10
12/7	57	58	54	59	61	57.8	7	1/4	55	51	44	53	58	52.2	14
12/8	56	58	54	59	61	57.6	7	1/5	52	58	48	49	52	51.8	10
12/9	58	50	51	52	66	55.4	16	1/6	44	46	51	46	46	46.6	7
12/10	58	53	52	58	56	55.4	6	1/7	57	58	46	46	56	52.6	12
12/11	56	62	53	59	60	58.0	9	1/8	59	65	52	56	52	56.8	13
12/14	57	58	58	58	60	58.2	3	1/11	62	57	56	60	58	58.6	6
12/15	64	64	53	54	60	59.0	11	1/12	58	53	43	43	62	51.8	19
12/16	64	61	66	48	51	58.0	18	1/13	52	63	48	54	54	54.2	15

The engineer arbitrarily took the pressures at the start of each of five hours each day, called this a subgroup of size five, and constructed Average and Range charts. Therefore, each subgroup represents a single day's data, and consecutive subgroups are consecutive days.

(a) Plot the running records for the Subgroup Averages and Subgroup Ranges.

(b) The engineer decided to use the first 12 subgroups to compute the control limits. Why do you think he did this? Use the first 12 subgroups to compute control limits for the Averages and Ranges.

(c) Now use all 24 subgroups to compute control limits for the Averages and Ranges.

(d) What effect did the out-of-control Averages have on the limits found in part (c)?

(e) What effect did the out-of-control Ranges have upon the limits found in part (c)?

Exercise 3.3:

A data set consisting of 44 subgroups of size $n = 2$ has a Grand Average of 936.08 units, and an Average Range of 27.84 units. Compute control limits for an Average and Range Chart.

Exercise 3.4:

A certain chemical is produced in batches, and the batch identity is maintained in shipping to each customer (batches are not blended together). Since each batch is well-stirred and logically homogeneous, every batch is characterized by a single test value. These test values for the past 15 batches are:

35 39 38 42 37 37 39 37 37 40 39 39 38 42 36

(a) Since these data are used to characterize *each* batch, it would be inappropriate to arrange them into subgroups. Place these 15 values on an Individual and Moving Range Chart.

(b) If batch 16 had a value of 34, would that batch be judged to be consistent with the previous 15 batches?

(c) If batch 17 had a value of 44, would that batch be judged to be consistent with the previous batches?

Exercise 3.5:

Complex data can often be changed into numbers which are much easier to work with by subtracting off a constant and moving the decimal place. Consider the data of Table 2.3, page 32: The first five values are: 1.3750, 1.3751, 1.37505, 1.3749, and 1.3750. In each case, the 1.37xx portion of the number does nothing but hold the place. By subtracting 1.3700 from each value, and then moving the decimal over four places, these five values can be rewritten as: 50, 51, 50.5, 49, and 50.

Using this re-expression of these data, the fifty values in Table 2.3 become:

50	43	46	52	52	46	42	50	49	52
51	42	50	50	46	42	43	51	50	50
50.5	45	52	49	42	44	42	52	49.5	48
49	47	52.5	54	43	43	45	54	51	49.5
50	49	51	51	45	46	49	51	50	49

Arranging these fifty values into 10 subgroups of size five, the Subgroup Averages and Subgroup Ranges are:

$\bar{X}$	50.1	45.2	50.3	51.2	45.6	44.2	44.2	51.6	49.9	49.7
R	2	7	6.5	5	10	4	7	4	2	4

(a) Compute the control limits and plot the Average and Range Chart for these data.

(b) Is the process for producing Camshaft Bearing Number Three operating as consistently as possible?

Chapter Four

The Whys and Wherefores of Control Charts

Much of what has been written about control charts in both the technical journals and the trade press is contradictory. Some authors will allow just about anything (*PreControl*, *Zone Charts*, *two-sigma limits*, *Modified Control Limits*, etc.), while others would hedge the charts about with so many caveats that they would be impossible to use ("*the data must be normally and independently distributed*," "*you need 3.09 sigma limits*," "*you must use averages*", etc.). Moreover, distortions and perversions of the control chart are repeatedly offered up as "alternatives" and "modifications" even though they ignore or contradict the philosophical underpinnings of control charts. Any careful reading of this body of material will inevitably lead one to the conclusion that there is an appalling and widespread misunderstanding of Shewhart's control charts. The teaching of control charts can only be described as an example of Rule Four of the Funnel—a case of novices teaching neophytes and the blind leading the blind.

The purpose of this chapter is to provide the reader with an antidote to the confusion that surrounds control charts. While a full treatment of some of these topics is beyond the scope of this text, this chapter will outline some of the fundamental concepts behind Shewhart's charts. The intent of these discussions is to help the reader toward a more effective utilization of the charts.

The first section demonstrates, by means of three examples, the importance of using the right method of computation for the control limits. Two wrong methods are illustrated and the essential difference between the right and wrong methods is clearly defined.

The second section provides an explanation of why three-sigma limits are so effective in practice. Section Three shows what happens when the data are not normally distributed. This is done by presenting the results of a simulation study as a sequence of histograms. An appreciation of Sections Two and Three will lead to an understanding of why the control chart is so robust in practice.

Section Four lists some common myths about control charts and explains why they are myths. Finally, Section Five lists the Four Foundations of Shewhart's charts, and connects them to Deming's Fourteen Points.

4.1 Charts Done Right

The control chart formulas were not arbitrarily selected. They were instead carefully constructed to contain certain features which result in very robust limits. The notion of robustness used here is robustness of computation: *even though "out-of-control" data are used to compute the control limits, the limits will still be good enough to detect that lack of control.* It is this robustness that makes the control chart technique so effective in practice, since one can never know in advance if the data display a lack of control or not. The following example illustrates two of the right ways of computing control chart limits.

EXAMPLE 4.1:   *Average Charts Done Right:*

Three subgroups of size 8 are listed below:

Subgroup	Values	Average	Range	s
I	4 5 5 4 8 4 3 7	5	5	1.690
II	0 2 1 5 3 2 0 3	2	5	1.690
III	6 9 9 7 8 7 9 9	8	3	1.195

The Grand Average is $\overline{\overline{X}} = 5.0$, *and the Average Range is* $\overline{R} = 4.333$.
Limits for Average and Range Charts are found as follows:
$n = 8$ *gives* $A_2 = 0.373$, $D_3 = 0.136$, $D_4 = 1.864$ *from Table A.2, so:*

$$UCL_{\overline{X}} = \overline{\overline{X}} + A_2 \overline{R} = 5.0 + 0.373\,(4.333) = 6.62$$

$$CL_{\overline{X}} = \overline{\overline{X}} = 5.0$$

$$LCL_{\overline{X}} = \overline{\overline{X}} - A_2 \overline{R} = 5.0 - 0.373\,(4.333) = 3.38$$

$$UCL_R = D_4 \overline{R} = 1.864\,(4.333) = 8.08$$

$$CL_R = \overline{R} = 4.333$$

$$LCL_R = D_3 \overline{R} = 0.136\,(4.333) = 0.59$$

One could also use the data on the preceding page to compute limits for Averages and Standard Deviations as follows:

The Grand Average is $\bar{\bar{X}}$ = 5.0, and the Average Standard Deviation is $\bar{s}$ = 1.525. Limits for Average and Standard Deviation Charts are found as follows:

n = 8 gives A_3 = 1.099, B_3 = 0.185, B_4 = 1.815 from Table A.5, so:

$$UCL_{\bar{X}} = \bar{\bar{X}} + A_3\,\bar{s} = 5.0 + 1.099\,(1.525) = 6.68$$

$$CL_{\bar{X}} = \bar{\bar{X}} = 5.0$$

$$LCL_{\bar{X}} = \bar{\bar{X}} - A_3\,\bar{s} = 5.0 - 1.099\,(1.525) = 3.32$$

$$UCL_S = B_4\,\bar{s} = 1.815\,(1.525) = 2.768$$

$$CL_S = \bar{s} = 1.525$$

$$LCL_S = B_3\,\bar{s} = 0.185\,(1.525) = 0.282$$

These limits are shown in Figure 4.1:

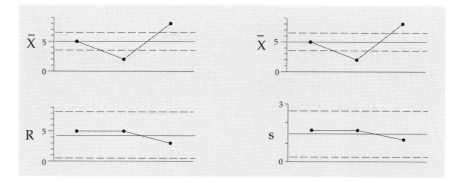

Figure 4.1: $\bar{X}$ and R Chart and $\bar{X}$ and s Chart for Example 4.1

Both of the Average Charts in Figure 4.1 display a lack of control. *Both methods of computing the limits detected this lack of control in spite of the fact that the out-of-control data were used to compute the limits!* This is a characteristic of the right way to compute control limits. The purpose of a control chart is to detect a lack of control when it exists, and it should be able to do so, at least most of the time, even when the out-of-control data are used to compute the limits. Otherwise, the technique would not be of much use. This ability to detect a lack of control is closely tied up with the manner in which the control limits are computed.

One should also note that the control limits computed for these two Average Charts are essentially the same even though different dispersion statistics were used. Moreover, both the Range Chart and the Standard Deviation Chart convey the same message.

The following examples illustrate two wrong ways of computing control limits.

EXAMPLE 4.2:   *Average Charts Done Wrong:*

The data from Example 4.1 will be used again.
Three subgroups of size 8 are listed below:

Subgroup	Values	Averages
I	4 5 5 4 8 4 3 7	5
II	0 2 1 5 3 2 0 3	2
III	6 9 9 7 8 7 9 9	8

This incorrect method computes the standard deviation of all 24 values and constructs the formulas for limits for the Average Chart from scratch:

$$\text{supposed control limits for } \bar{X} = \bar{\bar{X}} \pm 3 \frac{s}{\sqrt{n}}$$

Grand Average $= \bar{\bar{X}} = 5.0$

Standard Deviation for all 24 observations $= s = 2.904$

$$\text{"supposed" } UCL_{\bar{X}} = 5.0 + 3 \frac{2.904}{\sqrt{8}} = 8.08$$

$$CL_{\bar{X}} = 5.0$$

$$\text{"supposed" } LCL_{\bar{X}} = 5.0 - 3 \frac{2.904}{\sqrt{8}} = 1.92$$

These Limits are shown in Figure 4.2.

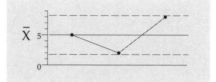

Figure 4.2: Incorrect Limits for the Average Chart (Example 4.2)

The limits computed in Example 4.2 and shown in Figure 4.2 obscure the fact the the Subgroup Averages are out-of-control! This is because these limits have been inflated by over 90% compared to the limits shown in Figure 4.1.

Even though many novices, and several computer programs, use the method of Example 4.2 for computing control chart limits, it is nevertheless completely and totally incorrect. There is absolutely no way that this approach can be justified. The use of this method *requires* the data to be completely homogeneous. This is why it will always be useless in any attempt to examine the data for possible non-homogeneity. Shewhart deliberately rejected the use of this method on page 302 of *Economic Control of Quality.*

While the flowchart in Figure 3.1 begins with the assumption of a stable process, one must remain skeptical about this assumption. It is an assumption made for the sake of argument, not because one actually believes the process is in statistical control.

EXAMPLE 4.3:   *Average Charts Done Wrong—Another Way:*

The data from Example 4.1 are:

Subgroup	Values	Averages
I	4 5 5 4 8 4 3 7	5
II	0 2 1 5 3 2 0 3	2
III	6 9 9 7 8 7 9 9	8

This incorrect method computes the standard deviation of the Subgroup Averages and constructs the formulas for limits for the Average Chart from scratch:

$$\text{supposed control limits for } \bar{X} = \bar{\bar{X}} \pm 3\, s_{\bar{x}}$$

$$\text{Grand Average} = \bar{\bar{X}} = 5.0$$

$$\text{Standard Deviation for 3 subgroup averages} = s_{\bar{x}} = 3.0$$

$$\text{"supposed" } UCL_{\bar{X}} = 5.0 + 3\,(3.0) = 14.0$$

$$CL_{\bar{X}} = 5.0$$

$$\text{"supposed" } LCL_{\bar{X}} = 5.0 - 3\,(3.0) = -4.0$$

These Limits are shown in Figure 4.3.

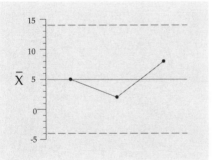

Figure 4.3: More Incorrect Limits for the Average Chart (Example 4.3)

The limits in Figure 4.3 are over 455% wider than the limits in Figure 4.1. They totally obscure the fact that the Subgroup Averages are out-of-control. Yet every (computerized) control chart in a plant in Indiana had limits computed in the manner of Example 4.3. Is it any wonder that they never found anything to be out-of-control?

Just as the method of Example 4.2 requires that the data be completely homogeneous, the method of Example 4.3 requires the Subgroup Averages to be completely homogeneous. Both of these requirements are totally inconsistent with the purpose of a control chart—the detection of differences between the subgroups—thus these methods are unreliable for detecting a lack of control. They presume that there is no possibility that the subgroups might be different. This is what makes them inappropriate for the computation of control chart limits.

What then is the difference between the right ways and the wrong ways of computing control chart limits? The wrong methods invariably use a *single dispersion statistic*. The right methods will invariably use the *average of k dispersion statistics* (or possibly a median of *k* dispersion statistics). The use of an average dispersion statistic is one of the foundations of Shewhart's control charts.

4.2 Why Three Sigma Limits?

The decision to use three-sigma limits on the control charts was not based *solely* upon probability theory. This point has been repeatedly misunderstood by those who would use probability theory to "adjust" the control chart limits. In order to present some of Shewhart's own thoughts, several excerpts follow which bear upon the choice of three sigma limits. [1]

"Hence we must use limits such that through their use we will not waste too much time looking unnecessarily for trouble."

"The method of attack is to establish limits of variability. . . such that, when [an observation] is found outside these limits, looking for an assignable cause is worth while."

"If more than one statistic is used, then the limits on all the statistics should be chosen so that the probability of looking for trouble when any one of the chosen statistics falls outside its own limits is economic."

". . .we usually choose a symmetrical range characterized by limits

$$\bar{\theta} \pm t\,\sigma_\theta \text{ ."}$$

"Experience indicates that *t* = 3 seems to be an acceptable economic value."

"Hence the method for establishing allowable limits of variation in a statistic θ depends upon theory to furnish the expected value $\bar{\theta}$ and the standard deviation σ_θ of the statistic θ and upon empirical evidence to justify the choice of limits

$$\bar{\theta} \pm t\,\sigma_\theta \text{ "}$$

Three-sigma limits are not probability limits. While we will resort to some theory to demonstrate some of the properties of three-sigma limits, it is important to remember that there are other considerations which were used by Shewhart in selecting this criterion. As indicated by the last quotation above, the strongest justification of three-sigma limits is the empirical evidence that three-sigma limits work well in practice—that they provide effective action limits when applied to real world data. Thus, the following arguments

---

[1] *Economic Control of Quality of Manufactured Product*, pp.147-148, 276-277.

cannot further justify the use of three-sigma limits, but they can reveal one of the reasons why they work so well.

While it is not a rigorous probabilistic argument, the Empirical Rule provides a useful way of characterizing data using a measure of location and a measure of dispersion.

THE EMPIRICAL RULE: Given a homogeneous set of data:

Part One: Roughly 60% to 75% of the data will be located within a distance of one sigma unit on either side of the average.

Part Two: Usually 90% to 98% of the data will be located within a distance of two sigma units on either side of the average.

Part Three: Approximately 99% to 100% of the data will be located within a distance of three sigma units on either side of the average.

A "sigma unit" is a measure of scale for the data. The common dispersion statistics can be converted into sigma units by the use of the formulas in Appendix Table A.1. By shifting from measurement units into sigma units, it is possible to characterize how much of the data will be within a given distance on either side of the average. **Thus, sigma units express the number of measurement units which correspond to one standard unit of dispersion.**

Notice that there is no requirement of normality (or even approximate normality) in the Empirical Rule. It is general enough to apply to many different sorts of data. However, since it is difficult to illustrate this robustness with sets of data, we will resort to the use of probability models instead. When applied to a probability model the percentages in the Empirical Rule refer to areas under the curve, the sigma unit is replaced by the dispersion parameter, SD(X), and the average is replaced by the location parameter, MEAN(X).[2]

In order to display the robustness of the Empirical Rule six different probability models are used. All are constructed so as to have MEAN(X) = 0 and SD(X) = 1.0. Therefore, the interval defined by part one of the Empirical Rule will go from –1 to 1, the interval defined by part two will range from –2 to 2, while the interval defined by part three will range from –3 to 3.

The three parts of the Empirical Rule will be illustrated in Figures 4.4, 4.5, and 4.6.

---

[2] Parameters are descriptive constants for a theoretical probability model. For a discussion of the relationships between histograms and their statistics and theoretical models and their parameters see Section 9.9.

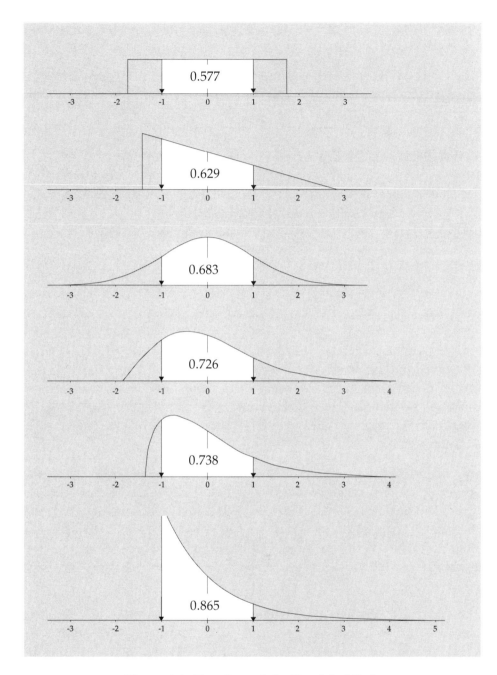

Figure 4.4: Part One of the Empirical Rule

Part One of the Empirical Rule is the weakest part. Only four of the six distributions shown in Figure 4.4 satisfy Part One. Nonetheless, Part One is still a useful guide for describing where the bulk of the distribution (or the data) will be.

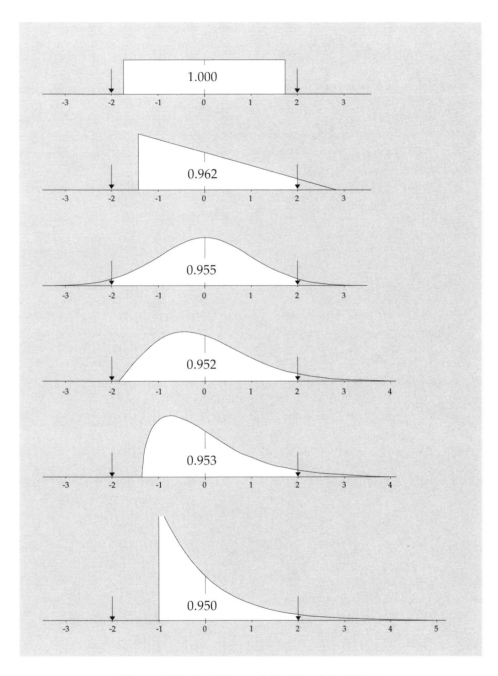

Figure 4.5: Part Two of the Empirical Rule

Part Two is stronger than Part One. Only one of the six distributions in Figure 4.5 does not satisfy Part Two.

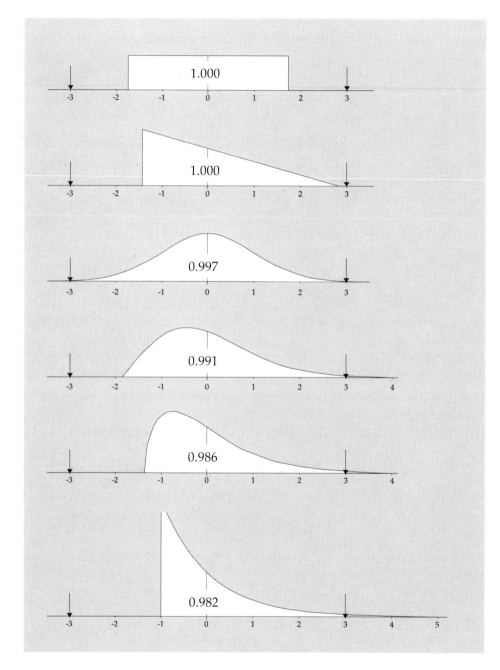

Figure 4.6: Part Three of the Empirical Rule

Part Three is the strongest part of the Empirical Rule. With regard to probability models, Part Three suggests that no matter how skewed, no matter how "heavy-tailed," virtually all of the distribution will fall within 3 standard deviations of the mean.

When applied to homogeneous sets of data, the third part of the Empirical Rule suggests that no matter how the data "behave," virtually all of the data will fall within three sigma units of the average. Since data which display statistical control are, by definition, reasonably homogeneous, the Empirical Rule provides an explanation why the control chart will yield very few "false alarms." At the same time, when a point falls outside the three-sigma limits it is very likely to be due to the presence of an Assignable Cause.

As was indicated by the formulas in the preceding section and the observations about the choice of three-sigma limits at the beginning of this section, there is more to the control chart than just the application of the third part of the Empirical Rule. Nonetheless, the third part of the Empirical Rule is a powerful reason why three-sigma limits work.

4.3 What if the Data are not Normally Distributed?

What if the data are not normally distributed? For those who use control charts this question will be of interest mainly because so many have used the supposed requirement of normality as an obstacle to the use of control charts. They have prescribed elaborate rituals for verifying and establishing normality—rituals such as plotting the data on probability paper, or using lack-of-fit tests to check for normality, or transforming the data using logarithms or other complex mathematical functions. Of course these rituals are all more complex than the control chart itself, but at least complexity sounds profound, even when it is nonsense.

The assumption of normally distributed data is introduced into the control chart formulas through the use of the control chart constants (see Appendix Tables A.1 to A.7 for these constants). The values for these constants are computed using a normal probability distribution for the original data. Fortunately, the assumption of normality is not a critical assumption. The control chart constants will not change appreciably even when the data are non-normal.[3]

Control charts work well even if the data are not normally distributed. This issue was addressed by Shewhart in his first book, and it should never have been an issue. However, since it has continued to be an issue, this section will consider just how the Average and Range Charts behave when the data are not normally distributed.

Shewhart resorted to simulation studies to examine the robustness of the control chart approach. While he used two non-normal distributions, the study presented here uses

---

[3] Irving Burr examined 26 non-normal distributions and found that A_2 varied less than 2% on the average, and that D_4 varied less than 6% on the average. Before discrepancies of this size will have a detectable impact upon the control limits, the limits would have to be computed using at least 150 subgroups of size 5.

five non-normal distributions and a normal distribution (the six distributions shown in Figure 4.7).

These six distributions are, respectively, from top to bottom, the Uniform distribution, the Right Triangular distribution, the Normal distribution, a Burr distribution, the Chi-Square distribution with 2 degrees of freedom, and the Exponential distribution.

The first three of these distributions are the same ones that Shewhart used in his simulation studies. The last three were included to consider the behavior of the control charts in the presence of "heavy-tailed" distributions.

Each simulation run was begun by generating observations from one of the six distributions (by means of a pseudo-random number generator). These observations were then grouped in subgroups of size n, and the Subgroup Average and the Sub-

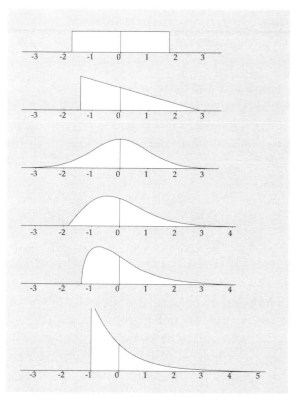

Figure 4.7: Six Theoretical Distributions

group Range were calculated. Continuing in this manner, histograms for the measurements, the averages, and the ranges were generated. This whole process was repeated for subgroup sizes of $n = 2, 4,$ and 10. Since these data were obtained from a homogeneous source, they will, *a priori*, display statistical control. Thus, as one looks at the histograms below, most of the Individual Values, Subgroup Averages, and Subgroup Ranges *should* fall within the three sigma limits shown.

Six distributions and three subgroup sizes give a total of 18 simulations. Each of these simulations is summarized by three histograms—one for the Individual Values, one for the Subgroup Averages, and one for the Subgroup Ranges. Each histogram shows the appropriate three-sigma limits, and the percentage of the values which fell within these limits. Each of the following figures gives the results for two of the 18 simulations. The six simulations with $n = 2$ are given first, followed by the six with $n = 4$, and then the six with $n = 10$.

Following each figure a short summary of the two simulation studies is given.

We begin with the results for subgroups of size $n = 2$. The results for the Uniform distribution and the Right Triangular distribution are shown in Figure 4.8.

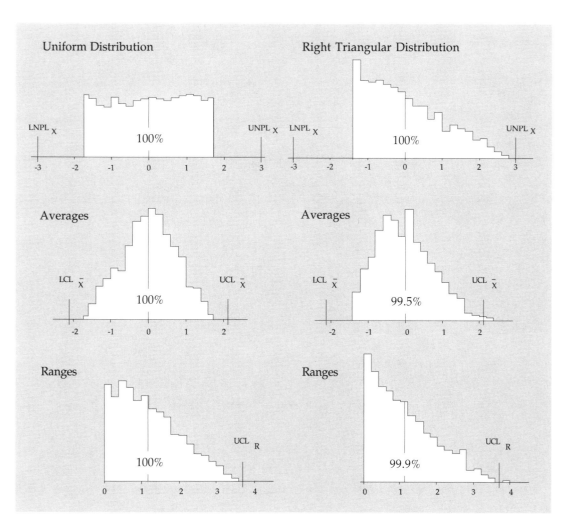

Figure 4.8: Results for Uniform and Triangular Dist. when $n = 2$

With the Uniform distribution and subgroups of size $n = 2$, *all* of the 2000 Individual Values fell inside the interval [-3,3], *all* of the 1000 Subgroup Averages fell within the interval [-2.12, 2.12], and *all* of the 1000 Subgroup Ranges fell within the interval [0, 3.68].

With the Triangular distribution and subgroups of size $n = 2$, *all* of the 2000 Individual Values fell inside the interval [-3,3], 995 of the 1000 Subgroup Averages fell within the interval [-2.12, 2.12], and 999 of the 1000 Subgroup Ranges fell within the interval [0, 3.68].

The results for subgroups of size $n = 2$ drawn from the Normal distribution and the Burr distribution are shown in Figure 4.9.

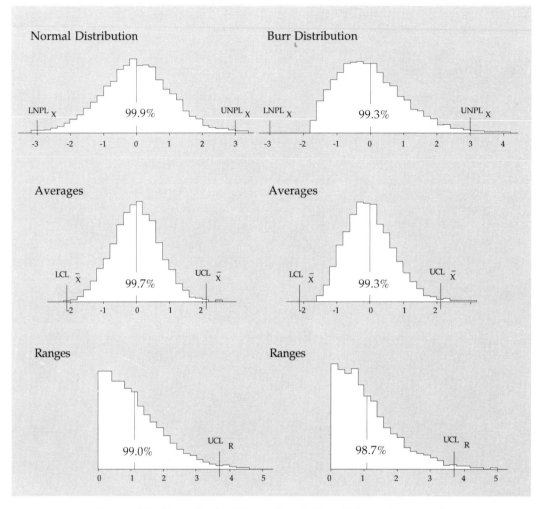

Figure 4.9: Results for Normal and Burr Dist. when $n = 2$

With the Normal distribution and subgroups of size $n = 2$, 9987 of the 10,000 Individual Values fell inside the interval [-3,3], 4985 of the 5000 Subgroup Averages fell within the interval [-2.12, 2.12], and 4948 of the 5000 Subgroup Ranges fell within the interval [0, 3.68].

With the Burr distribution and subgroups of size $n = 2$, 9926 of the 10,000 Individual Values fell inside the interval [-3,3], 4964 of the 5000 Subgroup Averages fell within the interval [-2.12, 2.12], and 4937 of the 5000 Subgroup Ranges fell within the interval [0, 3.68].

The results for subgroups of size $n = 2$ drawn from the Chi-Square distribution and the Exponential distribution are shown in Figure 4.10.

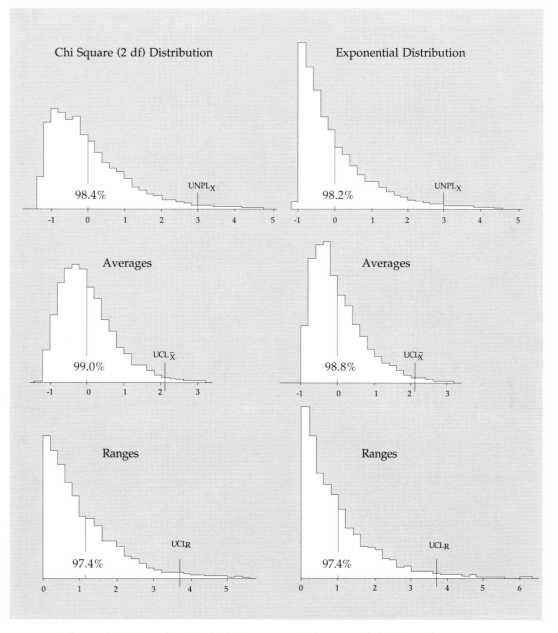

Figure 4.10: Results for Chi-Square and Exponential Dist. when *n* = 2

With the Chi-Square distribution and subgroups of size *n* = 2, 9840 of the 10,000 Individual Values fell inside the interval [-3,3], 4952 of the 5000 Subgroup Averages fell within the interval [-2.12, 2.12], and 4872 of the 5000 Subgroup Ranges fell within the interval [0, 3.68].

With the Exponential distribution and subgroups of size *n* = 2, 9817 of the 10,000 Individual Values fell inside the interval [-3,3], 4939 of the 5000 Subgroup Averages fell within the interval [-2.12, 2.12], and 4868 of the 5000 Subgroup Ranges fell within the interval [0, 3.68].

The results for subgroups of size $n = 4$ drawn from the Uniform distribution and the Right Triangular distribution are shown in Figure 4.11.

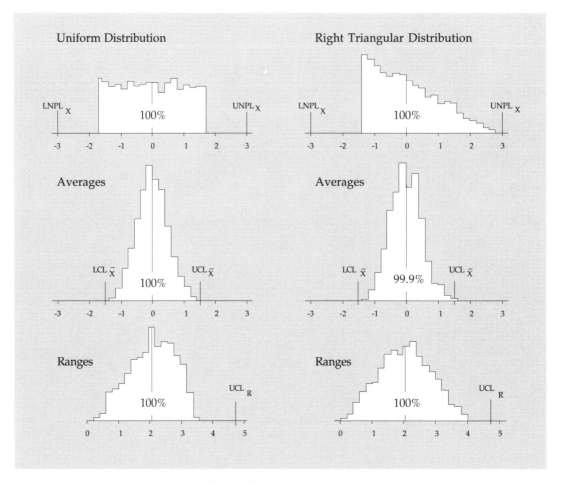

Figure 4.11: Results for Uniform and Triangular Dist. when $n = 4$

With the Uniform distribution and subgroups of size $n = 4$, *all* of the 4000 Individual Values fell inside the interval [-3,3], *all* of the 1000 Subgroup Averages fell within the interval [-1.5, 1.5], and *all* of the 1000 Subgroup Ranges fell within the interval [0, 4.70].

With the Triangular distribution and subgroups of size $n = 4$, *all* of the 4000 Individual Values fell inside the interval [-3,3], 999 of the 1000 Subgroup Averages fell within the interval [-1.5, 1.5], and *all* of the 1000 Subgroup Ranges fell within the interval [0, 4.70].

The results for subgroups of size $n = 4$ drawn from the Normal distribution and the Burr distribution are shown in Figure 4.12.

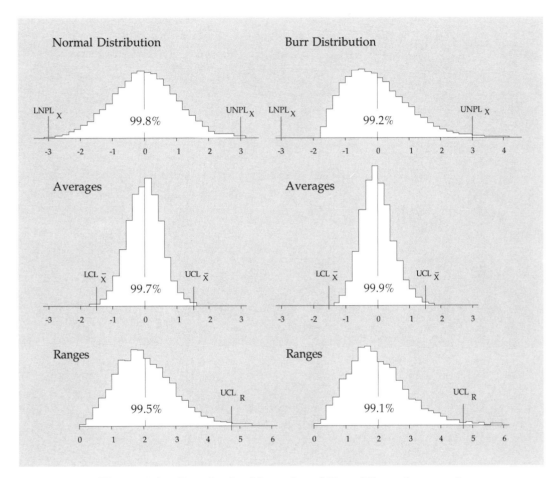

Figure 4.12: Results for Normal and Burr Dist. when $n = 4$

With the Normal distribution and subgroups of size $n = 4$, 19,960 of the 20,000 Individual Values fell inside the interval [-3,3], 4987 of the 5000 Subgroup Averages fell within the interval [-1.5, 1.5], and 4977 of the 5000 Subgroup Ranges fell within the interval [0, 4.70].

With the Burr distribution and subgroups of size $n = 4$, 19,838 of the 20,000 Individual Values fell inside the interval [-3,3], 4996 of the 5000 Subgroup Averages fell within the interval [-1.5, 1.5], and 4954 of the 5000 Subgroup Ranges fell within the interval [0, 4.70].

The results for subgroups of size $n = 4$ drawn from the Chi-Square distribution and the Exponential distribution are shown in Figure 4.13.

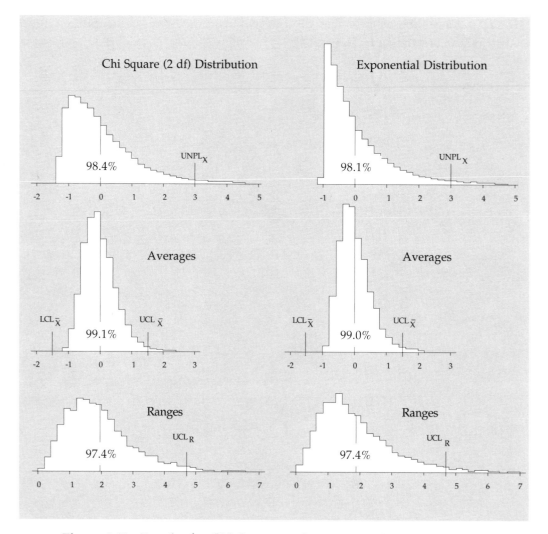

Figure 4.13: Results for Chi-Square and Exponential Dist. when *n* = 4

With the Chi-Square distribution and subgroups of size *n* = 4, 19,686 of the 20,000 Individual Values fell inside the interval [-3,3], 4956 of the 5000 Subgroup Averages fell within the interval [-1.5, 1.5], and 4868 of the 5000 Subgroup Ranges fell within the interval [0, 4.70].

With the Exponential distribution and subgroups of size *n* = 4, 19,619 of the 20,000 Individual Values fell inside the interval [-3,3], 4949 of the 5000 Subgroup Averages fell within the interval [-1.5, 1.5], and 4868 of the 5000 Subgroup Ranges fell within the interval [0, 4.70].

The results for subgroups of size *n* = 10 drawn from the Uniform distribution and the Right Triangular distribution are shown in Figure 4.14.

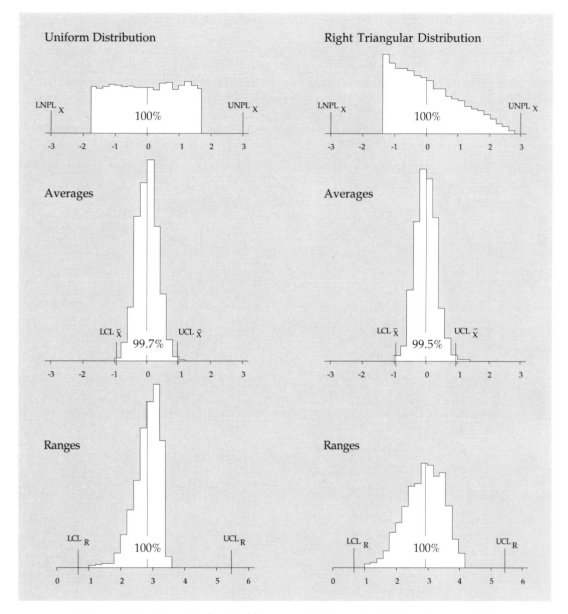

Figure 4.14: Results for Uniform and Triangular Dist. when *n* = 10

With the Uniform distribution and subgroups of size *n* = 10, *all* of the 10,000 Individual Values fell inside the interval [-3,3], 997 of the 1000 Subgroup Averages fell within the interval [-.95, .95], and *all* of the 1000 Subgroup Ranges fell within the interval [0.69, 5.47].

With the Triangular distribution and subgroups of size *n* = 10, *all* of the 10,000 Individual Values fell inside the interval [-3,3], 995 of the 1000 Subgroup Averages fell within the interval [-.95, .95], and *all* of the 1000 Subgroup Ranges fell within [0.69, 5.47].

The results for subgroups of size $n = 10$ drawn from the Normal distribution and the Burr distribution are shown in Figure 4.15.

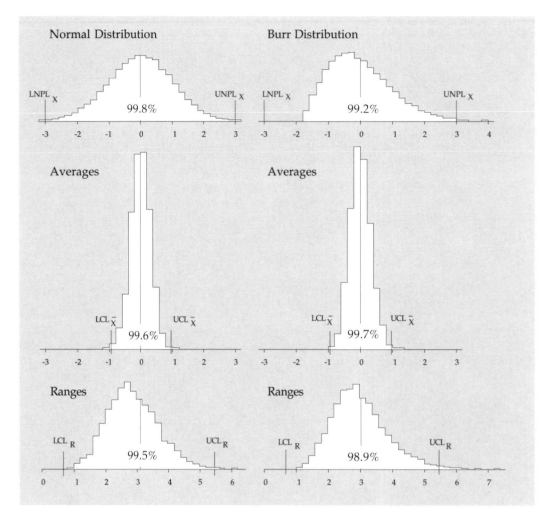

Figure 4.15: Results for Normal and Burr Dist. when $n = 10$

With the Normal distribution and subgroups of size $n = 10$, 49,897 of the 50,000 Individual Values fell inside the interval [-3,3], 4982 of the 5000 Subgroup Averages fell within the interval [-.95, .95], and 4977 of the 5000 Subgroup Ranges fell within the interval [0.69, 5.47].

With the Burr distribution and subgroups of size $n = 10$, 49,603 of the 50,000 Individual Values fell inside the interval [-3,3], 4984 of the 5000 Subgroup Averages fell within the interval [-.95, .95], and 4946 of the 5000 Subgroup Ranges fell within the interval [0.69, 5.47].

The results for subgroups of size $n = 10$ drawn from the Chi-Square distribution and the Exponential distribution are shown in Figure 4.16.

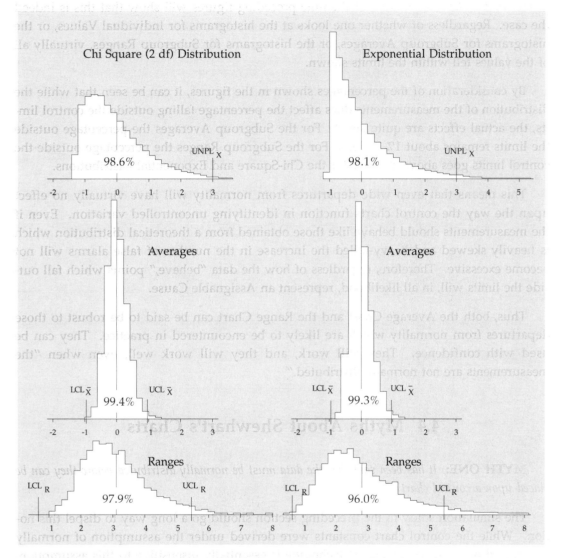

Figure 4.16: Results for Chi-Square and Exponential Dist. when $n = 10$

With the Chi-Square distribution and subgroups of size $n = 10$, 49,310 of the 50,000 Individual Values fell inside the interval [-3,3], 4972 of the 5000 Subgroup Averages fell within the interval [-.95, .95], and 4896 of the 5000 Subgroup Ranges fell within the interval [0.69, 5.47].

With the Exponential distribution and subgroups of size $n = 10$, 49,070 of the 50,000 Individual Values fell inside the interval [-3,3], 4964 of the 5000 Subgroup Averages fell within the interval [-.95, .95], and 4800 of the 5000 Subgroup Ranges fell in [0.69, 5.47].

Due to the way the preceding data were obtained they can be logically said to display statistical control. Therefore, one would expect most of the data to fall within the appropriate limits. An examination of the nine preceding figures will show that this is indeed the case. Regardless of whether one looks at the histograms for Individual Values, or the histograms for Subgroup Averages, or the histograms for Subgroup Ranges, virtually all of the values fell within the limits shown.

By consideration of the percentages shown in the figures, it can be seen that while the distribution of the measurements does affect the percentage falling outside the control limits, the actual effects are quite small. For the Subgroup Averages the percentage outside the limits remains about 1% or less. For the Subgroup Ranges the percentage outside the control limits goes above 2% only for the Chi-Square and Exponential Distributions.

This means that even wide departures from normality will have virtually no effect upon the way the control charts function in identifying uncontrolled variation. Even if the measurements should behave like those obtained from a theoretical distribution which is heavily skewed and heavy-tailed the increase in the number of false alarms will not become excessive. Therefore, regardless of how the data "behave," points which fall outside the limits will, in all likelihood, represent an Assignable Cause.

Thus, both the Average Chart and the Range Chart can be said to be robust to those departures from normality which are likely to be encountered in practice. They can be used with confidence. They will work, and they will work well, even when "the measurements are not normally distributed."

4.4 Myths About Shewhart's Charts

MYTH ONE: *It has been said that the data must be normally distributed before they can be placed upon a control chart.*

The simulation study in the preceding section should go a long way to dispel this notion. While the control chart constants were derived under the assumption of normally distributed data, the control chart technique is essentially insensitive to this assumption. This insensitivity is part of what makes the control chart robust enough to work in the real world as a procedure for inductive inference.

This myth is an expression of a misunderstanding of the relationship between the control chart and the techniques of statistical inference. As Shewhart noted, *"we are not concerned with the functional form of the universe, but merely with the assumption that a universe exists."* [4]

---

[4] *Statistical Method from the Viewpoint of Quality Control*, p.54. Emphasis in the original.

"Some of the earliest attempts to characterize a state of statistical control were inspired by the belief that there existed a special form of frequency function f(x) and it was early argued that the normal law characterized such a state.[5] When the normal law was found to be inadequate, then generalized functional forms were tried. Today, however, all hopes of finding a unique functional form f(x) are blasted."[6]

Therefore, the data do not have to be normally distributed before one can place them on a control chart. The computations are essentially unaffected by the normality, or non-normality of the data. At the same time, just because the data display a reasonable degree of statistical control does not mean that the data will follow a normal distribution. *The normality of the data is neither a prerequisite nor a consequence of a state of statistical control.*

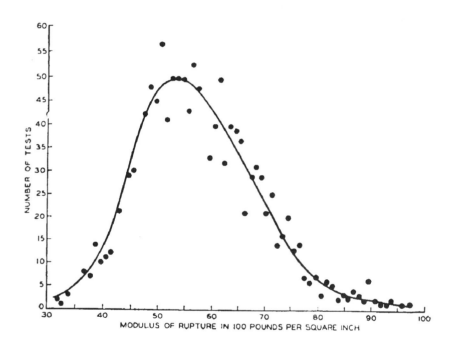

Figure 4.17: Shewhart's Figure 9: Variability in Modulus of Rupture of Clear Specimens of Green Sitka Spruce Typical of the Statistical Nature of Physical Properties

As a final bit of evidence against this myth we turn to page 23 of *Economic Control of Quality of Manufactured Product.* Here Shewhart presents the data shown in Figure 4.17. He characterizes these data as "at least approximately [in] a state of control." They are certainly not normally distributed!

---

[5] e.g. Adolphe Quetelet, circa 1845.
[6] *Statistical Method from the Viewpoint of Quality Control*, p.12.

MYTH TWO: *It has been said that the control chart works because of the central limit theorem.*

The central limit theorem does apply to Subgroup Averages: as the subgroup size increases, the histogram of the Subgroup Averages will, in the limit, become more "normal" regardless of how the individual measurements are distributed. This tendency can be seen in the histograms in Figure 4.18. (These histograms were drawn from those in Section 4.3.) Even though the distributions for the Individual Values are totally different, the distributions for the subgroup averages tend to look more and more alike as the subgroup size increases.

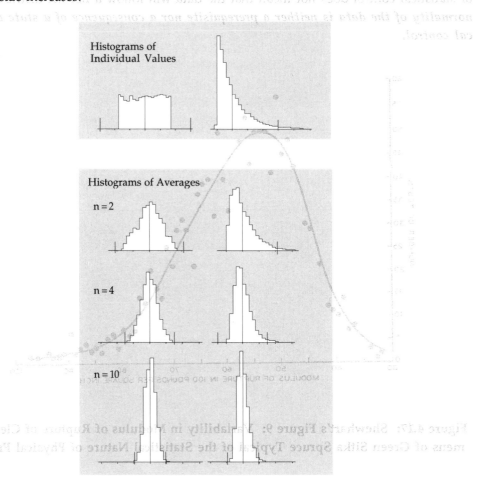

Figure 4.18: The Central Limit Theorem for Subgroup Averages

Many statistical techniques which are based upon averages utilize the central limit theorem. Because the central limit is so widely used, it is only natural to assume that it is also the basis for the control chart. However, this is not the case.

Even though the central limit theorem applies to the Subgroup Averages, it is not the reason why control charts work. First of all, the central limit theorem does *not* apply to Subgroup Ranges, therefore, if the central limit theorem was the basis for control charts, then the Range Chart would not work. This is illustrated in Figure 4.19. Using two distributions for Individual Values, and sample sizes of $n = 2$, $n = 4$, and $n = 10$, the histograms for the Subgroup Ranges do not display increasing similarity with increasing subgroup size. In fact it is just the opposite. As n increases the histograms for the Subgroup Ranges become more dissimilar.

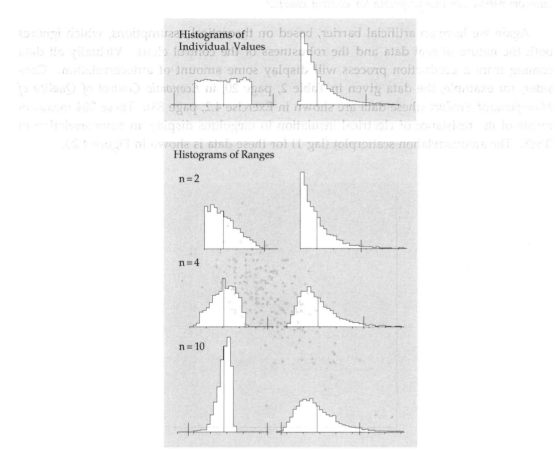

Figure 4.19: The Lack of a Central Limit Theorem for Subgroup Ranges

The second reason that the central limit theorem cannot be said to be the basis for control charts is the conservative nature of three-sigma limits. When you have already bracketed approximately 99% to 100% of the values by brute force, one does not need to appeal to any theoretical arguments to understand that a point outside the limits is very likely to represent a signal. The conservative nature of three-sigma limits makes the central limit theorem irrelevant. This was illustrated in Figure 4.6, page 64.

Undoubtedly, this myth has been one of the greatest barriers to the effective use of control charts with management data and process-industry data. Whenever data are obtained one-value-per-time-period it will be logical to use "subgroups of size one." However, if someone believes this myth, they will feel compelled to average something in order to invoke the blessing of the central limit theorem, and the rationality of the data analysis will be sacrificed to superstition.

MYTH THREE: *It has been said that the observations must be independent—data with autocorrelation are inappropriate for control charts.*[7]

Again we have an artificial barrier, based on theoretical assumptions, which ignores both the nature of real data and the robustness of the control chart. Virtually all data coming from a production process will display some amount of autocorrelation. Consider, for example, the data given in Table 2, page 20, in *Economic Control of Quality of Manufactured Product* (these data are shown in Exercise 4.2, page 88). These 204 measurements of the resistance of electrical insulation in megohms display an autocorrelation of 0.548. The autocorrelation scatterplot (lag 1) for these data is shown in Figure 4.20.

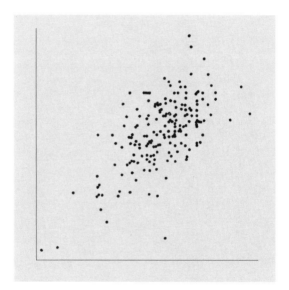

Figure 4.20: Autocorrelation of Data from *Economic Control of Quality*, page 20

Yet Shewhart organized these data into 51 subgroups of size four and plotted the control charts. The Average Chart for these data displayed a lack of control. This Average Chart was shown on page 21 of his book as the left hand portion of "Figure 7:"

---

[7] A large positive autocorrelation will exist when the data display two characteristics: (i) successive individual values are generally quite similar, while (ii) non-sequential individual values may be quite dissimilar. A more complete treatment of autocorrelation is given in Wheeler 1989.

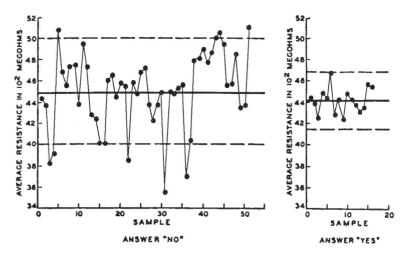

FIG. 7.—SHOULD THESE VARIATIONS BE LEFT TO CHANCE?

Figure 4.21: Shewhart's Average Chart for Correlated Data

In describing these data Shewhart wrote:

> "*Several of the observed values [averages] lie outside these limits. This was taken as an indication of the existence of causes of variability which could be found and eliminated.*
>
> "*Further research was instituted at this point to find these causes of variability. Several were found, and after these had been eliminated another series of observed values gave the results indicated in Fig. 7–b. Here we see that all of the points lie within the limits. We assumed therefore, upon the basis of this [chart], that it was not feasible for research to go much further in eliminating causes of variability. Because of the importance of this particular experiment, however, considerably more work was done, but it failed to reveal causes of variability. Here then is a typical case where the [control chart] indicates when variability should be left to chance.*"

Remember that the purpose of analysis is insight rather than numbers. The control chart is not concerned with probability models, but with using data for making decisions in the real world. Control charts have worked with autocorrelated data for over 60 years!

While a complete treatment of the effects of autocorrelation is beyond the scope of this text, the following observation is in order. Even though it is true that excessive positive autocorrelation (say greater than 0.80) will tighten the control limits, it will also simultaneously create a running record that is easy to interpret at face value. Thus, in those cases where autocorrelation contaminates the limits, it also makes the running record more useful in its own right. This increased interpretability of the running record will usually provide the insight needed for process improvement, and further computations become unnecessary.

MYTH FOUR: *It has been said that the data must be in control before one can plot them on a control chart.*

This myth can only have come from the use of one of the wrong methods of computing limits which were detailed in section one of this chapter. Among the absurdities which have been perpetrated in the name of this myth are the censoring of the data prior to placing them on the chart and the use of "two-sigma" or "2.33 sigma" limits. Needless to say that these, and all the other, manipulations are unnecessary. The express purpose of the control chart is the detection of a lack of control. If a control chart cannot be used to detect a lack of control, then what is the reason for ever using a chart? Look at Figure 4.21 again.

Other myths exist. Additional myths will probably be created in the future. It has been the purpose of this chapter to combat the myths surrounding Shewhart's charts in order to help the reader to use these charts more effectively. Continuing in this vein, the next section will list the four foundations for Shewhart's charts.

4.5 Four Foundations for Shewhart's Charts

FOUNDATION ONE: *Shewhart's charts will always use control limits which are set at a distance of three sigma units on either side of the central line.*

Regardless of whether one is working with Individual Values, Subgroup Averages, Subgroup Ranges, Subgroup Standard Deviations, Moving Ranges or Moving Averages, the limits will be placed according to the same principle.

These three-sigma limits will always be based upon the data. They cannot be determined by any computation based upon specifications. This is the problem with both Modified Control Limits and the techniques which have been labeled "PreControl." By attempting to base action limits on specifications these techniques end up with limits that can never work as well as the data-based control limits. They will always have either more false alarms or more missed signals than the control chart.

Three sigma limits are action limits—they define the point at which one is justified in taking action on the process. They are not probability limits. While they have a basis in probability theory, three-sigma limits were essentially chosen because they provided reasonable action limits. They strike an economical balance between the two types of errors that one can make in interpreting data from a continuing process. They neither result in too many false alarms, nor do they miss too many signals.[8]

As was shown earlier, much of the robustness of the control charts comes from the use of three-sigma limits. These limits are conservative enough to be insensitive to non-normality of the data even when the subgroup size is one. This is why there is simply no need to appeal to the central limit theorem to justify the use of the control chart. Three-sigma limits have been thoroughly proven in over 60 years of practice to be the best action limits for production processes. Accept no substitutes.

FOUNDATION TWO: *In computing three-sigma control limits one must always use an average dispersion statistic.*[9]

By computing several dispersion statistics and using either an average or a median dispersion statistic one introduces considerable stability into the computations. More-over, this use of the within subgroup variation will provide measures of dispersion which are much less sensitive to a lack of control than any other approach. This was demon-strated in Section 4.1.

The choice of dispersion statistic is unimportant. One may use Ranges, Standard Devi-ations, or Root Mean Square Deviations—these choices do not matter. If one uses the proper approach, the different statistics will yield similar results. If one uses the wrong approach, the different statistics will also yield similar *incorrect* results. Thus, it is impera-tive that the student learn and use the correct approach (see Tables A.2 through A.7).

When the subgroup size is $n = 1$, one must use the Average Moving Range to con-struct the limits. (The right and wrong ways of computing limits for Individual Values is discussed in Section 9.2.)

FOUNDATION THREE: *The conceptual foundation of Shewhart's control charts is the notion of rational sampling and rational subgrouping.*

How the data are collected, how they are arranged into subgroups, and how these subgroups are placed on the charts must be based upon a consideration of the context for the data, the sources of variation present in the data, the questions to be addressed by the charts, and the use to be made of the knowledge gained.

Failure to consider these factors when placing data on a control chart can result in

---

[8] For further reading on this topic see *Economic Control of Quality* pp.147, 148, 276, 277 and 304.

[9] The only exceptions for this are the Attribute Charts, which use location statistics to compute the limits instead of dispersion statistics. See Section 10.2, page 258.

control charts which are nonsense. It is only by respecting these factors that one gains the leverage to make the control chart informative and useful. It is this flexibility which gives Shewhart's charts the ability to provide the maximum amount of insight with the least effort. Unfortunately, the novice can get tangled up in this flexibility.

The effective use of Shewhart's charts requires an appreciation of rational sampling and rational subgrouping. These topics are discussed more completely in Chapter Five.

FOUNDATION FOUR: *Control charts are effective only to the extent that the organization can use, in an effective manner, the knowledge gained from the charts.*

Without an organization which can disseminate and act upon knowledge gained, the knowledge is gained in vain. Knowledge is only useful as a basis for action, and without the ability to respond to knowledge by changing the organization's actions as appropriate, SPC will not be as effective as it can be. As long as there are internal barriers and obstacles that prevent the organization from utilizing the charts, nothing will happen. This is why so many of Dr. Deming's 14 points bear directly upon this one foundation.

This is why SPC alone is not enough. If one cornerstone is missing, the whole building will be crooked. On the other hand, working at any program for increasing organizational effectiveness and efficiency without using SPC is doomed to failure. This is because old habits die hard. There needs to be some catalyst to promote organizational change, and that is just what SPC can provide. Each piece of knowledge gained by SPC makes a demand upon the organization. As the organization responds to this demand, it will be reinforcing new habits to replace the old. With new habits, SPC becomes more effective, more knowledge is gained, and more demands are made upon the organization. This feedback cycle is the basis for continual improvement.

This Fourth Foundation of Shewhart's Charts was only implicit in Shewhart's work—there was always the assumption that organizations would behave in a rational manner. However, Dr. Deming came to see that this was not the case. Just giving businessmen effective methods of collecting, organizing, and analyzing data was not enough. In the absence of such methods, businesses had come to be run by the emotional interpretation of the visible figures—a universal "My mind is made up, don't bother me with the facts" syndrome.

As he contrasted his experience in Japan with that in the United States, Dr. Deming began to characterize just what was needed before an organization could behave in a rational manner. In 1967 he authored a paper entitled "What Happened In Japan?" In it nine characteristics were listed. These nine characteristics then evolved into "Some New Principles in Administration" published in 1975 in an article entitled "On Some Statistical Aids Toward Economic Production," and finally into the "14 points" in the early 1980's.

While these 14 points do not constitute the whole of Dr. Deming's philosophy, they are a profound starting point. They are not techniques, they are not a list of instructions, nor or they a checklist. They are a vision of just what can be involved in "using SPC." And they ultimately lead to radically different and better ways of organizing businesses and working with people. However, a deep understanding is required before these 14 points can be used to accomplish the "total transformation." The need is not to "adopt the 14 points," individually, or collectively, but rather to create a new environment which is conducive to them and consistent with them.

Dr. Deming's Fourteen Points

1. Create constancy of purpose for continual improvement of products and service to society, allocating resources to provide for long-range needs rather than only short-term profitability, with a plan to become competitive, to stay in business, and to provide jobs.

2. Adopt the new philosophy. We are in a new economic age, created in Japan. We can no longer live with commonly-accepted levels of delays, mistakes, defective materials, and defective workmanship. Transformation of Western management style is necessary to halt the continued decline of industry.

3. Eliminate the need for mass inspection as the way of life to achieve quality by building quality into the product in the first place. Require statistical evidence of built-in quality in both manufacturing and purchasing functions.

4. End the practice of awarding business solely on the basis of price tag. Instead, require meaningful measures of quality along with the price. Reduce the number of suppliers for the same item by eliminating those that do not qualify with statistical and other evidence of quality. The aim is to minimize *total* cost, not merely initial cost, by minimizing variation. This may be achievable by moving toward a single supplier for any one item, on a long-term relationship of loyalty and trust. Purchasing managers have a new job, and must learn it.

5. Improve constantly and forever every process for planning, production, and service. Search continually for problems in order to improve every activity in the company, to improve quality and productivity, and thus to constantly decrease costs. Institute innovation and constant improvement of product, service, and process. It is the management's job to work continually on the system (design, incoming materials, maintenance, improvement of machines, supervision, training, retraining).

6. Institute modern methods of training on the job for all, including management, to make better use of every employee. New skills are required to keep up with changes in materials, methods, product design, machinery, techniques, and service.

7. Adopt and institute leadership aimed at helping people to do a better job. The responsibility of managers and supervisors must be changed from sheer numbers to quality. Improvement of quality will automatically improve productivity. Management must ensure that immediate action is taken on reports of inherited defects, maintenance requirements, poor tools, fuzzy operational definitions, and all conditions detrimental to quality.

8. Encourage effective two-way communication and other means to drive out fear throughout the organization so that everybody may work effectively and more productively for the company.

9. Break down barriers between departments and staff areas. People in different areas, such as Research, Design, Sales, Administration, and Production, must work in teams to tackle problems that may be encountered with products or service.

10. Eliminate the use of slogans, posters and exhortations for the work-force, demanding Zero Defects and new levels of productivity, without providing methods. Such exhortations only create adversarial relationships; the bulk of the causes of low quality and low productivity belong to the system, and thus lie beyond the power of the work-force.

11. Eliminate work standards that prescribe quotas for the work-force and numerical goals for people in management. Substitute aids and helpful leadership in order to achieve continual improvement of quality and productivity.

12. Remove the barriers that rob hourly workers, and people in management, of their right to pride of workmanship. This implies, *inter alia*, abolition of the annual merit rating (appraisal of performance) and of Management by Objective. Again, the responsibility of managers, supervisors, foremen must be changed from sheer numbers to quality.

13. Institute a vigorous program of education, and encourage self-improvement for everyone. What an organization needs is not just good people; it needs people that are improving with education. Advances in competitive position will have their roots in knowledge.

14. Clearly define top management's permanent commitment to ever-improving quality and productivity, and their obligation to implement all of these principles. Indeed, it is not enough that top management commit themselves for life to quality and productivity. They must know what it is that they are committed to—that is, what they must do. Create a structure in top management that will push every day on the preceding 13 Points, and take action in order to accomplish the transformation. Support is not enough: action is required.

To delve deeper into the issues involved in these 14 points see *The Deming Dimension* by Henry Neave and *Out of the Crisis* by Dr. Deming.

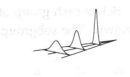

Exercise 4.1:

On page 29 the fifty diameters for Camshaft Bearing Number Three are summarized with an Average and a Root Mean Square Deviation. The Average is 1.37482, and the Standard Deviation is 0.000354.

Transforming the data as shown in Exercise 3.5, page 54, these summary statistics would also be transformed:

the Grand Average of 1.37482 would become 48.20,

and the Standard Deviation of 0.000354 would become 3.54.

(a) In Exercise 3.4 the 50 Camshaft Bearing Number Three diameters were arranged into 10 subgroups of size five. The 10 Subgroup Averages were:

$\bar{X}$ 50.1   45.2   50.3   51.2   45.6   44.2   44.2   51.6   49.9   49.7

Use the Grand Average of 48.2 and the Standard Deviation of 3.54 to compute INCORRECT limits for Subgroup Averages using the following formula (based on Example 4.2, page 58).

$$\text{supposed control limits for } \bar{X} = \bar{\bar{X}} \pm 3\frac{s}{\sqrt{n}}$$

(b) Do any of these Subgroup Averages fall outside these INCORRECT control limits? Compare this result with that found in Exercise 3.5, page 54.

(c) Compute the standard deviation of the 10 Subgroup Averages shown above, and use the following formula, obtained from Example 4.3, page 59, to compute another set of INCORRECT control limits for the Subgroup Averages.

$$\text{supposed control limits for } \bar{X} = \bar{\bar{X}} \pm 3 s_{\bar{x}}$$

Exercise 4.2:

The data from Table 2, page 20, of Shewhart's 1931 book are shown below arranged into 51 subgroups of size four. Below each group of four values the Subgroup Average and Subgroup Range are shown. The subgroup numbers indicate the time-order sequence for these data.

-1-	-2-	-3-	-4-	-5-	-6-	-7-	-8-	-9-	-10-	-11-	-12-	-13-
5045	4290	3980	3300	5100	4635	4410	4725	4790	4110	4790	4740	4170
4350	4430	3925	3685	4635	4720	4065	4640	4845	4410	4340	5000	3850
4350	4485	3645	3463	5100	4810	4565	4640	4700	4180	4895	4895	4445
3975	4285	3760	5200	5450	4565	5190	4895	4600	4790	5750	4255	4650
4430.0	*4372.5*	*3827.5*	*3912.0*	*5071.25*	*4682.5*	*4557.5*	*4725.0*	*4733.75*	*4372.5*	*4943.75*	*4722.5*	*4278.75*
1070	*200*	*335*	*1900*	*815*	*245*	*1125*	*255*	*245*	*680*	*1410*	*745*	*800*

-14-	-15-	-16-	-17-	-18-	-19-	-20-	-21-	-22-	-23-	-24-	-25-	-26-
4170	4175	2920	4090	4640	4215	4615	4700	4095	4445	4560	5000	4850
4255	4550	4375	5000	4335	4275	4735	4700	3940	4000	4700	4575	4850
4170	4450	4375	4335	5000	4275	4215	4700	3700	4845	4310	4700	4570
4375	2855	4355	5000	4615	5000	4700	4095	3650	5000	4310	4430	4570
4242.5	*4007.5*	*4006.25*	*4606.25*	*4647.5*	*4441.25*	*4566.25*	*4548.75*	*3846.25*	*4572.5*	*4470.0*	*4676.25*	*4710.0*
205	*1695*	*1455*	*910*	*665*	*785*	*520*	*605*	*445*	*1000*	*390*	*570*	*280*

-27-	-28-	-29-	-30-	-31-	-32-	-33-	-34-	-35-	-36-	-37-	-38-	-39-
4855	4100	4050	4430	3075	4425	4840	4700	4450	3635	4340	5000	4770
4160	4340	4050	4300	2965	4300	4310	4440	4450	3635	4340	4850	4500
4325	4575	4685	4690	4080	4430	4185	4850	4850	3635	3665	4775	4770
4125	3875	4685	4560	4080	4840	4570	4125	4450	3900	3775	4500	5150
4366.25	*4222.5*	*4367.5*	*4495.0*	*3550.0*	*4498.75*	*4476.25*	*4528.75*	*4550.0*	*3701.25*	*4030.0*	*4781.25*	*4797.5*
730	*700*	*635*	*390*	*1115*	*540*	*655*	*725*	*400*	*265*	*675*	*500*	*650*

-40-	-41-	-42-	-43-	-44-	-45-	-46-	-47-	-48-	-49-	-50-	-51-
4850	5000	5075	4925	5075	5600	4325	4500	4850	4625	4080	5150
4700	4700	5000	4775	4925	5075	4665	4765	4930	4425	3690	5250
5000	4500	4770	5075	5250	4450	4615	4500	4700	4135	5050	5000
5000	4840	4570	4925	4915	4215	4615	4500	4890	4190	4625	5000
4887.5	*4760.0*	*4853.75*	*4925.0*	*5041.25*	*4835.0*	*4555.0*	*4566.25*	*4842.5*	*4343.75*	*4361.25*	*5100.0*
300	*500*	*505*	*300*	*335*	*1385*	*340*	*265*	*230*	*490*	*1360*	*250*

(a) The Average Range is 658.6. Compute control limits for the Subgroup Ranges.

(b) Do any of the Subgroup Ranges exceed the Upper Control Limit?

(c) The Grand Average is 4498.18. Using the formulas from Example 4.1, page 56, compute the correct control limits for the Subgroup Averages. Do these limits agree with those shown in Figure 4.21 on page 81?

(d) The standard deviation statistic of all 204 Individual Values is $s = 466.4$. Use this value and the procedure shown in Example 4.2, page 58, to construct a set of INCORRECT limits for the Subgroup Averages above.

(e) The standard deviation of the 51 Subgroup Averages shown above is $s_{\bar{x}} = 352.3$. Use the procedure shown in Example 4.3, page 59, to compute another set of INCORRECT control limits for the Subgroup Averages.

(f) Which set of limits for the Subgroup Averages is most sensitive to the lack of control in these data?

Chapter Five

Using Control Charts Effectively

Control charts are powerful tools for detecting uncontrolled variation. The previous chapter outlined the whys and wherefores of control charts, and illustrated that they are effective with virtually any type of data. This is one of the reasons that the control chart can be used in an endless variety of situations.

This flexibility means that there may well be several different ways of applying the charts in any one case. Usually, some of these ways will be more effective than others. However, until one has acquired a certain amount of experience, these differences in effectiveness may not be apparent.

This chapter will discuss two ways of increasing the efficiency of the control chart. The first consists of a way to make the control charts more sensitive to changes in the process. The second is a way of using the charts to get answers to specific questions.

5.1 Patterns in the Running Record

Shewhart's control charts give very few false alarms. This is why three-sigma limits are such effective action limits. Whenever a point falls outside the limits, it is most likely due to the presence of some Assignable Cause, and it is appropriate to identify and remove this Assignable Cause. On the other hand, whenever the running record stays within the three-sigma limits, and varies above and below the central line in a random manner, it is safe to say that the process appears to be stable.

But what if the running record does not vary above and below the central line in a random manner? What if a pattern is apparent in the running record? If the pattern can be meaningfully interpreted in the context of the process, it should be taken as an indication of an Assignable Cause. If the "pattern" makes no sense in the context of the process and subgrouping, and if it does not persist over an extended period of time, then it needs no interpretation.

In order to avoid interpreting "patterns" that are due to chance alone, guidelines describing non-random patterns are used. In the following sections some of these guidelines are discussed.

5.2 Simple Run Tests

Run tests are the basic tools for detecting patterns in the running record. There are different types of runs, but the most common is the run about the central line.

A run about the central line consists of a group of successive points that are all on the same side of the central line. Two points in a row on the same side of the central line is said to be a run of length two. A single point on one side of the central line is said to be a run of length one.

To see how runs about the central line provide evidence of a process change, consider the game of tossing a coin. Tossing two heads in succession is not remarkable. Even three heads in a row will happen fairly often. But four in a row is more interesting, as would be five, or six, or seven. As the length of the run of heads increases, a pattern begins to appear. Finally, if one were to toss eight heads in a row, most would suspect that there was something nonrandom about the game. (The theoretical odds of getting either eight heads or eight tails in a row in eight tosses of a fair coin is 1 out of 128.)

In the same way, when eight or more successive points fall on the same side of the central line of the Average Chart, they may be considered to be evidence of a sustained shift in the process average, even when no point falls outside the control limits.

When applying this run test to the Range Chart (or to a chart for any other measure of dispersion) some allowance must be made for the lack of symmetry in the distribution of the ranges. This lack of symmetry increases the chance of long runs *below* the central line. There are two ways to remedy this problem. The simplest remedy is to be more conservative when interpreting runs below the central line of the Range Chart. Instead of 8 points, one might require 12 successive values below the central line before looking for an Assignable Cause. A slightly better, yet more complicated, remedy is to use the Median Range as the central line. With this new central line, runs of length 8 or more below or above the central line will continue to be indications of a shift.

These simple run tests will be illustrated using the following data.

Table 5.1 Ninety-Nine Measurements of Blast Furnace Silicon

Subgroup	Measurements			Average	Range	Subgroup	Measurements			Average	Range
1	144	80	72	98.67	72	19	88	128	157	124.33	69
2	150	101	97	116.00	53	20	111	113	139	121.00	28
3	180	106	112	132.67	74	21	120	104	121	115.00	17
4	193	95	126	138.00	98	22	138	113	131	127.33	25
5	210	90	132	144.00	120	23	160	122	125	135.67	38
6	225	107	144	158.67	118	24	179	108	111	132.67	71
7	235	127	156	172.67	108	25	200	135	118	151.00	82
8	233	142	163	179.33	91	26	245	145	115	168.33	130
9	228	159	170	185.67	69	27	248	158	92	166.00	156
10	198	167	181	182.00	31	28	211	133	99	147.67	112
11	190	178	180	182.67	12	29	201	125	79	135.00	122
12	178	199	202	193.00	24	30	155	112	111	126.00	44
13	168	181	250	199.67	82	31	145	105	127	125.67	40
14	137	173	205	171.67	68	32	102	95	135	110.67	40
15	121	163	175	153.00	54	33	83	63	130	92.00	67
16	116	158	157	143.67	42						
17	85	147	148	126.67	63						
18	65	134	140	113.00	75						

EXAMPLE 5.1:   *Blast Furnace Silicon Data: Runs of Length 8 or More:*

The data in Table 5.1 consist of 99 measurements of the silicon content of the hot metal drawn from a blast furnace. These values have been arranged into 33 subgroups of size n = 3. The control charts for these data are shown in Figure 5.1.

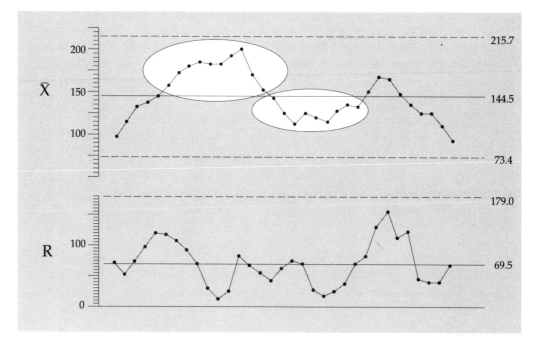

Figure 5.1: Control Charts for Blast Furnace Silicon Data

Even though no point falls outside the control limits, the running record on the Average Chart does not behave in the expected manner. In fact, there are two long runs, one of ten points above the central line, and one of nine points below the central line. Both of these runs are interpreted as indications of a lack of control.

The Range Chart shows ten runs about the central line. Two of the runs above the central line consist of six values. Neither of these satisfy the run test outlined above.

For runs about the central line a new run begins every time the running record crosses the central line. When a point falls right on the central line it is taken to be the start of a new run.

Some books suggest using "runs-up and runs-down" in addition to runs about the central line. A "run-up" would consist of a sequence of points where each value is larger than the preceding value. Figure 5.1 contains several runs-up and runs-down. Recent work suggests, however, that the use of runs-up and runs-down (1) will not appreciably increase the sensitivity of the control chart and (2) will result in many more false alarms than are commonly expected from the procedure. As will be seen on page 97, these are undesirable characteristics.

5.3 More Complex Run Tests

The run tests described in this section are more complicated than the ones given above, since they use both the *length* of the run and the *distance* from the central line as the criterion for a lack of control. These tests are based on the idea that a short run, consisting of points that are far away from the central line, provides as much evidence of a shift as a longer run consisting of points that are closer to the central line.

The first of these two run tests will be said to indicate a shift in the process whenever:
(a) at least two out of three successive values are on the same side of the central line,
(b) and these two values are also more than two sigma units away from the central line. (The third value may fall on either side of the central line.)

EXAMPLE 5.2:   *Blast Furnace Silicon Data: Runs Beyond 2-Sigma Lines:*

Returning to the data of Table 5.1, the control limits for the Average Chart are 215.69 and 73.40. The central line is 144.54. Since the distance from the central line to the control limits is 3 Sigma($\overline{X}$),[1] the two-sigma lines can be easily calculated in the following manner:

$$3 \; Sigma(\overline{X}) \; = \; UCL_{\overline{X}} \; - \; CL_{\overline{X}} = 215.69 \; - \; 144.5 = 71.15 \; units.$$

Thus, a value for Sigma($\overline{X}$) is $\frac{1}{3}$ (71.15) = 23.72 units.

The two-sigma lines for the Average Chart are 144.54 $\pm$ 47.43 = 191.97 and 97.11. These lines are shown in Figure 5.2. To use the run test given above, look for at least two out of three successive points beyond these lines. Subgroups 12 and 13 are both beyond 191.97, so they satisfy this run test. These two points identify one of the shifts in the process average that was found earlier.

The upper control limit of the Range Chart can be used in the manner shown above.

$$3 \; Sigma(R) \; = \; UCL_R \; - \; CL_R = 179.0 \; - \; 69.5 \; = \; 109.5 \; units.$$

Sigma(R) is thus $\frac{1}{3}$ (109.5) = 36.50 units.

The two-sigma lines are 69.54 + 73.00 = 142.54 and 69.54 − 73.00 = −3.46. The upper line is shown in Figure 5.2. The lower line is not shown since ranges cannot be negative. The Range Chart does not show any evidence of a shift based on this run test.

---

[1] *Sigma($\overline{X}$)* and *Sigma(R)* denote specific measures of dispersion defined in Appendix Table A.1. Here they are computed from the limits instead of being directly obtained from an average dispersion statistic.

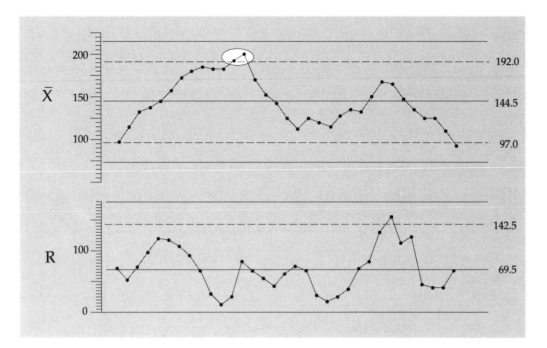

Figure 5.2:   Blast Furnace Silicon Data with 2-Sigma Lines

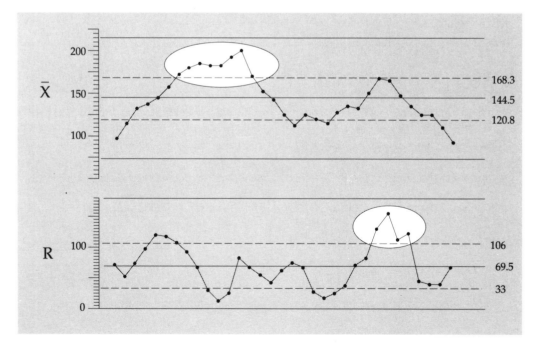

Figure 5.3:   Blast Furnace Silicon Data with 1-Sigma Lines

The second of the two run tests given in this section is said to indicate a shift in the process whenever:

   (a) at least four out of five successive values are on the same side of the central line,

   (b) and these four values are more than one sigma unit away from the central line. (The fifth value may fall on either side of the central line.)

This rule identifies a shift by using a longer run made up of points that are closer to the central line. The logic and the application are essentially the same as for the preceding run test, as can be seen in the following example.

EXAMPLE 5.3:   *Blast Furnace Silicon Data: Runs Beyond 1-Sigma Line:*

Again using the data from Table 5.1, the Sigma($\overline{X}$) and Sigma(R) values will be computed as in Example 5.2 above.

For the Average Chart, the one-sigma lines will be:

$$144.54 \pm 23.72 = 168.26 \text{ and } 120.82.$$

These lines are shown in Figure 5.3. Look for at least four out of five successive values that are beyond these one-sigma lines. Subgroups 7 through 14 are above the upper line. These points indicate the same shift that was found in Examples 5.1 and 5.2. Subgroups 18 and 21 fall below the lower line. Since this is only two out of four successive values, they cannot be taken as sufficient evidence of a shift. Likewise, subgroups 32 and 33 are not enough to satisfy this run test.

For the Range Chart, the one-sigma lines will be:

$$69.54 \pm 36.50 = 106.04 \text{ and } 33.04.$$

*These lines are shown on Figure 5.3. Subgroups 5, 6, and 7 are above the upper line, but three out of three is **not** sufficient to satisfy this run test. Likewise, subgroups 10, 11, 12, and subgroups 20, 21, 22 do **not** satisfy this test. But subgroups 26, 27, 28, and 29 do satisfy this run test. Thus, these four successive subgroups indicate an increase in the process dispersion that was not detected in any other manner.*

5.4 Four Rules for Defining Lack of Control

When these three run tests are combined with the original criterion of a lack of control, four rules for detecting Assignable Causes are obtained. In the interest of clarity, the following nomenclature will be used:[2]

DETECTION RULE ONE: A lack of control is indicated whenever a single point falls outside the (three-sigma) control limits.

DETECTION RULE TWO: A lack of control is indicated whenever at least two out of three successive values fall on the same side of, and more than two sigma units away from, the central line.

DETECTION RULE THREE: A lack of control is indicated whenever at least four out of five successive values fall on the same side of, and more than one sigma unit away from, the central line.

DETECTION RULE FOUR: A lack of control is indicated whenever at least eight successive values fall on the same side of the central line.

When the four rules are arranged in this order, a logical progression is apparent. Going from Rule 1 to Rule 4, progressively longer runs are required as the points are allowed to fall nearer to the central line. These four rules form a consistent set of decision rules for detecting shifts in the process. Unfortunately, they are not all uniformly easy to apply.

Since Rules 1 and 4 do not require any additional computations, they are the logical ones to be used initially. Then, at a later date, if greater sensitivity and quicker responses are needed, Rule 2, and possibly Rule 3, can be added.

Finally, it should be kept in mind that the objective is to gain insight from the control chart. This means that the most important part of detecting a lack of control on the chart is the ability to interpret the chart in the context of the process. Without this ability, a significant run test will be of little value. Thus, these rules, and any other run tests, must always be used with discretion.

It should also be noted that each run test is sensitive to one type of pattern. The run tests given in this chapter are oriented toward detecting sustained shifts. Other run tests are sensitive to oscillation, while still others are suitable for detecting trends.

---

[2] These four Rules are sometimes known as the Western Electric Zone Tests.

The list is endless. Many more could have been included. However, each time another criterion for a lack of control is applied to the charts, the chance of a false alarm increases. If one uses enough run tests, one will always find something that appears to be a signal.

A common way of characterizing a given set of Detection Rules is to compute the Average Run Length between false alarms. These Average Run Length (ARL) values are *theoretical* values. As such, they are at best only rough guides to what happens in practice. However, they do give an indication of the problem of what happens as the number of run tests proliferate.

If Detection Rule One is used by itself, the theoretical Average Run Length between false alarms is 370 subgroups on the Average Chart.

If Detection Rules One and Four are used together, this theoretical Average Run Length between false alarms drops to 153 subgroups on the Average Chart.

If Detection Rules One, Two, Three and Four are all used together, the theoretical Average Run Length between false alarms drops to 92 subgroups on the Average Chart. While a theoretical ARL of 92 is still acceptable, additional run tests will tend to make this quantity drop even further, and smaller values would soon become unacceptable. Therefore, while some have suggested using as many as a dozen rules, the authors recommend using the rules given in this section, subject to the qualifications explained in the following section.

5.5 Other Patterns in the Running Record

Since the interpretation of any particular run test depends upon the structure of the data, it is almost impossible to provide a set of run tests that would be appropriate for all situations. *If the structure of the data suggests that certain patterns would be meaningful, be sure to look for such patterns in the running record.* The following examples show how this was done in two instances.

EXAMPLE 5.4:   *Three Operators:*

Three operators, running the same rubber mill, had their batches of rubber checked by the lab each day. Five samples were obtained from each operator, and the durometer readings were obtained for each sample. When control charts were introduced into the laboratory, the lab personnel decided to use the five daily samples they were already collecting from each operator on their control charts. This naturally resulted in separate subgroups for each operator. The Range Chart for the first eight days of the chart is shown in

Figure 5.4.

Since the different subgroups represented different workers, any differences between the workers could be expected to show up as a detectable pattern on the charts. Therefore, it is appropriate to look for patterns that can be associated with the individuals. When the lab supervisor did this, he found that every out-of-control range came from Operator 27's subgroups. Moreover, Operator 27 was always above the central line on the Range Chart, while Operators 65 and 75 were always below the central line. Since the Range Chart tracks the subgroup dispersion, this meant that Operator 27 was producing less homogeneous product than were the other operators.

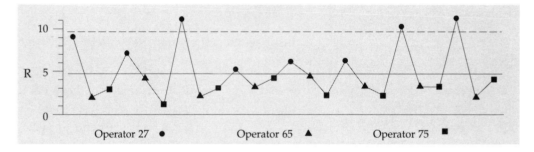

Figure 5.4: Range Chart for Three Operators

Now Operator 27 was the senior operator, a 30 year veteran, and was considered by the supervisor to be an outstanding operator. When shown the control chart, the supervisor was skeptical of the results. Nevertheless, due to the persistence of this pattern, he began to observe Operator 27 more closely. He soon noticed that Operator 27 stood well back from the rubber mill, and that he always got someone else to read the specifications for each batch.

It turned out that Operator 27's vision had deteriorated to the point that he was legally blind. He couldn't read the specifications, he couldn't see to get his batches thoroughly mixed, and he couldn't see well enough to stay out of danger. Therefore, he would load a batch of rubber, start the mill, and step back. Once the company discovered that it had a blind man running a hazardous piece of equipment, it moved quickly to get Operator 27 a medical retirement. Fortunately, Operator 27 lived to take the retirement.

EXAMPLE 5.5: *The Automatic Thickness Controller:*

The thickness of an extruded sheet is controlled by an automatic controller. A sensor measures the sheet thickness, and in response to these readings the controller adjusts the speed of the extrusion screw. The thickness measurements are stored electronically, and a summary report is generated for each roll of material. Unfortunately, this summary averages the thicknesses over an hour-long period, so the report does not show the short-term behavior of the extruder.

In an effort to understand what was happening with this equipment, a production engineer decided to read the measurements off the screen as they occurred and plot them on a control chart. The Average Chart is shown in Figure 5.5. As the engineer recorded the thicknesses and plotted the points, he became aware of a definite oscillation in the sheet thickness. Acting on a hunch, he turned off the automatic thickness controller and collected the rest of the data while in the manual mode. The control limits shown in Figure 5.5 are based on the data obtained while the equipment was in the automatic mode. Clearly something was wrong with the automatic thickness control system.

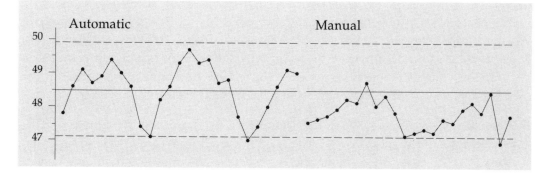

Figure 5.5: Average Sheet Thicknesses

In the first of these two examples a *persistent* pattern was the stimulus to look for the Assignable Cause. (One guideline for persistence is the recurrence of the pattern eight times.) In the second, the pattern was *consistent* enough to suggest a particular experiment. In both, it was not the routine use of run tests, but rather the interpretation of the charts in their context that led to the discoveries. This alertness for patterns which fit in with the way the data are collected and plotted cannot be programmed. It depends on someone's taking the effort to look at, *and to think about,* the charts. This has always been, and always will be, an essential part of the effective use of control charts.

5.6 Rational Subgrouping

Another aspect of the efficient use of the control charts is making the charts answer the right questions. In order to do this, the way the data are organized into subgroups must be matched with the structure present in the data. This usually means that each subgroup will be selected from some small region of space, or time, or product, in order to assure relatively homogeneous conditions within the subgroup.

The emphasis on minimizing the variation within the subgroups comes from the fact that it is the variation *within* the subgroups that is used to set the control limits. In particular, the limits depend upon the Average Range, which in turn depends upon the individual Subgroup Ranges, which measure the variation within the subgroups. Thus, the control chart uses the *within subgroup variation* to put limits on how much variation should exist *between* the subgroups.

To expand on this, the control chart for averages asks the question: "Do the Subgroup Averages vary more than they should, based on the variation within the subgroups?" Or put another way, "Making allowance for the amount of variation within the subgroups, are there detectable differences between the Subgroup Averages?"

The control chart for ranges asks the question: "Is the variation within subgroups consistent from subgroup to subgroup?" Or alternatively, "Making allowance for the *average* amount of variation within the subgroups, are there detectably different amounts of variation in the different subgroups?" Since these questions are couched in rather general terms, we return to Examples 5.4 and 5.5 to make their meaning clear.

A portion of the Average Chart for Example 5.5 is reproduced in Figure 5.6. The extruded sheet was thirty inches wide. The scanner cycled from side to side, measuring the thickness at specified positions along the way. The engineer collected all data generated when the scanner was 10 inches from the extruder's right side. Each subgroup consisted of five consecutive readings for that position. The elapsed time represented by these five readings was about 90 seconds. Thus, the points on the Average Chart represent the average thickness over consecutive ninety-second intervals.

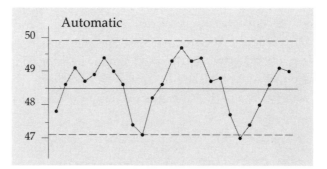

Figure 5.6: Average Chart for Example 5.5

The control limits shown define the region within which the averages should fall if the long-term variation in sheet thickness (several minutes duration) is essentially the same as the short-term variation (90 seconds duration). While on automatic operation, two of the 28 averages fell outside the limits. Thus, in addition to the cyclic pattern, there is evidence that the long-term variation is greater than the short-term variation: the averages vary more than they should, based on the variation between successive readings.

The Range Chart of Example 5.4 is reproduced in Figure 5.7. The ranges measure the variation in a physical characteristic for five samples drawn from the product produced by each operator. The Average Range summarizes these Subgroup Ranges, and the control limits are based upon the Average Range. If all of the subgroups display the same amount of dispersion, then the ranges should all fall within the control limits. In other words, if the variation in the product is consistent from subgroup to subgroup, these ranges should be consistent. Three ranges fall above the upper control limit, providing evidence that the variation in the product is not consistent from subgroup to subgroup. Since different subgroups represent different operators, this is conclusive evidence that the different operators are producing product with different degrees of consistency.

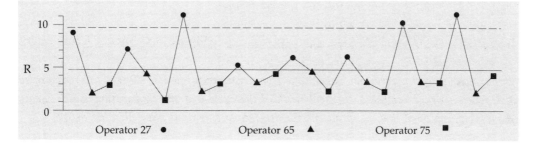

Figure 5.7: Range Chart for Example 5.4

Notice that in each of the examples above, the structure of the data and the way the data were organized into subgroups formed an essential part of the explanation. Without this information the charts would have been meaningless.

Returning to the guideline given above, it is the variation *within* the subgroups that determines how sensitive the control charts will be. Thus, one must consider the sources of variation for a particular measurement, and then organize the subgroups accordingly. For some measurements there will be a natural way to subgroup the data. For other measurements there may be several possible ways of subgrouping. An illustration of this latter case is provided by the following example.

Injection molding is used to make a particular socket, four pieces at a time. At the time these data were collected this method of fabrication represented a shift in both material and technology. Therefore, a process certification run was required prior to going into full production. Dave, the supervisor, decided to use control charts to evaluate this process certification run.

Since there was only one mold, the process certification run involved only one press, and only one operator. The data consisted of the effective thickness of a socket, measured in hundredths of a millimeter. Since one side of the socket was convex, a special gauge had to be designed and built to measure this thickness. Because of the way this gauge was built, the measurements represent the thickness in excess of 12.00 millimeters. Four times a day Dave would go to the press and gather up the parts produced by five consecutive cycles of the press.

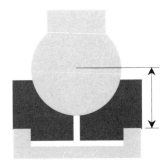

Figure 5.8: Socket Cross-Section

Since each cycle produced four parts, (one from each cavity) he had 20 parts to measure every two hours. Being careful, Dave kept track of the cycle and the cavity from which each part came. Having done this, he wrote his twenty measurements in the following array.

	Cycle of Press				
(Hour of Collection)	*A*	*B*	*C*	*D*	*E*
Cavity I	15	16	17	16	18
Cavity II	10	13	11	10	10
Cavity III	7	8	10	7	10
Cavity IV	8	9	10	10	10

Figure 5.9: Hourly Socket Thickness Data

There are three identifiable sources of variation within these data. There is the Hour-to-Hour variation that is represented by the different sets of 20 parts. There is the Cycle-to-Cycle variation that is represented by the different columns in Figure 5.9. And there is the Cavity-to-Cavity variation that is represented by the different rows in Figure 5.9.

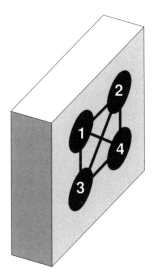

Figure 5.10: Socket Mold

The supervisor then had to choose how he would organize these data into subgroups, and how he would organize the subgroups into control charts. For purposes of illustration, this will be done in three different ways.

The first organization is shown in Table 5.2. Here the columns are used to form the subgroups. This organization allocates some sources of variation to be represented by differences between subgroups, and it allocates others to be represented by differences within the subgroups.

For example, the data for Hour 1 fall in different subgroups from that of Hour 2, therefore, the Hour-to-Hour differences will show up *between* the subgroups. Likewise, for any given hour, the data for Cycle A is in a different subgroup from that for Cycle B, etc., therefore the Cycle-to-Cycle differences will show up *between* the subgroups. Finally, for any given hour and cycle, the data for Cavity I falls within the same subgroup as that for Cavities II, III, and IV. Therefore, the Cavity-to-Cavity differences show up *within* the subgroups.

Table 5.2: First Organization of the Socket Data

1:	A	B	C	D	E
I	15	16	17	16	18
II	10	13	11	10	10
III	7	8	10	7	10
IV	8	9	10	10	10
$\bar{X}$	10	11.5	12	10.75	12
R	8	8	7	9	8

2:	A	B	C	D	E
I	13	18	15	15	15
II	9	10	11	8	9
III	7	11	10	10	9
IV	10	13	13	10	9
$\bar{X}$	9.75	13	12.25	10.75	10.5
R	6	8	5	7	6

3:	A	B	C	D	E
I	14	14	18	14	14
II	9	10	10	12	9
III	8	10	9	10	8
IV	8	9	10	8	9
$\bar{X}$	9.75	10.75	11.75	11	10
R	6	5	9	6	6

4:	A	B	C	D	E
I	14	15	15	15	14
II	10	10	11	11	10
III	7	9	12	10	10
IV	11	12	11	10	13
$\bar{X}$	10.5	11.5	12.25	11.5	11.75
R	7	6	4	5	4

5:	A	B	C	D	E
I	12	13	13	12	13
II	8	7	8	7	7
III	5	6	8	5	4
IV	4	4	5	3	4
$\bar{X}$	7.25	7.5	8.5	6.75	7
R	8	9	8	9	9

6:	A	B	C	D	E
I	14	15	17	14	13
II	7	11	12	8	6
III	6	4	7	6	5
IV	4	7	6	5	4
$\bar{X}$	7.75	9.25	10.5	8.25	7
R	10	11	11	9	9

7:	A	B	C	D	E
I	12	12	13	13	11
II	6	6	6	6	7
III	4	5	4	4	6
IV	4	4	5	4	5
$\bar{X}$	6.5	6.75	7	6.75	7.25
R	8	8	9	9	6

8:	A	B	C	D	E
I	13	15	16	14	13
II	9	8	7	7	8
III	10	8	6	7	5
IV	6	6	8	6	5
$\bar{X}$	9.5	9.25	9.25	8.5	7.75
R	7	9	10	8	8

9:	A	B	C	D	E
I	15	16	17	14	13
II	11	13	11	13	8
III	9	9	6	8	10
IV	9	10	11	9	5
$\bar{X}$	11	12	11.25	11	9
R	6	7	11	6	8

10:	A	B	C	D	E
I	13	13	14	13	13
II	7	8	7	6	7
III	4	5	6	5	5
IV	5	5	6	6	5
$\bar{X}$	7.25	7.75	8.25	7.5	7.5
R	9	8	8	8	8

11:	A	B	C	D	E
I	13	16	13	16	18
II	10	8	10	10	11
III	8	7	8	7	11
IV	11	10	9	10	10
$\bar{X}$	10.5	10.25	10	10.75	12.5
R	5	9	5	9	8

12:	A	B	C	D	E
I	16	18	18	16	13
II	13	8	8	10	7
III	13	10	10	6	7
IV	9	6	8	7	7
$\bar{X}$	12.75	10.5	11	9.75	8.5
R	7	12	10	10	6

13:	A	B	C	D	E
I	13	18	18	14	13
II	11	10	9	10	10
III	14	9	10	9	7
IV	9	12	11	11	6
$\bar{X}$	11.75	12.25	12	11	9
R	5	9	9	5	7

14:	A	B	C	D	E
I	13	13	14	14	14
II	7	8	9	8	8
III	6	6	7	6	6
IV	6	7	6	6	6
$\bar{X}$	8	8.5	9	8.5	8.5
R	7	7	8	8	8

15:	A	B	C	D	E
I	13	15	18	15	14
II	7	12	10	10	7
III	7	8	12	12	6
IV	11	12	12	12	6
$\bar{X}$	9.5	11.75	13	12.25	8.25
R	6	7	8	5	8

Table 5.2 Continued: First Organization of the Socket Data

16:	A	B	C	D	E	17:	A	B	C	D	E	18:	A	B	C	D	E
I	15	14	15	14	12	I	14	16	14	13	14	I	12	15	15	15	14
II	6	7	8	6	10	II	9	10	13	7	6	II	9	7	8	10	9
III	7	10	8	6	6	III	6	5	5	7	5	III	5	7	6	6	10
IV	6	8	7	9	7	IV	7	7	4	7	5	IV	6	8	7	12	12
$\overline{X}$	8.5	9.75	9.5	8.75	8.75	$\overline{X}$	9	9.5	9	8.5	7.5	$\overline{X}$	8	9.25	9	10.75	11.25
R	9	7	8	8	6	R	8	11	10	6	9	R	7	8	9	9	5

19:	A	B	C	D	E	20:	A	B	C	D	E
I	17	15	18	18	17	I	18	16	17	14	13
II	10	10	12	12	6	II	8	10	11	10	7
III	5	9	7	8	7	III	7	7	7	10	5
IV	7	7	5	12	8	IV	10	7	9	8	8
$\overline{X}$	9.75	10.25	10.5	12.5	9.5	$\overline{X}$	10.75	10	11	10.5	8.25
R	12	8	13	10	11	R	11	9	10	6	8

Thus, the subgroups defined in Table 5.2 allocate the major sources of variation in these data in the following manner:

Source of Variation	First Allocation
Hour to Hour	Between Subgroup
Cycle to Cycle	Between Subgroup
Cavity to Cavity	Within Subgroup

The Hour-to-Hour and Cycle-to-Cycle differences correspond to differences between subgroups while the Cavity-to-Cavity differences correspond to differences within the subgroups. One should not go on until this allocation is understood, for it is the key to understanding this example.

This first allocation yields 100 subgroups of size $n = 4$. The Grand Average is 9.74 units, and the Average Range is 7.90 units. The control limits for the Average Chart are 3.98 units to 15.50 units. The upper control limit for the Range Chart is 18.03 units. These control charts are shown in Figure 5.11.

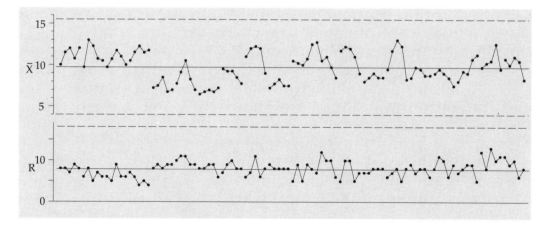

Figure 5.11: Control Charts for First Organization of Socket Data

Table 5.3: Second Organization of the Socket Data

1:

	A	B	C	D	E	X̄	R
I	15	16	17	16	18	16.4	3
II	10	13	11	10	10	10.8	3
III	7	8	10	7	10	8.4	3
IV	8	9	10	10	10	9.4	2

2:

	A	B	C	D	E	X̄	R
I	13	18	15	15	15	15.2	5
II	9	10	11	8	9	9.4	3
III	7	11	10	10	9	9.4	4
IV	10	13	13	10	9	11	4

3:

	A	B	C	D	E	X̄	R
I	14	14	18	14	14	14.8	4
II	9	10	10	12	9	10	3
III	8	10	9	10	8	9	2
IV	8	9	10	8	9	8.8	2

4:

	A	B	C	D	E	X̄	R
I	14	15	15	15	14	14.6	1
II	10	10	11	11	10	10.4	1
III	7	9	12	10	10	9.6	5
IV	11	12	11	10	13	11.4	3

5:

	A	B	C	D	E	X̄	R
I	12	13	13	12	13	12.6	1
II	8	7	8	7	7	7.4	1
III	5	6	8	5	4	5.6	4
IV	4	4	5	3	4	4	2

6:

	A	B	C	D	E	X̄	R
I	14	15	17	14	13	14.6	4
II	7	11	12	8	6	8.8	6
III	6	4	7	6	5	5.6	3
IV	4	7	6	5	4	5.2	3

7:

	A	B	C	D	E	X̄	R
I	12	12	13	13	11	12.2	2
II	6	6	6	6	7	6.2	1
III	4	5	4	4	6	4.6	2
IV	4	4	5	4	5	4.4	1

8:

	A	B	C	D	E	X̄	R
I	13	15	16	14	13	14.2	3
II	9	8	7	7	8	7.8	2
III	10	8	6	7	5	7.2	5
IV	6	6	8	6	5	6.2	3

9:

	A	B	C	D	E	X̄	R
I	15	16	17	14	13	15	4
II	11	13	11	13	8	11.2	5
III	9	9	6	8	10	8.4	4
IV	9	10	11	9	5	8.8	6

10:

	A	B	C	D	E	X̄	R
I	13	13	14	13	13	13.2	1
II	7	8	7	6	7	7	2
III	4	5	6	5	5	5	2
IV	5	5	6	6	5	5.4	1

11:

	A	B	C	D	E	X̄	R
I	13	16	13	16	18	15.2	5
II	10	8	10	10	11	9.8	3
III	8	7	8	7	11	8.2	4
IV	11	10	9	10	10	10	2

12:

	A	B	C	D	E	X̄	R
I	16	18	18	16	13	16.2	5
II	13	8	8	10	7	9.2	6
III	13	10	10	6	7	9.2	7
IV	9	6	8	7	7	7.4	3

13:

	A	B	C	D	E	X̄	R
I	13	18	18	14	13	15.2	5
II	11	10	9	10	10	10	2
III	14	9	10	9	7	9.8	7
IV	9	12	11	11	6	9.8	6

14:

	A	B	C	D	E	X̄	R
I	13	13	14	14	14	13.6	1
II	7	8	9	8	8	8	2
III	6	6	7	6	6	6.2	1
IV	6	7	6	6	6	6.2	1

15:

	A	B	C	D	E	X̄	R
I	13	15	18	15	14	15	5
II	7	12	10	10	7	9.2	5
III	7	8	12	12	6	9	6
IV	11	12	12	12	6	10.6	6

16:

	A	B	C	D	E	X̄	R
I	15	14	15	14	12	14	3
II	6	7	8	6	10	7.4	4
III	7	10	8	6	6	7.4	4
IV	6	8	7	9	7	7.4	3

17:

	A	B	C	D	E	X̄	R
I	14	16	14	13	14	14.2	3
II	9	10	13	7	6	9	7
III	6	5	5	7	5	5.6	2
IV	7	7	4	7	5	6	3

18:

	A	B	C	D	E	X̄	R
I	12	15	15	15	14	14.2	3
II	9	7	8	10	9	8.6	3
III	5	7	6	6	10	6.8	5
IV	6	8	7	12	12	9	6

19:

	A	B	C	D	E	X̄	R
I	17	15	18	18	17	17	3
II	10	10	12	12	6	10	6
III	5	9	7	8	7	7.2	4
IV	7	7	5	12	8	7.8	7

20:

	A	B	C	D	E	X̄	R
I	18	16	17	14	13	15.6	5
II	8	10	11	10	7	9.2	4
III	7	7	7	10	5	7.2	5
IV	10	7	9	8	8	8.4	3

The second organization of these data is shown in Table 5.3. Here the rows are used to define the subgroups and the allocation of the sources of variation is as follows: the Hour-to-Hour variation is represented by differences between subgroups; the Cycle-to-Cycle variation is represented by differences within the subgroups; and the Cavity-to-Cavity variation is represented by differences between subgroups.

Source of Variation	Second Allocation
Hour to Hour	Between Subgroup
Cycle to Cycle	Within Subgroup
Cavity to Cavity	Between Subgroup

This second allocation yields 80 subgroups of size $n = 5$. The Grand Average is unchanged at 9.74 units, and the Average Range is now 3.51 units. The control limits for the Average Chart are 7.71 to 11.77 units, and the upper control limit for the Range Chart is 7.42 units. The control charts for this arrangement of the data are shown in Figure 5.12.

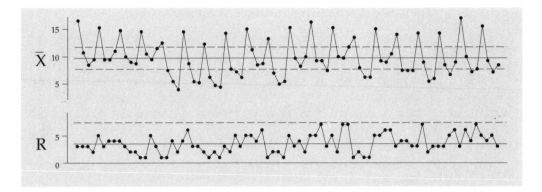

Figure 5.12: Control Charts for Second Organization of Socket Data

The control charts in Figures 5.11 and 5.12 are considerably different, yet they portray the same data. The difference is due to the way the data are organized into subgroups.

The Average Chart in Figure 5.12 shows an obvious pattern: every fourth average is out of control on the high side. Based on the order in which the subgroups were plotted, these high averages all correspond to Cavity I. Thus, Cavity I is producing sockets that are detectably thicker than those produced by the other three cavities.

Why isn't this difference seen in the charts in Figure 5.11? Because the right question wasn't asked. The allocation for the first control chart was:

Source of Variation	First Allocation
Hour to Hour	Between Subgroup
Cycle to Cycle	Between Subgroup
Cavity to Cavity	Within Subgroup

And this allocation results in charts which ask the following questions:
  (1) Are there detectable differences from Hour-to-Hour?
  (2) Are there detectable differences from Cycle-to-Cycle?
  (3) Are the Cavity-to-Cavity differences consistent?
The charts in Figure 5.11 do **not** ask if there are detectable differences between the cavities.

In contrast, the control charts in Figure 5.12 have the following allocation:

Source of Variation	Second Allocation
Hour to Hour	Between Subgroup
Cycle to Cycle	Within Subgroup
Cavity to Cavity	Between Subgroup

And this allocation results in charts which ask the following questions:

(1) Are there detectable differences from Hour-to-Hour?

(2) Are the Cycle-to-Cycle differences consistent?

(3) Are there detectable differences from Cavity-to-Cavity?

Since the Cycle-to-Cycle differences are so much smaller than the Cavity-to-Cavity differences, the control limits in Figure 5.12 are much tighter than those in Figure 5.11. Thus, in addition to considering different questions, the charts in 5.12 are more sensitive.

The third organization of these data is simply a rearrangement of the subgroups in Table 5.3. The subgroups for each cavity were collected together and separate control charts were made for each of the four cavities.

Table 5.4: Third Organization of the Socket Data

Cavity I:

	A	B	C	D	E	$\bar{X}$	R		A	B	C	D	E	$\bar{X}$	R		A	B	C	D	E	$\bar{X}$	R
1:	15	16	17	16	18	16.4	3	2:	13	18	15	15	15	15.2	5	3:	14	14	18	14	14	14.8	4
4:	14	15	15	15	14	14.6	1	5:	12	13	13	12	13	12.6	1	6:	14	15	17	14	13	14.6	4
7:	12	12	13	13	11	12.2	2	8:	13	15	16	14	13	14.2	3	9:	15	16	17	14	13	15	4
10:	13	13	14	13	13	13.2	1	11:	13	16	13	16	18	15.2	5	12:	16	18	18	16	13	16.2	5
13:	13	18	18	14	13	15.2	5	14:	13	13	14	14	14	13.6	1	15:	13	15	18	15	14	15	5
16:	15	14	15	14	12	14	3	17:	14	16	14	13	14	14.2	3	18:	12	15	15	15	14	14.2	3
19:	17	15	18	18	17	17	3	20:	18	16	17	14	13	15.6	5								

Cavity II:

	A	B	C	D	E	$\bar{X}$	R		A	B	C	D	E	$\bar{X}$	R		A	B	C	D	E	$\bar{X}$	R
1:	10	13	11	10	10	10.8	3	2:	9	10	11	8	9	9.4	3	3:	9	10	10	12	9	10	3
4:	10	10	11	11	10	10.4	1	5:	8	7	8	7	7	7.4	1	6:	7	11	12	8	6	8.8	6
7:	6	6	6	6	7	6.2	1	8:	9	8	7	7	8	7.8	2	9:	11	13	11	13	8	11.2	5
10:	7	8	7	6	7	7	2	11:	10	8	10	10	11	9.8	3	12:	13	8	8	10	7	9.2	6
13:	11	10	9	10	10	10	2	14:	7	8	9	8	8	8	2	15:	7	12	10	10	7	9.2	5
16:	6	7	8	6	10	7.4	4	17:	9	10	13	7	6	9	7	18:	9	7	8	10	9	8.6	3
19:	10	10	12	12	6	10	6	20:	8	10	11	10	7	9.2	4								

Cavity III:

	A	B	C	D	E	$\bar{X}$	R		A	B	C	D	E	$\bar{X}$	R		A	B	C	D	E	$\bar{X}$	R
1:	7	8	10	7	10	8.4	3	2:	7	11	10	10	9	9.4	4	3:	8	10	9	10	8	9	2
4:	7	9	12	10	10	9.6	5	5:	5	6	8	5	4	5.6	4	6:	6	4	7	6	5	5.6	3
7:	4	5	4	4	6	4.6	2	8:	10	8	6	7	5	7.2	5	9:	9	9	6	8	10	8.4	4
10:	4	5	6	5	5	5	2	11:	8	7	8	7	11	8.2	4	12:	13	10	10	6	7	9.2	7
13:	14	9	10	9	7	9.8	7	14:	6	6	7	6	6	6.2	1	15:	7	8	12	12	6	9	6
16:	7	10	8	6	6	7.4	4	17:	6	5	5	7	5	5.6	2	18:	5	7	6	6	10	6.8	5
19:	5	9	7	8	7	7.2	4	20:	7	7	7	10	5	7.2	5								

Cavity IV:

	A	B	C	D	E	$\bar{X}$	R		A	B	C	D	E	$\bar{X}$	R		A	B	C	D	E	$\bar{X}$	R
1:	8	9	10	10	10	9.4	2	2:	10	13	13	10	9	11	4	3:	8	9	10	8	9	8.8	2
4:	11	12	11	10	13	11.4	3	5:	4	4	5	3	4	4	2	6:	4	7	6	5	4	5.2	3
7:	4	4	5	4	5	4.4	1	8:	6	6	8	6	5	6.2	3	9:	9	10	11	9	5	8.8	6
10:	5	5	6	6	5	5.4	1	11:	11	10	9	10	10	10	2	12:	9	6	8	7	7	7.4	3
13:	9	12	11	11	6	9.8	6	14:	6	7	6	6	6	6.2	1	15:	11	12	12	12	6	10.6	6
16:	6	8	7	9	7	7.4	3	17:	7	7	4	7	5	6	3	18:	6	8	7	12	12	9	6
19:	7	7	5	12	8	7.8	7	20:	10	7	9	8	8	8.4	3								

Instead of looking for differences between the cavities, this organization explicitly allows for such differences by placing different cavities on different charts.

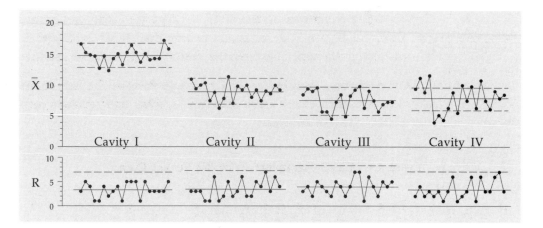

Figure 5.13: Control Charts for Third Organization of Socket Data

Cavity I has a Grand Average of 14.65, and an Average Range of 3.30, giving control limits for averages of 16.55 and 12.75, and an upper control limit for ranges of 6.98.

Cavity II has a Grand Average of 8.97, and an Average Range of 3.45, giving control limits for averages of 10.96 and 6.98, and an upper control limit for ranges of 7.29.

Cavity III has a Grand Average of 7.47, and an Average Range of 3.95, giving control limits for averages of 9.75 and 5.19, and an upper control limit for ranges of 8.35.

Cavity IV has a Grand Average of 7.86, and an Average Range of 3.35, giving control limits for averages of 9.79 and 5.93, and an upper control limit for ranges of 7.08.

By drawing the Average Charts on the same scale, the difference between Cavity One and the other three cavities becomes immediately apparent. Moreover, a lack of control is still indicated. With this organization, the long-term (Hour-to-Hour) variation is being directly compared with the short-term (Cycle-to-Cycle) variation. The charts show very clearly that the long-term variation is excessive. There is some Assignable Cause present that is making the press produce parts that are thinner one hour, and thicker the next hour. By identifying and removing this Assignable Cause, greater product consistency can be achieved with virtually no additional expense.

Of the three organizations, the third is the most sensitive, since it explicitly allows for the Cavity-to-Cavity variation. This allows the Hour-to-Hour lack of control to show up. This lack of control is present in all three charts, but it can be detected in the first chart, Figure 5.11, only by the use of Detection Rule III, and it is overwhelmed by the Cavity-to-Cavity variation in the second chart, Figure 5.12.

EXAMPLE 5.7:   *The Rest of the Story:*

Dave used the third organization shown in Figure 5.13. He could see that Cavity One was making thicker parts, and he could see that the process was out of control. In his words: "I didn't know what to do to get the process into control—I'd never gotten a process into control before—but I knew what to do about Cavity One!"

So, ignoring the out-of-control condition for the moment, he decided to tackle the problem of the difference between the cavities. The histograms for the four cavities is shown in Figure 5.14. On the scale used in this figure, the specifications are 0 to 15. Cavity One is centered near the upper specification, with 28 of its 100 values outside the specifications. Cavity Two is centered in the upper two-thirds of the specifications, and Cavities Three and Four appear to be well-centered relative to the specifications.

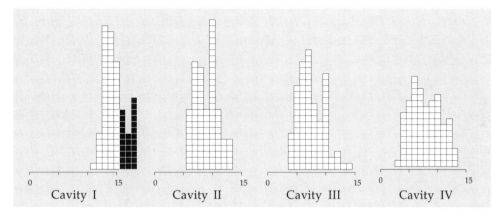

Figure 5.14: Histograms for Four Cavities

Based on these data, Dave took the mold off the press and sent it to the tool room. He wanted to move the histogram for Cavity One down 7.5 hundredths of a millimeter, so he asked for a 3-thousandths inch shim to be placed behind cavity one. He also wanted to shift the histogram for Cavity Two down by 2.5 hundredths of a millimeter, so he asked for a 1-thousandth inch shim to be placed behind Cavity Two. In a couple of days he got the mold back. He put it on the same press, and began to gather data as before. When he had filled up his control charts (organized as in Figure 5.13) he recomputed his limits and looked to see what his shims had done.

Cavity One showed an average that was lower than before. The average had shifted down an amount equal to 5 thousandths of an inch. Cavity Two showed an average that was 3 thousandths of an inch lower than before. Cavity Three showed an average that was 1 thousandth of an inch lower than before, while Cavity Four's average had shifted down 2 thousandths of an inch!

"What have you done to the mold?" Dave asked the toolmaker.

"Just what you asked." he replied.

"Then why are Cavities Three and Four thinner than before?"

"I don't know, I just put a 3 thousandths inch shim behind Cavity One, and a 1 thousandth inch shim behind Cavity Two."

"You didn't do anything else to the mold?"

"Not really."

"What do you mean?"

"Well—I did clean it up real good—there was a wax build-up on the face of the mold. I cleaned that off for you."

Dave said that it was at this point that the light bulb went on in his mind. Of course there would be a wax build-up. The operator would occasionally clean off this wax build-up. But they were not cleaning it off often enough. This was what was driving the process out of control from Hour-to-Hour. When they changed the cleaning interval for this operation the out of control points disappeared. Confident that he now had a process that was both stable and capable, Dave was ready to go into full production.

Date	January 3								January 4										1/5		1/6		1/7	
Cavity I	4	4	3	7	4	3	3	3	3	3	2	8	5	3	9	3	4	3	3	4	4	4	3	3
Cavity II	7	6	4	6	7	4	9	4	6	5	5	6	10	9	6	8	7	6	7	6	7	7	6	5
Cavity III	6	6	3	4	4	4	3	2	3	3	2	7	5	6	5	5	4	5	4	5	6	3	3	2
Cavity IV	7	7	5	7	3	3	4	3	7	3	5	3	2	2	4	4	4	3	3	6	3	6	3	2
Averages	6	5.8	3.8	6	4.5	3.5	4.8	3	4.8	3.5	3.5	6	5.5	5	6	5	4.8	4.2	4.2	5.2	5	5*	3.8	3
Ranges	3	3	2	3	4	1	6	2	4	2	3	5	8	7	5	5	3	3	4	2	4	4	3	3

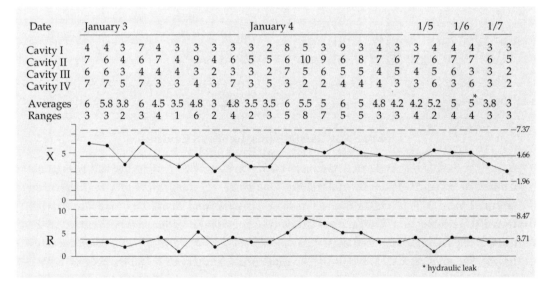

* hydraulic leak

Figure 5.15: Operator's Control Chart for Socket Thicknesses

When they did start production the control chart was placed in the hands of the operator. For his convenience they changed to the organization shown in Figure 5.11, with all four cavities in one subgroup. This chart is shown in Figure 5.15. It shows a process that displays a reasonable degree of statistical control. This chart covers a period of four days some 120 days after the start of production. In fact, it begins with the start-up following the two-week shut-down for Christmas and the New Year. The first nine points come from the first day after the break. The next nine points come from day two, and then they shifted back to two subgroups per day.

There is a fundamental difference between the chart in Figure 5.11 and the chart in Figure 5.15. In Figure 5.11, it was not known if the cavities were the same or not. When the four cavities were subgrouped together in Figure 5.11 there was an implicit *assumption* that the four cavities were performing the same. Since the four cavities were not equivalent, this assumption made the chart in Figure 5.11 insensitive. It is always dangerous to assume that parallel operations are equivalent. It is much better to use the control charts to examine this assumption.

In Figure 5.15, the four cavities had been adjusted to the point that they were *known* to be equivalent, and so they could be subgrouped without obscuring a signal. This equivalence can be seen in the following manner. The Average Range of 3.71 units in Figure 5.15 is a cavity-to-cavity difference. This yields a *Sigma(X)* value of 1.80 units for Cavity-to-Cavity variation. The Average Range of 3.51 in Figure 5.12 is a Cycle-to-Cycle difference. This yields a *Sigma(X)* value of 1.51 units for Cycle-to-Cycle variation. Thus, the cavity-to-cavity variation is essentially the same as the Cycle-to-Cycle variation in a single cavity. This means that the four cavities produce parts which have essentially the same average thicknesses. Under such conditions, placing the four cavities together in a single subgroup does not seriously degrade the sensitivity of the control chart, and, in this case, it makes it easier for the operator to maintain the control chart.

When parallel operations are represented in the data, it is always best to keep the parallel operations in separate subgroups. The control chart will be more sensitive, and easier to interpret, when each of the parallel operations are identifiable on the chart. However, if one has solid evidence that the parallel operations are operating alike, and if there is some advantage to doing so, then one may place the parallel operations together within the subgroups of a control chart.

Another lesson from Example 5.7 is the variable spacing of the subgroups. On the first two days after a two week shutdown they collected data from the process much more frequently than they did on the following days. This gets more data for computing limits, and it allows them to monitor the process more closely at first. Once they were satisfied that the process was behaving as expected, they slowed down on their sampling.

Thus, the manner in which the data are organized into subgroups, and the manner in which these subgroups are organized into control charts determine just what questions will be answered by the data. The sources of variation that are represented by differences *within* the subgroups should be those that are the least interesting, while the sources of variation that are represented by differences *between* the subgroups should be the ones that are most interesting. Differences that are fixed, such as the differences between cavities, can be accounted for by using different charts.

Finally, it should always be possible to express, in English, just what sources of variation exist between the subgroups and within the subgroups. If this cannot be done, it is unlikely that much will be gained from the use of the control charts.

5.7 Questions Regarding Data

No control chart makes sense by itself. It will always need a context before it can be interpreted. Whether one is constructing a control chart, or sharing a control chart with someone else, there are certain questions that will need to be answered before the chart can be interpreted. Some of these questions are the following:

1. What do the individual values represent? What are these numbers?

2. How are the values obtained? Who obtains them? How often? At which location? By what method? With what instrumentation?

3. What sources of variation are present in these data?

4. How are these data organized into subgroups? Which sources of variation occur *within* the subgroups? Which sources of variation occur *between* the subgroups?

5. How should such data behave? Are there natural barriers within the range of observed values?

In addition to these questions, there are some principles of subgrouping that should be used in constructing control charts.

SUBGROUPING PRINCIPLE NUMBER ONE:
Never knowingly subgroup unlike things together.

Each subgroup must be logically homogeneous. While nobody is likely to average a height and a weight together, there are more subtle ways that unlike things can be combined. For example, the amount trimmed off on the right side (by one operation) and the amount trimmed off on the left side (by another operation) do not belong in the same subgroup. These two values represent two different processes. Subgrouping them will simply obscure the difference between these two processes.

The control chart in Figure 5.11 has subgroups which consist of cavities which are definitely different. One of the tell-tale signs of this problem a running record which hugs the central line. The Range Chart from Figure 5.11 is shown in Figure 5.16. Notice that the 100 range values do not spread out to fill up the middle two-thirds of the limits as one would expect. Instead they all fall close to the central line. (Remember that the Empirical Rule suggests that approximately two-thirds of the data should be within one sigma unit of the central line, and approximately 95% of the data should be within two sigma units of the central line. Here we find 95 of the 100 values within one sigma unit of the central line, as indicated by the grey band in Figure 5.16.) When 15 or more successive values display this type of behavior on either an Average Chart, or a Range Chart, it is wise to consider if the subgrouping is appropriate.

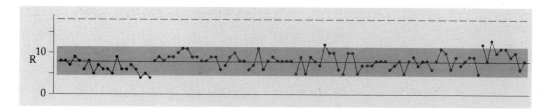

Figure 5.16: Range Chart from First Organization of Ball Joint Socket Data

Occasionally some characteristic of the data will naturally result in a running record which hugs the central line, but when first placing data on a control chart one should look for this signal that the subgrouping might be inappropriate.

SUBGROUPING PRINCIPLE NUMBER TWO:
Minimize the variation within each subgroup.

It is the variation within each subgroup that will define the background noise level for the data. Any signals that may be in the data will have to be found against this background of noise. Therefore, by minimizing the variation within the subgroups one will be creating a control chart that will be sensitive to the presence of signals. Of course this principle must be applied with reason. It will be shown later that one may occasionally define subgroups which are too homogeneous. Just what this does to the chart, and how to deal with this problem will be discussed in Chapter Nine.

SUBGROUPING PRINCIPLE NUMBER THREE:
Maximize the opportunity for variation between the subgroups.

If there is any possibility that two things may differ, make sure that they are in different subgroups. If one wishes to explicitly compare two things, say A and B, make sure that A and B show up in different subgroups. The control chart looks for differences between subgroups. It uses the variation within the subgroups to define how much variation to ignore in this quest. Therefore, by minimizing the variation within each subgroup and maximizing the opportunity for variation from subgroup to subgroup one will get useful and sensitive control charts.

SUBGROUPING PRINCIPLE NUMBER FOUR:
Average across noise, not across signals.

The purpose of using a Subgroup Average is to average out noise in order to concentrate the signal and make it easier to detect. One should never average across measurements which were obtained in such a manner that one knows, *a priori*, that the measurements are not logically equivalent. It is always a mistake to average across signals or potential signals.

SUBGROUPING PRINCIPLE NUMBER FIVE:
Treat the chart in accordance with the use of the data.

The subgroup frequency should reflect the monitoring and decision frequency which is appropriate for the process. If single values are collected, then subgroups of size one may be the most appropriate for the data. If multiple measurements are collected all at the same time, from the same process, then these multiple measurements may be logically subgrouped together. Whenever one is faced with limited amounts of data, as in process trials, experiments, or certification runs, it is always advisable to look at a running record of the Individual Values. A running record of the Individual Values can reveal things that are obscured by subgrouping. This is why the automatic subgrouping of limited amounts of data is not a good practice.

SUBGROUPING PRINCIPLE NUMBER SIX:
Establish operational definitions for the sampling procedure.

When there is subjectivity in the process of obtaining the measurements the values are likely to change with each change in operator. Systematic procedures for obtaining samples, and carefully defined measuring techniques are important foundations for useful data.

Exercise 5.1:

The Blast Furnace Silicon Data, given in Table 5.1, page 91, represents 99 successive measurements of the silicon level in one particular furnace. Since a sample of the molten iron is sent to the lab from the first tap on each shift, there are exactly three silicon values for each day. The arrangement of the 99 values in Table 5.1 into 33 subgroups of size $n = 3$ was motivated by the desire to let each subgroup represent a single day. Therefore, each row of the data was made into a subgroup, with the result being the charts shown in the text.

The only problem with this arrangement of the subgroups is that the data were not recorded in rows. They were written in columns. Consider the first block of nine values in Table 5.1:

144	80	72	The silicon levels for the first day were [144, 150, 180] rather
150	101	97	than [144, 80, 72]. In fact, the values of [80, 101, 106] were
180	106	112	obtained on day 12, while the values [72, 97, 112] were

obtained on day 23. Thus, the subgrouping shown in Table 5.1 is a non-rational subgrouping. This subgrouping occurred because the subgroups were formed without consideration of the structure of the data as they were recorded on the laboratory record. These data have been rearranged into rational subgroups in the following table. Each subgroup represents one day, and successive subgroups represent successive days.

Day	Measurements			Average	Range	Day	Measurements			Average	Range
1	144	150	180	158.00	36	18	128	113	104	115.00	24
2	193	210	225	209.33	32	19	113	122	108	114.33	14
3	235	233	228	232.00	7	20	135	145	158	146.00	23
4	198	190	178	188.67	20	21	133	125	112	123.33	21
5	168	137	121	142.00	47	22	105	95	63	87.67	42
6	116	85	65	88.67	51	23	72	97	112	93.67	40
7	88	111	120	106.33	32	24	126	132	144	134.00	18
8	138	160	179	159.00	41	25	156	163	170	163.00	14
9	200	245	248	231.00	48	26	181	180	202	187.67	22
10	211	201	155	189.00	56	27	250	205	175	210.00	75
11	145	102	83	110.00	62	28	157	148	140	148.33	17
12	80	101	106	95.67	26	29	157	139	121	139.00	36
13	95	90	107	97.33	17	30	131	125	111	122.33	20
14	127	142	159	142.67	32	31	118	115	92	108.33	26
15	167	178	199	181.33	32	32	99	79	111	96.33	32
16	181	173	163	172.33	18	33	127	135	130	130.67	8
17	158	147	134	146.33	24						

(a) Compute the control limits for the Average and Range charts and plot these charts.

(b) What source of variation is represented on the Range Chart?

(c) What source of variation is represented on the Average Chart?

(d) Allowing for the average amount of variation within-a-day, how much variation in the average daily silicon levels would you expect if this process was in control?

Exercise 5.2:

The end-to-end consistency of the thickness of a baked part is important to subsequent operations. Thickness measurements are available from a process trial in which 10 pieces from one batch of compound were baked in the same cavity. The thickness of each part was measured at eight locations, according to the scheme shown in the sketch below.

During this study, the parts were loaded into the cavity so that positions 1, 2, and 3 were at the hinge end of the cavity, and positions 6, 7, and 8 were at the clamp end of the cavity.

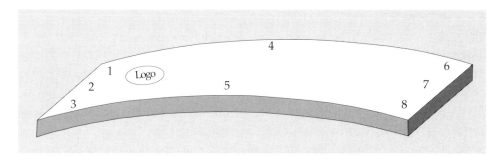

Position	Piece									
	A	B	C	D	E	F	G	H	I	J
1	.311	.311	.309	.311	.310	.310	.311	.311	.310	.310
2	.311	.312	.313	.312	.310	.310	.310	.312	.311	.311
3	.312	.312	.314	.312	.312	.312	.312	.313	.313	.312
4	.315	.314	.310	.313	.312	.310	.313	.314	.313	.315
5	.312	.312	.314	.313	.315	.313	.311	.315	.312	.314
6	.315	.319	.315	.318	.313	.316	.316	.316	.316	.315
7	.312	.314	.313	.314	.312	.312	.314	.314	.313	.313
8	.314	.314	.314	.315	.313	.313	.314	.315	.315	.314

(a) Use the data above to obtain a control chart that will answer the question "Is there a detectable difference between the average end thicknesses?"

(b) What is your answer to the question in part (a)?

(c) How would you organize these data in order to compare the average thicknesses at each of the 8 positions?

Chapter Six

Capability, Stability, and
World Class Quality

Can the process produce product that meets specifications? This question has been around as long as there have been specifications. Many procedures for answering this question have been proposed, yet most of these fall short of a complete answer because they do not deal with the issue of prediction. Before a process can be said to have a well-defined capability, it must display a reasonable degree of statistical control. Therefore, the *capability* of a process depends upon both the *conformity* of the product and the *stability* of the process.

6.1 The Capability of a Stable Process

A stable process is a process which displays a reasonable degree of statistical control—that is, we may predict, within limits, how the process will perform in the future. Given this predictability which is the essence of statistical control, a stable process can be said to possess a well-defined capability—virtually all of the Individual Values will fall within the Natural Process Limits as long as the process displays some degree of statistical control.

The simplest and easiest way to assess the capability of a *stable* process is to plot a histogram of the Individual Values directly from the control chart. The axis of this histogram can show the Specification Limits, and the relationship between the histogram and these limits will portray the capability of the stable process.

EXAMPLE 6.1:   *Capability of the Ball Joint Socket Process:*

The control chart shown in Figure 6.1 shows a process consisting of four parallel operations described in Examples 5.6 and 5.7.

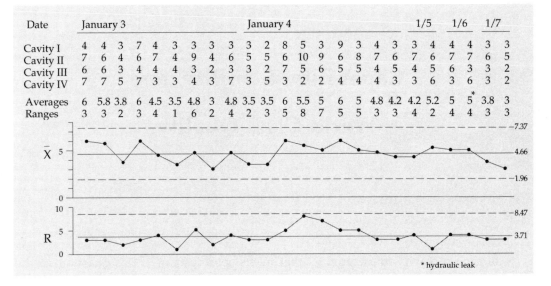

Date	January 3									January 4									1/5		1/6		1/7	
Cavity I	4	4	3	7	4	3	3	3	3	3	2	8	5	3	9	3	4	3	3	4	4	4	3	3
Cavity II	7	6	4	6	7	4	9	4	6	5	5	6	10	9	6	8	7	6	7	6	7	7	6	5
Cavity III	6	6	3	4	4	4	3	2	3	3	2	7	5	6	5	5	4	5	4	5	6	3	3	2
Cavity IV	7	7	5	7	3	3	4	3	7	3	5	3	2	2	4	4	4	3	3	6	3	6	3	2
Averages	6	5.8	3.8	6	4.5	3.5	4.8	3	4.8	3.5	3.5	6	5.5	5	6	5	4.8	4.2	4.2	5.2	5	5*	3.8	3
Ranges	3	3	2	3	4	1	6	2	4	2	3	5	8	7	5	5	3	3	4	2	4	4	3	3

X̄   5 —7.37
— —4.66
— —1.96
    0

    10
R   5 —8.47
— —3.71
    0

* hydraulic leak

Figure 6.1: Operator's Control Chart for Socket Thicknesses

These four parallel operations are subgrouped together on this chart because they have been adjusted so that the four cavities are essentially equivalent.

The histogram for the data from the control chart in Figure 6.1 is shown plotted against the Specification Limits in Figure 6.2. The 0.0 point for these data was set to be equal to the Lower Specification Limit, so the Specifications for this dimension are 0 to 15 hundredths of a millimeter.

*Clearly, this **stable** process is **capable** of meeting these specifications.*

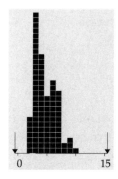

Figure 6.2: Histogram for Socket Thicknesses

If some of the Individual Values fall outside the Specification Limits, then the fraction nonconforming on this histogram will be the best estimate of the process fraction nonconforming. In addition to this graphic summary of the capability of a stable process, one may also compute numerical summaries of capability. These numerical values may be used alone, but they are more effective when combined with a histogram such as Figure 6.2.

The Natural Process Limits may be used to characterize the *actual capability* of a stable process. These limits may be directly computed from the Grand Average and the Average Range:

$$\text{Natural Process Limits for Individual Values} = \overline{\overline{X}} \pm 3 \; Sigma(X) = \overline{\overline{X}} \pm 3 \; \frac{\overline{R}}{d_2}$$

No matter how the data behave, the Empirical Rule assures us that virtually all of the Individual Values will fall within the interval defined by the Natural Process Limits. This part of the Empirical Rule is summarized in Figure 6.3.

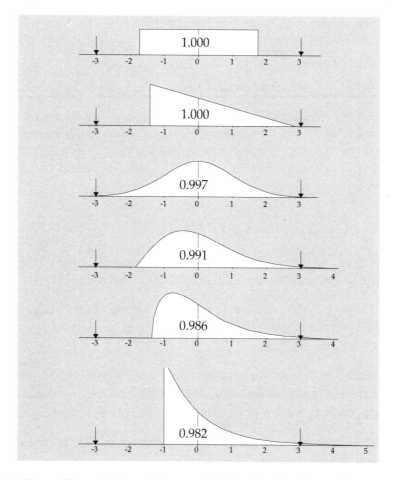

Figure 6.3: Three Sigma Natural Process Limits for Six Theoretical Distributions

EXAMPLE 6.2:   *Natural Process Limits for the Ball Joint Socket Data:*

The Grand Average of the Control Chart in Figure 6.1 is 4.66 units, while the Average Range is 3.71 units. Thus, the Natural Process Limits for these data are:

$$4.66 \pm 3 \left(\frac{3.71}{2.059} \right) = -0.75 \text{ to } 10.07.$$

According to the Empirical Rule, virtually all of the thicknesses should fall between these values. For the histogram in Figure 6.2, 96 out of 96 points fall within this interval.

The symmetric formula for Natural Process Limits shown above is customary. It will be appropriate for most applications. The generality of these symmetric Natural Process Limits is shown in Figure 6.3. However, if a process has displayed a reasonable degree of statistical control over an extended period of time, and if the historical data from this process display a skewed histogram, then one might be willing to modify the formula for the Natural Process Limits to reflect this skewness. Inspection of Figure 6.3 shows that, when a distribution is skewed, *the short tail is always abbreviated to a greater degree than the long tail is extended.* Therefore, even with customized formulas for Natural Process Limits, the distance between the Natural Process Limits will not exceed 6 *Sigma(X).*

EXAMPLE 6.3:   *Modified Natural Process Limits for the Ball Joint Socket Data:*

Examination of the Histogram in Figure 6.2 suggests a skewed histogram. The lower tail appears to be shorter than the upper tail. Since the nature of this process is such that there is a limit on how thin the parts may be, this shortened lower tail is thought to be characteristic of this process. Therefore, one could define the Natural Process Limits for this process to be:

$$4.66 - 2 \left(\frac{3.71}{2.059} \right) \quad to \quad 4.66 + 3 \left(\frac{3.71}{2.059} \right) \quad = \quad 1.06 \text{ to } 10.07 \text{ units.}$$

All 96 of the values in Figure 6.2 fall within this interval. This stable process operates within an interval that is defined by −2 Sigma(X) to +3 Sigma(X).

The Natural Process Limits are the "voice of the process." As such, an obvious and direct way of assessing the capability of a stable process is to compare the Natural Process Limits with the Specification Limits.

If the Natural Process Limits for a stable process fall entirely within the Specification Limits, then the process can be said to be in the Ideal State: it is in control and producing 100% conforming product. Such a process is said to be both *stable* and *capable.*

If one or both of the Natural Process Limits for a stable process fall outside the Specification Limits, then the process may be said to be in the Threshold State: It is in control, but it is likely to be producing some nonconforming product. Such a process is *stable,* but *not capable.*

There are two ways that a stable process may fail to be capable.

When there is both an Upper Specification Limit and a Lower Specification Limit, the Specification Limits may simply be too close together. The spread of the Natural Process Limits may exceed the tolerance defined by the specifications. In short, the process may not have enough "elbow room" between the Specification Limits. When a process is not capable because of this problem, one will have to work on reducing the process variation and/or loosening the specifications. Setting the Process Aim appropriately may help to reduce the amount of nonconforming product on one side or the other, but the nonconforming product cannot be eliminated by any setting of the Process Aim. Without a reduction in the process variation, or a widening of the specifications, some nonconforming product will be inevitable.

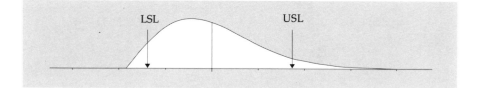

Figure 6.4: Not Enough Elbow Room for Process

The elbow room for a process is the distance between the Specification Limits. This distance may be denoted as the Specified Tolerance, and may be expressed in either measurement units or in sigma units.

Specified Tolerance (in measurement units) = Upper Spec. – Lower Spec.

$$\text{Specified Tolerance (in sigma units)} = \frac{\text{Upper Spec.} - \text{Lower Spec.}}{Sigma(X)}$$

where $Sigma(X)$ is some within-subgroup dispersion statistic[1] such as $\dfrac{\overline{R}}{d_2}$.

Figure 6.5 shows that if the Specified Tolerance exceeds 6 sigma units, then the process has adequate elbow room. If the process also happens to be properly centered, it can produce virtually 100% conforming product.

Stable processes with a Specified Tolerance of less than 6 sigma units are commonly considered to have inadequate elbow room. Even when such a process is "properly centered," it is possible that some nonconforming product will be produced. The smaller the Specified Tolerance becomes, the greater the likelihood of nonconforming product becomes.

---

[1] See Appendix Table A.1 for other formulas for $Sigma(X)$.

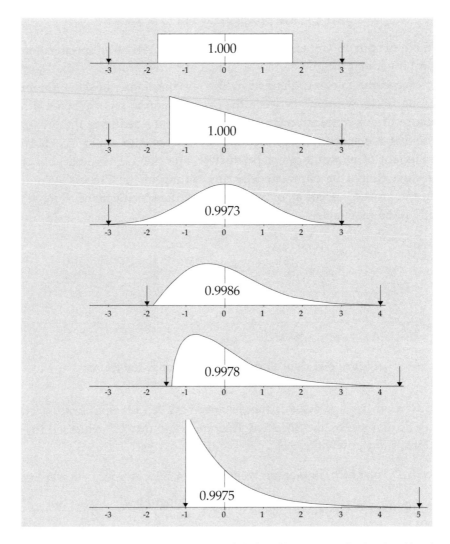

Figure 6.5: The Coverage of 6 Sigma(X) for Six Theoretical Distributions

The Specified Tolerance describes the elbow room for a stable process in terms of the standard unit of dispersion for Individual Values, *Sigma(X)*. This makes the Specified Tolerance easy to understand and use. A Specified Tolerance of 6 sigma units is generally considered to be the bare minimum for a process to be said to be capable. The Specified Tolerance is related to some other values which are associated with process capability. These relations are discussed in Section 6.2.

EXAMPLE 6.4:   *Specified Tolerance for the Ball Joint Socket Data:*

For the Ball Joint Socket Data: $Sigma(X) = \dfrac{\overline{R}}{d_2} = \dfrac{3.71\ units}{2.059\ sigma} = 1.80\ units/sigma.$

Therefore, Specified Tolerance $= \dfrac{15.0\ units - 0.0\ units}{1.80\ units/sigma} = 8.33\ sigma\ units$

Clearly the Ball Joint Socket Process has adequate elbow room relative to the thickness dimension specifications.

The other way that a stable process may fail to be capable is due to the Process Average being in the wrong place. When this happens it may be possible to reduce or eliminate the nonconforming product by simply changing the Process Aim. Of course, if such a change in the Process Aim leads to increased operating costs, one will need to also work on the problem by reducing the process variation. With reduced variation, the Process Aim can be brought closer to the Specification Limit without creating nonconforming product.

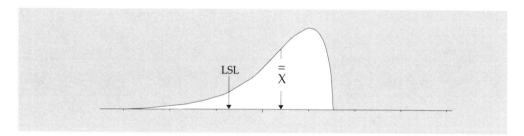

Figure 6.6: Process Average in Wrong Place

The way the process is centered relative to the Specification Limit (or Limits) may be described by the Distance to Nearest Specification.

The distance (in sigma units) between the Grand Average and the Upper Specification Limit is defined to be:

$$Z_U = \frac{\text{Upper Specification Limit} - \text{Grand Average}}{Sigma(X)}$$

The distance (in sigma units) between the Grand Average and the Lower Specification Limit is defined to be:

$$Z_L = \frac{\text{Grand Average} - \text{Lower Specification Limit}}{Sigma(X)}$$

When the Grand Average is on the correct side of the Specification Limit(s) the two values above will be positive. When the Grand Average is on the wrong side of a Specification Limit one of the formulas above will result in a negative value.

The Distance to Nearest Specification (expressed in sigma units) may be defined to be the minimum of the two values above:

$$DNS = \text{minimum of } \{ Z_U, Z_L \}$$

(The minimum of these two values will be the smallest value when both values are positive, and it will be the negative value when one of these values is negative.)

Based upon the Empirical Rule, it is generally desirable for the Distance to Nearest Specification to exceed 3 sigma units. If it does, then it is likely that the process will produce virtually 100% conforming product (as long as it continues to display a reasonable degree of statistical control). If the *DNS* value drops below 3.0 there is an increasing possibility that some nonconforming product may be produced. Of course, the interpretation of *DNS* should always be done in conjunction with a histogram such as the one shown in Figure 6.2.

The Distance to Nearest Specification expresses how the process is centered relative to the specifications, and it does this in terms of the scale units which characterize the process. The *DNS* value is related to several other values which are commonly associated with process capability. These relationships are discussed in the following section.

EXAMPLE 6.5:   *DNS for the Ball Joint Socket Data:*

The Distance to Nearest Specification for the Ball Joint Socket Thicknesses is found as follows:

$$Z_U = \frac{15.0 \text{ units} - 4.66 \text{ units}}{1.80 \text{ units/sigma}} = 5.74 \text{ sigma}$$

$$Z_L = \frac{4.66 \text{ units} - 0.0 \text{ units}}{1.80 \text{ units/sigma}} = 2.59 \text{ sigma}$$

$$DNS = min \{ 5.74, 2.59 \} = 2.59 \text{ sigma}$$

This indicates that the Process Average is approximately 2.5 sigma units above the Lower Specification Limit. Since the thicknesses possess a skewed distribution (see Figure 6.2) this value does not indicate a current problem with nonconforming product. However, since a drop in the Process Average of about 1 unit (1 one-hundredth of a millimeter) to 3.6 units will place the process right against the Lower Specification Limit, it is time to schedule the re-tooling of this mold.

When a process has both Upper and Lower Specification Limits, it is possible to compute both a Specified Tolerance and a Distance to Nearest Specification.

When both values are possible, the *DNS* value will always be less than or equal to one-half of the Specified Tolerance (when both the *DNS* and the Specified Tolerance are expressed in the same units, i.e., when both are expressed in sigma units).

$$DNS \leq {}^1/_2 \text{ Specified Tolerance}$$

The advantage of using the Specified Tolerance and the Distance to Nearest Specification to characterize the capability of a stable process is that they focus attention on the areas needing improvement when the process is not capable. Moreover, they do this without resorting to jargon. Instead of using index numbers or percentages, they use the natural scale of sigma units. Once one has mastered the Empirical Rule, this use of sigma units makes it easy to understand just how the process is performing relative to the specifications.

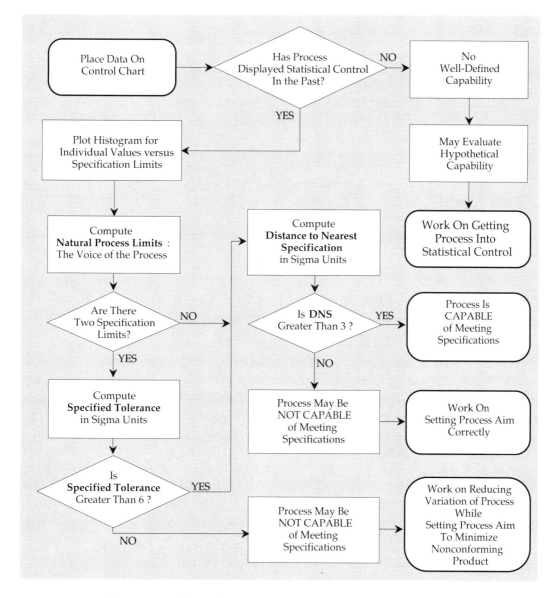

Figure 6.7: Assessing the Capability of a Stable Process

The logic of assessing the capability of a stable process is outlined by the flowchart in Figure 6.7. As the flowchart shows, the question of capability is not a simple, one-dimensional question. There are several possible paths through the flowchart, and they all end in different places. An unstable process does not possess a well-defined capability. A stable process may be capable, or it may be not-capable due to poor process aim, or it may be not-capable due to a lack of elbow room. When confronted with a stable but not-capable process, there are certain courses of action that are indicated if one is to move toward having a stable and capable process.

6.2 Capability Confusion

Both the Specified Tolerance and the Distance to Nearest Specification, expressed in either measurement units or sigma units, may be easily and clearly interpreted. However, both of these values are commonly transformed (and occasionally distorted) into other capability measures.

Capability ratios are intended to be a simple way of expressing the relationship between the voice of the process and the voice of the customer. The result is usually expressed as either a dimensionless number or a percentage.

One way of computing a capability ratio is to divide the spread between the Specification Limits by the spread between the Natural Process Limits. This capability ratio is usually denoted by the symbol C_p:

$$C_p = \frac{\text{Upper Specification} - \text{Lower Specification}}{6\ Sigma(X)}$$

One should note that this value is just the Specified Tolerance, expressed in sigma units, and divided by 6.0.[2] The symbol C_p is quite widely used, and it most often is used for the quantity above. However, it goes by different names in different books. Moreover, most textbooks also impose a requirement of normally distributed data upon the computation of C_p. Inspection of Figure 6.3 should show that $6\ Sigma(X)$ is an appropriate, if slightly conservative, value for estimating the spread between the Natural Process Limits even for non-normally distributed data.

Another way of computing a capability ratio is to divide the spread between the Natural Process Limits by the spread between the specification limits. This capability ratio is sometimes denoted by the symbol *PCI:*

$$PCI = \frac{6\ Sigma(X)}{\text{Upper Specification} - \text{Lower Specification}} \cdot$$

---

[2] The value for *Sigma(X)* used in this formula is an average within-subgroup dispersion statistic.

(Yes, this is just the inverse of C_p!) When one group uses C_p, and another group uses *PCI*, and these two groups attempt to use these ratios to communicate with each other, everyone becomes confused.

Ratios are fairly straightforward quantities. There are two ways to use two values to form a ratio—either A is divided by B, or B is divided by A. In many instances this does not create confusion. For example, one may express fuel economy in miles-per-gallon or in gallons-per-mile. Both ratios make the same comparison, and both do it with equal efficiency, yet these two numbers cannot be used interchangeably. You have to be specific about which one you are using in any one application.

The choice between miles-per-gallon and gallons-per-mile is facilitated by the fact that each ratio has its own units attached. There is little chance of confusing these two ratios because their units help to differentiate between them. However, when the units in a ratio cancel, the ratio will become a dimensionless number. Given a dimensionless ratio, it is inevitable that someone will get confused and invert it. When this happens, confusion is multiplied until all are confused. This is exactly what has happened with the capability ratio.

In fact, the very existence of both C_p and *PCI* says something about the clarity with which these ratios communicate! With the confusion created by C_p and *PCI*, many individuals have decided to invent their own ratios. Both of the authors have been intercepted in plant parking lots by individuals who have invented "new" ways of computing capability ratios. There seems to be no end to the ways people try to dress up the basic comparisons between the voice of the process and the voice of the customer. Therefore, one will always have to question just how a given index or ratio is constructed. *This questioning should also cover what dispersion statistic was used and how it was computed.*

As if things were not bad enough, another quantity, commonly denoted by the symbol C_{pk} (and also called a capability ratio) is defined to be the Distance to Nearest Specification (in sigma units) divided by 3.0:

$$C_{pk} = \frac{DNS}{3.0}$$

This ratio characterizes the process centering relative to the specifications. Some authors do not distinguish between this measure of process centering and the earlier measures of elbow room.

Of course, for those product characteristics having both Upper and Lower Specification Limits (bilateral tolerances) one can have both a C_p value and a C_{pk} value. A stable process which has a Specified Tolerance which exceeds 6 sigma units of elbow room will have a C_p value which exceeds 1.00. If this stable process also has a Distance to Nearest Specification which exceeds 3 sigma units, then it will have a C_{pk} value which also exceeds 1.00. (The fact that *DNS* is limited to one-half of the value of the Specified Tolerance will automatically limit C_{pk} to be less than or equal to C_p.)

It is worth noting just what has happened in the previous paragraph. Both the Specified Tolerance and the Distance to Nearest Specification were converted into index ratios (numbers where 1.00 is the boundary condition between two different situations). These "capability ratios" blur the distinction between the two measures. The fact that one measure describes the "elbow room" for the process, while the other describes the "process location" is obscured by these transformations. So even without the gymnastics of unintentional inversion to confuse the issue, the use of a common boundary condition obscures the different roles for the two basic measures.

How can these problems be solved? The easiest way, by far, is to use quantities which have units attached. Which communicates more clearly:

"The Specified Tolerance is 4.5 sigma units wide, and
the Distance to Nearest Specification is 2 sigma units."
or
"The C_p value is 0.75, the *PCI* value is 1.33,
and the C_{pk} value is 0.67."

The first sentence is self contained. The last sentence is jargon—it only has meaning relative to some external framework not included in the sentence. In fact, without careful thought, one is not sure if the situation revealed in the last sentence is good or bad.

EXAMPLE 6.6: "*Capability Ratios*" *for the Ball Joint Socket Data:*

The Ball Joint Socket Thicknesses had a Specified Tolerance of 8.33 sigma units and a Distance to Nearest Specification of 2.59 sigma units. The histogram in Figure 6.8 portrays a process which was shown to be stable by a control chart. It is also capable.

The C_p value for this process is 1.39.
The PCI value for this process is 0.720.
The C_{pk} value for this process is 0.86.

(Note that this process has 100% conforming product even though C_{pk} is less than 1.0.)

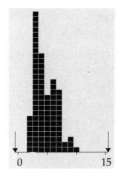

Figure 6.8: Histogram for Socket Thicknesses

None of the numerical summaries of capability should be interpreted without reference to a histogram of the Individual Values plotted against the Specification Limits. Likewise, none of the numerical summaries of capability are meaningful in the absence of a reasonable degree of statistical control (which can only be ascertained by a control chart.)

6.3 Converting Capabilities Into Fraction Nonconforming

Most books convert the capability measures listed in the previous section into fractions of nonconforming product. These statements come in two flavors: ordinary fantasies and outright hallucinations. In the ordinary fantasy category are statements like: "When the C_p value is 1.00 the process will produce 99.7 percent conforming parts." In the hallucination category are statements like: "When the C_p value is 1.50 the process will produce 6.8 parts per million nonconforming."

The conversion of a capability number into a specific fraction of nonconforming product will always require the use of some assumed distribution. Of course, the common assumption is that of normally distributed data. However, such assumptions are essentially unverifiable. As Shewhart noted, the normal distribution characterizes the *limiting* behavior of an *infinite* sequence of values—it can never be said to be a characteristic of a finite sequence.[3] Since we shall always be working with finite sequences, this means that there is no way to ever assert that a given set of data "are normally distributed." So any computation which is based upon the normal distribution (or any other distribution) will be no better than an assumption, and assumptions rarely deserve to be carried out to more than one or two digits (one or two significant figures). Assumptions certainly cannot support computations in the parts per million range.

Now, it is true that certain general probability laws, such as Tchebycheff's Inequality, do place a *bound* on the percentage of values that may fall outside a given interval. Moreover, rough guidelines such as the Empirical Rule may be used to characterize the *approximate* percentages which will fall outside certain intervals. For example, if approximately 99% to 100% of the values fall within three sigma units of the average, then a C_p value of 1.00 will imply that approximately 1% or less will be nonconforming. There is a substantial difference between this statement and saying that "no more than 3 in a 1000 will be nonconforming." The "3 in 1000" statement implies a knowledge and precision that is not available to mere mortals. The "approximately 1% or less" statement conveys the assurance that nonconforming products will be rare, without promising or implying more than is known.

Moreover, it is not necessary to convert the capability values into fictitious fractions nonconforming. If one has a process that is *stable*, but *not capable*, then there will be a rework pile, or a scrap budget, or warranty costs, or a pile of returned goods to quantify the problem of nonconforming product. These knowable figures may only be the tip of the iceberg, but they are definitely visible. One does not need any esoteric computations

---

[3] *Statistical Method from the Viewpoint of Quality Control*, p.12.

to know that a problem exists. If there is a 100% inspection of outgoing product, then the ratio of nonconforming items found to the number of items examined will be a far better estimate of the process fraction nonconforming than any number obtained from a capability value.

On the other hand, if one has a process that is *stable* and *capable*, it will not be necessary to compute an estimated fraction nonconforming. By reducing the variation, or properly setting the process aim, one can assure that there will be virtually no nonconforming product. Maintaining a process in a reasonable degree of statistical control will require a certain amount of continual attention. With this level of attention, one is not likely to be caught napping by any excursion that is likely to produce nonconforming product. This is why the practice of evaluating suppliers based upon C_p values and the like, without regard for process stability, is both flawed and inappropriate.

Finally, when dealing with a process which is both *stable* and *capable*, any attempt to convert a capability ratio into a fraction nonconforming is doomed to failure. This is because such attempts will have to rely upon the extreme tails of the distribution, and the extreme tails of a probability distribution are mathematical entities which simply do not characterize the real world. Even with 10,000 observations, the percentiles of the histogram and the percentiles of an appropriate theoretical distribution will match closely only within the middle 90 percent of the distribution. In the outer 5 percent of each tail, considerable discrepancies will occur. This is why, no matter how much data one has, one can never fully specify a probability distribution function for a stable process. In fact, as Dr. Deming has said: "with enough data, no curve will fit the results of an experiment."[4]

Therefore, the conversion of capability values into fractions nonconforming is an operation that has no contact with reality. It is nothing more than fantasy, and the results are illusions, if not outright delusions.

6.4 What Can Be Said for Unstable Processes?

Not much.

If a process is out of control, it has failed to display a reasonable degree of consistency in the *past*. Therefore, it is illogical to expect that it will spontaneously begin to do so in the *future*. This severely limits the ability to predict the conformity of future product. In fact, since all data analysis is historical, all that can be done is to summarize past performance.

---

[4] "On Probability As a Basis for Action," *American Statistician*, v.29, p.148, 1975.

As indicated in the flowchart of Figure 6.7, an out-of-control process does not possess a well-defined capability. Therefore, it is meaningless to attempt to characterize such processes as being either *capable* or *not capable*. About all that can be done is to try to use the historical data to describe what was. Even this will be chancy. If the data collected are inconsistent, how well will they characterize the process behavior during the same period?

If the past measurements fell within the specification limits, the process may be said to have been on the Brink of Chaos. If some of the past measurements fell outside of the specifications, then the process may be said to have been in the State of Chaos. In either case, future performance cannot be predicted because, by definition, the process is subject to unpredictable changes. Therefore, knowledge of what happened yesterday tells very little about what to expect today. This unpredictability of an unstable process is illustrated by the following example from a plant in Europe.

EXAMPLE 6.7:   *The Batch Weight Data:*

The raw materials for the process are dry mixed, and then blended with a phenolic resin, in batches that should weigh 1000 kilograms each. The weights of all batches run during one week are shown in Table 6.1. (The time order sequence for the values in Table 6.1 is given by reading the values row by row, 15 values per row.)

Table 6.1: Batch Weights for 259 Batches

```
 905  930  865  895  905    885  890  930  915  910    920  915  925  860  905
 925  925  905  915  930    890  940  860  875  985    970  940  975 1000 1035
1020  985  960  945  965    940  900  920  980  950    955  970  970 1035 1040
1000 1000  990 1000  950    940  965  920  920  925    900  905  900  925  885
1005 1005  950  920  875    865  880  960  925  925    875  900  905  990  970

 910  980  900  970  900    895  885  925  870  875    910  915  900  950  880
 910  965  910  880  900    920  940  985  965  925    925  975  905  890  950
 975  935  940  900  915    980  880  905  915  960    900  915  920  865  980
 935  840  900  965  890    875 1020  780  900  900    800  960  845  820  910
 885  940  930  925  850    965 1010 1030  980 1010    950  940 1005  880  930

 845  935  905  965  975    985  975  950  905  965    905  950  905  995  900
 840 1050  935  940  920    985  970  915  935  950   1030  875  880  955  910
1050  890 1005  915 1070    970 1040  770  940  950   1040 1035 1110  845  900
 905  910  860 1045  820    900  860  875 1005  880    750  900  835  930  860
 960  950 1020  975  950    960  950  880 1000 1005    990 1020  980 1020  920

 960 1000 1000  860 1130    830  965  930  950  945    900  990  865  945  970
 915  975  940  870  890    915  935 1060 1015 1100    810 1010 1140  805 1020
1110  975  970 1090
```

The first 45 mix weights were used to compute limits for the XmR chart shown in Figure 6.9. These computations are shown on pages 214–215.

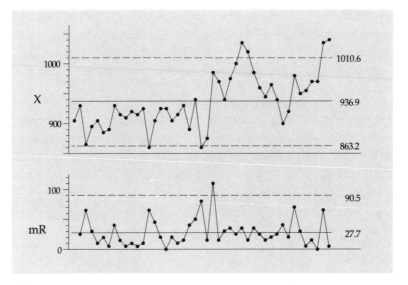

Figure 6.9: *XmR* **Chart for 45 Batch Weights**

The Individual Values chart contains several indications of a lack of control. Six of the 45 weights are outside the control limits, and there are runs about the central line of length 21 and 12. The process for producing batches that weigh 1000 kg is clearly out of control, and is therefore unpredictable.

The control limits for the Individual Values in Figure 6.9 are the computed values for the Natural Process Limits. However, in this case, these limits merely PASS JUDGMENT upon the process—it is judged to be out of control—rather than being PREDICTORS of what the process will produce. So while the calculations are the same, the interpretation will depend upon the message of the chart. When the process is not in statistical control, the limits for Individual Values cannot be interpreted as predictors of what will be. When a process is out of control, there is simply no reliable way to predict how it will perform in the future.

To clarify this point further, consider trying to use the computed Natural Process Limits of 863 kg to 1010 kg as predictors. Figure 6.10 shows all 259 of the batches for the week plotted against these limits.

In the top row, the limits of 863 to 1010 roughly define the region where many of the batch weights occur. However, in the middle row there are more points that fall far out-side this region. Finally, in the bottom row the process is operating over a much wider region than 863 kg to 1010 kg.

In fact, on Friday afternoon, 8 of the last 12 batches had weights which fell outside the interval of 863 kg to 1010 kg calculated from Monday's data!

When a process is out of control, it is characterized by random and erratic changes. For this reason, it is only a matter of time before it will wander outside *any* limits which are calculated using historical values. The only predictable thing about an unstable process is its unpredictability.

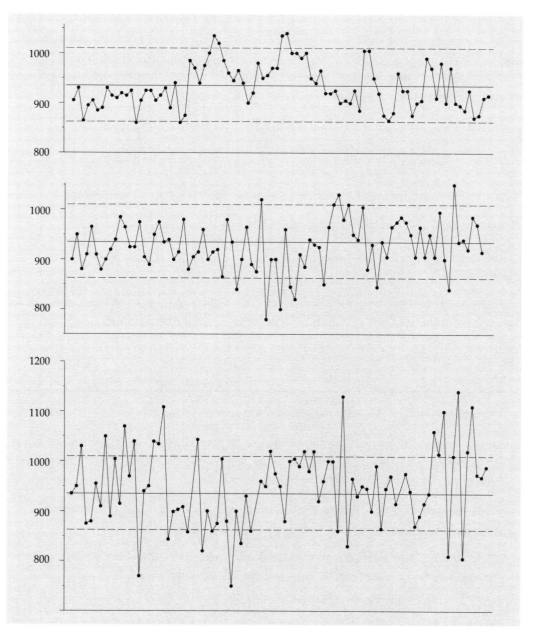

Figure 6.10: X Chart for 259 Batch Weights

Unfortunately, many people can and do compute "capability values" for processes which behave like the batch weight data. Such values are, at best, descriptive of the past, rather than being predictive of the future. For this reason some have labeled these values as "performance values" rather than "capability values." Moreover, unlike capability values, it is appropriate to use the overall dispersion statistic *s* in the computation of these performance values instead of an average within-subgroup dispersion statistic.

The computation of the following values is essentially an exercise in frustration, since they will have no predictive value. However, if one is determined to compute performance values for out-of-control processes, then one should use the following formulas instead of the capability formulas.

Instead of C_p, one could compute a Process Performance Ratio: P_p

$$P_p = \frac{\text{Upper Specification} - \text{Lower Specification}}{6\,s}$$

where *s* is the usual standard deviation statistic computed using all of the data.

Instead of C_{pk}, one could compute the Centered Performance Ratio: P_{pk}

$$P_{pk} = \frac{\text{minimum of } (USL - \bar{\bar{X}}) \text{ and } (\bar{\bar{X}} - LSL)}{3\,s}$$

These values attempt to characterize the *past performance* of an out-of-control process. They may or may not do a very good job depending upon the data used.

EXAMPLE 6.8:   *Performance Ratios for Batch Weight Data:*

The specifications for the Batch Weights are 900 kg to 1100 kg.

The Average Range for the first 44 moving ranges was 27.84 kg. Based on this, a value for Sigma(X) is 24.7 kg. The Average of the first 45 weights is 936.9 kg. Using these values, the P_p value is 1.35, while the P_{pk} value is 0.50.

Using the first 45 Batch Weights, the s statistic is s = 45.8 kg. Using this value the P_p value is 0.73, and using the Average of 936.9 the P_{pk} value is 0.27.

Using all 259 Batch Weights, the Average is 937.0 and the s statistic is s = 61.3. With these values, the P_p value becomes 0.54, and the P_{pk} value becomes 0.20

While these last values do the best job of describing how miserably this process performed during the past week, the considerable variation in the values computed serves to point out the futility of these calculations. What you get depends upon the data you use, and since the data are out-of-control, the results can vary all over the place.

This same unpredictability applies to any computation of the fraction nonconforming for an unstable process. In the first 129 values for the Batch Weight Data there were 20 values below the Lower Specification Limit, and none above the Upper Specification Limit. This translates into a total of 15.5% nonconforming Batch Weights. In the last 129 values of the Batch Weight Data there were 33 values below the Lower Specification Limit, and 5 values above the Upper Specification Limit, for a total of 29.5% nonconforming Batch Weights. Thus, the first half of the week does not even predict the last half of the week.

So just what can one say about an unstable process? Not much.

6.5 The Hypothetical Capability of an Unstable Process

When a process is unstable, the computed values for the Natural Process Limits may be used to pronounce judgement, but they are not predictors of what *will* be. An unstable process has only the record of its past performance, which is virtually worthless as a prediction of the future. The one thing that can be said for such a process is that it can be improved. By finding and eliminating the Assignable Causes of excessive variation, the consistency of the product stream can often be dramatically increased.

If there is a need to approximate how much improvement might result from getting a process in control, then one may calculate the *hypothetical process capability*. To do this, begin with the Range Chart, and carry out the following cycle of operations:

1. Delete any ranges that are out of control, and recalculate the Average Range.

2. Recalculate the control limits for the Range Chart.

3. Repeat step 1 as long as additional range values are found outside the revised control limits.

When no additional ranges are found outside the revised limits, then one may approximate the Hypothetical Process Spread using the most recent value of the Average Range:

$$\text{Hypothetical Process Spread} = \frac{6\,\bar{R}}{d_2}$$

If the process is one in which the Process Aim can be easily changed, then this value of the Hypothetical Process Spread is likely to be all that is needed. On the other hand, if the Process Average is very hard to change, then it may be helpful to find Hypothetical Process Limits. To do this, continue with the Average Chart:

4. Delete any averages that are out of control, and recalculate the Grand Average.

5. Recalculate the control limits for the Average Chart, using the new value for the Grand Average, and the last revised value for the Average Range.

6. Repeat step 4 as long as additional average values are found outside the revised control limits.

When no more averages are found outside the revised limits, use the last value of the Grand Average, along with the last value of the Average Range, to approximate the Hypothetical Process Limits by:

$$\text{Hypothetical Process Limits} = \bar{\bar{X}} \pm 3 \frac{\bar{R}}{d_2}$$

One should note that the formulas above are the same as for the computations for stable processes. The difference is in the treatment of the data. The Hypothetical Process Limits and the Hypothetical Process Spread are simply indications of what might be if and when the process is actually brought into control. They have absolutely no bearing on what is currently being produced.

EXAMPLE 6.9   *Hypothetical Capability of Socket Cavity Four:*

The thicknesses for the Ball Joint Sockets produced in Cavity Four were given in Table 5.4 and are reproduced in Table 6.2. The control chart for these data is shown in Figure 6.11. The Grand Average is 7.86, and the Average Range is 3.35 units.

Table 6.2 Ball Joint Socket Thicknesses for Cavity Four

	A	B	C	D	E	$\bar{X}$	R		A	B	C	D	E	$\bar{X}$	R		A	B	C	D	E	$\bar{X}$	R
1:	8	9	10	10	10	9.4	2	8:	6	6	8	6	5	6.2	3	15:	11	12	12	12	6	10.6	6
2:	10	13	13	10	9	11	4	9:	9	10	11	9	5	8.8	6	16:	6	8	7	9	7	7.4	3
3:	8	9	10	8	9	8.8	2	10:	5	5	6	6	5	5.4	1	17:	7	7	4	7	5	6.0	3
4:	11	12	11	10	13	11.4	3	11:	11	10	9	10	10	10.0	2	18:	6	8	7	12	12	9.0	6
5:	4	4	5	3	4	4.0	2	12:	9	6	8	7	7	7.4	3	19:	7	7	5	12	8	7.8	7
6:	4	7	6	5	4	5.2	3	13:	9	12	11	11	6	9.8	6	20:	10	7	9	8	8	8.4	3
7:	4	4	5	4	5	4.4	1	14:	6	7	6	6	6	6.2	1								

Since the Range Chart for the Thicknesses from Cavity Four is in-control, there is no revision of the Average Range necessary. It can be used directly to estimate the Hypothetical Process Spread. This value will still be hypothetical because the lack of control on the Average Chart will result in product distribution which is more widely spread than the Hypothetical Process Spread would suggest.

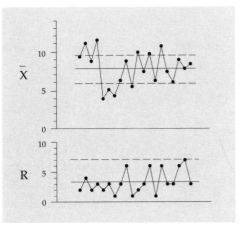

Figure 6.11: Cavity Four Thicknesses

$$\text{Hypothetical Process Spread} = \frac{6\ (3.35)}{2.326} = 8.6\ \text{units}$$

Since the Specified Tolerance is equal to 15 units of measurement, this process should be capable of meeting specifications if it is brought into control and is properly centered. However, since the process is not in-control, it is not currently operating with a spread of 8.6 units. The histogram of the Individual Values from Table 6.2 is shown in Figure 6.12. The range of this histogram is 10 units.

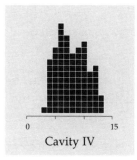

Cavity IV

Figure 6.12
Thickness Histogram
for Cavity Four

The computation of the Hypothetical Process Limits would proceed as follows:

Step 4. Delete the out-of-control averages and recompute the Grand Average:

$$\overline{\overline{X}} = \frac{85.4}{11} = 7.76\ \text{units}.$$

Step 5. Recompute the Limits for the Average Chart.

$$\overline{\overline{X}} \pm A_2\ \overline{R} = 7.76 \pm 0.577\ (3.35) = 5.83\ \text{to}\ 9.69$$

Step 6. None of the remaining Subgroup Averages fall outside these control limits.

Thus, the Hypothetical Process Limits for Cavity Four may be taken to be:

$$\overline{\overline{X}} \pm 3\ \frac{\overline{R}}{d_2} = 7.76 \pm 3\ \frac{3.35}{2.326} = 3.44\ \text{to}\ 12.08$$

Shortly after the data in Table 6.2 were collected the process was brought into a state of statistical control. It was then maintained in this state. The data shown in Figure 6.13 consist of the thicknesses of 24 parts from Cavity Four. These data were collected some nine months after the data shown in Table 6.2. The range of the histogram in Figure 6.13 is seen to be 6 units. This is better than the Hypothetical Process Spread of 8.6 units. Thus, when it was brought into a state of statistical control, the process did better than was predicted by the hypothetical computation above. (The Grand Average of 4.125 units is less than the value of 7.76 computed above because of tool wear during the intervening nine months.)

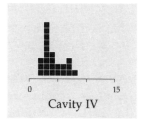

Cavity IV

Figure 6.13: Cavity Four
When Process Was In Control

In fact, the data from all four cavities combined have the histogram shown in Figure 6.2, page 118. There the range of thicknesses for parts produced in all four cavities is seen to be only 9 units. Thus, all four cavities are now more consistent than Cavity Four was initially. This is typical of what happens to a process when it is brought into, and maintained in, a reasonable degree of statistical control.

Thus, the Hypothetical Process Limits and the Hypothetical Process Spread are only approximations of what might be. Until the effort is made to identify and remove the Assignable Causes of uncontrolled variation, the process will never actually achieve the capability predicted by these hypothetical values.

Any procedure for evaluating capability that does not also consider process stability will invariably yield a faulty picture of the process. Unstable processes are not predictable, while stable processes are predictable. No computation, no manipulation of the data, can ever overcome this fact.

6.6 Short Term Capability Studies

Occasionally, the performance of a particular machine may need to be evaluated when there is no operating history available from a control chart. A procedure for such situations will be outlined in this section.

First of all, one must realize that any short-term study of a machine or process will only reveal part of the story. Factors which commonly result in variation for the product or the process may not have an opportunity to do so during a short-term study. This is why any short-term study must be considered to be a "best-case" scenario.

A short-term study will typically generate anywhere from 25 to 50 values. These values might be dimensions of parts produced in sequence, or repeated measurements of the same thing, or values obtained from repeatedly cycling through the same operation.

A naive approach to short-term capability places these 25 to 50 values in a histogram and computes some numerical summaries. The problem with this approach is its total disregard for process stability. Remember, one is not really interested in the 50 numbers in this study, but in the ability to predict what the process will do in the future. The question of capability cannot be divorced from the question of stability. If data are to be collected from some trial runs, then one should examine these data for evidence of instability. If the machine or process is unstable under relatively ideal conditions, what will it be like in a production environment?

Other procedures will attempt to remedy this oversight by automatically placing the data on an Average and Range Chart (say 5 or 10 subgroups of size 5). While this is an improvement over the naive approach, it is still not the best practice.

Since even Average and Range Charts can miss some signals, especially when used with finite amounts of data, it is wise to look at a running record of the individual values.[5]

Thus, with 25 to 50 values, one should begin with a running record of these 25 to 50 values plotted in their time order sequence. This running record should be examined for any obvious patterns such as trends or sustained shifts. If nothing is seen in the running record, one may continue by computing the Moving Ranges and turning the running record into a chart for Individual Values. The Individual Values Chart is then examined for out-of-control points, and the Moving Range Chart is examined for evidence of breaks in the sequence of values.

Finally, if one still desires to do so, one may place the data into subgroups and create an Average and Range Chart. Of course, with sequential values, the subgrouping is essentially arbitrary, but occasionally this will be required in order to show an out-of-control condition most clearly.

Therefore, any approach to a short-term capability study should begin with a plot of the Individual Values, and proceed to examine these values for any indications of a lack of statistical control. If the control chart shows the machine or process to be out of control, then that machine or process does not have a well-defined capability.

If the control chart does not show any indication of a lack of control, then it may be assumed that the machine or process does have a well-defined capability when it is operated under the conditions of the test. In order to approximate this capability calculate the Natural Process Limits from the data on the control chart. Of course these limits only apply to the experimental unit. Moreover, these limits will apply to the machine or process only for the conditions under which the data were collected. These conditions usually involve operation by one operator, using one batch of raw material, at a time when the machine or process has just been adjusted to operate properly by the engineers who designed it. Under these relatively ideal conditions, the capability should describe the best that this machine or process can ever do without being modified in some way. If this capability is insufficient, the machine or process should not be purchased.

If this rather ideal capability is good enough, then the machine or process might work as planned on the production floor. The limited conditions of the evaluation make it very hard to generalize to just how much worse the machine or process may perform in practice. All that is known is that the short-term capability is a best-case analysis, and allowances will have to be made for the other sources of variation that exist in every manufacturing operation.

---

[5] Dr. Deming's recommendation in a letter to the author.

The Vision System Study:

One company bought a vision system to measure the circular inserts being fabricated out of steel wire. The insert was placed on a backlighted panel, and a video camera recorded the image. A computer then began to count the number of pixels within the circular image of the insert. Once this count was obtained, the effective diameter for the insert was computed.

Because of problems after installation, an engineer and a statistician decided to study the measurement system. The statistician suggested repeatedly measuring the same part. The engineer simply picked up a part from the production line and they began to measure it over and over again. In less than an hour they had collected and plotted 30 measurements of this part. The XmR chart for these data is shown in Figure 6.14.

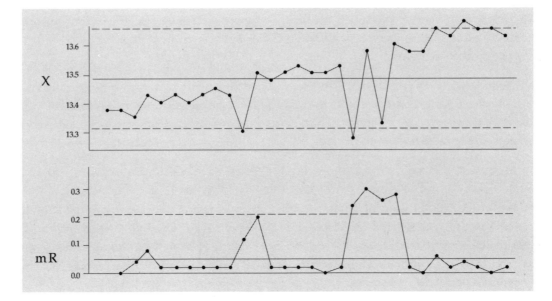

Figure 6.14: XmR Chart for Vision Measurement System

Since each measurement was made using the same part, the running record for X values should be a flat line except for measurement error, and the Moving Ranges should be in control. The definite trend on the X chart, and the out-of-control Moving Ranges both indicate problems with the Vision Measurement System.

The measured diameter of this steel part grew about one-quarter of an inch during this one hour period. This "growth" was a problem with the design of the vision system—the pixel size was slowly changing over time, causing the computed area to drift and the apparent diameter to change.

The Moving Ranges represent pure measurement error in this case. The out-of-control Moving Ranges represent a problem with the way the vision system was installed. The computer would loose count of the pixels when a nearby stamping press would shake the building in the middle of a measurement. This would result in a bad value and a correspondingly large Moving Range. Thus, this short-term capability study revealed that this vision system was essentially a high-tech, electronic, rubber ruler. This measurement system has no well-defined capability.

6.7   World Class Quality

Variation always creates costs. Actions taken to deal with variation after the fact will inevitably increase the costs, while actions that reduce variation at the source will reduce subsequent costs while increasing product quality. The further upstream one works to reduce variation, the lower the Costs of Variation will be.

Say, for example, that X denotes a performance characteristic for a particular product, and let the target value for X be denoted by τ. If the target value has been properly defined, and if a particular unit of the product has a value of $X = \tau$, then there should be no problem with that unit. The problem comes when the product performance characteristic is not equal to τ. Assume, for the purposes of this discussion, that any deviation of X from τ will result in a degradation in the performance of the product. Generally, small differences will result in small amounts of degradation, while greater deviations will result in greater degradations.

The traditional approach to the problem of product variation has been that of specifications. By using specification limits to define some neighborhood of τ, say $\tau \pm \Delta x$, manufacturers have hoped to place acceptable bounds upon the degradation in performance for the product. As long as the quality characteristic X falls within these specification limits, the product is said to be satisfactory. When the value for X falls outside these limits, the product is suddenly deemed to be unsatisfactory and certain actions are invoked to remedy the situation.

To understand the natural consequences of the Specification Approach consider a stream of units produced and evaluated according to specifications of $\tau = 100$ and $\Delta x = 10$. The first unit has a value of 108 and is therefore deemed to be satisfactory. The next unit has a value of 102, and it also is passed. The third unit has a value of 96, so it is passed. Say the next unit has a value of 92. It is passed. The fifth unit has a value of 90, which is still within specifications, so it is passed and everything is still deemed to be satisfactory for the production process. However, when the sixth unit has a value of 89 the whole department is thrown into an uproar to find out why they are making nonconforming product! Inspectors are sent to inspect all incoming products. Engineers are assigned to project teams to work on the process. Managers consider if a recall is needed. And the workers adjust the process to increase the value for X. This sudden cascade of actions will of course greatly increase the costs associated with the production of this product. (One should note that the difference between the fifth unit (90) and the sixth unit (89) was less than any of the differences between earlier successive units, yet the fifth unit was deemed to be satisfactory and the sixth unit was deemed to be unsatisfactory!)

Thus, specification limits are actually *artificial* boundaries used to make *arbitrary* decisions about what product to use. They are a naive attempt to deal with the problems created by the variation of product characteristics. All product is considered to be either good or bad, and the dividing line between good stuff and bad stuff is seen to be a sharp cliff.

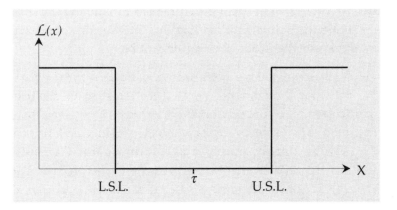

Figure 6.15: Loss Function for Conformance to Specifications Concept of Quality

The graph in Figure 6.15 shows the Loss Function for the Specification Approach to product variation. The loss associated with using a given item is viewed to be a function of the value of the product characteristic, X. In Figure 6.15 the loss is shown on the vertical scale and is labeled as $L(x)$, while values for X are shown on the horizontal scale. With the Specification Approach to product variation the cost of using an item is defined to be zero whenever the value for X is within the specification limits [$L(x)$ is zero when X is within the specifications]. The loss is defined to be some definite (nonzero) value whenever the value for X is outside the specification limits. And the step function of Figure 6.15 is the result.

The world view shown in Figure 6.15 is reinforced by the cascade of actions which are initiated whenever the value for X falls outside the specification limits. Sorting, blending, rework, scrapping of product and adjusting the process will all contribute to the loss associated with nonconforming product, and this sudden shift in the way the product is treated will essentially create a step-function in any cost curve. However, one should notice that this step-function is created by a reaction on the part of management, rather than by any sudden and dramatic change in the product characteristic, X. The changes from 108 to 102, from 102 to 96, from 96 to 92, and from 92 to 90 were all larger than the change from 90 to 89 which triggered the responses. According to the specification world view, 108, 102, 96, 92 and 90 are equivalent, but 89 is different from 90. The shift from "operating okay" to operating "in trouble" is always seen as sudden and unexpected.

Therefore, the very nature of the Specification Approach fosters periods of neglect of the process broken by periods of intense process scrutiny. During the periods of neglect any insights into the process are usually lost, process improvements come unravelled, and the product quality begins to drift away from the target value once again. This is why Conformance to Specifications is no longer enough to remain competitive in today's world. The Conformance to Specifications Approach does not engender the constancy of purpose required to learn from, and to continually improve the production process. As long as the conformance to specifications is regarded as the main objective for any operation, it will be impossible to sustain any real process improvements. (This is why designed experiments are always more successful in an environment which has demonstrated the constancy of purpose needed to get at least some of its processes into a reasonable state of statistical control. If a plant has not demonstrated the ability to use Shewhart's Control Charts in a sustained program of process improvement, what hope is there that they can use more sophisticated and complicated techniques, and on what basis can one expect that the knowledge gained from the experiments will continue to be utilized in the weeks and months to come?)

Therefore, a different approach to the problem of product variation was needed.

In September of 1960, Dr. Genichi Taguchi introduced an elegant way to approach the problem of variation. His approach used a well known mathematical construction in a new setting, and resulted in a powerful new perspective on the problem of variation in production.

Again let X denote some performance characteristic for a particular product, and let τ represent the target value for X. As X varies about τ there will be some loss associated with each particular value of X. When $X = x$, denote this loss as $\mathcal{L}(x)$. The loss function, $\mathcal{L}(x)$, is generally assumed to be;

(1) non-negative for all values of x,
(2) equal to zero when $x = \tau$, and
(3) piecewise smooth near τ.

Under these rather general conditions, one may use a Taylor series expansion to approximate $\mathcal{L}(x)$ within some region close to τ. When this is done, the first three terms of the approximation are:

$$\mathcal{L}(x) \approx \mathcal{L}(\tau) + \mathcal{L}'(\tau)\,[(x-\tau)] + \tfrac{1}{2}\,\mathcal{L}''(\tau)\,[(x-\tau)^2]$$

Assumption (2) results in the first term on the right, $\mathcal{L}(\tau)$, being zero. Assumptions (1) and (2) imply that the loss is minimum at $x = \tau$, and since the first derivative disappears at a minimum, $\mathcal{L}'(\tau) = 0$ and the second term vanishes. Thus, the first non-zero term in the Taylor series expansion for $\mathcal{L}(x)$ in the neighborhood of τ is the term involving $(x-\tau)^2$. From this it follows that the simplest form for $\mathcal{L}(x)$ is the function

$$\mathcal{L}(x) = K\,(x - \tau)^2$$

for some constant K.

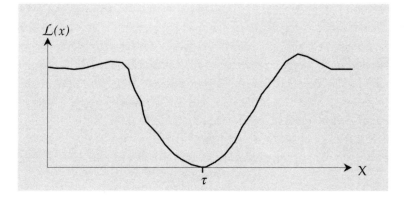

Figure 6.16: A Piecewise Smooth Loss Function

Since the units for $(x-\tau)^2$ will be [measurement units squared], the constant K will be expressed in terms of [dollars per measurement unit squared]. By the appropriate consideration of the costs associated with given deviations of X from τ, one may actually define the value for K for a specific application.

It should be emphasized that the loss function $\mathcal{L}(x)$ is not likely to be represented by the quadratic function over all values for X. It is logical to assume that there is some maximum loss that will eventually place an upper bound upon $\mathcal{L}(x)$. However, even though $\mathcal{L}(x)$ may well be more complex than the simple quadratic function defined above, this approximation will suffice in some region close to τ.

While $\mathcal{L}(x)$ defines the loss, in dollars, associated with a particular value of X, it does not take into account the likelihood that a particular value of X will occur. To do this one will have to consider the notion of a distribution of values for X.

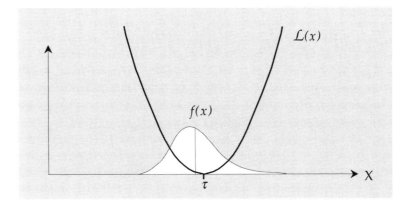

Figure 6.17: A Quadratic Loss Function with a Product Distribution

To begin with, consider a production run of 100 pieces. Each piece would have some value for the performance characteristic, $X = x$. For each value of X there would be some loss, say $L(x)$. The 100 loss values associated with these 100 pieces could be summed up to obtain the total loss for this production run. If this total loss was divided by 100, one would then obtain an "average loss per piece" for this production run.

This same approach can be generalized to yield an average loss value for any production process which displays a reasonable degree of statistical control.

To see how to do this in practice it is helpful to first consider an idealized process which displays exact stability. Imagine that the probability density function, $f(x)$, for this process is known. Then the probability density function will define the likelihood that X will take on each value along the horizontal axis, while the Loss Function, $L(x)$, will define the loss for each value of X. Therefore, the Average Loss per Unit of Production will be found by integrating the product of $L(x)$ and $f(x)$. This integral is called the Expected Value of $L(x)$:

$$E[L(x)] = \int_{all\ x} L(x)\, f(x)\, dx$$

When the quadratic Taguchi Loss Function, $L(x) = K(x-\tau)^2$, is placed in this expression the Average Loss may be rewritten as

$$E[L(x)] = \int_{all\ x} K(x-\tau)^2 f(x)\, dx = K[\sigma^2 + (\mu-\tau)^2]$$

where σ^2 is the *square of the standard deviation* (or *variance*) of the distribution of X, and

$(\mu - \tau)^2$ is the *square of the bias* of the distribution of X. This result holds regardless of the form for the distribution of X. Thus, under conditions of exact process stability, the Average Loss Per Unit of Production Due to Variation in the Product Performance Characteristic may be expressed in terms of parameters of the distribution of X. In particular, the Average Loss due to product variation is seen to be proportional to the square of the process standard deviation and the square of the amount by which the process average deviates from the target value. ***This means that the Average Loss will always be minimized by operating on target with minimum variance.***

Since the Average Loss is an actual cost of production, its reduction will be a desirable objective, and the equations above suggest a particular strategy for doing this. In terms of an existing process, one operates on target when the Process Aim is properly set, and one operates with minimum variation when one operates a process in a state of statistical control. When a process displays a reasonable degree of statistical control, it is operating as consistently as possible.

Thus, Dr. Taguchi's concept of a more realistic Loss Function leads unavoidably to a new definition of world class quality—"On Target With Minimum Variance." "On Target" will require that one knows the Process Average, and sets the Process Aim in such a way to get the Process Average to be as close to the Target as possible. Some control chart techniques for doing this will be described in Chapter 8. "Minimum Variance" will require that a process be operated in such a way that it will display a reasonable degree of statistical control.

The failure to operate a process *on target with minimum variance* will inevitably result in dramatic increases in the Average Loss Per Unit of Production. Such losses may be severe, and are always unnecessary.

Conformance to Specifications, Zero Defects, Six Sigma Quality, Cost of Quality and *all other specification based nostrums miss this point.* World Class Quality has been defined by "On Target With Minimum Variance" *for the past thirty years!* The sooner one wakes up to this fact of life, the sooner one can begin to compete.

The equation for the Average Loss Per Unit of Production is:

$$E\{\mathcal{L}(x)\} = \int \mathcal{L}(x)\, f(x)\, dx = K\left\{ \sigma^2 + (\mu - \tau)^2 \right\}$$

This equation is a function of the parameters of a probability model. As such it cannot be calculated in practice. However, it is possible to approximate this quantity using the statistics which are the basis for control charts. In particular, the approximate Average Loss may be defined to be:

$$K\left\{ MSD(\tau) \right\}$$

where $MSD(\tau)$ denotes the Mean Square Deviation About Target for a stable process:

$$MSD(\tau) = \left[\ (Sigma(X))^2 + (\bar{\bar{X}} - \tau)^2 \ \right].$$

where *Sigma(X)* and $\bar{\bar{X}}$ come from the control chart for the characteristic *X*.

The Mean Square Deviation About Target characterizes how a stable process is performing relative to "On Target With Minimum Variance." Moreover, this measure is directly proportional to the average cost due to variation in the product characteristic. This measure does not replace the Specified Tolerance and the Distance to Nearest Specification, but it does surpass them in tracking process improvements and the subsequent reductions in costs.

In order to find a value for *K* one will need to be able to connect a definite cost with a specific deviation from target. One way to do this is to define the cost of scrapping an item, and connect this cost with the deviation from target which will result in scrap. Once a cost, C_{scrap}, is connected with a specific value for *X*, say x_{scrap}, then:

$$C_{scrap} = K \ (x_{scrap} - \tau)^2 \qquad \text{and} \qquad K = \frac{C_{scrap}}{(x_{scrap} - \tau)^2}$$

Given a value for *MSD(τ)* and a value for *K*, one may compute an estimated Average Loss Per Unit of Production by multiplying these two values together.

6.8 Summary

In characterizing the capability of a process, the question of statistical control is basic. A process that is in a state of statistical control exists as a well-defined entity. The continuity provided by a state of statistical control is the basis for using the past to predict the future. As long as the process continues to operate in a state of statistical control, the Natural Process Limits describe the amount of variation that will exist in the product stream.

On the other hand, when the process is out of control, it must be considered to be schizophrenic. It will continually change in unpredictable ways, at random times, as the Assignable Causes come and go. In this kind of situation, numerical summaries will merely represent the historical data. They cannot be meaningfully generalized to represent anything beyond the data. They may (or may not) summarize past performance, but they definitely will not provide reliable guides to the future. Any procedure for characterizing a production process that does not recognize these realities, will of necessity yield a flawed picture of the process.

With stable processes, the Natural Process Limits, the Specified Tolerance, the Distance to Nearest Specification, and the Mean Square Deviation About Target may all be used to characterize different aspects of the process. They will all be indicative of both the past and the future as long as the process continues to display statistical control.

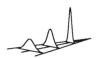

Exercise 6.1:

The control chart for the data of Example 3.1, page 43 is shown in Figure 3.7 on page 45. The Grand Average is 4.763, and the Average Range is 4.05 based upon subgroups of size $n = 4$. These data display a reasonable degree of statistical control. The Specification Limits for this thickness are -5 to 15 units.

(a) Compute *Sigma(X)* for this process.

(b) Compute Natural Process Limits for this thickness.

(c) Express the Specified Tolerance in sigma units, and compute the value for C_p.

(d) Express the Distance to Nearest Specification in sigma units, and compute the value of C_{pk}.

(e) Given a target value of 5 units, compute the $MSD(\tau)$ value for this process.

(f) Assume that an item is scrapped when the thickness is out-of-specification, and that the cost of scrapping an item is $0.05 per piece. Compute the Average Loss Per Unit of Production using the result from part (e). Extend this Average Loss over the daily production figure of 50,000 pieces per day to find the Average Daily Loss due to variation.

Exercise 6.2:

The 15 test values on page 54, Exercise 3.4, show a process that has demonstrated statistical control in the past. If the supplier maintains this process in statistical control it will continue to perform in the future as it has in the past. The Minimum Specification Limit for these test values is 25. The Average is 38.33 pounds, and the Average Moving Range is 2.36 pounds.

(a) Compute *Sigma(X)* for this process.

(b) Express the Distance to Nearest Specification in sigma units,
and compute the value of C_{pk}.

(c) What would your target value be if you set the target to get a C_{pk} of 1.33?

(d) When a characteristic may be characterized as "the bigger, the better," it is customary to define the *MSD* value to be:[6]

$$MSD(\infty) = \frac{1}{n} \sum \frac{1}{X^2}$$

The 15 values from p.54 are: *35, 39, 38, 42, 37, 37, 39, 37, 37, 40, 39, 39, 38, 42 and 36.*
Use these values to compute the *MSD(∞)* value for this supplier.

---

[6] The *MSD* value for non-negative characteristics for which zero is desirable (as in zero shrinkage) is
customarily defined to be $MSD(0) = \frac{1}{n} \sum X^2$

Exercise 6.3:

Using the data of Table 6.1, on page 131:

(a) Construct a grouped frequency histogram for the first six rows of data. Use intervals with a width 20 pounds.

(b) Construct a grouped frequency histogram for rows 7 through 12 of the data. Use 20 pound intervals again.

(c) Construct a grouped frequency histogram for rows 13 through 18 of the data. Use 20 pound intervals.

(d) Do these histograms suggest that the production process is stable and predictable?

Exercise 6.4:

(a) For the bottom three theoretical distributions shown in Figure 6.5, page 122, the mean is zero and the standard deviation is 1.0. Assume that the arrows shown are the upper and lower specification limits for these "processes" and compute the C_p and C_{pk} values for these three distributions.

(b) For each of the three distributions used in part (a): what proportion of the distribution falls within the specification limits?

Chapter Seven

Using Control Charts for
Continual Improvement

In the flowchart in Figure 6.7 reference is made to reducing process variation. In the past the lack of adequate tools has caused this task to be regarded as very difficult. This is no longer true. The control chart provides a systematic way to reduce process dispersion. In fact, the continual reduction of process variation is a natural consequence of the effective use of the charts.

7.1 A Flowchart for Using Control Charts

Figure 7.1 presents a flowchart that outlines the use of control charts for continual improvement. The flowchart begins with the characteristic to be studied, and proceeds to the collection of the data. The question of how to get started will be addressed later, as will the question of having measurement units which are small enough. The focus for this chapter is on the use of control charts for continual improvement.

Notice the cycles on the right side of the chart. Continual improvement comes as the result of a long sequence of small steps. Some of these steps will result in dramatic improvements. Most improvements, however, will rest on the preceding steps as well as the most recent one.

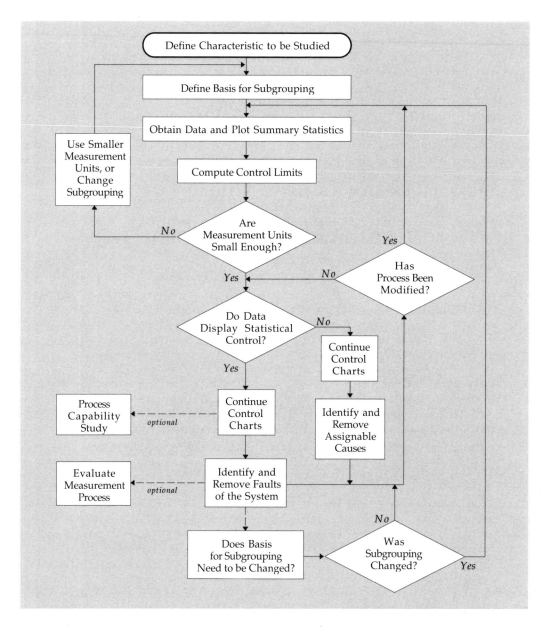

Figure 7.1: Using Shewhart's Charts for Continual Improvement

For this reason, one can rarely leap from current conditions to the ultimate process potential. Instead, one must persevere in using the chart to better understand the process. The cycles on the flowchart show the sequence of decisions and options possible after each subgroup on the charts. Each of these cycles could be subdivided into three portions: keeping the charts, interpreting the charts, and implementing the knowledge gained from the charts.[1]

The first portion of these cycles consists of obtaining the data and maintaining the control charts. Some of the considerations involved in selecting the variables for charting will be discussed later. The concepts behind the subgrouping, and the mechanics of actually keeping the control charts have already been covered. The second portion of these cycles concerns the interpretation of the control charts. Again, this topic has been covered in considerable detail in the previous chapters. It is the implementation portion of these cycles that is the key to whether or not the control charts will be used as powerfully as they can be in any particular application. If the process is out of control, the chart can do nothing but prompt. The *users* have to identify and remove the Assignable Causes of the uncontrolled variation. Likewise, if the process is in control, the control chart can be used to evaluate the results of process experimentation, but it is the producer who must perform the experiments and then follow up by removing the faults of the system. The control chart simply provides information in a form that is easy to understand. The power of the control chart comes from the way in which such understanding is put into practice.

On the flowchart, the implementation of the knowledge provided by the control chart is represented by the loop going back up to the question about process modification. In any company, the ability to move from the point of identifying Assignable Causes to the point of making the necessary changes will primarily depend on the organizational environment. If management does not actively support these efforts, they will not be effective. Some companies will implement the information provided by the control charts smoothly and efficiently. Others will implement the information sporadically and inconsistently. Some will implement the information only if that information is made known to, and is understood by, the right people.

Thus, the power of the control chart depends on how effectively the company is organized to utilize the insights offered by the chart. If these insights are fully utilized, there are virtually no limits to possible improvements. As one cycles through the various steps of the flowchart in Figure 7.1, the control chart will continue to track the process, and each departure from statistical control will provide additional information about how the process operates. The cumulative effect will be a never-ending cycle of process improvement.

Whenever the information provided by the charts is not effectively used, the cycle of improvement is broken. These breaks allow entropy to degrade the process, and as new Assignable Causes continue to occur, the sporadic improvements obtained from the charts

---

[1] These three portions are parallel with Shewhart's Three Steps of Quality Control as given on page 1 of *Statistical Method from the Viewpoint of Quality Control*.

will not suffice to overcome these negative forces. Therefore, the process will slowly deteriorate.

One final comment regarding the flowchart in Figure 7.1 is appropriate. The dotted branches on the left side of the chart denote optional analyses based on the control chart. These include process capability studies and the evaluation of the measurement process. Both of these optional analyses pertain to one point in time. While both are based upon control charts, and while both may be useful in characterizing certain aspects of a process, neither is *necessarily* a part of using the charts for process improvement. All too often organizations get distracted by these side issues and fail to ever get around to using control charts to actually improve processes.

In this chapter you will read about two companies that used control charts for continual improvement. The first case history focuses on the use of the control chart itself, and the second case history describes the consequences of an organizational philosophy of continual improvement.

7.2 Continual Improvement

The following control chart was brought to this country by a group of executives from the Body and Assembly Division of Ford Motor Company, following a visit to the Tokai Rika Company in March, 1982. As the Ford group was touring the Tokai Rika plant, they observed eight production workers gathered around this control chart "engaged in active discussion." To the people from Ford, it seemed that something must be wrong with the process represented by the chart, so they asked about it. They expected there to be an internal production problem, or an assembly plant problem, or a problem of too many rejects. However, they were told that this was simply a routine review of an ongoing process, and in fact, the process was currently operating in statistical control, and well within the specifications. To substantiate this, their hosts translated the chart, and presented a copy to the Ford group.

The process represented by the control chart is the fabrication of a cigar lighter socket. The dimension tracked by the chart is the distance between the flange and the detent, as shown in Figure 7.2. The target value for this dimension is 15.90 mm, and the specified tolerance is ± 0.10 mm. The measurements shown on the chart were made with a snap gauge, and are recorded to the nearest 0.01 mm.

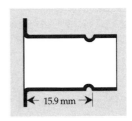

Figure 7.2: Tokai Rika Cigar Lighter Socket

The chart, as we have it, begins in August, 1980, and is shown in Figure 7.3. The specifications are clearly indicated at the top of the chart. Subgroups of size $n = 4$ were used, and one subgroup was collected each day. In August and early September the process appeared to be in a state of statistical control.

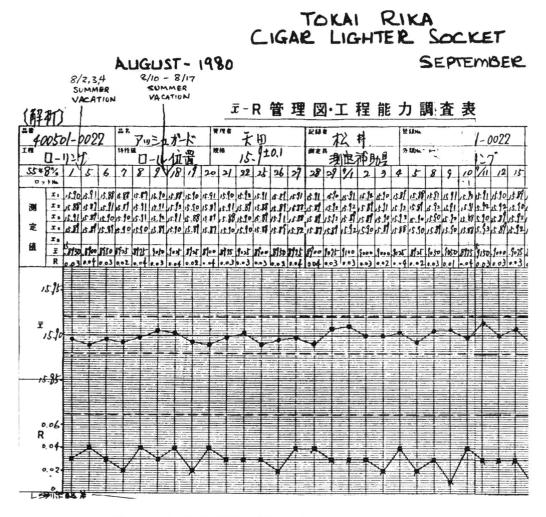

Figure 7.3: Tokai Rika Chart, Aug. 1, to Sept. 15, 1980

Based on production data given later, about 17,000 pieces were being produced each day. The four pieces for the daily subgroup were drawn out of this product stream at 10 a.m., 11 a.m., 2 p.m., and 4 p.m.

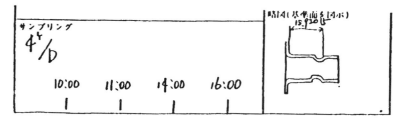

Figure 7.4: Sampling Times for Cigar Lighter Socket

One might well wonder how four pieces per day could be adequate. It would appear that this question occurred to the Tokai Rika personnel since their answer is recorded at the bottom of the chart for August.

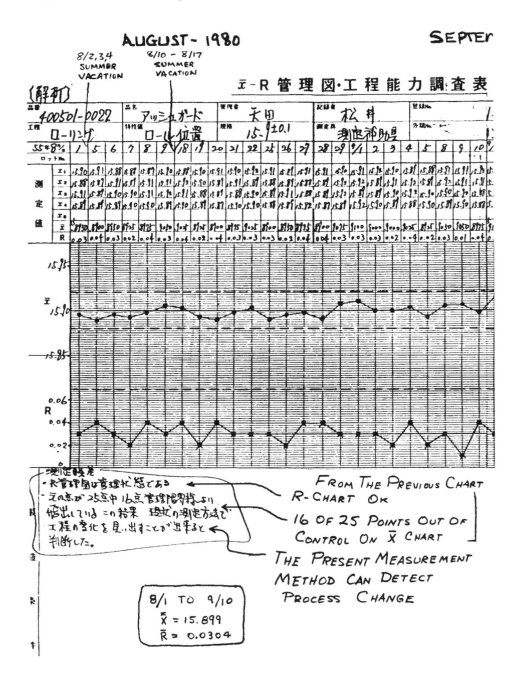

Figure 7.5: Tokai Rika Footnote for Aug. 1, 1980

As long as a control chart is capable of detecting a lack of control, it is sensitive enough to use in monitoring a process. There is no need to increase sensitivity by increasing subgroup size. Furthermore, one subgroup per day had proven to be adequate since this process was one that usually went out of control slowly, over a period of days. For these reasons, the subgroup size and the subgroup frequency were not changed.

Figure 7.3 shows the process to be in control during August. In addition to being in statistical control, they were operating well inside the specifications. This can be seen from the histogram constructed using the 244 measurements recorded on the chart during the months of August, September, and October, 1980. This histogram is shown in Figure 7.6.

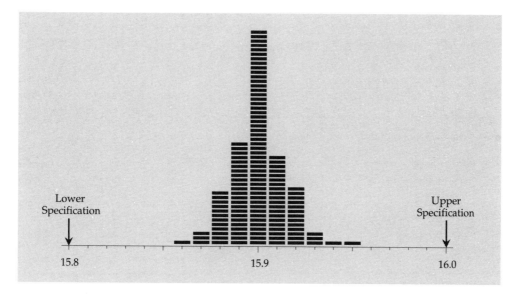

Figure 7.6: Tokai Rika Histogram for Aug., Sept., and Oct. 1980

Clearly, the process was well within the specifications, and it was centered relative to those specifications. Since the process was in control as well, it could be classified as being in the Ideal State. While this is desirable, it is not irreversible. A state of statistical control is not a natural state for a production process. It is, instead, an achievement, and therefore it must be maintained. Assignable causes will always occur from time to time. To keep the process in the Ideal State these Assignable Causes will have to be identified and removed.

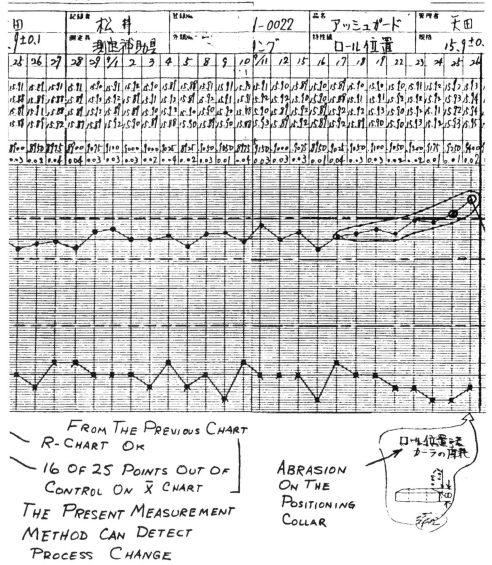

Figure 7.7: Tokai Rika Chart, Aug. 25 to Sept. 26, 1980

A lack of control is noted on September 25 and 26, 1980. While the first point outside the limits occurs on Sept. 25, the run containing this point starts on Sept. 17. By marking the run associated with the out-of-control point, the Tokai Rika personnel identified a period during which the Assignable Cause may have been present. Following this identification of an out-of-control condition, they looked for the Assignable Cause. The notes at the bottom of the control chart document these efforts. In order to clarify these notes at the bottom of the control chart, Figure 7.8 shows a portion of the rolling machine. A pressure pad holds the socket blank in place against the positioning collar while the outer roller forms the crimp.

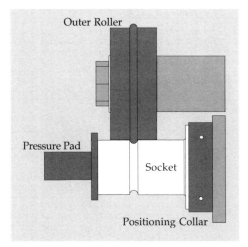

Figure 7.8: The Rolling Operation

Given the design of the equipment shown in Figure 7.8, it is clear that the wear will be concentrated on the positioning collar. In fact, wear on the positioning collar is the Assignable Cause for the lack of control noted in late September, 1980.

This Assignable Cause was duly noted on the chart, and the very next day the process average shifted back to the target of 15.90 mm. Again, a note tells what was done.

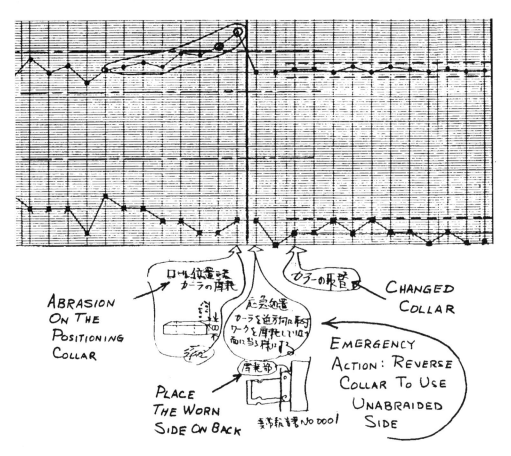

Figure 7.9: Tokai Rika Footnotes for Sept. 29 and Oct. 1, 1980

As a temporary solution, the worker turned the worn collar over to use the back side. Two days later a new collar was installed. This incident displays a desire on the part of the Tokai Rika personnel to operate at the target. The process was in no danger of producing nonconforming product, yet they took the trouble to fix it so that it would stay centered on the target value of 15.90 mm. Moreover, just as the shift on September 29 shows the desire of the workers to operate at the target value, the replacement of the collar on October 1 shows the support of the management for this policy.

Why do the operators and their supervisors want to operate right at the target when they have such wide specifications? Isn't this excessive? Would it not be cheaper to let the process run until the process average was above 15.95 mm? While it might be cheaper for this one operation, it would eventually prove to be more expensive for the company. Remember the definition of World Class Quality: "On Target with Minimum

Variance." This example shows how this concept is put into practice.

The cost of using any part will increase as the dimensions of that part deviate from the target values. This happens because once variation is built into a stream of product, subsequent operations must always allow for this variation. This affects the design of jigs and fixtures. If affects the way the parts assemble with other (variable) parts. Finally, it affects the way the product will function in service. All of these allowances for product variation accumulate to increase the cost of using the variable parts in manufacturing, and the cost of selling the variable products to customers who demand warranty coverage.

The Taguchi Loss Function provides a satisfactory approximation for the losses due to deviations from target—for a given deviation, there will be a given loss, and the greater the deviation, the greater the loss. A Taguchi Loss Function is shown in Figure 7.10.

For a stream of product, each item will have a certain value, and the histogram of these values will characterize the product stream as a whole (if the process displays statistical control). An approximation to the histogram of a centered process is also shown in Figure 7.10.

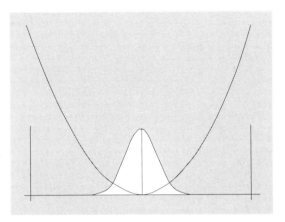

Figure 7.10: Taguchi Loss Function and Centered Process

Combining the Taguchi Loss Function and the product histogram (or a suitable approximation thereunto) one can obtain the Average Loss Per Unit of Production. This is done by multiplying each loss value by the percentage of product with the corresponding variation. That is, the Average Loss Per Unit of Production will be defined by the area under a curve which is found by multiplying the two curves in Figure 7.10 together point by point. This area is shown in Figure 7.11 for a centered process.

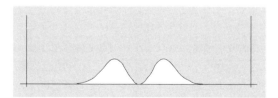

Figure 7.11: The Average Loss Per Unit for a Centered Process

As the production process drifts away from the Target value this Average Loss Per Unit of Production will inevitably increase. For example, Figures 7.10 and 7.11 were drawn to represent the Tokai Rika Cigar Lighter process during the period of August 1 to September 15, 1980.

Beginning around September 17, this process began to drift away from the target value of 15.90 mm. On September 26 the Subgroup Average was 15.94 mm. Since the Average Range in August was 0.0304 mm, the computed value for *Sigma(X)* would be:

$$Sigma(X) \;=\; \frac{\overline{R}}{d_2} \;=\; \frac{0.0304 \text{ mm}}{2.059 \text{ sigma}} \;=\; 0.0148 \text{ mm/sigma unit.}$$

Therefore, a shift of 0.04 mm in the Subgroup Average amounts to a shift of:

$$\frac{0.04 \text{ mm}}{0.0148 \text{ mm/sigma}} \;=\; 2.7 \text{ sigma units.}$$

If the production process shifts so that it has an average of 15.94 mm, as happened on September 26, then it is off-center by 2.7 sigma units. This situation is shown in Figure 7.12.

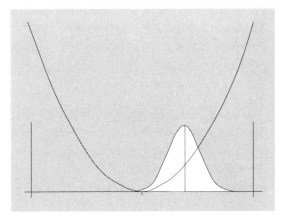

Figure 7.12: Taguchi Loss Function and Shifted Process

One should note that the process shown in Figure 7.12 is still operating well within the specification limits. However, conformance to specifications is not the definition of world class quality. The reason for this can be seen in the comparison of the Average Losses Per Unit of Production shown in Figure 7.13.

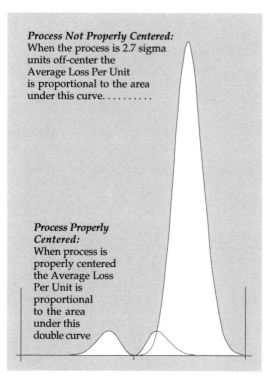

Process Not Properly Centered:
When the process is 2.7 sigma units off-center the Average Loss Per Unit is proportional to the area under this curve. . . . .

Process Properly Centered:
When process is properly centered the Average Loss Per Unit is proportional to the area under this double curve

Figure 7.13: Two Average Losses Per Unit

When the Process Average is 2.7 sigma units away from the target, the Average Loss Per Unit of Production is over 8 times larger than when the process is centered on the target.

This is the reason many Japanese companies strive to keep their processes centered on the target even when the specifications may be twenty or thirty sigma units wide. There is simply no advantage to allowing the process to function below its capability. A process which displays a reasonable degree of statistical control is performing up to its potential, and the product stream will be a homogeneous as possible given the current process. When a process goes out of control this homogeneity is lost. The process is performing at less than its potential. The product stream will show more variation than is inherent in the process, and the company will experience a definite increase in the cost of production. This cost may well be shifted to later operations, or even to warranty service, but it is a real cost.

Of course, once the process is in control and properly centered relative to the specifications, the only way to further reduce the Average Loss Per Unit is by changing the process (to reduce the process variation). This is the reason that continual improvement leads to increased productivity. This happened at the Tokai Rika plant in the Fall and Winter of 1980-1981. The control chart shows how they did it.

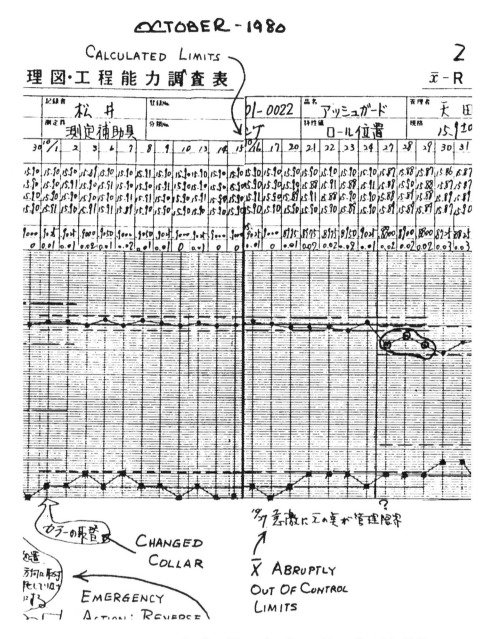

Figure 7.14: Tokai Rika Chart for Sept. 30 to Oct 31, 1980

Following the installation of the new collar on October 1, data were collected for recalculating the control limits. The process stayed within these new limits until October 27. At that time it suddenly went out of control. The fact that it was a sudden change in the process was a clue to the nature of the problem, and as such it was noted at the bottom of the chart.

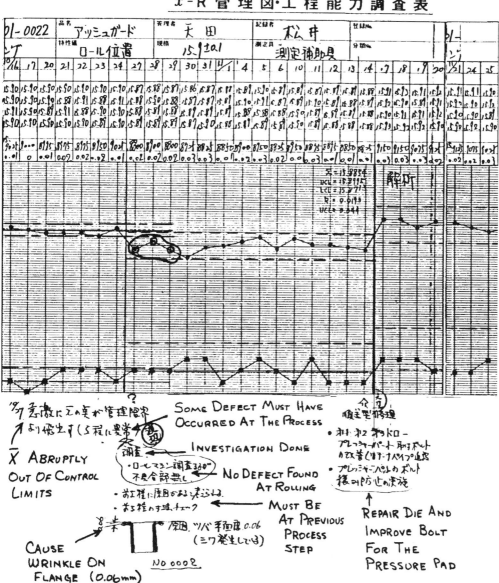

Figure 7.15: Tokai Rika Chart for Oct. 16 to Nov. 25, 1980

The search for the Assignable Cause led back to the preceding step, a blanking operation. When a problem was found, it was checked to see if it corresponded to the indications given by the control chart. Since this problem involved the repair of a die, the fix was postponed until the weekend of November 15 and 16.

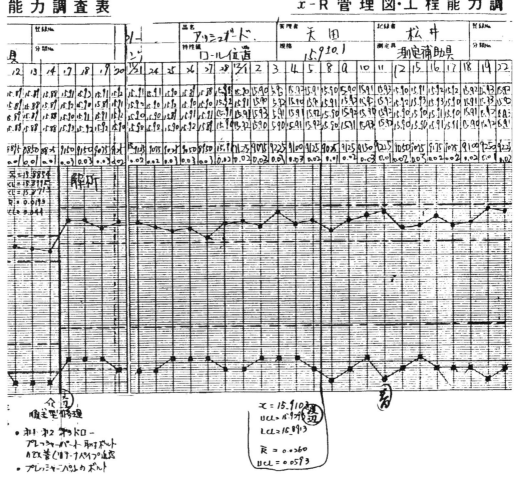

Figure 7.16: Tokai Rika Chart for Nov. 12 to Dec. 22, 1980

Following the repairs noted on the chart, data for new control limits were collected. When these limits were calculated, the process was seen to have returned to the Ideal State where it remained for the rest of the year.

Since a state of statistical control is not a natural state for a production process, it was only a matter of time until the process went out of control again. This time it happened on January 16, 1981. The note for this date indicates that in this instance, they let the process run out of control and off-center because a new type of collar had been ordered. Based on their earlier actions and those that came later, this period of off-center production can only be explained by assuming that they had no replacement collar to use while waiting for the new collar. With respect to the specifications, they knew that as long as the average did not exceed 15.95 mm, and the range remained in control, they were in no danger of producing any nonconforming sockets. Both of these requirements were satisfied during this period of off-center production.

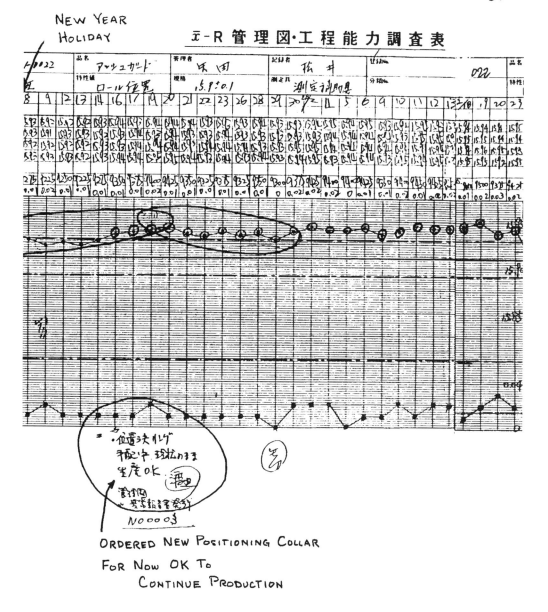

Figure 7.17: Tokai Rika Chart for Jan. 8 to Feb. 23, 1981

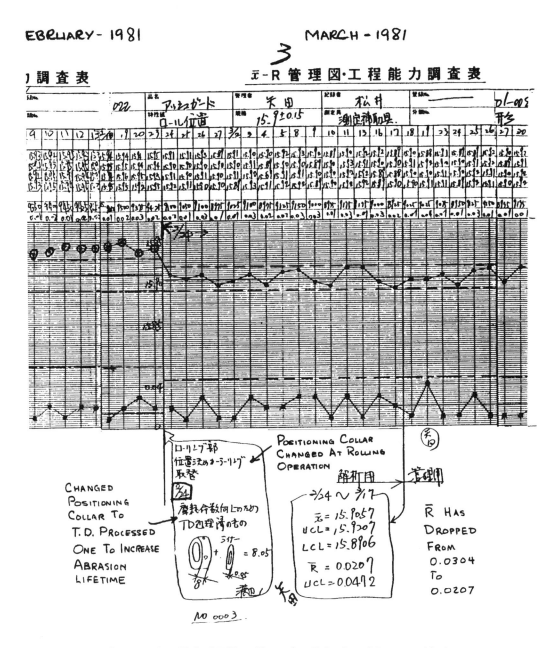

Figure 7.18: Tokai Rika Chart for Feb. 9 to Mar. 30, 1981

Finally, on February 24, the new collar had been installed, and they proceeded to collect data for new control limits. The central lines and control limits are shown at the bottom of the chart. Of particular interest is the value for the Average Range. In August of 1980, the average range was 0.0304 mm. In March of 1981, it was 0.0207 mm. This 32 percent reduction in the process variation is shown in Figure 7.19 by a comparison of the histogram from August through October 1980 with that from April through June 1981.

Since both of these periods had some out-of-control excursions there are a few points outside the Natural Process Limits on each histogram.

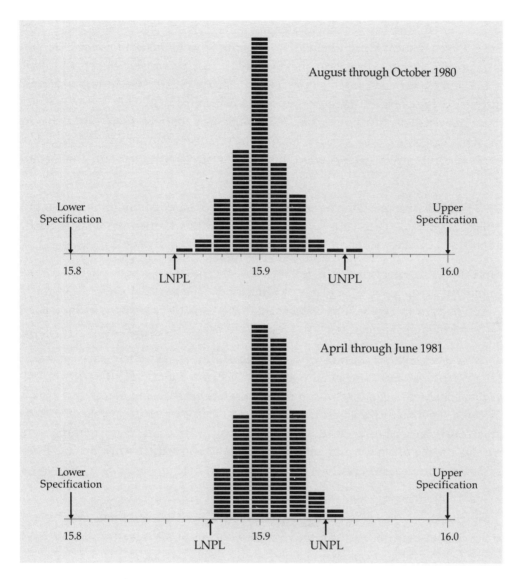

Figure 7.19: Process Histograms, 1980 and 1981

How did they improve this process? What did they have to do to make it better? They simply responded to those signals of a lack of control that were given by the control chart. By finding and removing the Assignable Causes of uncontrolled variation, they made the stable process even better than it was before. This is a natural consequence of the proper use of the control charts. This attentive use of the control charts is the key to continual process improvement. Not only did they keep the charts, and interpret the charts, but they also implemented the changes that were indicated by the charts.

This process was not a special target for improvement. It already spent most of its time in the Ideal State. In fact, the operators seem to have plotted the points only every two or three days. The basis for this statement is the fact that when the process went out of control, the runs seem to lag behind the first indication of a lack of control. In particular, in Figure 7.7 the circled run contains two points that are outside the control limits; in Figure 7.15 the circled run contains three points that are outside the limits; and in Figure 7.17 the circled run contains three or four out-of-control points. This means that in each case, the runs were identified one or more days *after* the first point fell outside the limits. Such benign neglect is hardly consistent with a special program for improving a process. However, when they finally responded, they did not rest until they found something to fix.

The Tokai Rika people have discovered the secret of successfully improving a process with minimum effort. They simply use the control charts to identify areas of need in a routine manner. As they respond to these needs, they improve their process.

It might also be interesting to note that while the Tokai Rika personnel were successfully improving their process, the specifications were relaxed to 15.90 ± 0.15 mm. This change can be seen in Figure 7.20. This change was essentially immaterial to Tokai Rika, for they continued to concentrate on making all the parts virtually alike.

Many Western manufacturers will ask if this didn't make their parts more costly. Since the Western approach to quality has been "Burn the toast and then scrape it," this feeling that consistent quality results in extra costs has been deeply ingrained. This is not the case with the Tokai Rika Cigar Lighter Socket. This process is capable of performing with the consistency shown on the preceding page. It costs them nothing extra to achieve this degree of uniformity, and it does make the product work better. They are simply getting the consistency which their process can deliver—nothing more—and nothing less.

Thus, with their process operating well inside the specification limits, they continued to use the control chart to maintain their process in control. While operation in the Ideal State is indeed desirable, it certainly makes for dull control charts!

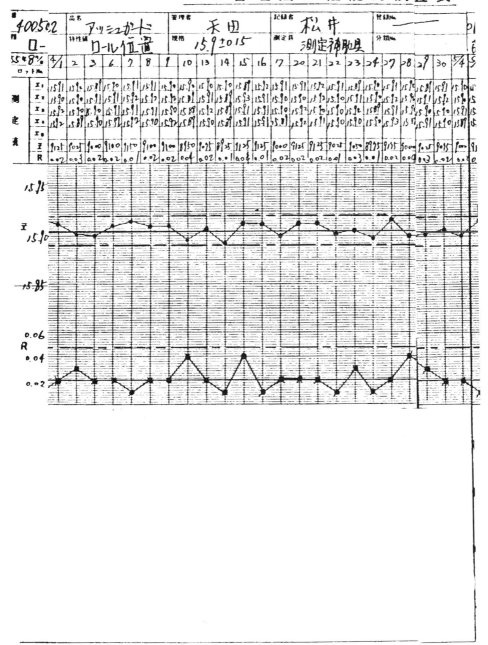

Figure 7.20: Tokai Rika Chart for April 1 to May 4, 1981

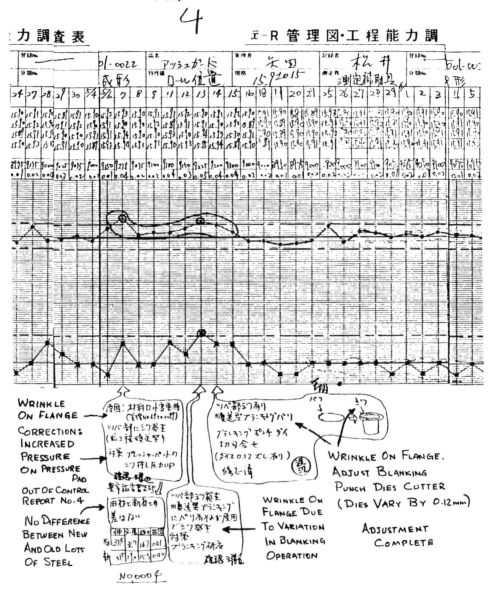

Figure 7.21: Tokai Rika Chart for April 24 to June 5, 1981

There was some excitement in May. A wrinkle occurred on the flange and they tried to fix it, only to have the problem recur a few days later.

Here the recurrence of the problem indicates that the fix was not effective. Thus, they continued to look for the Assignable Cause. One additional insight is provided by the note about the out-of-control report. If they are required to write reports regarding every out-of-control point, it is safe to assume that such points are relatively rare throughout their operations.

In this instance, the problem was in the blanking operation, and it could only be fixed by repairing the die. When this job was done the tool-maker noted it on the chart.

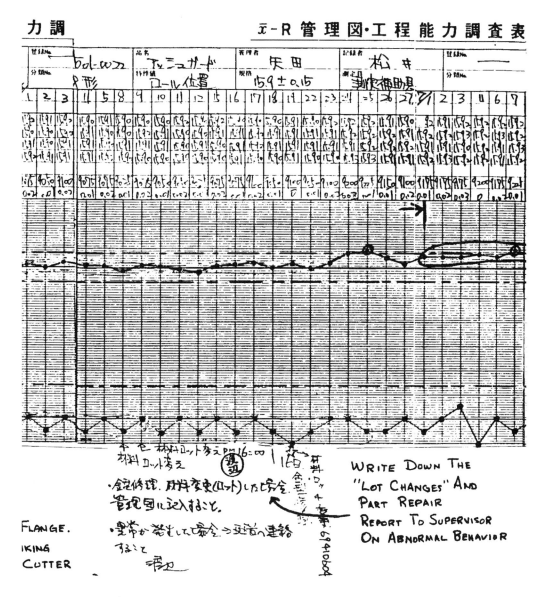

Figure 7.22: Tokai Rika Chart for June 1 to July 7, 1981

After the problem with the blanking operation had been fixed, the process returned to operation within the Ideal State.

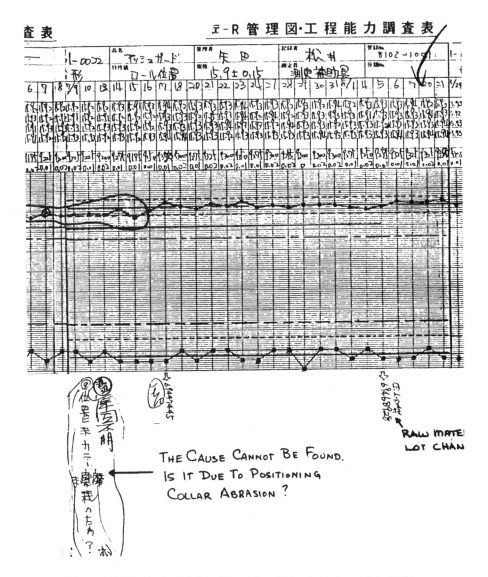

Figure 7.23: Tokai Rika Chart for July 6 to Aug. 24, 1981

In early July the process began to drift to the high side. Since the collar in place was the new collar (with the "TD" processing), the workers were not sure whether the out-of-control points were caused by collar wear. Therefore, they let the process run without taking any further action. On August 29 they recalculated control limits using the data collected since July 9. These limits show that the process average had shifted to 15.93 millimeters.

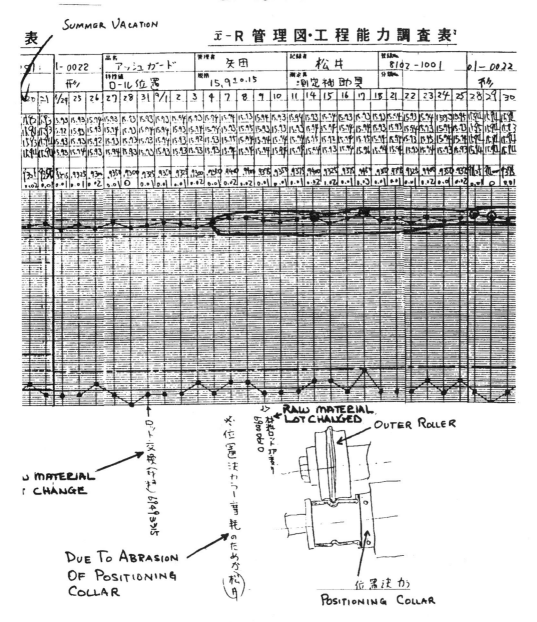

Figure 7.24: Tokai Rika Chart for Aug. 20 to Sept. 30, 1981

The process continued to drift upward until it finally went above the new limits in September. This time the cause was clear. The positioning collar had been worn down sufficiently to be clearly identified as the source of the problem.

A new collar was ordered and installed on October 5, 1981.

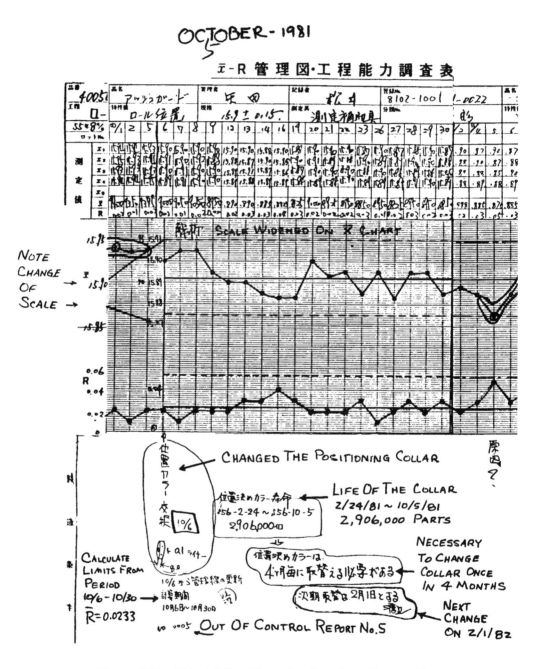

Figure 7.25: Tokai Rika Chart for Oct. 1 to Nov. 6, 1981

Since the collar with the TD processing was a new tool, they used the control chart to evaluate its performance.

While the original collar was in service for seven and one-half months, they decided to replace the new collar every four months. They based this decision on the four months of operation without any problems at rolling (March through June). The gradual upward drift, seen in July, August and September, represented tool wear. They did not want, as a rule, to allow the process to drift away from the target value. Even though there were times in the past when they had to live with such a drift, they considered it to be undesirable because of the Average Loss Per Unit of Production. Changing the collar every four months allowed the process to perform at its best. Once again, they were simply not interested in having the process perform less consistently than it was capable of doing.

Points continued to fall outside the control limits during November, 1981. Some of these points represent specific problems, which were pinpointed by specific notes on the chart. These notes helped the maintenance workers know just what to fix.

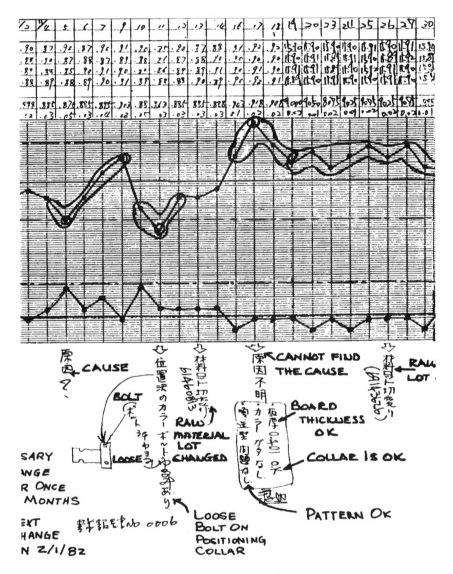

Figure 7.26: Tokai Rika Footnotes for November, 1981

The note for November 17 may seem somewhat strange. Here the operator listed everything which he found to be OK, but not what was wrong. The clue to the reason for this note is found by inspecting the handwriting in the data portion of the control chart. Several different operators are keeping this chart. They each rotate through the different jobs in this department, and the note on November 17 is one operator telling another that he has not found anything to have caused these out-of-control points.

The next operator does not have the out-of-control points, but he does have a long run above the central line. In spite of his running record being consistently above the central line, it is perfectly centered on 15.90 mm. A clue to the nature of this problem is found in the note for December 15.

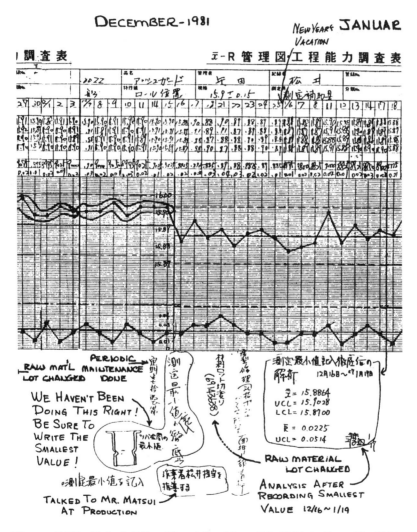

Figure 7.27: Tokai Rika Chart for Nov. 26, 1981 to Jan. 18, 1982

The note for Dec. 15, 1981, is very emphatic. "We haven't been doing this right! Be sure to record the smallest value found for each piece!" Another note indicates that Mr. Matsui came down and discussed this change in the measurement procedure.

These strongly pointed notes seem to indicate a problem with the way the measurements were being recorded. In any case, the Tokai Rika personnel attributed the apparent shift between December 15 and December 16 to the new method of measuring the parts. One might also note that the Average Range is still in the neighborhood of 0.02 millimeters.

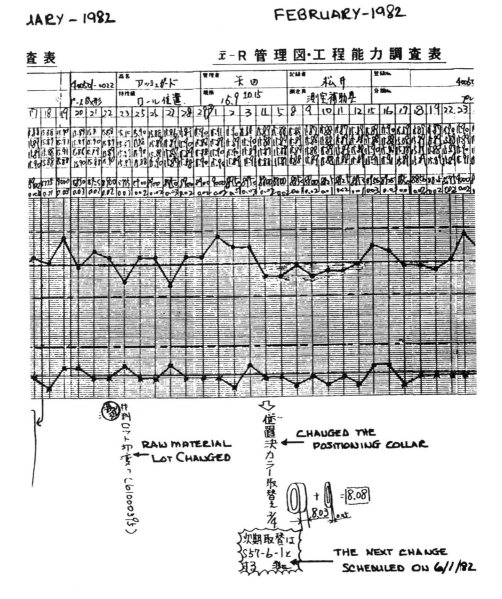

Figure 7.28: Tokai Rika Chart for Jan 17 to Feb. 23, 1982

The positioning collar was changed on February 4, 1982, and the next change was scheduled for early June.

Unlike the earlier changes, however, the process did not go out of control first. Neither did they stop to recalculate new control limits. There was no need because they were changing the part before the part could change their process.

MARCH - 1982

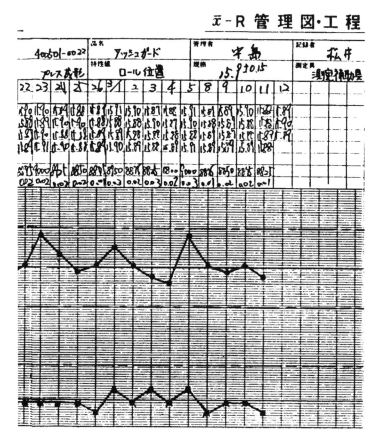

Figure 7.29: Tokai Rika Chart for Feb. 22 to March 12, 1982

Figure 7.29 brings us to the point where the Ford team walked through the plant some time between 2 and 4 in the afternoon of March 12. The process under discussion was in the Ideal State, and it had been there at least since December. The specifications were essentially 30 sigma units wide, and the process was properly centered relative to those specifications.

During the last thirteen months of this control chart, the process maintained a consistency that is characterized by the histogram in Figure 7.30. This histogram comes from the time period following their shift to recording the smallest observed value. This is why the histogram is no longer centered at 15.90. The Natural Process Limits shown were computed from the summary statistics for January 19, 1982 (see Figure 7.27). The 232 measurements used in this histogram show a process that is (1) operating within the Natural Process Limits and (2) using the middle 20 percent the specification limits.

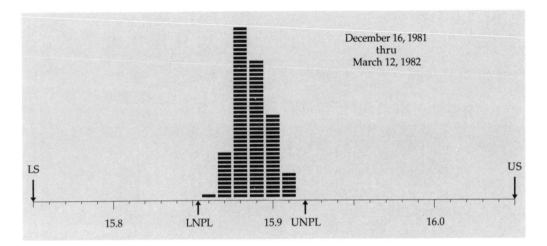

Figure 7.30: Process Consistency, March 1981 to March 1982

The spread of the Natural Process Limits is about 0.06 mm. The measurements are made to the nearest 0.01 mm. This means that $Sigma(X)$ is roughly equal to the smallest unit of measurement. Therefore, the process has been improved to the point where the part-to-part variation is beginning to be obscured by the round-off in the measurement process. To detect any further improvements in process consistency the Tokai Rika company would have to upgrade the measurement device.

Finally, the effective use of this one control chart was no accident. Before the workers can operate a process in this manner, they must be allowed to do so by management. Before the managers can respond to the needs indicated by the chart, they must be free to use the charts as a basis for action. Before maintenance, or engineering, or sales, or purchasing can use the charts, they must understand the charts. In short, the use of control charts makes demands on the whole organization.

Statistical tools do not exist in a vacuum. They have to be used in order to be effective. The way a company is organized, and the attitudes of its managers, will determine how the knowledge created by the control charts is used. Since most American companies are full of internal barriers to cooperation and communication, there is little hope that these tools will be used as effectively as they have been in Japan, unless the corporate culture is changed from top to bottom.

The next section, however, illustrates what can happen in this country when the company president understands that the use of statistical tools involves a totally new way of thinking about how to run the business, and then actively promotes this understanding throughout the organization.

7.3 But Will This Work in North America?

The following examples show how one U.S. company continually improved both the quality of their products and the productivity of their plants. The key factor for these transformations was the understanding and leadership of the company president, who had been personally tutored by Dr. Deming. Without this continuing pressure and guidance from the top, much of what follows would never have happened.[2]

The first example concerns the manufacture of carbonless paper. The progression shown by this example is the same one emphasized throughout this book. The first step was to bring the process into a state of statistical control. (Once a process is brought into control it becomes much easier to work on improving the process.)

In making carbonless paper a water-based coating is applied to a moving web of paper. The paper coating machine was applying an average of 3.60 pounds of dry coating per 3000 square feet, while running at 1100 linear feet per minute. Historically, the machine operator made adjustments based on measurements of the amount of coating material on a sample taken from the end of each roll of paper. In addition to the operator's test, quality control technicians made tests to determine the mark intensity. These tests were made on a sample taken right off the coater and on a sample that had been oven-aged. If the off-the-coater test was too light or too dark, the quality control technician could request that the operator make an adjustment to the machine. This method of operation generally resulted in a good quality product, but the average coating weight of 3.60 pounds per 3000 square feet was high, and there were frequent changes in the machine settings.

The manager knew that something needed to be done, but he did not know how to reduce the average coating weight. The purchase of a new coating head, costing $700,000, was being considered when the plant manager decided to utilize control charts to study the operation. Beginning in August of 1979, the coater was allowed to run untouched for hours at a time to provide data for the charts. At the same time, an intensive program was begun to bring the viscosity of the coating into statistical control. Follow-

---

[2] The details in this section were collected from the various public speeches made by the president of this company.

ing work with the supplier of the chemicals, this viscosity was lowered dramatically, and its variation was minimized.

With this improved coating mixture, the control charts showed that the coating head could be operated in a state of statistical control with a natural process variation of 0.4 pounds either side of the average. These data also showed that by using the sample taken right off the coater, the operators and technicians were actually adjusting the process the wrong way each time they made an adjustment.

Following these initial studies, the operator was able to use the control chart to run the process. Process adjustments were now made on the basis of out-of-control points, using measurements that were positively correlated with the product quality, rather than being made in reaction to noise. Moreover, persons connected with the process realized that they could reduce the average coating weight without hurting the product quality.[3]

These studies took seven months to complete. When the conclusions were published within the company, there was tremendous opposition on the part of some technical, quality control, and management personnel. Yet, because of the president's understanding and support, the program continued. As time passed, it became increasingly hard for detractors to argue with success.

By April, 1980, the coater was operating at an average of 2.8 pounds of dry coating per 3000 square feet. This saving of 0.8 pounds of coating was worth $800,000 per year. In addition, the product quality was both good and consistent. The operator's job was both easier and more important, since he was controlling his own quality. Fewer machine adjustments were needed, and quality control technicians were now free for other work.

Early in 1981, the manager of the coating department realized that the control charts showed the coating head could be improved. By studying Pareto charts and Cause and Effect diagrams on sources of coater down-time and coater waste, he determined that coating streaks were a major source of waste. Additional opportunities for improvement included excessive down-time for cleaning and changing rubber rolls. Using this information, he developed a simple and inexpensive modification for the coating head. This modification reduced the variation to 0.3 pounds per 3000 sq. ft., allowing the average to be dropped to 2.7 pounds, and saving an additional $100,000. Moreover, these changes substantially reduced streaks, down-time and cleaning time.

During this process it became clear that as the coat weight dropped, further speed increases were possible. By the summer of 1981, the coater was running at 1400 linear feet

---

[3] The use of control charts as an adjustment mechanism requires that one knows how to make specific adjustments to the process. Moreover, it is a weak use of the charts. The Tokai Rika chart shows the more powerful usage—nothing was done until the Assignable Cause was found. Then steps were taken to fix the problem, not just to compensate and continue on.

per minute. The savings from this increase in productivity amounted to about $750,000 per year.

With the process now under statistical control, and making good quality products with reduced coating material, reduced waste, reduced downtime and higher speeds, plant personnel were able to give some thought to making further improvements. People began to wonder why they needed 2.7 pounds of coating. Tests suggested that about half of the 2.7 pounds was taken up in substrate penetration. With some research into ways to reduce this penetration loss, additional material savings, reduced drying time, and increased operating speeds would be possible. By the fall of 1981, speeds of 2000 linear feet per minute seemed to be possible in the near future.

Following the initial success outlined above, the president decided to make a major effort to utilize control charts in another product line. In 1980, this company was producing magnetic disk packs for computers in much the same way that its major U.S. competitors were producing them. At first the plant yield had been only 20 percent. By using all the technical expertise available this had been improved to an average of 66 percent before leveling off. Since the industry-wide average yield was 55 percent, this company was doing slightly better than average. Yet because of high scrap costs, thirty technicians, chemists, and engineers were working full-time, attempting to increase the yield.

At the end of 1980, the president set a new goal for this magnetic disk operation. Productivity was to be doubled within two years time. This goal included both the production area and the administrative services portion of the magnetic disk organization. In order to meet this goal, an average growth of three percent per month would need to be maintained. Of course, merely setting a goal without also providing the means to improve the system is a sure-fire way to distort the data and the system. In this case the president did provide the means to improve the system—he hired a competent statistician to help the personnel in this division to learn how to improve their processes, and he did this in spite of a company-wide hiring freeze.

As it entered this two-year quest for increased productivity, this division had sales of $40 million per year, with pretax profits of 11 percent. It employed 225 salaried and 225 hourly workers, and was housed in a 100,000 square foot plant.

The first control charts were started in January of 1981. By the end of the month, 30 control charts were being kept by the workers, and another 100 control charts were being kept by the 30 members of the technical staff who had been struggling to improve the process during the previous 18 months.

The yield in January was 71 percent. The skeptics noted that the yields had been that high before, and predicted a drop for February. The yield in February was 75 percent. The skeptics were somewhat quieter. The yield in March stayed at 75 percent, but in April, it moved up to 80 percent. In May, the yield was 82 percent. In June, it was 85 percent, and in July, 90 percent. In August, the yield reached 94 percent.

In eight months time, the same people in the same plant were producing 42 percent more certifiable product. The reduction in scrap costs amounted to $450,000 per month. Throughout the rest of 1981, and into early 1982, the average yield stayed around 94 percent, varying from 91 percent to 98 percent month to month.

Out of the 130 control charts started in January, 25 were being used to control the production process. Most of the rest were no longer needed and had been discontinued. Only 6 of the technical personnel were now needed in the magnetic disk operation. The other 24 technical personnel had been borrowed from other divisions, and so they left the fire-fighting brigade and returned to their regular positions.

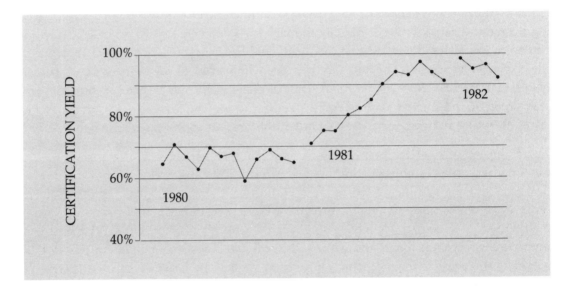

Figure 7.31: Monthly Yields for Disk Packs

By the end of 1981, this division was in a position to cut the price of its disk packs by approximately 20 percent. As a result of this price cut, this division's physical sales volume increased by 50 percent between August 1981 and April 1982. Since their customers only had a 15 percent increase in physical volume during this same period, this increase represents an increased market share. This increased market share came about because the company had the most consistent quality in the market, and it had it at the lowest price.

To meet this increased demand, more disk packs had to be produced. The plant personnel had to get more out of their processes. Fortunately, this was now possible because the control charts kept identifying problems before they got out of hand. The processes ran more smoothly than they had ever done before. As a result, the division was able to keep up with the growing demand.

By the end of 1982, this division still had 225 salaried and 225 hourly workers. It was still housed in the same 100,000 square foot plant. Yet its sales were running at the rate of $100 million per year, with pretax profits averaging 18 percent. Allowing for the 20 percent price cut, it was selling *three* times as many disk packs as it had been at the end of 1980, and it was doing it using the same plant and the same work force.

Thus, the division had exceeded the president's goal.[4] Productivity had been tripled within two years. Moreover, productivity was still increasing at the rate of 30 percent per year.

The improvements were apparent everywhere. Inventory days dropped from 94 to 34. On-time shipments increased from 50 percent to over 80 percent. The number of direct labor man-hours per unit dropped from 7.4 to 2.0. Similar improvements were seen in a dozen other common measures of plant activity.

In 1980, this company had not been one of the major manufacturers of computer disk packs in the U.S. They faced stiff domestic competition, and the Japanese were trying to enter the U.S. market. By the end of 1982, the three major domestic manufacturers had dropped out of the business, and the Japanese had given up. They simply could not compete with a company that produced the most consistent quality product at the lowest price.

7.4 Summary

Ultimately, all statistical techniques presume that the organization will behave in a rational manner. To the extent that organizations do not behave this way, they will be ineffective in using statistics. Whole books have been written about this inability of organizations to react to knowledge in a rational manner. In particular, this is the thrust of Dr. Deming's "Fourteen Points," "Five Deadly Diseases," and "Seven Deadly Sins." Any organization which wants to become effective in the use of control charts will be working on removing the barriers that Dr. Deming has described.

This is why it is impossible to "install SPC." The control charts do not work in a vacuum. They make demands of both workers and management, and the organization must enable these groups to respond. When the attitudes that are part of the corporate culture, or the organizational structure itself, handicap the workers or the managers in responding to these demands, the use of control charts will be less than effective.

---

[4] This is why it is futile to try and set a goal on an unstable process—one cannot know what it can do. Likewise it is futile to set a goal for a stable process—it is already doing all that it can do! The setting of goals by managers is usually a way of passing the buck when they don't know how to change things.

Statistical Process Control is primarily a way of thinking with some techniques attached. It is the way of thinking that is the key. Without this way of thinking the techniques will ultimately be useless.

The development of a company-wide sensitivity to the need to utilize control charts for continual improvement is likely to occur only if it is initiated and maintained by the top levels of management. When this happens, the potential power of the control chart staggers the imagination!

Exercise 7.1:

For the Tokai Rika Cigar Lighter Socket Process:

Figure 7.3 shows Specifications of 15.9 mm ± 0.1 mm. Figure 7.5 shows a Grand Average of 15.899 mm, and Average Range of 0.0304 mm. Compute the following quantities for the Tokai Rika Cigar Lighter Socket as of September 12, 1980:

(a) Compute *Sigma(X)* for this process.

(b) Compute the Natural Process Limits.

(c) Express the Specified Tolerance in sigma units and compute C_p.

(d) Express the Distance to Nearest Specification in sigma units and compute C_{pk}.

(e) Compute the $MSD(\tau)$ value for a target value of 15.90 mm.

(f) Consider the cost of scrapping a socket to be ¥20. Also, assume that a socket is scrapped if the detent dimension falls outside the specification limits. Find a value for K and compute the Average Loss Per Socket due to variation about the target of 15.90 mm.

Exercise 7.2:

For the Tokai Rika Cigar Lighter Socket Process:

As of March 17, 1981, the Grand Average was 15.9057 mm and the Average Range was 0.0207 mm based upon subgroups of size $n = 4$. Use the original Specification Limits of 15.90 mm ± 0.10 mm, and compute the following quantities for the Tokai Rika Cigar Lighter Socket as of March 17, 1981:

(a)   Compute *Sigma(X)* for this process.

(b)   Compute the Natural Process Limits.

(c)   Express the Specified Tolerance in sigma units and compute C_p.

(d)   Express the Distance to Nearest Specification in sigma units and compute C_{pk}.

(e)   Compute the $MSD(\tau)$ value for a target value of 15.90 mm.

(f)   Use the K value from Exercise 7.1 and compute the Average Loss Per Socket due to variation about target.

(g)   What effect did this reduction in the process dispersion have upon C_p? Upon C_{pk}? Upon $MSD(15.90)$?

Exercise 7.3:

For the Tokai Rika Cigar Lighter Socket Process:

As of January 17, 1982, the Specification Limits shown in Figure 7.27 are 15.90 mm ± 0.15 mm, while the Grand Average is 15.8864 mm following the change in the measuring technique, and the Average Range is 0.0225 mm based upon subgroups of size $n = 4$.

(a) Compute *Sigma(X)* for this process.

(b) Compute the Natural Process Limits.

(c) Express the Specified Tolerance in sigma units and compute C_p.

(d) Express the Distance to Nearest Specification in sigma units and compute C_{pk}.

(e) Compute the $MSD(\tau)$ value for a target value of 15.88 mm. The shift in target allows for the effect of changing the measurement technique.

(f) Use the value of K from Exercise 7.1 and compute the Average Loss Per Socket due to variation about the target.

(f) What effect does the relaxation of the specifications have upon the C_p and C_{pk} values? Upon the MSD value?

Chapter Eight

Setting the Process Aim

With shorter and shorter production runs the ability to set up a run so that it will operate on-target may make the difference between success and failure. Without a bank of in-process inventory to cushion the impact, and without adequate lead time to allow for reworking or re-fabricating the product, a single faulty run can close down a whole assembly operation. Thus, in today's short-run environment, it becomes even more critical to set-up each run properly. Some ways to use the data generated by the process to assess the Process Aim will be described in this chapter. While these procedures will be especially useful with short production runs, they may be used in virtually any manufacturing environment.

8.1 The Difference Between Aim and Consistency

The following example shows three processes. Two of these production processes have great consistency, yet are not meeting the specifications because of poor process aim. The third operation has neither good consistency nor good aim.

The control chart shown in Figure 8.1 was made by a process engineer who was investigating a problem with the length of a connecting wire. The wires were purchased from three different suppliers, and were supposed to be 100 mm long, with a specified tolerance of ± 4 mm.

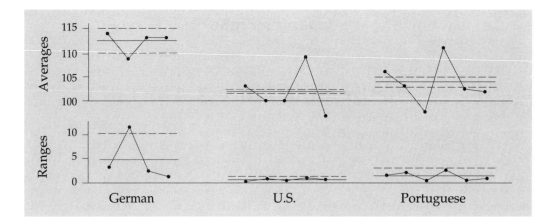

Figure 8.1: Control Charts for Connecting Wire Lengths

The data for each subgroup consist of the lengths of five pieces of wire. Each subgroup represents exactly one shipment.

The four shipments from the German supplier had a Grand Average of 112.7 mm and an Average Range of 4.6 mm. Although there were only four subgroups, there is a detectable lack of control on both the Average Chart and the Range Chart.

The five shipments from the U.S. supplier had a Grand Average of 102.2 mm and an Average Range of 0.6 mm. Here, the Average Chart is so completely out of control that none of the Subgroup Averages are within the control limits.

The six shipments from the Portuguese supplier had a Grand Average of 104.0 mm and an Average Range of 1.4 mm. Once again, the Average Chart is badly out of control.

So what was to be done? The U.S. and Portuguese suppliers showed great consistency within shipments, but a total lack of consistency between shipments. The German supplier showed very poor consistency within each shipment, and a lack of consistency between shipments.

Since the wires from all suppliers were out of control, the engineer decided to consider whether they might all be able to improve their products. The Hypothetical Process Spread for the U.S. supplier was about 1.6 mm. For the Portuguese supplier, it was about 3.6 mm, and for the German supplier, it was about 5.9 mm. Based on this analysis, the plant stopped buying from the German supplier, and the other two suppliers were told that while they had great consistency within each shipment, they needed to improve the quality of their product by consistently setting their Process Aim at 100 mm.

Dr. Taguchi's notion of a Quadratic Loss Function leads directly to the result that operating on-target with minimum variance will always minimize the costs due to variation from target. A rigorous treatment is not required—one does not need to know precisely the actual shape of the loss function, nor does one need to know the distribution for product characteristic. As long as the loss function is minimum at the target, non-negative, and piecewise smooth, the minimum average loss per unit of production will occur when the process is operating on-target with minimum variance. Thus, in addition to operating with a reasonable degree of statistical control, one must know how to get the process on-target.

For the sake of clarity, the following nomenclature will be used throughout this chapter. The "Process Aim" denotes that value or values at which the adjustable process controls are set. Thus, the Process Aim represents all that is directly manipulated by the operator as he is making his adjustments. The "Process Average" is the average value of some product characteristic, averaged over all the product produced at a given Process Aim. The "Target" is the desired value for the Process Average.

In the preceding example, the Target value was 100 mm. The average for each subgroup approximates the Process Average for a given shipment, and the Process Aim would consist of those controls over the fabrication of the connecting wires which the operator can manipulate.

An easy way to distinguish between these three quantities is given by the following: the "Process Aim" is what you set, the "Process Average" is what you get, and the "Target" is what you want. Using this nomenclature, the objective of a set-up procedure is to adjust the Process Aim until the Process Average is close enough to the Target to result in a satisfactory production run.

Why settle for close enough? Why not make the Process Average equal to the Target? Simply because in practice, one must *estimate* the Process Average with an average, and averages are always subject to sampling variation. This guarantees that no procedure will ever be able to consistently make the Process Average exactly equal to the Target. The best that can ever be achieved in practice is to get the Process Average close to the Target most of the time. In order to do this, the procedure must use an adequate amount of data in conjunction with the proper decision rule or rules. (An inadequate amount of data can be worse than guessing, and the wrong decision rules will waste effort through an excessive number of wrong decisions.)

Thus, the problem of setting the Process Aim is one of using both the right amount of information and the right decision rules for interpreting that information. The following sections will detail several techniques for setting the Process Aim. Some of these techniques will use control charts, while others will use a separate data collection procedure.

8.2 The Necessity of Process Stability

The whole procedure of setting the Process Aim will be futile if the process does not display statistical control. If the process is not in control, then the notion of a Process Average is not well-defined. In effect, there is not one Process Average, but many. In short, no process exists as a well-defined entity unless it is in statistical control. Trying to set the aim of an unstable process is simply wasted effort. When a process is known to be unstable, one should work to identify and remove the Assignable Causes of this instability rather than waste time continually tweaking the controls.

Therefore, one should not attempt to use the following procedure on a process that is not being tracked by a control chart. Moreover, the Range Chart should display a reasonable degree of statistical control, and any points that are out of control on the Average Chart should correspond to known adjustments of the process. If this is not the case, then one must identify and remove the Assignable Causes of the uncontrolled variation before proceeding further.

8.3 Setting the Process Aim Using a Sequence of Values

The nature of the problem of setting the Process Aim is slightly different from the usual problem connected with a control chart. In general, an out-of-control signal indicates the presence of an assignable cause. Since one does not want to react to false alarms, the control chart is set up to avoid false alarms. However, when one has definitely and deliberately changed the Process Aim, the question is not whether there is an assignable cause present, but whether or not the change has had the desired effect.

Since it is always easier to obtain a contradiction than a confirmation, we shall assume that the change in the Process Aim had the desired effect—so that the Process Average is in the neighborhood of the Target value—and then look for evidence that might contradict this assumption. One of the easiest ways to do this is to use a chart for Individual Values.

Say that the Process Aim has been adjusted and the process is now stabilized at the new level. Periodically a sample is obtained from the product stream and measured. This single measurement can be placed on a special chart for Individual Values and used to judge if the Process Average is detectably off-Target.

This special chart for Individual Values will have the following features:

1. The central line for the X chart will be set at the Target value.

2. A historic *Sigma(X)* value for Individual Values will be used to establish the three-sigma limits on either side of this central line.

3. One-sigma and two-sigma lines will be drawn, centered on the central line, on both sides of the chart for Individual Values.

4. Individual Values will be obtained and plotted on this X chart.

5. As each point is plotted, Detection Rules I, II, III, IV will be used to examine the data for a lack of control. (See page 96 for these four rules.)

6. Any lack of control on the Individual Chart will represent an off-Target process. When a lack of control is detected, the average of the observations will provide a reasonable estimate of where the Process Average is located relative to the Target, and the Process Aim should be adjusted accordingly. Following each adjustment, additional data are collected and analyzed to see if the Process Average is still detectably different from the Target.

7. When 10 successive measurements fail to indicate a lack of control, using all four detection rules, the Process Average may be said to be reasonably close to the Target. At this point one may shift from the "aim setting mode" back to a "monitoring mode" where the control chart tracks the process for potential upsets.

Since this is a procedure for setting the Process Aim, we will naturally be concerned primarily with the Individuals Chart. One can also compute the Moving Ranges and plot them on a Moving Range Chart, but this chart will only be of secondary interest in this case. The upper control limit for the Moving Ranges would be:

$$[\, d_2 + 3\, d_3\,]\ Sigma(X) = 3.686\ Sigma\ (X),$$

while the central line for the Moving Ranges would be:

$$d_2\ Sigma(X)\ =\ 1.128\ Sigma(X).$$

EXAMPLE 8.2:   *Setting the Process Aim With An XmR Chart:*

Product 15F is made on Unit 15. The Target value for Product 15F is 9.0 units.
A control chart for Product 15F has shown a Sigma(X) value of 1.84 units.
Therefore, an Individual Chart is set up with the following lines:

$$UNPL_X\ =\ 9.0 + 3\ (1.84)\ =\ 14.52$$
$$upper\ 2\text{-}sigma\ line =\ 9.0 + 2\ (1.84)\ =\ 12.68$$
$$upper\ 1\text{-}sigma\ line =\ 9.0 + 1.84\ =\ 10.84$$
$$Central\ Line\ =\ Target\ Value\ =\ 9.0$$
$$lower\ 1\text{-}sigma\ line =\ 9.0 - 1.84\ =\ 7.16$$
$$lower\ 2\text{-}sigma\ line =\ 9.0 - 2(1.84)\ =\ 5.32$$
$$LNPL_X\ =\ 9.0 - 3(1.84)\ =\ 3.48$$

And a moving Range chart is set up with the following limits:

$$UCL_R = 3.686 (1.84) = 6.78$$
$$CL_R = 1.128 (1.84) = 2.08$$

After the Process Aim has been adjusted to hopefully achieve a Process Average near the Target value of 9.0, data are collected and plotted on the XmR chart.

The first value is 11.

This value does not, by itself, suggest that the Process Average is off-Target. Therefore, no action will be taken at this point.

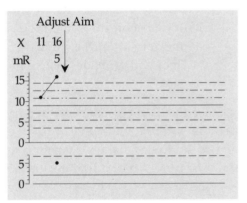

Figure 8.2: Setting the Process Aim I

The next measured value is 16.

This value signals the need to further adjust the Process Aim.

The combined average of the values collected at this setting will suggest the magnitude of the needed adjustment.
This average is:

$$\frac{(11+16)}{2} = 13.5 \ .$$

Figure 8.3: Setting the Process Aim II

The Process Aim is adjusted downward by an amount which is thought to be about 4 units.

Following this adjustment the next value is 8.

This value is plotted on the chart.

At this time the chart does not indicate the need for further adjustment.

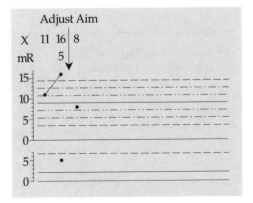

Figure 8.4: Setting the Process Aim III

The next value is 11.

This value is plotted on the chart.

The value of 11, by itself or in conjunction with the previous value of 8, does not indicate a need for further adjustment.

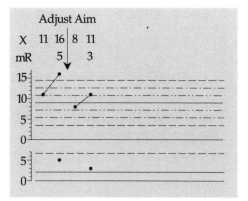

Figure 8.5: Setting the Process Aim IV

The next value is 8.

This value is plotted on the chart.

The values obtained since the last adjustment do not suggest a need for further adjustment.

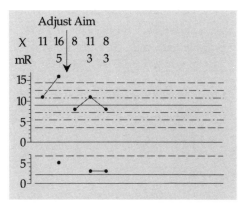

Figure 8.6: Setting the Process Aim V

The next seven values are:
11, 6, 9, 8, 9, 10, and 9.

These values do not suggest a need for further adjustment.

Since a total of ten values have failed to detect a need for an adjustment, consider the Process Aim to be set sufficiently close to the Target for a satisfactory production run.

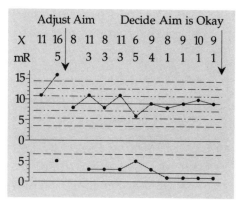

Figure 8.7: Setting the Process Aim VI

Before adjusting the Process Aim one should collect some data from the process itself. These data should be plotted on a control chart. If this has been done, then the control chart will provide a value for *Sigma(X)* to use in constructing the limits for the chart for Individual Values. In particular:

$$Sigma(X) = \frac{\bar{R}}{d_2} \,.$$

In the absence of any prior knowledge about the process, one will have to use the data as they are collected to determine both the Process Dispersion and the Process Average. Any failure to first determine the Process Dispersion will inevitably result in incorrect and inappropriate adjustments of the Process Aim. One simply cannot make an intelligent decision as to whether the Process Average is close to the Target value without some measure of Process Dispersion. One way of doing this is shown in the procedure below:

M1. The central line for the X chart will be set at the Target value. From 5 to 10 Individual values will be obtained and plotted in a running record against this central line. (If eight or more successive values are all on one side of the Target, skip to Step M7 below.)

M2. The Moving Ranges for these 5 to 10 Individual Values are computed and plotted on a Moving Range Chart. The Average Moving Range is found and used to compute a value for *Sigma(X):*

$$\frac{\overline{mR}}{1.128} = Sigma(X).$$

M3. The computed *Sigma(X)* value for Individual Values will be used to establish the three-sigma limits on either side of the central line on the X-Chart.

M4. One-sigma and two-sigma lines will be drawn, centered on the central line, on both sides of the chart for Individual Values.

M5. The initial 5 to 10 values will be examined for evidence of a lack of control relative to these limits using Detection Rules I, II, III, and IV. If any evidence of a lack of control is found, the Process Aim will need to be adjusted. Skip to Step M7 below.

M6. If the initial values fail to detect a lack of control, additional values may be collected. As each new point is plotted, Detection Rules I, II, III, and IV will be used to examine the data for a lack of control. Any lack of control on the Individual Chart will represent an off-Target process.

M7. When a lack of control is detected, the average of the observations will provide a reasonable estimate of where the Process Average is located relative to the Target, and the Process Aim should be adjusted accordingly. Following each adjustment of the Process Aim, return to Step M6 above.

M8. When 10 successive measurements fail to indicate a lack of control, using all four detection rules, the Process Average is said to be reasonably close to the Target. At this point one may shift from the "aim setting mode" back to a "monitoring mode" where the control chart tracks the process for potential upsets.

While the *Sigma(X)* value found in the procedure above may not be based upon very much data, it will still be better than guesswork, especially when needless adjustments can result in excess nonconforming product. Yes, one wants to react as soon as possible. Yes, one cannot afford to wait too long before making a needed adjustment. But how will one know when it is needed?

It will always be a mistake to adjust the Process Aim
        before one has a detectable signal that the Process Average is off-Target.

The control chart provides (among other things) an operational definition of when the Process Aim needs to be adjusted. Children yank the steering wheel back and forth when they play like they are driving. Drivers adjust the steering only when they want to change course, *or when they have a signal* that they are headed in the wrong direction. One does not have to weave back and forth to prove that one is not asleep at the wheel! When timeliness of adjustment is important, then one should collect the measurements as quickly as possible. In the absence of a prior value for *Sigma(X)*, one will have to collect some data before even attempting to adjust the Process Aim. Of course, in the absence of a control chart for a given process, one may try to adjust the aim of an out-of-control process—generally an exercise in frustration—but if such is necessary, the steps above are the best way of attempting to do this.

Many years ago Frank Grubbs published a procedure for setting the Process Aim which does not require a value for *Sigma(X)*.[1] While Grubbs' Rule is fairly simple, it is essentially a modified form of tampering. This is because it has one adjust the Process Aim without first attempting to filter out the noise.

Grubbs' Rule can take a process which is on-Target and move it off-Target. Thus, like all procedures that do not take the natural variation in the numbers into account, it is capable of misleading the user. With Grubbs' Rule the operator will start making adjustments after the first measurement, and will continue to make adjustments following each additional measurement for some finite period of time. While this may give the illusion of action, the actions may well be the wrong actions.

---

[1] Frank E. Grubbs, "An Optimum Procedure for Setting Machines or Adjusting Processes," *Journal of Quality Technology,* V.15, No.4, October 1983, pp.186-189, reprinted from the July 1954 issue of *Industrial Quality Control.*

So, even though one may chafe at having to collect 5 to 10 values without readjusting the Process Aim, it is the only prudent course of action. It will always be folly to make adjustments in the absence of a signal indicating that an adjustment is needed.

8.4 Setting the Process Aim Using Multiple Measurements

The basic procedure for adjusting the Process Aim with multiple measurements is:

1. Set the Process Aim.

2. Measure the specified number of pieces, n, and calculate the average.

3. If the average is NOT within some critical distance, D, of the Target, then return to Step 1 above.

4. Proceed with the production run when the average of n measurements is less than D units away from the Target.

Once an operator has been given consistent values for n and D, he can use this procedure to set the Process Average as close to the Target as is necessary, and he can do it quickly and efficiently. Moreover, as long as he continues to use this procedure, both the operator and his supervisor can be confident that the Process Aim is being set correctly.

How then does the supervisor provide the operator with the values for n and D? Since one must have a decision rule that is appropriate for the amount of data available, one cannot arbitrarily choose values for n and D. The plans given below combine values of n and D that work.

Even with the following plans, there is still the problem of which plan to use. The Process Average will, in general, end up closer to the Target when more data are used. Just how close does one need to be to the Target? This is the question that needs to be answered in practice. But how does one decide on a "degree of closeness?" Isn't perfection the goal? As was observed earlier, we can never get the Process Average to exactly coincide with the Target, so we must learn to live with "close enough." Thus, we need a measure of closeness. A way to do this is provided by Dr. Taguchi's Loss Function.

Based on a quadratic approximation to the loss function in the neighborhood of the Target value, the Average Loss Per Unit of Production will be proportional to the Mean Square Deviation About Target:

$$MSD(\tau) = \left\{ \left[Sigma(X) \right]^2 + \left[\text{Process Average} - \text{Target} \right]^2 \right\}$$

For any given process, the best that one can do (without modifying the process) is to have the process in a state of statistical control and perfectly centered on the Target. As the Process Average deviates from the Target, the $MSD(\tau)$ value will increase. When a plan for setting the Process Aim does a good job of getting the Process Average close to the Target, it will have a small $MSD(\tau)$ value.

Thus, each time one of the following plans is used to set the Process Aim, the Process Average will end up somewhere (hopefully close to the Target), and there will be a single $MSD(\tau)$ value. If these $MSD(\tau)$ values for a given plan are averaged, then this Average $MSD(\tau)$ value may be used to characterize this plan for setting the Process Aim. This Average $MSD(\tau)$ value for a given plan will be called the Average Taguchi Loss. These Average Taguchi Loss values will be expressed as percentages of the minimum loss (that loss which occurs when the Process Average is equal to the Target). For a procedure to get an Average Taguchi Loss of 100% it would have to set the Process Average equal to the Target value every time without error.

The key to an effective procedure for setting the Process Aim is the relationship between the amount of data collected and the decision rule used to interpret these data. If the amount of data is appropriate for the decision rule used, the decisions will tend to be correct most of the time. If the decision rule and the amount of data are mismatched, then the decisions will tend to be incorrect more often. Eight plans for setting the Process Aim are shown on the following pages. These eight plans match up the decision rule with the amount of data, so that one will generally get a Process Average that is reasonably close to the Target value.

For the sake of generality, the distance between the Process Average and the Target is expressed in *Sigma(X)* units (that is, it is written as some multiple of *Sigma(X)*). This means that in order to use these plans for setting the Process Aim, one must first compute a *Sigma(X)* value. The best place to obtain this *Sigma(X)* value is from a control chart for the product or process.

PLAN A: If one wants the Process Average to be within 2.88 *Sigma(X)* units of the Target, use $n = 1$ and $D = 1.44$ *Sigma(X)*. The Average Taguchi Loss for this plan is estimated to be less than 495% of minimum.

PLAN B: If one wants the Process Average to be within 2.0 *Sigma(X)* units of the Target, use $n = 3$ and $D = 1.0$ *Sigma(X)*. The Average Taguchi Loss for this plan is estimated to be less than 260% of minimum.

PLAN C: If one wants the Process Average to be within 1.5 *Sigma(X)* units of the Target, use $n = 5$ and $D = 0.75$ *Sigma(X)*. The Average Taguchi Loss for this plan is estimated to be less than 190% of minimum.

PLAN D: If one wants the Process Average to be within 1.0 *Sigma(X)* units of the Target, use $n = 10$ and $D = 0.5$ *Sigma(X)*. The Average Taguchi Loss for this plan is estimated to be less than 140% of minimum.

PLAN E: If one wants the Process Average to be within 0.75 *Sigma(X)* units of the

Target, use $n = 15$ and $D = 0.37$ *Sigma(X)*. The Average Taguchi Loss for this plan is estimated to be less than 129% of minimum.

PLAN F: If one wants the Process Average to be within 0.5 *Sigma(X)* units of the Target, use $n = 25$ and $D = 0.25$ *Sigma(X)*. The Average Taguchi Loss for this plan is estimated to be less than 114% of minimum.

PLAN G: If one wants the Process Average to be within 0.33 *Sigma(X)* units of the Target, use $n = 40$ and $D = 0.17$ *Sigma(X)*. The Average Taguchi Loss for this plan is estimated to be less than 110% of minimum.

PLAN H: If one wants the Process Average to be within 0.20 *Sigma(X)* units of the Target, use $n = 71$ and $D = 0.10$ *Sigma(X)*. The Average Taguchi Loss for this plan is estimated to be less than 103% of minimum.

These adjustment procedures will be adequate for most of the routine adjustment problems where multiple measurements may be easily obtained. By choosing a plan further down the list, the Process Average will be set closer to the Target. Of course, this in turn, requires more measurements.

Figure 8.8 shows the Average Taguchi Loss for each plan, and the Number of Measurements required by each plan.

Table 8.1: Plans for Setting the Process Aim

Plan	Number of Measurements n	Critical Distance D	Average Taguchi Loss
A	1	1.44 *Sigma(X)*	495%
B	3	1.00 *Sigma(X)*	260%
C	5	0.75 *Sigma(X)*	190%
D	10	0.50 *Sigma(X)*	140%
E	15	0.37 *Sigma(X)*	129%
F	25	0.25 *Sigma(X)*	114%
G	40	0.17 *Sigma(X)*	110%
H	71	0.10 *Sigma(X)*	103%

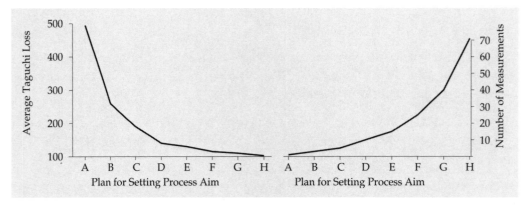

Figure 8.8: Average Taguchi Loss and Number of Measurements for Plans for Setting the Process Aim

If the cost of variation from Target is high relative to the cost of collecting the measurements and adjusting the Process Aim, then a situation similar to that shown in Figure 8.9 will hold. Here Plans D, E, and F appear to be reasonable.

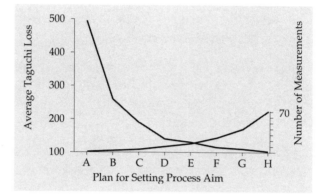

Figure 8.9: Large Cost of Variation and Small Cost of Measurements

If the cost of variation from Target is small relative to the cost of collecting the measurements and adjusting the Process Aim, then a situation similar to that shown in Figure 8.10 will hold. In this case it is Plans B, C, and D that appear to be reasonable.

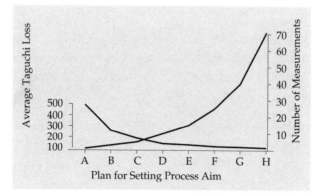

Figure 8.10: Small Cost of Variation and Large Cost of Measurements

If one is not certain just what the costs of variation are relative to the cost of collecting the measurements and adjusting the Process Aim, the two graphs above suggest that Plan D is reasonable in any case.

A sample worksheet for using these plans to adjust the Process Aim is shown in

Figure 8.11. The information shown on this worksheet will greatly simplify the actual decision-making process on the production floor.

If the nature of the process, or the nature of the measurement, dictates the use of single measurements in setting the Process Aim, then one will be limited in the ability to verify that the Process Average is close to the Target. Plan A shows a value of $D = 1.44$ Sigma(X) for $n = 1$. This means that if one gets a single measurement within D units of the Target, it is very likely that the Process Average is within $2D$ units of the Target.

Using a smaller value for D will not deliver any greater certainty. With only one measurement there is only a limited amount of information available, and nothing can change this limitation. The only real consequence of using a smaller value for D would be an increased number of needless adjustments.

If one can use a *sequence* of single measurements, then rather than repeatedly using Plan A, it is generally better to use the Individual Values Chart described in Section 8.3.

8.5 Summary

The procedures for setting the Process Aim given in this chapter, when used in conjunction with a control chart to monitor the stability of the production process, will allow the worker to operate the process "On-Target with Minimum Variance." Of course, while a process is operated On-Target with Minimum Variance it will produce a minimum amount of nonconforming product. *No other mode of operation can make this promise.*

The control chart is unsurpassed in detecting the presence of Assignable Causes that represent opportunities for improving the process. The simple procedures for setting the Process Aim discussed in this chapter provide a reliable way to get a stable process located at a desired point.

However, as powerful as these procedures may be, they must be combined with commitment and constancy of purpose. When this combination is used to reduce the product variation, the Average Loss Per Unit of Product will drop and increased productivity will be the result. This has been proven in practice thousands of times over. Those organizations which fail to institutionalize this motivation and constancy of purpose in action will simply become increasingly noncompetitive.

Date _____ Part Number _____ Operator _____

Process or Machine _____ other ID _____

Dimension Measured _____ Target Value _____

Sigma(X) Value _____ Plan Used _____

Sample Size n = _____ Critical Distance D = _____

Adjust Process Aim if Average of n Measurements is Outside Decision Interval:

Decision Interval: Target $- D$ = _____ Target $+ D$ = _____

	First Sample Measurements	Second Sample Measurements	Third Sample Measurements	Plan	n	D
1	_____	_____	_____			
2	_____	_____	_____	A	1	1.44 Sigma(X)
3	_____	_____	_____	B	3	1.00 Sigma(X)
4	_____	_____	_____	C	5	0.75 Sigma(X)
5	_____	_____	_____	D	10	0.50 Sigma(X)
6	_____	_____	_____	E	15	0.37 Sigma(X)
7	_____	_____	_____	F	25	0.25 Sigma(X)
8	_____	_____	_____	G	40	0.17 Sigma(X)
9	_____	_____	_____	H	71	0.10 Sigma(X)
10	_____	_____	_____			
11	_____	_____	_____			
12	_____	_____	_____			
13	_____	_____	_____			
14	_____	_____	_____			
15	_____	_____	_____			

Average _____ _____ _____

Decision _____ _____ _____

Figure 8.11: Worksheet for Setting the Process Aim Using Multiple Measurements

Exercise 8.1:

You operate a filling operation. The containers have a label net weight of 16 ounces. By law at least 95% of your containers must meet or exceed this net weight. Past measurements of the fill weights from your operation have shown (when placed on a control chart) that the filling operation displays a reasonable degree of statistical control with a *Sigma(X)* value of 0.36 oz.

(a) Using the Empirical Rule, what Target weight could you use in order to safely meet the legal requirement for these fill weights?

(b) If you were to use Plan D from page 202 with the Target weight specified above, what range of values for the average fill weights of ten containers would lead to the decision "Do not adjust the Process Aim"?

(c) If you were to use the procedure in Section 8.3, and outlined on page 195, compute the values for the central line, the one-sigma lines, the two-sigma lines, and the three-sigma limits for the X Chart and the central line and Upper Control Limit for the Range Chart.

(d) What is the implicit assumption in the use of the use of 0.36 oz. as the basis for the targeting and monitoring procedures?

(e) How will you detect any changes in average fill weight for this process?

(f) How will you detect any changes in variation in the fill weights for this process?

(g) How could you reduce the "give-away" due to overfill without violating the legal requirement on fill weights?

Chapter Nine

Special Topics Concerning
Control Charts for Measurements

This chapter is a collection of additional topics concerning control charts for measurement data. The first section describes the one situation where the control chart does not "fail-safe"—Inadequate Measurement Units. The next section shows the right and wrong ways of computing limits for XmR Charts. The third section discusses when to use an XmR Chart and makes a distinction between "Regular Control Chart Data" and "Periodically Collected Data." A table is given to help with the choice of which chart to use in a given situation. The fourth section shows a Moving Average Chart. Section Five discusses "Three-Way Control Charts" with an application to chemical batches. Section Six discusses the revision of initial control limits while Section Seven discusses the issue of updating existing control limits. Section Eight shows a Median and Range Chart. And the last section shows the structure of the control chart formulas in terms of basic constants, expresses the tabled control chart constants in terms of these same basic constants, and then shows the origin of these basic constants.

9.1 Inadequate Measurement Units

The purpose of this section is to explain the problem of Inadequate Measurement Units. This will require the answers to two basic questions: What happens to the control chart when the measurement units used are too large? And, what is the effect on control charts of measurement "round-off." The answers to these two questions will lead to certain tell-tale signs for Inadequate Measurement Units. They will also show why this problem exists, and will suggest what can be done to remedy this problem when it is present.

The easiest way to see the effect of Inadequate Measurement Units is to manipulate a data set to create measurement units which are too large. One may then compare the control charts before and after the manipulation of the data to discover the effect of excessively large measurement units. The Rheostat Knob Data will be used to demonstrate this effect.

EXAMPLE 9.1:   *The Rheostat Knob Data:*

A particular rheostat knob had a pin hole on the shaft housing. The dimensions recorded in Table 9.1 are the distances from the back of the piece to the far side of the pin hole. These measurements were made to the nearest thousandth of an inch. The same measurements, rounded to the nearest hundredth of an inch, are shown in Table 9.2. These rounded measurements represent the values that would have been obtained if the parts had only been measured to the nearest hundredth of an inch. The control charts for the data in Tables 9.1 and 9.2 are shown in Figure 9.1.

Table 9.1: Rheostat Knob Data Recorded to 0.001 inch

Subgroup						$\overline{X}$	R	Subgroup						$\overline{X}$	R
1	.140	.143	.137	.134	.135	*.1378*	*.009*	15	.144	.142	.143	.135	.144	*.1416*	*.009*
2	.138	.143	.143	.145	.146	*.1430*	*.008*	16	.133	.132	.144	.145	.141	*.1390*	*.013*
3	.139	.133	.147	.148	.149	*.1432*	*.016*	17	.137	.137	.142	.143	.141	*.1400*	*.006*
4	.143	.141	.137	.138	.140	*.1398*	*.006*	18	.137	.142	.142	.145	.143	*.1418*	*.008*
5	.142	.142	.145	.135	.136	*.1400*	*.010*	19	.142	.142	.143	.140	.135	*.1404*	*.008*
6	.136	.144	.143	.136	.137	*.1392*	*.008*	20	.136	.142	.140	.139	.137	*.1388*	*.006*
7	.142	.147	.137	.142	.138	*.1412*	*.010*	21	.142	.144	.140	.138	.143	*.1414*	*.006*
8	.143	.137	.145	.137	.138	*.1400*	*.008*	22	.139	.146	.143	.140	.139	*.1414*	*.007*
9	.141	.142	.147	.140	.140	*.1420*	*.007*	23	.140	.145	.142	.139	.137	*.1406*	*.008*
10	.142	.137	.134	.140	.132	*.1370*	*.010*	24	.134	.147	.143	.141	.142	*.1414*	*.013*
11	.137	.147	.142	.137	.135	*.1396*	*.012*	25	.138	.145	.141	.137	.141	*.1404*	*.008*
12	.137	.146	.142	.142	.146	*.1426*	*.009*	26	.140	.145	.143	.144	.138	*.1420*	*.007*
13	.142	.142	.139	.141	.142	*.1412*	*.003*	27	.145	.145	.137	.138	.140	*.1410*	*.008*
14	.137	.145	.144	.137	.140	*.1406*	*.008*								

Table 9.2: Rheostat Knob Data Recorded to 0.01 inch

Subgroup						$\bar{X}$	R	Subgroup						$\bar{X}$	R
1	.14	.14	.14	.13	.14	.138	.01	15	.14	.14	.14	.14	.14	.140	.00
2	.14	.14	.14	.14	.15	.142	.01	16	.13	.13	.14	.14	.14	.136	.01
3	.14	.13	.15	.15	.15	.144	.02	17	.14	.14	.14	.14	.14	.140	.00
4	.14	.14	.14	.14	.14	.140	.00	18	.14	.14	.14	.14	.14	.140	.00
5	.14	.14	.14	.14	.14	.140	.00	19	.14	.14	.14	.14	.14	.140	.00
6	.14	.14	.14	.14	.14	.140	.00	20	.14	.14	.14	.14	.14	.140	.00
7	.14	.15	.14	.14	.14	.142	.01	21	.14	.14	.14	.14	.14	.140	.00
8	.14	.14	.14	.14	.14	.140	.00	22	.14	.15	.14	.14	.14	.142	.01
9	.14	.14	.15	.14	.14	.142	.01	23	.14	.14	.14	.14	.14	.140	.00
10	.14	.14	.13	.14	.13	.136	.01	24	.13	.15	.14	.14	.14	.140	.02
11	.14	.15	.14	.14	.14	.142	.01	25	.14	.14	.14	.14	.14	.140	.00
12	.14	.15	.14	.14	.15	.144	.01	26	.14	.14	.14	.14	.14	.140	.00
13	.14	.14	.14	.14	.14	.140	.00	27	.14	.14	.14	.14	.14	.140	.00
14	.14	.14	.14	.14	.14	.140	.00								

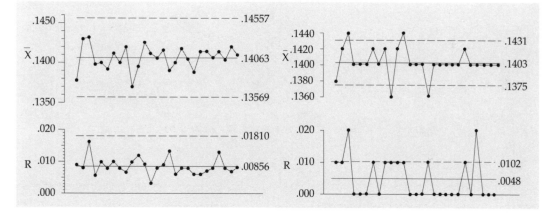

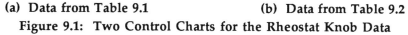

(a) Data from Table 9.1   (b) Data from Table 9.2

Figure 9.1: Two Control Charts for the Rheostat Knob Data

It is immediately apparent that the two charts do not look alike. One would hardly guess that they represented the same dimension on the same parts. The running records in Figure 9.1(b) have fewer levels. This is due to the fact that the smallest unit of measurement is ten times larger than its counterpart in Figure 9.1(a). Secondly, the control limits in Figure 9.1(b) are narrower than those in Figure 9.1 (a).

The out-of-control points in Figure 9.1(b) have nothing to do with the underlying physical process. Instead, they were created by the excessive round-off in Table 9.2.

Excessive round-off in the measurements can make a control chart appear to be out-of-control even when the underlying process is in a state of statistical control.

Fortunately, when this problem exists, it is easy to identify. Ordinary control charts signal the presence of inadequate discrimination due to measurement units which are too large: they do this by showing too few possible values within the control limits on the range chart.

If there are only 1, 2, or 3 possible values for the range within the control limits, then the measurement units are too large for the purposes of the control chart. Moreover, if the subgroup size is three or larger ($n \geq 3$), and there are only 4 possible values for the range within the control limits, then the measurement units are too large for the purposes of the control chart.

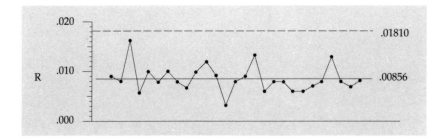

Figure 9.2: Range Chart for Data Recorded to 0.001 inch

In Figure 9.2, the tick marks on the vertical axis define the possible values for the Subgroup Ranges. There are 19 possible values for the range within the control limits. This is evidence that there is no problem with Inadequate Measurement Units.

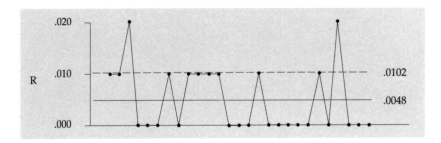

Figure 9.3: Range Chart for Data Recorded to 0.01 inch

In Figure 9.3, the tick marks again define the possible values for the Subgroup Ranges. There are only two possible values for the range within the control limits. This is sufficient evidence that these charts suffer from Inadequate Measurement Units. In other words, the measurement units are too large for the purposes of the chart. When this happens, one cannot safely interpret the control chart as reflecting the behavior of the process. (Any out-of-control points may be due to the round-off in the measurements.) This problem must be corrected before the control chart will be of any real use.

The problem seen on the control charts in Figures 9.1(b) and 9.3 is due to the inability of the measurements to properly detect and reflect the process variation. When the measurements are rounded off to the nearest 0.01 inch, most of the information about dispersion is lost in the round-off. As a result, the rounded data have many zero ranges even though the original data have no zero ranges. These zero ranges deflate the Average Range and tighten the control limits. At the same time, the greater discreteness for both the averages and the ranges will spread out the running records. Eventually it becomes inevitable that some points will fall outside the limits, even though the process itself is **not** out-of-control.

Since this problem arises out of the inability to detect variation within the subgroups, the solution consists of increasing the ability to detect that variation. This can be done in one of two ways. **Either use smaller Measurement Units, or increase the variation within the subgroups to a detectable level.** The latter approach will usually be accomplished by collecting values for a subgroup over a longer time span. By increasing the time span, one often increases the variation enough to make it detectable with the original Measurement Units.

Detection Rules for Inadequate Measurement Units

In order to justify the rules for detecting Inadequate Measurement Units we shall consider the theoretical model of an exactly stable process. Of course, in practice, no process ever displays exact stability. In spite of this, the theoretical model is useful for discovering basic relationships. In this case, there is a special relationship between the smallest actual unit of measurement and the standard deviation of an exactly stable process.

To understand this relationship, consider a subgroup of size $n = 2$. The Average Range for such subgroups will be approximately 1.128 SD(X) [1.128 times the Standard Deviation of the Distribution of X]. Since the range is just the distance between the two measurements in a subgroup, and since any collection of measurements from a stable process could be arbitrarily arranged into subgroups of size $n = 2$, we can say that the average distance between any two randomly selected measurements is about 1.1 SD(X). (1.128 is the value for d_2 for subgroups of size 2.)

At the same time, consider two measurements which are rounded off to the same value: two measurements will be rounded to the same value when they both differ from that value by less than one-half measurement unit. For example, in measuring to the nearest millimeter, the measurements of 14.51 mm and 15.49 mm will both be rounded off to the value of 15 mm. Thus, measurements might be rounded to the same value when they differ by less than one measurement unit.

The observations in the two preceding paragraphs can be combined to discover the root of the problem created by Inadequate Measurement Units. When the Process Standard Deviation, SD(X), is smaller than the Measurement Unit, the measurements will begin to be rounded to the same values. This rounding will begin to contaminate the estimate of the Process Standard Deviation by deflating the Average Range. Moreover, the smaller the Process Standard Deviation is relative to the Measurement Unit, the greater the contamination will be.

Therefore, the problem of Inadequate Measurement Units (inadequate discrimination due to a measurement unit which is too large) begins to affect the control chart when the Measurement Unit exceeds the Process Standard Deviation.

The control charts are on the borderline of Inadequate Measurement Units when the Process Standard Deviation is equal to the Measurement Unit. The rule for detecting this problem is based upon the borderline condition. The origin of this rule is outlined below.

Consider the formulas for the upper and lower control limits for the range chart:

$$UCL_R = D_4 \; MEAN(R)$$
$$LCL_R = D_3 \; MEAN(R)$$

where MEAN(R) represents the mean of the distribution of R. Figure 9.19 shows this mean to be related to SD(X) by:

$$MEAN(R) = d_2 \; SD(X).$$

Combining these equations, we get:

$$UCL_R = D_4 \; d_2 \; SD(X)$$
$$LCL_R = D_3 \; d_2 \; SD(X).$$

When SD(X) = Measurement Unit, these equations become:

$$\text{UCL}_R = D_4 \; d_2 \text{ measurement units}$$
$$\text{LCL}_R = D_3 \; d_2 \text{ measurement units.}$$

These values are tabled for subgroup sizes of $n = 2$ to $n = 10$ in Table 9.3.

Table 9.3: Control Limits for Range Chart When SD(X) = Measurement Unit

Subgroup Size	LCL	UCL	Possible Values for Range Within Limits	Number of Possible Values for Range Within Limits
2	none	3.69	0, 1, 2, 3	4
3	none	4.36	0, 1, 2, 3, 4	5
4	none	4.70	0, 1, 2, 3, 4	5
5	none	4.92	0, 1, 2, 3, 4	5
6	none	5.08	0, 1, 2, 3, 4, 5	6
7	0.21	5.20	1, 2, 3, 4, 5	5
8	0.39	5.31	1, 2, 3, 4, 5	5
9	0.55	5.39	1, 2, 3, 4, 5	5
10	0.69	5.47	1, 2, 3, 4, 5	5

Since the values in Table 9.3 define the borderline condition, the following guidelines for detecting Inadequate Measurement Units can be established.

The measurement unit borders on being too large when there are only 5 possible values within the control limits on the Range Chart. Four values within the limits will be indicative of Inadequate Measurement Units, and fewer than four values will result in appreciable distortion of the control limits.

The only exception to this occurs when the Subgroup Size for the Range Chart is $n = 2$; here 4 possible values within the control limits on the Range Chart will represent the borderline condition. Three possible values within the limits will be indicative of Inadequate Measurement Units, and fewer than three values will result in appreciable distortion of the control limits.

Thus, there need be no confusion about whether or not the measurement unit being used is sufficiently small for the application at hand. The control chart clearly shows when it is not. Fortunately, when this problem exists, the solutions are straightforward. But one must implement one of these solutions before the control charts will be of any real use.

One other note is needed. Occasionally the measurement unit will be too large simply because the data are truncated to a certain level in order to avoid reporting "noise." When such truncation creates inadequate discrimination, it is also cutting off part of the signal! Recording one extra digit will usually be sufficient to eliminate this source of inadequate discrimination.

The Tokai Rika Control Chart, shown in Chapter 7, operates on the borderline of Inadequate Measurement Units throughout most of the period covered. The Average Range drops to the neighborhood of 0.02 mm in March, 1981, and remains there throughout the next year. Since $n = 4$ the upper control limit for the Range Chart is 0.046 mm. With measurements made to the nearest 0.01 mm, there are exactly five possible values for the range within the control limits (0.00, 0.01, 0.02, 0.03, and 0.04). One might also note that the Tokai Rika personnel have already spread the collection of the sample pieces out over time. The four pieces selected were chosen at 10, 11, 2 and 4 o'clock. Without this hour-to-hour variation within the subgroup, it is likely that the measurement units would be too large to detect the part-to-part variation.

Thus, there need be no confusion about whether or not the measurement units used are small enough for the application at hand. The Range Chart clearly shows when they are not. Moreover, the solution for the problem of Inadequate Measurement Units is fairly straightforward: either smaller units of measurement must be used, or the variation within the subgroups must be increased.

9.2 Individual and Moving Range Charts Done Right

Individual and Moving Range Charts were introduced in Section 3.6, page 48. They were illustrated in Section 6.4, page 131. Here a distinction will be made between the right and the wrong ways of computing limits for these charts. We return to the Batch Weight Data of Example 6.7.

EXAMPLE 9.2:   *XmR Charts Done Right:*

The weights of the first 45 sequential batches run during one week are shown below arranged in columns by time order. These values were used to obtain the XmR Chart. With an Average of 936.89, and an Average Moving Range of 27.84, the limits for the XmR Chart are:

$$UNPL_X = 936.89 + 2.66\,(27.84) = 1010.94$$
$$CL_X = 936.89$$
$$LNPL_X = 936.89 - 2.66\,(27.84) = 862.84$$
$$UCL_R = 3.268\,(27.84) = 90.98$$
$$CL_R = 27.84$$

The XmR Chart for these data is shown in Figure 9.4. There are several indications of a lack of control on both charts. Thus, the chart is able to detect a lack of control, even though the out-of-control data were used to compute the limits! As was noted in Chapter 4, this is a distinguishing characteristic of the right way of computing control limits.

X	mR		X	mR		X	mR		X	mR		X	mR
905	—		910	5		915	10		975	35		900	40
930	25		920	10		930	15		1000	25		920	20
865	65		915	5		890	40		1035	35		980	60
895	30		925	10		940	50		1020	15		950	30
905	10		860	65		860	80		985	35		955	5
885	20		905	45		875	15		960	25		970	15
890	5		925	20		985	110		945	15		970	0
930	40		925	0		970	15		965	20		1035	65
915	15		905	20		940	30		940	25		1040	5

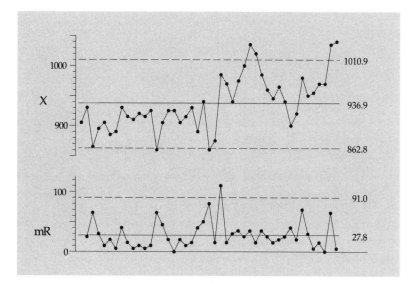

Figure 9.4: *XmR* Chart Done Right

The same data will be used to also illustrate the incorrect way of computing limits for an Individuals Chart in the following example.

EXAMPLE 9.3:   *Individuals Chart Done Wrong:*

An incorrect method of computing limits for an Individuals Chart uses both the Average and the Standard Deviation of ALL the data. The Average of the 45 observations shown in Example 9.2 is 936.89, while the Standard Deviation is s = 45.80. This incorrect approach computes limits for Individual Values as follows:

$$\text{"supposed" } UNPL_X = 936.89 + 3\,(45.80) = 1074.3$$
$$CL_X = 936.89$$
$$\text{"supposed" } LNPL_X = 936.89 - 3\,(45.80) = 799.5.$$

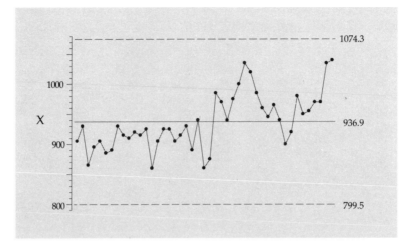

Figure 9.5: Individuals Chart Done Wrong

Since this approach uses a single dispersion statistic, there is no dispersion chart. The Individuals Chart with these incorrect limits is shown in Figure 9.5. These incorrectly computed limits are 86 percent wider than those in Figure 9.4. While there are long runs in these data, the incorrectly computed limits themselves completely obscure the out-of-control points, and therefore do their best to ignore the lack of control in these data.

Any computation of control limits based upon a single dispersion statistic computed on a single pass through the data will always be incorrect. Such computations are subject to being inflated whenever a lack of control exists, and therefore would only be appropriate when one knew for certain that the data displayed statistical control. Since such knowledge is not available to mere mortals, the use of a single dispersion statistic to compute control limits will always be wrong.

The right way of computing limits for Individual Values will always use a two-point Moving Range. Three- or four-point Moving Ranges will not be as good as a two-point Moving Range for two reasons: they do not use the data as "efficiently" as a two-point Moving Range, and they are harder to compute (instead of just computing the successive differences, one must first find both the minimum and maximum of each moving subgroup before computing a three- or four-point Moving Range).

Moreover, a two-point Moving Standard Deviation (sometimes called a Mean Square Successive Difference) will be no better than a two-point Moving Range. It will not be more "efficient." It will not yield "better" limits. It will simply be more complex.

Thus, the right way of computing limits for Individual Values will always use a two-point Moving Range.

9.3 When Should One Use An *XmR* Chart?

To understand when to use an *XmR* Chart it is helpful to make a distinction between two types of data: Regular Control Chart Data and Periodically Collected Data.

Regular Control Chart Data are data for which one may choose both the subgroup size and the subgroup frequency. That is, the subgroup size is independent of the subgroup frequency. For such data, the Average and Range Chart will generally be the best chart to use. The ability to choose the subgroup frequency will allow one to obtain subgroups to match the time period which characterizes changes in the process. The ability to independently select the subgroup size will allow one to collect several observations in a short time period and thereby to use the increased sensitivity of the Average Chart.

Periodically Collected Data are data for which the choice of subgroup size is NOT independent of the choice of subgroup frequency. Each value is uniquely identified with a specific period of time. In such a case, any change in subgroup size will also require a change in the time period covered by the subgroup. Examples of this sort of data would be a series of monthly values, periodic measurements from a continuous process, or final test values from a series of batches.

Periodically Collected Data are obvious candidates for the *XmR* Chart. Rather than having to wait for two or more time periods between successive subgroups, the *XmR* Chart allows one to plot a point every time one gets a value. That is, Periodically Collected Data will often have a logical subgroup size of $n = 1$.

However, there is a more fundamental reason for the use of an *XmR* Chart with Periodically Collected Data—it is frequently the most sensitive chart for this type of data. With Regular Control Chart Data one may increase the subgroup size without changing the subgroup frequency. If one is to observe the principle of homogeneous subgroups, any increase in subgroup size will be subject to the constraint that the additional values are logically homogeneous with the original values. Thus, increasing the subgroup size with Regular Control Chart Data should not substantially change the questions addressed by the charts. This ability to select the subgroup size is what enables one to use the sensitivity of Subgroup Averages rather than having to work exclusively with Individual Values. This means that, for Regular Control Chart Data, the Average Chart will generally be the preferred chart.

With Periodically Collected Data things are different. Any increase in subgroup size will automatically require the subgroup to represent more time periods. Such a change not only opens up the possibility of non-homogeneous subgroups, but it also makes a fundamental change in the questions framed and answered by the chart. This change in the questions framed makes it impossible to directly compare different subgroup sizes.

Different subgroup sizes represent different sets of questions, and therefore fundamentally different charts. Thus, the regular comparisons cannot be applied to Periodically Collected Data. With Periodically Collected Data all comparisons must be made at a fixed point of time—given a specific amount of data available, what is the best way to organize it on a control chart to detect an out-of-control condition? The answer to this question is a bit surprising—with Periodically Collected Data the Individuals Chart has greater initial sensitivity than any other chart, and when used with Detection Rules I, II, III, and IV, the Individuals Chart is essentially as sensitive as any other control chart.[1]

Another situation in which the use of the Individual Values may be more sensitive than the traditional charts is a set of data for which the natural ordering is unknown. One typical example of this could be a set of data from pre-production samples, where the order of production is not known. Without the natural ordering, any treatment of the data will essentially use a haphazard ordering. Grouping the data into haphazard subgroups may obscure evidence of a lack of control, while plotting the individual values may show some of them to be unusual (even though the ordering is haphazard).

Table 9.4 When to Use the Different Charts for Measurement Data

Regular Control Chart Data: *May choose both subgroup size and subgroup frequency:*

Organize data into rational subgroups .... Use Average and Range Chart.

Periodically Collected Data: *Frequency for Individual Values is fixed:*
Choice of subgroup size determines subgroup frequency:

Organize data in rational manner .... Use *XmR* Chart:
or
For slowly changing process .... Use Moving Average Chart.
or
For historical summary .... Use Average and Range Chart:

A final technical note about this procedure is appropriate. The fact that successive Moving Ranges are computed using a common X value will tend to lengthen the runs on the Moving Range Chart. Since these longer runs are a consequence of the computations, rather than being a characteristic of the process itself, they are not of interest when interpreting the chart. Thus, it is best to simply use only Detection Rule One with the

---

[1] See "Comparing Control Charts for Individual Values and Control Charts for Moving Averages" by Donald J. Wheeler, 1988, for more information on this topic.

Moving Range Chart. When a Moving Range value falls outside the range control limits, it is an indication of a sudden change in the series of Individual Values. This identification of discontinuities in the original time series is the major contribution of any Moving Range Chart.

9.4 Control Charts for Moving Averages

Some authors suggest using Moving Average Charts with Periodically Collected Data. These are essentially ordinary Average and Range Charts constructed using a moving subgroup of size two or larger.

EXAMPLE 9.4:   *Moving Average and Moving Range Charts:*

The weights of the first 45 sequential batches run during one week are shown below. (The time order sequence for these values is given by reading the values row by row.) These values will be used to obtain a Moving Average Chart.

```
 905  930  865  895  905  885  890  930  915  910  920  915  925   860   905
 925  925  905  915  930  890  940  860  875  985  970  940  975  1000  1035
1020  985  960  945  965  940  900  920  980  950  955  970  970  1035  1040
```

The only unique aspect of the construction of a Moving Average and Moving Range Chart is the construction of the moving subgroups. The first 14 values are arranged into moving subgroups of size n = 2 below—each value is written down twice on a diagonal so that it occurs in exactly two successive subgroups—then averages and ranges are computed for each "subgroup."

```
905   930   865   895   905   885   890   930   915   910   920   915   925   860
      905   930   865   895   905   885   890   930   915   910   920   915   925   860

905   930   865   895   905   885   890   930   915   910   920   915   925   860
      905   930   865   895   905   885   890   930   915   910   920   915   925   860
```

$m\bar{X}$	917.5	897.5	880.0	900.0	895.0	887.5	910.0	922.5	912.5	915.0	917.5	920.0	892.5	...
mR	25	65	30	10	20	5	40	15	5	10	5	10	65	

With a Grand Moving Average of 936.08, and an Average Moving Range of 27.84, the limits for the Moving Average and Moving Range Chart are constructed just like those for an ordinary Average and Range Chart with subgroup size n = 2: (See Exercise 3.3 for the computations for these data.)

For an n-period Moving Average each value would be written down n times on a diagonal. When n values are stacked up they form a moving subgroup of size n. Then the average and range are computed for each subgroup and these values are plotted on a chart with the usual limits for subgroups of size n.

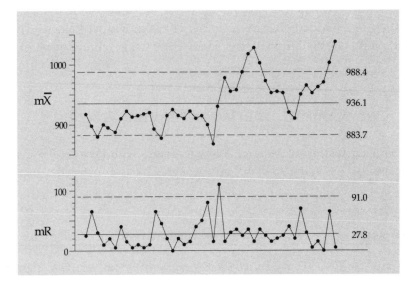

Figure 9.6: Moving Average and Moving Range Chart

The chart in Figure 9.6 may be compared to that in Figure 9.4 on page 215. Both the Individuals Chart and the Moving Average Chart detect the lack of control in these data. The Moving Range Chart is the same as that in Figure 9.4 because both charts are based upon n = 2.

Just as on the Moving Range Chart, successive Moving Averages are computed using some of the same Individual Values. This overlap in the data used for successive Moving Averages will undermine the use of detection rules which are based upon runs. For this reason, the authors do not recommend the use of Detection Rules Two, Three, or Four with the Moving Average Chart. It is best to use only Detection Rule One with Moving Average Charts and Moving Range Charts.

Moving Averages will, of necessity, lag behind any shift in the process. This makes the Moving Average Chart initially *less* sensitive to process changes than an *XmR* Chart. While the Moving Average Chart will eventually detect a sustained change or trend in the process, such changes are often seen more quickly on the Individuals Chart. Moreover, the Moving Average Chart will often obscure transitory phenomena. Before a Moving Average will detect a problem, that problem will have to persist for at least *n* time periods. Of course the Moving Range Chart is still available to detect sudden changes in the time series, but this sensitivity drops as the size of the moving subgroup increases.

The Moving Average is a smoothing technique for time series data. It will average out the short-term variation and concentrate attention on the underlying trend. With monthly data, a 12-period Moving Average will average out the seasonal effects and the month-to-month variation and show the basic annual trend based upon the past 12 month's performance. With quarterly data a 4-period Moving Average will work the same way.

Combining all these characteristics, the Moving Average Chart is recommended when the process is slowly changing relative to the sample frequency and the values themselves are subject to considerable variation.

9.5 Three-Way Control Charts

When bulk product is processed in batches there will generally be variation from batch to batch. If the processing itself is done so that there is considerable homogeneity within each batch, then the variation from one batch to the next may be many times greater than the variation within any one batch. When this happens, the regular control chart may not present a realistic picture of the process. In this situation, there is an appropriate way to modify the control chart.

The only way to know that batch-to-batch variation is actually greater than within-batch variation is to measure each. This will of necessity involve multiple observations per batch. If the producer is interested in the within-batch variation, he will have to collect two or more measurements per batch. If the producer is not interested in the within-batch variation, then he may use one measurement per batch.

The *XmR* Chart will be the best chart for data that may be characterized as "one-value-per-batch." When there are several observations per batch a different approach will be needed. Consider the following example:

EXAMPLE 9.5: _____ *The Steel Tensile Strength Data:*

The data in Table 9.5 are tensile strength values for five samples from each of twenty-five heats of steel. These twenty-five heats all met the same specifications, and the 125 samples were all tested by the same tester, on the same day, using the same equipment. The data are subgrouped in such a way that each subgroup uniquely represents one heat. The tensile strengths were measured to the nearest 500 pounds, and were expressed in units of 1000 pounds.

The Grand Average is 55.145, the Average Range is 1.016. With subgroups of size 5 the control limits for the Subgroup Averages are 54.559 to 55.731, and the control limit for the Subgroup Ranges is 2.148. The Average and Range Chart is shown in Figure 9.7.

Table 9.5: Steel Tensile Strength Data

	Tensile Strengths					$\bar{X}$	R		Tensile Strengths					$\bar{X}$	R
1	52.0	52.0	52.5	52.5	52.5	*52.30*	*0.5*	14	55.5	56.0	55.5	55.5	56.5	*55.80*	*1.0*
2	56.0	55.5	56.0	55.5	55.5	*55.70*	*0.5*	15	52.5	52.5	52.5	52.5	52.5	*52.50*	*0.0*
3	54.0	54.0	53.5	54.0	58.0	*54.70*	*4.5*	16	50.5	50.5	50.5	50.5	51.0	*50.60*	*0.5*
4	58.0	58.5	58.0	58.0	58.0	*58.10*	*0.5*	17	53.5	53.5	53.5	53.0	53.5	*53.40*	*0.5*
5	56.5	57.0	57.0	55.0	57.5	*56.60*	*2.5*	18	55.5	55.5	56.0	56.0	56.0	*55.80*	*0.5*
6	49.5	50.0	50.0	50.0	50.0	*49.90*	*0.5*	19	56.0	55.5	56.0	56.0	56.0	*55.90*	*0.5*
7	56.0	55.0	55.0	55.0	55.0	*55.20*	*1.0*	20	54.5	54.5	55.0	55.0	54.5	*54.70*	*0.5*
8	57.5	57.5	57.5	57.5	57.5	*57.50*	*0.0*	21	55.5	55.5	55.5	56.0	56.0	*55.70*	*0.5*
9	53.0	53.0	53.0	53.0	53.0	*53.00*	*0.0*	22	56.5	57.0	56.0	56.0	55.5	*56.20*	*1.5*
10	58.5	58.5	58.5	59.0	58.5	*58.60*	*0.5*	23	55.5	56.0	56.0	56.0	56.0	*55.90*	*0.5*
11	53.5	53.0	53.0	52.5	53.0	*53.00*	*1.0*	24	57.5	57.5	57.5	57.5	57.5	*57.50*	*0.0*
12	57.0	49.6	56.5	56.5	56.5	*55.22*	*7.4*	25	57.5	57.0	57.5	57.0	57.5	*57.30*	*0.5*
13	57.5	57.5	57.5	57.5	57.5	*57.50*	*0.0*								

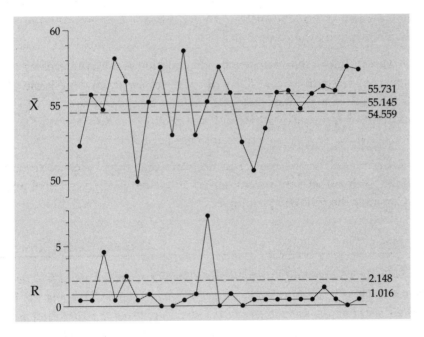

Figure 9.7: Regular Control Chart for Steel Tensile Data

The control chart in Figure 9.7 has the variation within each batch isolated within each subgroup, while the batch-to-batch variation shows up between successive subgroups. The chart shows that the batch-to-batch variation is much greater than the variation within the batches. Since it is the variation within the subgroups that determines the control limits, and since there is no allowance for batch-to-batch variation within the subgroups, one should expect that the control chart in Figure 9.7 would be out-of-control. The within-batch variation is not the proper yardstick for assessing the batch-to-batch variation.

Many situations in practice will result in data which contain more than one basic source of variation. In Chapter Five the Ball Joint Socket Data contained multiple sources of variation, and those data were placed on a control chart in three different ways. The difference between the Ball Joint Socket Data and the Steel Tensile Strength Data is the relationship between these multiple sources of variation. In the Ball Joint Data the Cavity-to-Cavity variation was reduced to the point that it was essentially the same as the Cycle-to-Cycle variation. In the Steel Tensile Strength Data it is unreasonable to expect different batches of steel to be as homogeneous as a single batch of steel. Using the variation within the batches of steel to construct limits will inevitably result in unrealistically tight limits on the Average Chart.

Thus, it comes down to a judgement call. If it is reasonable to assume that the "batch-to-batch" variation can be made as small as the "within-batch" variation, then the control chart in Figure 9.7 is the right chart to use. If this goal is not reasonable for a particular process, then the chart in Figure 9.7 is misleading. In the latter case, the solution for the problem is to obtain control limits which allow for the usual amount of "batch-to-batch" variation. Then the Range Chart will track the "within-batch" variation, and the Average Chart, with revised control limits, will look for excessive "batch-to-batch" variation.

The best way to allow for "batch-to-batch" variation is to measure it directly. This can be done by using a Moving Range on the Subgroup Averages.

EXAMPLE 9.6:   *Three-Way Control Charts for the Steel Tensile Strength Data:*

$\overline{X}$	mR	$\overline{X}$	mR	$\overline{X}$	mR	$\overline{X}$	mR	$\overline{X}$	mR
52.30	—	49.90	6.7	53.00	5.6	50.60	1.9	55.70	1.0
55.70	3.4	55.20	5.3	55.22	2.22	53.40	2.8	56.20	0.5
54.70	1.0	57.50	2.3	57.50	2.28	55.80	2.4	55.90	0.3
58.10	3.4	53.00	4.5	55.80	1.7	55.90	0.1	57.50	1.6
56.60	1.5	58.60	5.6	52.50	3.3	54.70	1.2	57.30	0.2

Using these Moving Ranges the control limits for the Subgroup Averages may be computed as follows:

$$\overline{mR} = 2.533$$

Since these Moving Ranges were computed using the Subgroup Averages:

$$Sigma(\overline{X}) = \frac{\overline{mR}}{d_2} = \frac{2.533}{1.128} = 2.246.$$

So Control Limits for Subgroup Averages are:

$$\overline{\overline{X}} \pm 3\ Sigma(\overline{X}) = 55.145 \pm 6.738 = 48.407\ to\ 61.883$$

It should be noted that while these limits are calculated in the same manner as Natural Process Limits, they are based on the Subgroup Averages. Thus, they are properly called control limits, rather than process limits. The upper control limit for the Moving Ranges is 8.28. If any Moving Range exceeded this limit, then that range would be identifying a sudden shift between subgroups, even if both averages remained within the control limits. The Three Way Control Chart is shown in Figure 9.8.

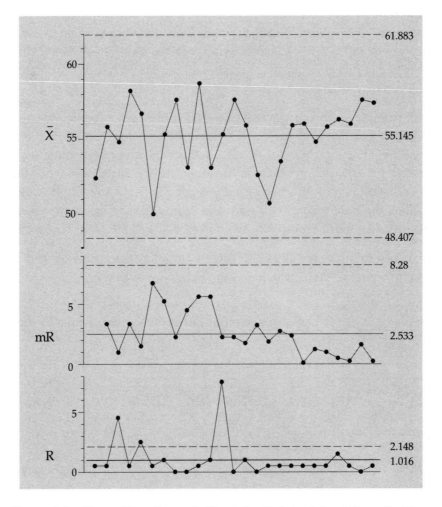

Figure 9.8: Three-Way Control Chart for Original Steel Tensile Data

The Average Chart and the Moving Range Chart monitor the batch-to-batch variation, while the regular Range Chart monitors the within-batch variation. Once these limits are established, they can then be used to monitor further production of the same product. This was done, and the Three Way Control Chart for the next twenty-five heats is shown in Figure 9.9.

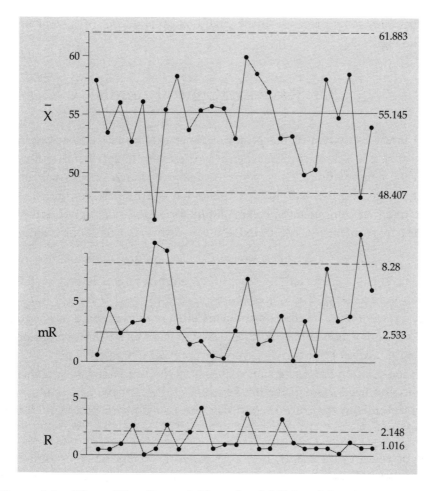

Figure 9.9: Three-Way Control Chart for Additional Steel Tensile Data

CAUTION: This approach should not be used indiscriminately. The Moving Range calculated from the Subgroup Averages should only be used when the physical situation warrants its use.

In particular, for chemical batches: (1) each subgroup should uniquely represent a batch, (2) there should be more than one measurement per batch, (3) the producer should want to monitor both the within-batch variation and the between-batch variation, and (4) it is unrealistic to expect the between-batch variation to be as small as the within-batch variation.

This Three-Way Control Chart approach should only be used when the data contain two inherently different sources of variation, and there is some overriding reason for tracking both sources of variation on one control chart. This technique must always be justified by an appeal to the context. It can never be justified by the behavior of the data alone. Remember, some processes are actually so severely out-of-control that the charts will look like Figure 9.7.

9.6 Revising Control Limits

Control limits computed in the proper manner are robust to a lack of control—they will usually detect a lack of control when it exists even though the out-of-control points are used in the computation. However, out-of-control Range values will tend to inflate the Average Range, and this will, in turn, inflate the width of the computed control limits. Thus, when one first computes the control limits for a particular set of data there may be some interest in revising the computed limits. Two ways of doing this will be given below.

Before one sets out to revise the computed control limits it is best to stop and ask if such revision is necessary. The objective of the control chart is insight in to the process, not practice in arithmetic. If the control chart already shows some out-of-control points the proper course of action is to look for the Assignable Causes of these out-of-control values. Revising the control limits may give you more out-of-control points to look at, but if you are not looking for the Assignable Causes for the out-of-control points you already have, why do you need more of them? Revision of the control chart limits will, in effect, turn up the volume on the control chart. Before you do this, you should ask if it isn't already loud enough.

Instead of revising the limits, it is best to work on finding the Assignable Causes which are already identified by the chart. As you find and remove Assignable Causes you will need to collect new data and compute new control limits following each change. (See Figure 4.21, page 81, to see how the removal of Assignable Causes does not just bring the process back to the status quo, but can actually result in process improvement.) Thus, if one is going to revise the limits as one finds and removes Assignable Causes, it is not imperative that the initial control limits identify *all* of the Assignable Causes. Rather, they just need to identify enough out-of-control points to help the user find some of the Assignable Causes.

Given these precautions, there are still times when the ability to revise the control limits is useful. The most straightforward way of doing this is to delete any out-of-control ranges from the computation of the Average Range, and then to recompute the limits. This cycle may be repeated until no further ranges fall outside the control limits.

(The same operation may be performed deleting the out-of-control Subgroup Averages to revise the Grand Average. However, since the impact of this operation will be only a slight adjustment in the central line for the Average Chart, it is considered to be optional.)

EXAMPLE 9.7:   *Revising the Limits for the Batch Weight Data:*

The Batch Weight Data were placed on an XmR Chart in Example 9.2. This chart is shown in Figure 9.4, page 215. The Moving Range Chart had an out-of-control value. When this out-of-control range value is deleted the Average Range becomes 25.93 and the revised limits for the XmR Chart are:

$$UNPL_X = 936.89 + 2.66\ (25.93) = 1005.9$$
$$CL_X = 936.89$$
$$LNPL_X = 936.89 - 2.66\ (25.93) = 867.9$$
$$UCL_R = 3.268\ (25.93) = 84.7$$
$$CL_R = 25.93$$

Since no additional range values are found to exceed 84.7, these limits may be used without further revision. The XmR Chart for these data is shown in Figure 9.10.

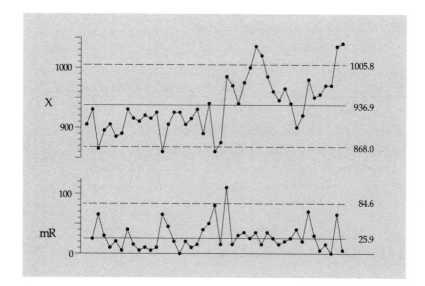

Figure 9.10: *XmR* Chart for Batch Weights with Revised Limits

Instead of the delete and revise approach, some prefer to revise the control chart limits by using the Median Range.

Since out-of-control ranges tend to be excessively large the Average Range tends to be inflated by such points. The Median Range depends upon the *ranking* of the range values rather than their specific values, and therefore is not so severely affected by extreme values as is the Average Range. Computing control limits using the Median Range will provide a revised set of limits without the necessity of going through one or more cycles of deletion and revision.

While it is possible to obtain a Median Range by inspection of the Range Chart, the best way to find a Median Range is to begin with a histogram of the range values. This will be less error prone, and easier to use should one need to check one's work. The Median Range is defined by the 50th percentile of the range histogram. Once the Median Range has been found, the control chart limits are computed using the control chart constants and formulas given in Tables A.1 and A.3 in the Appendix.

While some prefer to *always* use the Median Range instead of the Average Range, this is not the best practice. First of all, most people are not accustomed to finding a median. So while they know how to compute an average, they may need some coaching on how to find a Median Range. Secondly, the Median Range yields control limits which are effectively based upon only two-thirds of the data. So while the Median Range will do better when the ranges are out-of-control, it will be less efficient than the Average Range when the ranges are in-control. Thus, before one deliberately uses a procedure that is less efficient and more trouble, one should have a good reason for making the selection. This is why the authors recommend using the Median Range only when there is a definite reason for believing the Average Range to be inflated.

EXAMPLE 9.8:   *Limits for Batch Weights Using the Median Range:*

A Stem and Leaf Plot for the Moving Ranges for the first 45 values from the Batch Weight Data is shown in Figure 9.11. With 44 values, the median is the average of the 22nd and 23rd values from either end of the histogram. Thus, the Median Moving Range is:

$$\tilde{R} = 20$$

Using this value, the Sigma(X) value becomes:

$$Sigma(X) = \frac{\tilde{R}}{d_4} = \frac{20}{0.954} = 20.96$$

And the limits for the XmR Chart become:

$$\bar{\bar{X}} \pm \frac{3\,\tilde{R}}{d_4} \quad and \quad D_6\,\tilde{R}$$

$$UNPL_X = 936.89 + 3\,(20.96) = 999.8$$
$$CL_X = 936.89$$
$$LNPL_X = 936.89 - 3\,(20.96) = 874.0$$
$$UCL_R = 3.865\,(20) = 77.3$$
$$CL_R = 20$$

```
 0 | 00
 0 | 55555
 1 | 0000
 1 | 5555555
 2 | 00000
 2 | 5555
 3 | 000
 3 | 555
 4 | 000
 4 | 5
 5 | 0
 5 |
 6 | 0
 6 | 555
 7 |
 7 |
 8 | 0
 8 |
 9 |
 9 |
10 |
10 |
11 | 0
```

Figure 9.11

The XmR chart with these revised limits is shown in Figure 9.12.

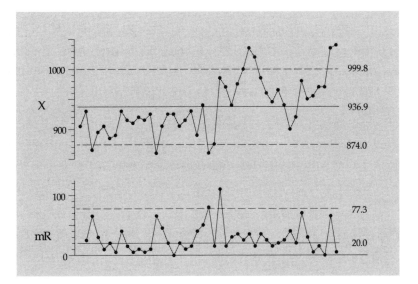

Figure 9.12: *XmR* **Chart for Batch Weight Data**
With Limits Based On Median Range

9.7 Updating Control Chart Limits

While the revision of control chart limits applies to the initial computation of limits for a given set of data, the updating of control chart limits pertains to the modification of existing limits on an ongoing chart.

An obvious time for updating the control limits is following a change in the process. It is a poor use of a control chart to make it prove what is already known. Instead, one should use the chart to discover that which is not known. So when a deliberate change is made, it is logical to collect data following the change and these new data may be used to compute new control limits. While the new data are being collected following the change, and prior to the computation of the new control limits, the new data may be plotted against the old limits as a means of verifying the change in the process. If a change is indicated, then the new limits are needed. If the new data "fit in with" the old limits, there is little need to update them.[2]

Another time to consider updating the control limits is when the limits are "trial control limits." Trial control limits are control limits computed from a limited amount of data. Of course, when there is only a finite amount of data available this issue is moot. One may always compute control limits using the data available, and any signals found

---

[2] For further information on how to accommodate deliberate process changes see *Short Run SPC*.

using trial control limits are likely to be real signals.[3] Thus, one does not have to wait until a large amount of data have been obtained before computing control limits. But when the limits for an ongoing control chart are computed from the first few subgroups, and then additional data are collected, it is generally recommended that the limits be updated when 20 to 30 subgroups are available. This recommendation of 20 to 30 subgroups is essentially a piece of insurance. By using 20 to 30 Subgroup Ranges in the computation of the Average Range the effect of any extreme value will be diluted and minimized. Of course, a single Subgroup Range that is, say, 10 times bigger than the Average Range will still dominate the computation and inflate the Average Range, but Subgroup Ranges that are just outside the control limits will have a fairly small impact when averaged in with 20 to 30 other values.

When updating trial control limits one may also elect to use either the delete and revise approach or the Median Range approach outlined in the preceding section. The objective is to use the data available to obtain reasonable and useful limits in as straightforward a manner as possible.

Finally, once the control limits are computed using about 100 observations there will generally be little change in the limits with further updates. Unless the process is changed, or changes in some fundamental way, the limits should not need further updates. The practice of automatically recomputing control limits every time a control chart form is filled up, and then using these latest limits on the next sheet, may result in the failure to detect slow trends in the process. Likewise, the automatic updating of control chart limits in some computer programs will, by default, use all of the data available, even though some of those data may no longer be appropriate for the current process.

The control chart is a versatile tool for use in real-time situations. Therefore, one should always actively control the manner in which the control chart limits are computed in order to be sure that the limits are appropriate for the current process. The computation of the limits cannot be divorced from the context for the chart.

---

[3] The reader is referred to the first example in Chapter Eight to see this in practice.

9.8 Charts for the Subgroup Median and Subgroup Range

While the computation of the Subgroup Average and the Subgroup Range is not very difficult, it can often be made easier by coding the data so as to avoid both negative numbers and numbers that are excessively large. If, however, the calculation of averages and ranges proves to be a barrier for those keeping a control chart, one may chart the Subgroup Medians and Subgroup Ranges instead.

The advantage of charting the Subgroup Medians and Subgroup Ranges is that, aside from the occasional computation of control limits, these charts can be maintained without any arithmetic.

A chart for the Subgroup Median begins with a graph on which every Individual Value is plotted. The observations in any particular subgroup are plotted in a column on the graph, and the median value for the subgroup is circled. In order to make it simple to find the Subgroup Median, the subgroup size should always be an odd number.

When there are three observations per subgroup, the Subgroup Median will be the middle value of the three. For five observations per subgroup, the median value will be the third from the largest. With seven observations, the median will be the fourth from the largest. Thus, in order to find the Subgroup Median, one only needs to count from the top down or from the bottom up.

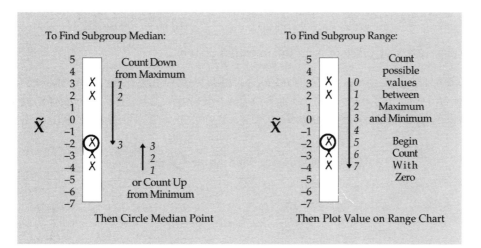

Figure 9.13: Finding Subgroup Medians and Subgroup Ranges

The Subgroup Range is also found by counting. Beginning with a count of *zero*, count all the *possible* values, starting with either the maximum observation and proceeding down through the minimum observation, or vice versa. The value for this Subgroup Range can then be plotted on a regular Range Chart.

When keeping charts for the Subgroup Median and Subgroup Range, it is important that whoever sets up the charts should be careful to make the job of plotting the points as easy as possible. Some obvious things to watch for are: Is the scale of the graph paper large enough? Do not use paper with closely spaced lines for these graphs. Is the scale clearly labeled? At least *every other possible value* should be written on *both* edges of the sheet, and in the middle as well. Are the possible values for both the Median Chart and the Range Chart sufficient to cover what will be seen in practice? If the plotting is made easy enough, then useful control charts can be obtained even though the Subgroup Median is not as efficient as the Subgroup Average.

The central line for the Median Chart is usually the average of the Subgroup Medians. (Occasionally one might use the median of the Subgroup Medians instead.) The central line for the Range Chart may be Average Range or the Median Range. The formulas for the control limits are:

$$UCL_{\tilde{X}} = \bar{\bar{X}} + A_6\,\bar{R} \qquad \text{or} \qquad UCL_{\tilde{X}} = \bar{\bar{X}} + A_9\,\tilde{R}$$

$$CL_{\tilde{X}} = \bar{\bar{X}} \qquad\qquad\qquad\qquad CL_{\tilde{X}} = \bar{\bar{X}}$$

$$LCL_{\tilde{X}} = \bar{\bar{X}} - A_6\,\bar{R} \qquad\qquad LCL_{\tilde{X}} = \bar{\bar{X}} - A_9\,\tilde{R}$$

$$UCL_R = D_4\,\bar{R} \qquad\qquad\qquad UCL_R = D_6\,\tilde{R}$$

$$CL_R = \bar{R} \qquad\qquad\qquad\qquad CL_R = \tilde{R}$$

$$LCL_R = D_3\,\bar{R} \qquad\qquad\qquad LCL_R = D_5\,\tilde{R}$$

One may use $\tilde{\tilde{X}}$ in place of $\bar{\bar{X}}$ in the formulas above.

The control chart constants for finding Median and Range Charts are shown in Table 9.6 below and also in Tables A.6 and A.7 in the Appendix. The use of these formulas will be illustrated in the following example.

Table 9.6: Factors for Median and Range Charts

n	A_6	D_3	D_4	n	A_9	D_5	D_6
3	1.187	—	2.574	3	1.265	—	2.745
5	0.691	—	2.114	5	0.712	—	2.179
7	0.509	0.076	1.924	7	0.520	0.078	1.967
9	0.412	0.184	1.816	9	0.419	0.187	1.850

EXAMPLE 9.9:   *Median and Range Charts:*

Exercise 3.1, p.52, gives the weights of 100 consecutively produced rubber parts. These 100 values have been arranged into 20 subgroups of size 5. The values recorded below are the deviations from the target weight, measured in grams.

subgroup	values					$\tilde{X}$	R	subgroup	values					$\tilde{X}$	R
1	3	−3	−2	2	−4	−2	7	11	2	2	−1	−8	−7	−1	10
2	−6	−2	−5	−2	5	−2	11	12	5	3	6	13	1	5	12
3	5	3	2	6	2	3	4	13	−2	−2	4	9	1	1	11
4	4	7	11	6	3	6	8	14	6	7	1	3	2	3	6
5	3	−2	3	−1	−3	−1	6	15	5	2	9	5	−3	5	12
6	4	−1	−2	2	3	2	6	16	−3	−5	−1	−2	−1	−2	4
7	−4	−11	−5	−7	−5	−5	7	17	3	−1	−1	1	−2	−1	5
8	−6	15	−5	−1	−1	−1	21	18	−3	2	−7	−9	−1	−3	11
9	1	3	7	−6	2	2	13	19	−3	−2	−6	−2	−6	−3	4
10	−1	−5	1	2	1	1	7	20	−8	−2	4	−1	−1	−1	12

For the first subgroup, the median is −2 and the range is 7 (see Figure 9.13). For the second subgroup, the median is −2 and the range is 11. The average of the Subgroup Medians is 0.30, and the Average Subgroup Range is 8.85. Using the control chart constants of A_6, D_3 and D_4 found in Table A.6 in the Appendix the control limits for the Median and Range Chart are:

$$UCL_{\tilde{X}} = \bar{\bar{X}} + A_6 \, \bar{R} = 0.30 + 0.691 \, (8.85) = 6.4$$

$$CL_{\tilde{X}} = \bar{\bar{X}} = 0.30$$

$$LCL_{\tilde{X}} = \bar{\bar{X}} - A_6 \, \bar{R} = 0.30 - 0.691 \, (8.85) = -5.8$$

$$UCL_R = D_4 \, \bar{R} = 2.114 \, (8.85) = 18.7$$

$$CL_R = \bar{R} = 8.85$$

While none of the Subgroup Medians falls outside these initial limits, one Subgroup Range is above its upper control limit.

Since the Range Chart is out of control, the possibility exists that the control limits based upon the Average Range may be inflated. As a check on this, the Median Range is used to find revised control limits. The Median Range is 7.5. Using the control chart constants of A_9, D_5 and D_6 found in Table A.7 in the Appendix the revised control limits for the Median and Range Chart are:

$$UCL_{\tilde{X}} = \bar{\bar{X}} + A_9 \, \tilde{R} = 0.30 + 0.712 \, (7.5) = 5.6$$

$$CL_{\tilde{X}} = \bar{\bar{X}} = 0.30$$

$$LCL_{\tilde{X}} = \bar{\bar{X}} - A_9 \, \tilde{R} = 0.30 - 0.712 \, (7.5) = -5.04$$

$$UCL_R = D_6 \, \tilde{R} = 2.179 \, (7.5) = 16.3$$

$$CL_R = \tilde{R} = 7.5$$

These slightly tighter limits show one Subgroup Median and one Subgroup Range to be out-of-control. These are the limits shown in Figure 9.14.

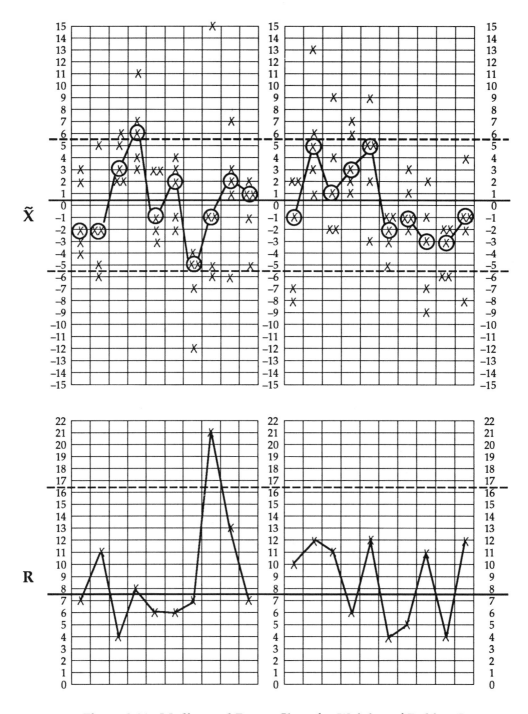

Figure 9.14: Median and Range Chart for Weights of Rubber Parts

Except for the calculation of the control limits, there is no arithmetic required to maintain the control charts for the Subgroup Median and the Subgroup Range. While this may be an advantage, there is one drawback to the use of these charts. The chart for the Subgroup Medians will never be as sensitive as the regular control chart for Subgroup Averages. It will always be slower in responding to changes in the process than the Average Chart would be. In general, shifting from the Subgroup Average to the Subgroup Median is roughly equivalent to reducing the subgroup size by two observations. This lack of sensitivity for the Median Chart can be seen by comparing the chart in Figure 9.14 with the Average Chart in Figure 9.15. While the Median Chart finally shows one Subgroup Median to be out of control, the Average Chart shows three Subgroup Averages to be out of control.

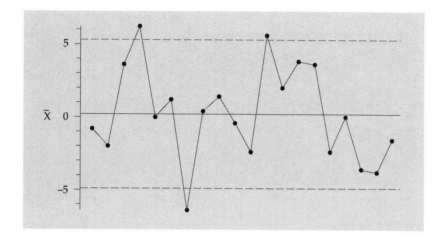

Figure 9.15: Average Chart for Weights of Rubber Parts

So, the Average Chart is more sensitive than the Median Chart. It should always be preferred over a Median Chart. However, a Median Chart should always be preferred over the alternative of no chart at all. If those keeping the charts can not or will not do the arithmetic required for Average and Range Charts, then Median and Range Charts can be used in their place.

Table 9.7: 100 Subgroups of Size 5 Drawn From A "Stable System"

Values	$\bar{X}$	R	Values	$\bar{X}$	R	Values	$\bar{X}$	R
12 9 9 8 9	9.4	4	9 10 10 11 10	10.0	2	10 12 11 9 13	11.0	4
11 13 11 11 11	11.4	2	11 8 11 9 11	10.0	3	10 7 11 8 13	9.8	6
14 6 11 8 9	9.6	8	12 11 13 8 10	10.8	5	12 10 9 8 13	10.4	5
10 12 13 8 10	10.6	5	9 11 11 11 11	10.6	2	12 10 11 10 10	10.6	2
11 10 12 11 8	10.4	4	13 11 10 7 7	9.6	6	11 10 12 10 9	10.4	3
7 10 7 7 9	8.0	3	10 9 13 10 12	10.8	4	7 8 12 10 10	9.4	5
12 12 14 7 10	11.0	7	8 9 7 10 11	9.0	4	8 9 11 9 8	9.0	3
11 10 9 10 10	10.0	2	7 15 7 8 11	9.6	8	9 14 12 12 11	11.6	5
9 9 11 11 9	9.8	2	11 9 10 11 13	10.8	4	7 8 9 9 9	8.4	2
11 12 10 9 11	10.6	3	10 13 10 9 11	10.6	4	12 9 10 10 9	10.0	3
9 10 11 11 10	10.2	2	12 9 7 13 13	10.8	6	10 8 12 9 11	10.0	4
9 9 10 11 7	9.2	4	9 11 9 10 9	9.6	2	12 10 10 10 13	11.0	3
7 10 12 11 10	10.0	5	8 15 11 10 9	10.6	7	8 9 9 11 7	8.8	4
8 10 11 9 10	9.6	3	7 9 5 12 13	9.2	8	9 9 10 8 9	9.0	2
10 8 11 12 11	10.4	4	10 9 10 11 10	10.0	2	10 9 7 9 9	8.8	3
11 8 9 11 7	9.2	4	12 12 10 11 11	11.2	2	11 7 5 9 8	8.0	6
9 9 11 11 8	9.6	3	11 11 12 10 14	11.6	4	9 11 11 10 9	10.0	2
12 9 11 10 6	9.6	6	12 9 12 9 9	10.2	3	12 10 13 12 13	12.0	3
12 11 10 15 12	12.0	5	8 10 14 13 9	10.8	6	12 10 11 8 12	10.6	4
9 12 11 9 9	10.0	3	10 10 10 14 11	11.0	4	10 9 12 9 13	10.6	4
13 11 12 7 8	10.2	6	11 11 8 11 7	9.6	4	11 12 9 11 7	10.0	5
9 9 13 8 7	9.2	6	10 9 11 8 10	9.6	3	7 8 13 10 10	9.6	6
10 12 9 11 10	10.4	3	11 11 10 10 13	11.0	3	9 9 8 7 9	8.4	2
8 8 12 10 8	9.2	4	12 11 5 9 7	8.8	7	9 10 11 9 7	9.2	4
9 13 7 10 13	10.4	6	11 9 9 11 12	10.4	3	10 11 11 9 10	10.2	2
11 10 12 10 10	10.6	2	14 11 14 10 8	11.4	6	12 9 13 9 8	10.2	5
11 9 9 8 8	9.0	3	9 10 10 15 11	11.0	6	11 13 11 11 7	10.6	6
11 12 8 12 10	10.6	4	10 13 7 12 10	10.4	6	7 8 9 10 8	8.4	3
11 14 8 13 8	10.8	6	11 9 12 10 13	11.0	4	9 11 12 11 9	10.4	3
14 12 9 9 10	10.8	5	6 10 11 10 10	9.4	5	9 10 9 10 10	9.6	1
9 11 13 10 7	10.0	6	10 10 11 7 10	9.6	4			
10 11 10 12 11	10.8	2	10 12 12 8 10	10.4	4			
9 10 9 13 14	11.0	5	13 7 11 12 11	10.8	6			
12 10 9 8 8	9.4	4	12 10 7 10 9	9.6	5			
9 7 14 12 9	10.2	7	9 9 9 10 10	9.4	1			

236

9.9 From Where Do Those Control Chart Constants Come?

The control limit formulas given in Appendix Tables A.2 through A.7 are cookbook formulas which depend upon tabled constants such as A_2, D_3, and D_4. While these constants make the computations easy, they do not make the structure of the control limits visible. While some are content to use the cookbook formulas, others want to know what the constants represent. This section is for this latter group. Here the structure of the control chart formulas will be explained, and the make-up of the control chart constants will be shown.

We begin with some data. Table 9.7 shows 100 subgroups of size five obtained from a quincunx (a bead board).

No changes were made in the settings of the quincunx while these data were obtained, thus they may be considered to have been obtained from a stable system of chance causes, and should therefore display a reasonable degree of statistical control. They do.

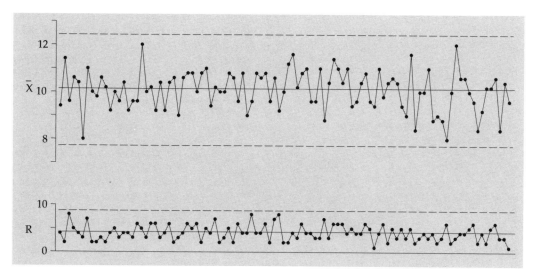

Figure 9.16: Average and Range Chart for Data of Table 9.7

The histograms for the 500 Individual Values, the 100 Subgroup Averages, and the 100 Subgroup Ranges are shown in Figure 9.17. The horizontal scales for the three histograms are the same, but the vertical scales differ in order to make the areas of the three histograms the same.

One should note that the histogram for Subgroup Averages will *always* be narrower than the histogram for Individual Values. This is why it is inappropriate to compare specification limits with control limits for Subgroup Averages.

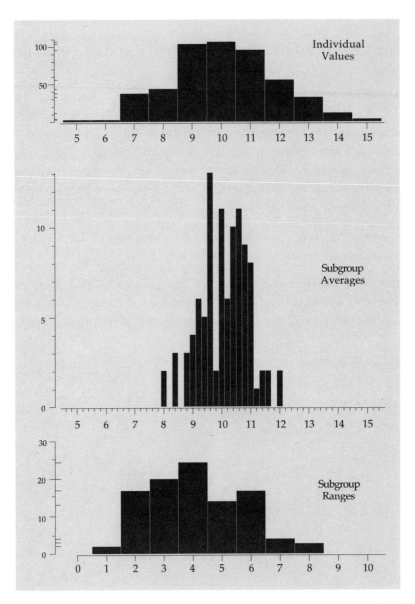

Figure 9.17: Histograms for Individuals, Averages, and Ranges of Table 9.7

The problem of constructing control limits is essentially the problem of how to place bounds on the three histograms in Figure 9.17. To do this we shall use certain theoretical relationships as a guide. Therefore, we shall need the traditional theoretical models for the three histograms shown in Figure 9.17. These three models are shown in Figure 9.18.

Each of the theoretical distributions in Figure 9.18 may be characterized by a location parameter and a dispersion parameter:

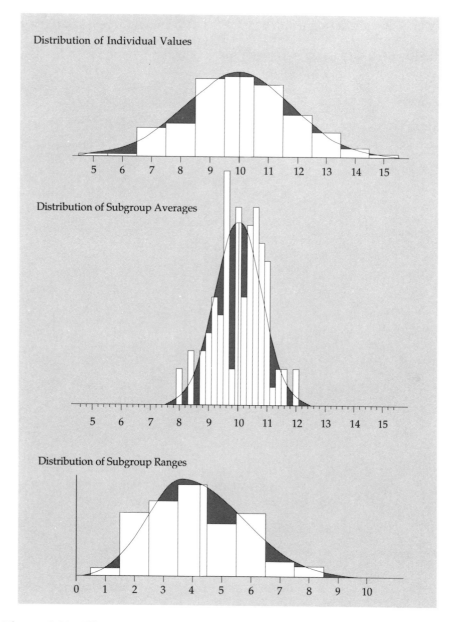

Figure 9.18: Theoretical Models for Individuals, Averages, and Ranges Drawn From A Stable Process

MEAN(X) = the location parameter for the distribution of Individual Values.

MEAN($\overline{X}$) = the location parameter for the distribution of Subgroup Averages.

MEAN(R) = the location parameter for the distribution of Subgroup Ranges.

SD(X) = the dispersion parameter for the distribution of Individual Values.

$SD(\bar{X})$ = the dispersion parameter for the distribution of Subgroup Averages.

$SD(R)$ = the dispersion parameter for the distribution of Subgroup Ranges.

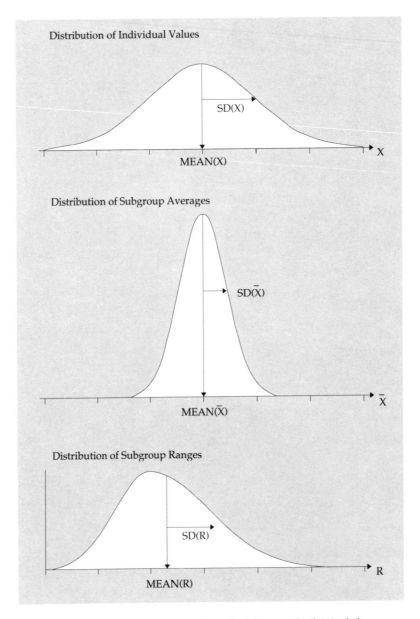

**Figure 9.19: Parameters for the Theoretical Models
for Individuals, Averages, and Ranges Drawn From A Stable Process**

The six parameters of Figure 9.19 are related. The parameters of the distribution of Subgroup Averages may be expressed in terms of those of the distribution of X. Likewise, the parameters for the distribution of Subgroup Ranges may be expressed in terms of SD(X).

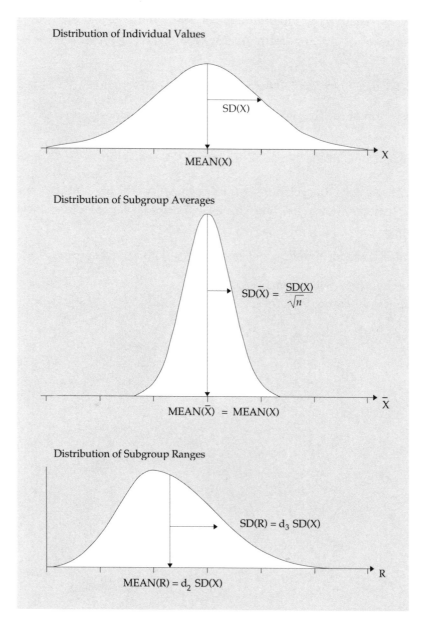

Figure 9.20: Relationships Between Parameters for the Theoretical Models for Individuals, Averages, and Ranges Drawn From A Stable Process

These relationships are shown in Figure 9.20. It is these relationships which we will use to develop formulas for the limits for the histograms in Figure 9.17.

Returning to the histograms of Figure 9.17 we begin our development of formulas for control chart limits with measures of location for each histogram. The two common measures of location are the balance point (averages) and the 50th percentile (medians). Here we shall use the balance point to define the location of the histograms.

The histogram of the Subgroup Averages will have a balance point defined by the Grand Average:

$$\text{Balance Point for } \bar{X} \text{ Histogram } = \text{ Grand Average } = \bar{\bar{X}} = 10.084$$

The histogram of the Subgroup Ranges will have a balance point defined by the Average Range:

$$\text{Balance Point for Range Histogram } = \text{ Average Range } = \bar{R} = 4.11$$

Finally, based upon the relationship between MEAN(X) and MEAN($\bar{X}$) shown in Figure 9.20, the histogram of Individual Values will also have a balance point defined by the Grand Average:

$$\text{Balance Point for Individuals Histogram } = \text{ Grand Average } = \bar{\bar{X}} = 10.084$$

Thus two averages will summarize the location of all three histograms. These balance points are shown in Figure 9.21.

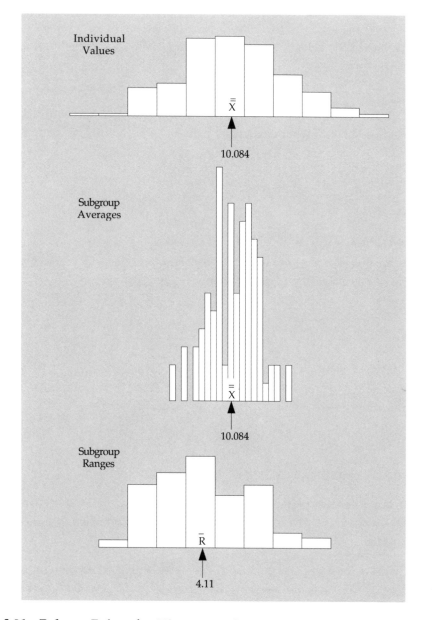

Figure 9.21: Balance Points for Histograms for Individuals, Averages, and Ranges

Next we must characterize the dispersion of each of these histograms. Rather than use the direct (and naive) approach of measuring the dispersion of each histogram directly, we use the information already available, based upon the relationships shown in Figure 9.20.

STEP ONE:

Figure 9.21 shows the balance point for the Range Histogram to be the Average Range:

$$\text{Balance point for Range Histogram} = \bar{R}$$

Figure 9.20 shows $\text{MEAN}(R) = d_2\,\text{SD}(X)$. Thus, these two relationships can be combined to obtain the following statistic as a measure of the dispersion of the Individual Values:

$$Sigma(X) \;=\; \frac{\bar{R}}{d_2}$$

STEP TWO:

Figure 9.20 shows $\text{SD}(\bar{X}) = \text{SD}(X)\big/\sqrt{n}$.

This relationship plus the measure of dispersion from Step One above yields the following statistic as a measure of dispersion for Subgroup Averages:

$$Sigma(\bar{X}) \;=\; \frac{\bar{R}}{d_2\sqrt{n}}$$

STEP THREE:

Figure 9.20 shows $\text{SD}(R) = d_3\,\text{SD}(X)$.

This relationship plus the measure of dispersion from Step One above yields the following statistic as a measure of dispersion for Subgroup Ranges:

$$Sigma(R) \;=\; \frac{d_3\,\bar{R}}{d_2}$$

These measures of dispersion are shown in Figure 9.22.

While the use of the Average Range as the basis for every measure of dispersion is very convenient, and while it offers a considerable economy of effort, there is a more fundamental reason for its use in the formulas above.

The use of an *average dispersion statistic* is a deliberate part of the control chart technique. Rather than directly summarizing the dispersion of each histogram with separate dispersion statistics, the control chart approach intentionally uses the average of the *k* subgroup dispersion statistics in the computation of limits.

As can be seen in the various examples where limits are deliberately computed in the wrong manner, alternatives to this deliberate use of an average dispersion statistic simply do not work. *With the exception of control charts for Count Data (see Chapter 10), control chart limits must be based upon either an average dispersion statistic or a median dispersion statistic.*

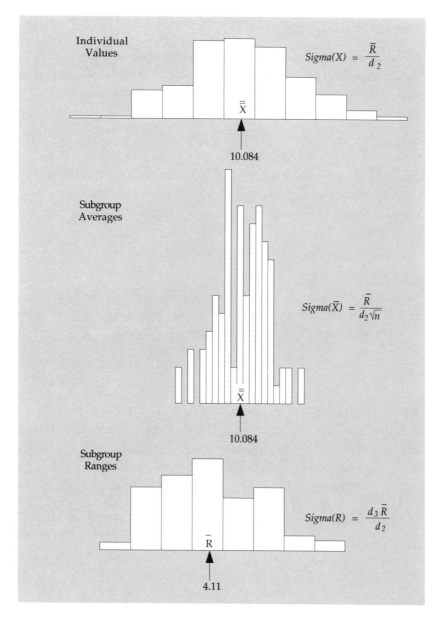

Individual Values

$$Sigma(X) = \frac{\bar{R}}{d_2}$$

$\bar{\bar{X}}$

10.084

Subgroup Averages

$$Sigma(\bar{X}) = \frac{\bar{R}}{d_2\sqrt{n}}$$

$\bar{\bar{X}}$

10.084

Subgroup Ranges

$$Sigma(R) = \frac{d_3\bar{R}}{d_2}$$

$\bar{R}$

4.11

Figure 9.22: Balance Points and Measures of Dispersion for Histograms for Individuals, Averages, and Ranges

Notice the economy of the formulas above. The location and dispersion of three different histograms (6 characteristics) are summarized using two basic statistics. While this simplifies the computation of control limits, the structure of these measures of dispersion is also the basis for the robustness of the traditional control chart formulas.

These measures of location and dispersion may be combined to obtain the formulas for three-sigma limits shown in Figure 9.23.

Three *Sigma(X)* values are added to, and subtracted from, the balance point for the Individual Values to obtain the three-sigma limits for Individual Values. These limits are properly called Natural Process Limits.

$$\text{Natural Process Limits for } X \ = \ \overline{\overline{X}} \pm 3 \ \frac{\overline{R}}{d_2}$$

Three *Sigma(X̄)* values are added to, and subtracted from, the balance point for the Subgroup Averages to obtain the three-sigma limits for Subgroup Averages. These limits are properly called Control Limits for Subgroup Averages.

$$\text{Control Limits for } \overline{X} \ = \ \overline{\overline{X}} \pm \frac{3 \, \overline{R}}{d_2 \sqrt{n}}$$

Three *Sigma(R)* values are added to, and subtracted from, the balance point for the Subgroup Ranges to obtain the three sigma limits for Subgroup Ranges. These limits are properly called Control Limits for Subgroup Ranges.

$$\text{Control Limits for } R \ = \ \overline{R} \pm \frac{3 \, d_3 \, \overline{R}}{d_2}$$

Thus, "three-sigma limits" is an approach rather than a fixed distance. Three-sigma limits are all found using the same principle, but different variables will have different sets of limits. The formulas above reveal the three-sigma structure of the control chart limits. The traditional computational formulas obscure this structure.

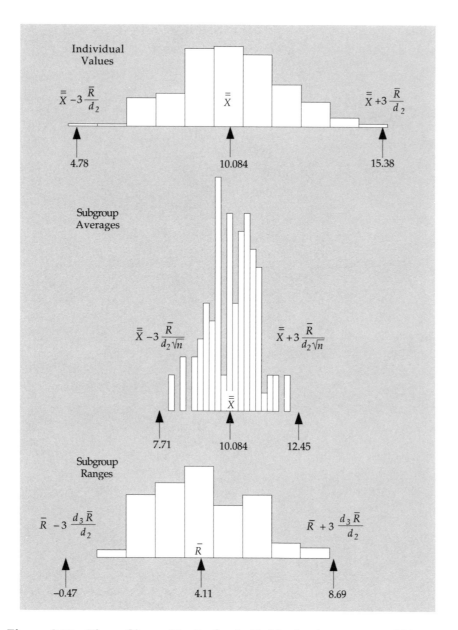

Figure 9.23: Three Sigma Limits for Individuals, Averages, and Ranges

By comparing the formulas in Figure 9.23 with the usual control chart formulas shown in Table A.2 the structure of the control chart constants for Average and Range Charts may be seen to be:

$$A_2 = \frac{3}{d_2 \sqrt{n}} \qquad D_3 = 1 - \frac{3d_3}{d_2} \qquad D_4 = 1 + \frac{3d_3}{d_2}$$

These formulas express the control chart constants for Average and Range Charts in terms of the basic quantities d_2, d_3 and the subgroup size n.

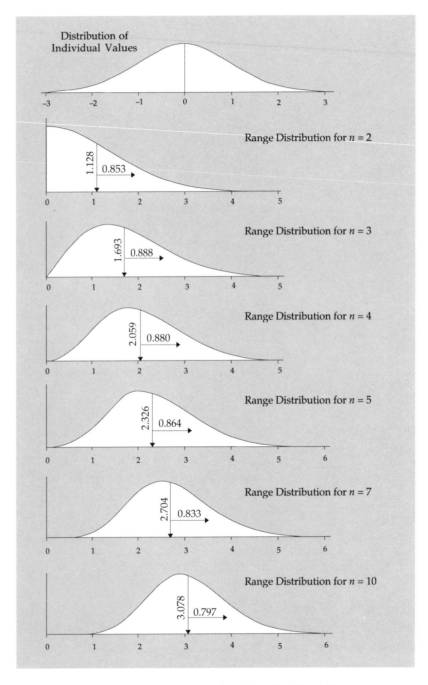

Figure 9.24: Distributions for Standardized Ranges

For a given subgroup size, n, the constants d_2 and d_3 are, respectively, the mean and standard deviation of the theoretical distribution for the standardized ranges (under the assumption of normally distributed Individual Values). Some of these distributions are shown in Figure 9.24. The values of d_2 and d_3 are shown in Table A.1 of the Appendix.

Graphs similar to Figure 9.24 could be drawn for the other fundamental constants given in Table A.1 of the Appendix. The formulas for the control chart constants are also given in Tables A.2 through A.7 of the Appendix.

Exercise 9.1:

Figure 7.14, p.164, shows a portion of the Tokai Rika Cigar Lighter Socket Chart where the limits were revised following the installation of a new positioning collar. The new limits are noticeably tighter than the earlier limits.

(a) How many possible values are found within the limits on the Range Chart?

(b) Did the process suddenly get better on October 1?

Exercise 9.2:

The Range Chart in Figure 9.7, page 222, is out-of-control.

(a) Delete the out-of-control values and revise the control limits for the Range Chart. Continue this procedure until all the ranges used in computing the Average Range are within the control limits.

(b) What problem do the revised Range Charts display?

(c) What source of variation is obscured by this problem? How could this problem be solved?

(d) Use the 25 Subgroup Ranges shown in Table 9.5, p.222, to find the Median Range, and use this value to compute revised control limits for the Range Chart.

(e) Which upper limit for the Range Chart was used in Figures 9.8 and 9.9?

(f) What do the out-of-control Subgroup Ranges in Figure 9.9 represent?

(g) What do the out-of-control Subgroup Averages in Figure 9.9 represent?

(h) Look at the original data in Table 9.5, p.222. Given the description of the data in the example, can you find the anomaly among the Individual Values?

Exercise 9.3:

Twenty-four hourly readings of the percent lime concentration are shown below.

Hour	%CaO	Hour	% CaO	Hour	%CaO
1	0.19	9	0.10	17	0.14
2	0.13	10	0.14	18	0.16
3	0.11	11	0.17	19	0.14
4	0.19	12	0.14	20	0.10
5	0.16	13	0.16	21	0.13
6	0.17	14	0.15	22	0.20
7	0.13	15	0.20	23	0.26
8	0.17	16	0.16	24	0.16

(a) Use these 24 values to construct an XmR Chart.

(b) The next 12 hourly readings for percent lime are:

0.01 0.18 0.18 0.20 0.11 0.30 0.21 0.11 0.17 0.18 0.13 0.28

Plot these values on a continuation of the XmR chart found in part (a).

(c) What does the continuation of the XmR Chart reveal about the behavior of this process?

Exercise 9.4:

Twenty-four hourly readings of the percent lime concentration are shown below.

Hour	%CaO	Hour	% CaO	Hour	%CaO
1	0.19	9	0.10	17	0.14
2	0.13	10	0.14	18	0.16
3	0.11	11	0.17	19	0.14
4	0.19	12	0.14	20	0.10
5	0.16	13	0.16	21	0.13
6	0.17	14	0.15	22	0.20
7	0.13	15	0.20	23	0.26
8	0.17	16	0.16	24	0.16

(a) Use these 24 values to construct a two-period Moving Average Chart.

(b) The next 12 hourly readings for percent lime are:
0.01 0.18 0.18 0.20 0.11 0.30 0.21 0.11 0.17 0.18 0.13 0.28

Plot these values on the continuation of the Moving Average Chart.

(c) What does the Moving Average Chart reveal about this process?

(d) Is the Moving Range Chart a useful addition to the Moving average Chart?

(e) Which chart is easier to use for these periodic data, the XmR Chart or the Moving Average Chart?

Exercise 9.5:

Twenty-four hourly readings of the percent lime concentration are shown below.

Hour	%CaO	Hour	% CaO	Hour	%CaO
1	0.19	9	0.10	17	0.14
2	0.13	10	0.14	18	0.16
3	0.11	11	0.17	19	0.14
4	0.19	12	0.14	20	0.10
5	0.16	13	0.16	21	0.13
6	0.17	14	0.15	22	0.20
7	0.13	15	0.20	23	0.26
8	0.17	16	0.16	24	0.16

(a) Use these 24 values to construct an Average and Range Chart with 12 subgroups of size 2.

(b) The next 12 hourly readings for percent lime are:

0.01 0.18 0.18 0.20 0.11 0.30 0.21 0.11 0.17 0.18 0.13 0.28

Use these 12 values to plot the next six subgroups on the Average and Range Chart.

(c) Where do the signals in these data show up on this Average and Range Chart?

(d) Which chart is the most revealing for these data, the XmR Chart, the Moving Average Chart, or the Average and Range Chart?

(e) Which principle of subgrouping is violated by this Average and Range Chart?

Exercise 9.6:

The first ten values in Table 2.3, page 32, are: 1.3750, 1.3751, 1.37505, 1.3749, 1.3750, 1.3743, 1.3742, 1.3745, 1.3747, and 1.3749. By subtracting 1.3700 from each value, and then moving the decimal over four places, these ten values can be rewritten as:

50, 51, 50.5, 49, 50, 43, 42, 45, 47, and 49.

(a) Compute the average of these ten transformed values.

(b) Use the ten transformed values to find 9 Moving Ranges, and compute the Average Moving Range.

(c) Compute the Natural Process Limits for these Individual Values, and compare them with the running record shown in Figure 2.4 on page 33 or the values on page 32.

(d) Do any of the Diameters for Camshaft Bearing Three fall outside these Natural Process Limits? What does this say about the fabrication process for Bearing Three?

(e) Are any of the Moving Ranges out-of-control? What impact does this have upon the computation of the Natural Process Limits? Did this prevent the computed limits from detecting the lack of control for the process?

(f) Delete the out-of-control range and recompute the Natural Process Limits for Camshaft Bearing Diameter Three.

Exercise 9.7:

There is little reason to subgroup the weights of the 100 consecutive rubber parts into subgroups of size 5, although this was done for both Average and Range charts and Median and Range charts. The first twenty weights are listed below along with their moving ranges:

X	3	-3	-2	2	-4	-6	-2	-5	-2	5	5	3	2	6	2	4	7	11	6	3
mR		6	1	4	6	2	4	3	3	7	0	2	1	4	4	2	3	4	5	3

(a) Use these 20 weights to compute limits for an *XmR* chart.

(b) The running record of all 100 values was assigned as part of Exercise 2.3. If you did Exercise 2.3 you may plot the limits computed in part (a) on that running record for X. Otherwise, use the remaining 80 values shown below to plot an *XmR* Chart for these data.

X	3	-2	3	-1	-3	4	-1	-2	2	3	-4	-11	-5	-7	-5	-6	15	-5	-1	-1
mR	0	5	5	4	2	7	5	1	4	1	7	7	6	2	2	1	21	20	4	0

X	1	3	7	-6	2	-1	-5	1	2	1	2	2	-1	-8	-7	5	3	6	13	1
mR	2	2	4	13	8	3	4	6	1	1	1	0	3	7	1	12	2	3	7	12

X	-2	-2	4	9	1	6	7	1	3	2	5	2	9	5	-3	-3	-5	-1	-2	-1
mR	3	0	6	5	8	5	1	6	2	1	3	3	7	4	8	0	2	4	1	1

X	3	-1	-1	1	-2	-3	2	-7	-9	-1	-3	-2	-6	-2	-6	-8	-2	4	-1	-1
mR	4	4	0	2	3	1	5	9	2	8	2	1	4	4	4	2	6	6	5	0

Exercise 9.8:

(a) Use the first 5 subgroups in the first column of Table 9.7, p.236, to compute control limits for the Subgroup Averages and Subgroup Ranges.

(b) Do any of the 100 Subgroup Averages or 100 Subgroup Ranges shown in Figure 9.17 fall outside these limits?

(c) Is it necessary to postpone the computation of control limits until hundreds of observations have been collected?

Exercise 9.9:

A film product is produced in wide rolls. Nine samples are cut from the end of each roll of film and tested for tensile strength. The control devices for this production process

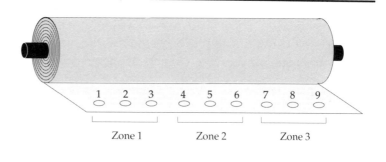

Zone 1   Zone 2   Zone 3

are set up in zones. Since tensile cannot be directly measured on line, these nine tensile values for each roll are used to answer several different questions about both the roll and the production process.

(a) The Zone controllers operate independently of each other. Would it be appropriate to use the ranges within each zone (R_1, R_2, R_3) to construct limits for the Zone Averages ($\bar{X}_1, \bar{X}_2, \bar{X}_3$) ?

$$
\begin{array}{ccc|cc}
X_1 & X_2 & X_3 & \bar{X}_1 & R_1 \\
X_4 & X_5 & X_6 & \bar{X}_2 & R_2 \\
X_7 & X_8 & X_9 & \bar{X}_3 & R_3
\end{array}
$$

(b) What would be a reasonable way of using the Zone Averages on a control chart? How would you construct limits for this chart, and what aspect of the production process would this chart track?

(c) What would be a reasonable way of using the Zone Ranges on a control chart? How would you construct limits for this chart, and what aspect of the production process would this chart track?

(d) In order to track the process roll-to-roll it was suggested that the nine values from a single roll could be used as a single subgroup on an ordinary Average and Range Chart. What is wrong with this suggestion?

(e) One chart which was suggested for these data was a range chart constructed using the range of the three Zone Averages. Just what characteristic would such a range chart track? Is this characteristic tracked in any of the other charts mentioned or devised above?

(f) If the Master Roll shown above is to be split into three Slave Rolls of equal width, would you still be interested in keeping the Range Chart described in Part (e)?

Exercise 9.10:

Use the data from Exercise 4.2, page 88:

(a) Delete the out-of-control ranges, revise the range control limit, and repeat until no more ranges are found to fall outside the revised limits.

(b) Use the latest revised Average Range to compute control limits for Subgroup Averages and also compute a Sigma(X) value.

(c) Using all 51 Subgroup Ranges, find the Median Range and compute control limits for Subgroup Averages and a Sigma(X) value.

Chapter Ten

Control Charts for Data

Based on Counts

The discussion in the preceding chapters has centered around Measurement Data. Such data consist of observations which come from a continuum. Some examples of Measurement Data are heights, weights, densities, times, temperatures, physical dimensions, and other similar quantities.

A second category of data consists of counts, and values based on counts. Obvious examples of these types of data are the number of blemishes in some amount of product or the number of nonconforming pieces out of some number examined. Since these data consist of counts of the occurrence of some attribute they are sometimes called Attribute Data. This chapter describes techniques for charting Attribute Data. The next chapter explains how to use Attribute Data effectively.

Attribute Data differ from Measurement Data in two ways. First of all Attribute Data have a certain irreducible discreteness which Measurement Data do not possess. Secondly, every count must have a known "Area of Opportunity" to be well-defined.

With Measurement Data, the discreteness of the values is basically a matter of choice. It can be reduced by using a smaller unit of measurement. This is not the case with count data, which are based on the occurrence of discrete events (so-called attributes). Count data always consist of integral values. This inherent and irreducible discreteness is, therefore, a characteristic of the data, and may be taken into account in establishing the control charts.

The "Area of Opportunity" for any given count will define the background against which the count must be interpreted. Before any two counts may be directly compared they must have corresponding (i.e. equal) Areas of Opportunity. If the Areas of Opportunity are not equal, or at least approximately equal, then the counts must be turned into rates before they may be meaningfully compared. This conversion from counts to rates is accomplished by dividing a count by its own Area of Opportunity.

Thus, there are two issues which are unique to data based upon counts. Is the inherent discreteness severe enough to intrude into the computations of the control charts? And are the Areas of Opportunity equal? When the counts get small, the discreteness will be severe and special charting techniques will be needed. If the Areas of Opportunity are not equal, or approximately equal, then the counts may not be directly compared until they have been converted into rates.

Table 10.1: Charts for Count Data

Data Characterized by Binomial Model		Data Characterized by Poisson Model		Other Data Based On Counts	
Area of Opportunity		Area of Opportunity		Area of Opportunity	
n constant	n variable	a constant	a variable	constant	variable
np-chart or XmR	*p*-chart or XmR	*c*-chart or XmR	*u*-chart or XmR	XmR for Counts	XmR for Rates

Table 10.1 lists the possibilities for charting Count Data. One should note that all count data consist of Individual Values. The control charts in Table 10.1 are all control charts for Individual Values. Therefore, we shall begin this chapter with the *XmR* Chart for Attribute Data.

10.1 A Simple Approach for Attribute Data

With count data, a single count is obtained for each sample. Since each count is an Individual Value, the *XmR* Chart can be used for the counts or for percentages based on the counts. Each count or each percentage is treated as the observation and a Moving Range is used to measure the variation from one value to the next.

EXAMPLE 10.1:   *The Premium Shipment Data:*

One plant receives thousands of shipments each month. Some of these shipments are handled as premium freight. Since premium freight costs about 3.5 times as much as regular freight the transportation manager keeps track of this expense as a line item in his monthly report. The data for 12 consecutive months are shown in Table 10.2. Since the total number of shipments differs from month to month the counts of the number of premium shipments cannot be directly compared—their Areas of Opportunity vary. Thus, the counts are converted into percentages by dividing by the total number of shipments each month (and moving the decimal over two places to the right).

Table 10.2 Premium Freight Data

month	total number of shipments	number of premium shipments	percentage premium shipments	premium percentage of total costs
1	7226	496	6.9	20.2
2	4440	161	3.6	28.8
3	4896	232	4.7	20.7
4	6019	352	5.9	23.3
5	4101	277	6.8	19.9
6	3775	252	6.7	18.2
7	5068	229	4.5	21.4
8	4040	239	5.9	19.6
9	4038	274	6.8	19.6
10	5275	324	6.1	23.4
11	4059	268	6.6	27.7
12	5133	361	7.0	25.3

The XmR Chart for these data is shown in Figure 10.1.

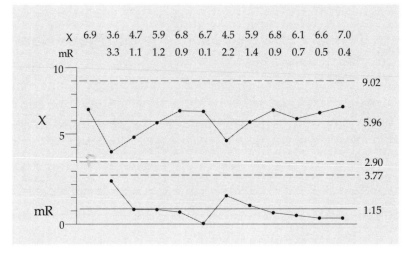

Figure 10.1: *XmR* Chart for Percentage Premium Freight

Whether this performance is good, bad, or indifferent, it was at least consistent. The percentage of shipments shipped via premium freight can be considered to have been stable with an average of 6 percent during this 12 month period.

The data for the next 8 months is shown in Table 10.3.

Table 10.3: Additional Premium Freight Data

month	total number of shipments	number of premium shipments	percentage premium shipments	premium percentage of total costs
13	5311	487	9.2	24.7
14	2977	290	9.7	26.5
15	4050	535	13.2	29.3
16	5546	654	11.8	32.2
17	5658	506	8.9	36.4
18	7357	588	8.0	30.2
19	7585	714	9.4	30.7
20	5196	480	9.2	34.3

The continuation of the XmR Chart for these data is shown in Figure 10.2.

The percentage premium freight has definitely increased during these past eight months. There is some assignable cause for this change, and it would be worthwhile to seek to find this cause. During the last eight months, 9 to 10 percent of the shipments have generated approximately 30 percent of the freight costs.

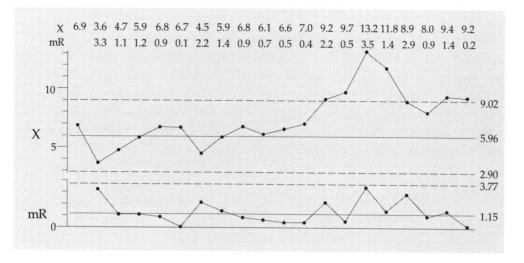

Figure 10.2: *XmR* Chart for Percentage Premium Freight Continued

The *XmR* Chart was introduced as a charting technique for Measurement Data. Its use with Count Data does not present a problem when the discreteness of the data is small relative to the magnitude of the counts. In other words, when the Average Count (per sample or time period) is large, the distinction between Count Data and Measurement Data is not as important as when the Average Count is small.

How large does the Average Count need to be? Large enough to prevent the discreteness of the counts from seriously affecting the control chart limits or the running record. In Section 9.1, the problems caused by discreteness in the Measurement Data were discussed. There it was shown that, for control charts, the detrimental effects of discreteness begin when the standard deviation is smaller than the smallest unit of measurement. For many counts, the standard deviation is roughly proportional to the square root of the Average Count. At the same time, the smallest unit of "measurement" for count data is an integer. Combining these facts, a case can be made for using the *XmR* Chart with Count Data whenever the Average Count exceeds 1.00. Certainly, if the Average Count exceeds 2.0 the discreteness of the counts will have a negligible impact upon the control chart limits.

This lower limit (of one to two counts per sample) is much lower than the cutoff generally cited. The reason this lower cutoff works with the control chart is the fact that control charts work to place *bounds* on the histogram rather than trying to pin down the *shape* of the histogram. The three-sigma limits are not appreciably affected by the discreteness of the Count Data until the Average Count per sample becomes *very* small.

This means that most Count Data can be recorded on *XmR* Charts. Only those situations in which there is a very small Average Count will actually *require* the special control charts given in the following sections.

This does not mean that the following approaches are not worthwhile. The control charts discussed in the following sections target specific types of Count Data. Because of this targeting, advantage can be taken of certain properties of the Count Data in order to make the computed control limits less variable. Thus, whenever the assumptions for an Attribute Chart are satisfied, that chart will be the most appropriate one to use. But when the assumptions are not satisfied, or when the user is not sure about the assumptions, the *XmR* Chart will provide a satisfactory alternative.

10.2 Charts for Data Based on Binomial Counts

No count exists in a vacuum. Each count must always have some Area of Opportunity. The primary distinction between the two major types of count data concerns the Area of Opportunity for the counts.

Consider a sample of **n** items, drawn at random times from the product stream at a particular point on the production line. If each item in this sample was classified as conforming or nonconforming, then the number nonconforming could be recorded as a count. Let this value be denoted by the symbol Y. The Area of Opportunity for the count Y is defined by the number of items examined. In particular, Y cannot be less than 0, and it cannot exceed **n**, but it can take on any integral value in between these two values. This set of possible values is the Area of Opportunity for count Y.

A sequence of such samples would therefore generate a sequence of observed values:
$$Y_1, Y_2, Y_3, Y_4, Y_5, \ldots .$$
When certain conditions are satisfied, a Binomial Probability Model may be used to characterize the behavior of the counts $Y_1, Y_2, Y_3, Y_4, Y_5, \ldots$.

Binomial Condition 1:
The Area of Opportunity for count Y must consist of **n distinct** items.

Binomial Condition 2:
Each of the **n** distinct items must be classified as possessing, or not possessing, some attribute. This attribute is usually some type of nonconformance to specifications.

Binomial Condition 3:
Let **p** denote the probability that an item has the attribute being counted. The value of **p** must be the same for all **n** items in any one sample. While the chart will check if **p** changes from sample to sample, the value of **p** must be constant *within each sample*.

Binomial Condition 4:
The likelihood of an item possessing the attribute will not be affected by whether or not the preceding item possessed the attribute. (Nonconforming items do not naturally occur together in clusters, and counts are independent of each other.)

When these four conditions are satisfied by the count data, it is feasible to use a Binomial Probability Model to compute control limits for the sequence of observed values Y_1, Y_2, Y_3, Y_4, Y_5, ... That is, we may use the known relationship between the Mean of the Binomial Distribution and the Standard Deviation of the Binomial Distribution in our computations. This will have the effect of making a Range Chart unnecessary.

The reader should notice that the symbol **n** is used here to denote the Area of Opportunity for a Binomial Count rather than the subgroup size (the number of values used to compute an average). The Binomial Count, Y, is an Individual Value, and there is exactly one count per "subgroup."

Given a sequence of observed values:

$$Y_1, Y_2, Y_3, Y_4, Y_5, ...$$

which satisfy the four conditions above, these values may be thought of as observations from a Binomial Distribution with parameters **n** and **p**. The Mean of this Binomial Distribution is:

$$MEAN(Y) = n\,p$$

while the Standard Deviation is:

$$SD(Y) = \sqrt{n\,p\,(1 - p)}$$

In practice, the observed Average Proportion Nonconforming from some baseline period, $\bar{p}$, is substituted for the parameter **p**.

The formula for the Average Proportion Nonconforming statistic, $\bar{p}$, is:

$$\bar{p} = \frac{\text{total number nonconforming in baseline samples}}{\text{total number items examined in baseline samples}}$$

Thus, the formulas for Three-Sigma Limits for the counts Y_i are:

$$UCL_{np} = n\bar{p} + 3\sqrt{n\bar{p}\,(1 - \bar{p})}$$

$$CL_{np} = n\bar{p}$$

$$LCL_{np} = n\bar{p} - 3\sqrt{n\bar{p}\,(1 - \bar{p})}$$

As suggested by the subscript, this control chart is called an *np*-chart. This traditional name makes it easy to distinguish the special control charts for Attribute Data from the control charts for Measurement Data.

EXAMPLE 10.2:   *The Number of Rejected Parts per Basket:*

At one inspect-and-pack operation, an np-chart was kept in the following manner. Twice each shift a data clerk came to the inspect-and-pack station. This clerk watched while sixty consecutive parts came to the inspect-and-pack operator. Each time the operator placed a part on the rework line she called out the reason for the rejection. The clerk recorded these rejections and plotted the total number rejected per sample on the np-chart shown in Figure 10.3. The sixty pieces constituted the Area of Opportunity for each count.

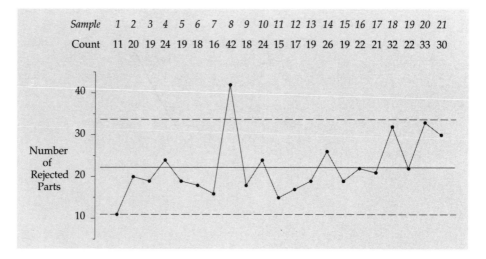

Sample	1	2	3	4	5	6	7	8	9	10	11	12	13	14	15	16	17	18	19	20	21
Count	11	20	19	24	19	18	16	42	18	24	15	17	19	26	19	22	21	32	22	33	30

Figure 10.3: *np*-Chart for Number of Rejected Parts per Basket

For these data the Average Proportion Nonconforming is:

$$\bar{p} = \frac{total\ number\ nonconforming\ in\ baseline\ samples}{total\ number\ items\ examined\ in\ baseline\ samples} = \frac{467}{1260} = 0.3706$$

with **n** = *60 one gets:*

$$n\,\bar{p} = 60\ (0.3706) = 22.24$$

and

$$\sqrt{n\,\bar{p}\ (1 - \bar{p}\ )} = 3.74$$

so that

$$UCL_{np} = n\,\bar{p} + 3\,\sqrt{n\,\bar{p}\ (1 - \bar{p}\ )} = 22.24 + 11.22 = 33.46$$

$$CL_{np} = n\,\bar{p} = 22.24$$

$$LCL_{np} = n\,\bar{p} - 3\,\sqrt{n\,\bar{p}\ (1 - \bar{p}\ )} = 22.24 - 11.22 = 11.02$$

Note that the use of an *np*-chart here assumes that each of the 60 pieces in a sample has the same likelihood of being defective, for any reason, as the other pieces in that sample. In other words, the likelihood of a defective piece is not changing during any single 60 piece sample. (The chart itself suggests that the likelihood is changing from sample to sample.)

10.3 Charts for Proportions Based on Binomial Counts

The *np*-chart should be used whenever the count data appear to be Binomially Distributed and the samples all have the same sized Areas of Opportunity. If the Area of Opportunity changes from sample to sample, then the counts cannot be directly compared. Each count has to be adjusted by the size of its Area of Opportunity. When the counts are divided by their Areas of Opportunity the result is a proportion, p_i. The Attribute Chart for these proportions is called a *p*-chart.

The *p*-chart is based on a running record that is made up of the sample proportions of nonconforming product, p_i. These values are obtained from the counts according to the formula:

$$p_i = \frac{Y_i}{n_i}$$

where Y_i is the count for sample i and n_i denotes the number of items examined for sample i.

The Average Proportion Nonconforming, $\bar{p}$, is computed in the same way as before, and the control limits for the p_i values are found using the formulas:

$$UCL_p = \bar{p} + 3\sqrt{\frac{\bar{p}(1-\bar{p})}{n_i}}$$

$$CL_p = \bar{p}$$

$$LCL_p = \bar{p} - 3\sqrt{\frac{\bar{p}(1-\bar{p})}{n_i}}$$

where the LCL_p is meaningful only if it is positive.

A problem with the *p*-chart is that the standard deviation depends upon the variable Area of Opportunity, n_i. As the Area of Opportunity changes, the computed value of the standard deviation changes, and the control limits get closer to, or farther away from, the central line. This means that new control limits are needed each time n_i changes. When n_i changes with each sample this can result in having to calculate control limits every time a new sample is taken. This makes the *p*-chart messy and tedious.

The computerized accounts payable system in one company was set up to index the invoices in several different ways. In order to enter the information from an invoice into the system, certain pieces of information had to be included on each invoice. When an invoice came in that did not have all of the necessary information, it was assigned to an incomplete file. Invoices in this file then required additional work. The data in Table 10.4 cover one four-week period.

The unequal number of invoices which arrived each day makes a direct comparison of the number of incomplete invoices misleading. Instead of comparing the counts, one must compare the rates, as expressed by the proportions of incomplete invoices. These are shown in Table 10.4.

Table 10.4 Daily Proportions for the Incomplete Invoice Data

Date	No. of Incomplete Invoices	Total No. of Invoices	Daily Proportion p_i	Date	No. of Incomplete Invoices	Total No. of Invoices	Daily Proportion p_i
9/27	20	98	0.204	10/11	7	50	0.140
9/28	18	104	0.173	10/12	7	53	0.132
9/29	14	97	0.144	10/13	9	56	0.161
9/30	16	99	0.162	10/14	5	49	0.102
10/1	13	97	0.134	10/15	8	56	0.143
10/4	29	102	0.284	10/18	9	53	0.170
10/5	21	104	0.202	10/19	9	52	0.173
10/6	14	101	0.139	10/20	10	51	0.196
10/7	6	55	0.109	10/21	9	52	0.173
10/8	6	48	0.125	10/22	10	47	0.213

To construct a p-chart for the proportion of incomplete invoices one must begin with a running record of the daily proportions. With the addition of limits for each point this running record is converted into a p-chart.

The Average Proportion of Incomplete Invoices for these data is the central line for the p-chart:

$$CL_p = \bar{p} = \frac{240}{1424} = 0.169$$

The control limits for each day are computed using this value of $\bar{p}$ and the appropriate value of n_i. In performing these calculations, it is not necessary to recalculate the numerator of the three-sigma term. The value of:

$$3 \sqrt{\bar{p} (1 - \bar{p})} = 1.124$$

remains the same for every sample. To obtain the three-sigma value for a specific sample, *divide the value 1.124 by the square root of n_i for that sample. The actual control limits are shown in Table 10.5, and are plotted in Figure 10.4.*

Table 10.5 Control Limits for the Incomplete Invoice Data

Date	Y_i	n_i	p_i	UCL_p	LCL_p	Date	Y_i	n_i	p_i	UCL_p	LCL_p
9/27	20	98	0.204	.282	.055	10/11	7	50	0.140	.327	.010
9/28	18	104	0.173	.279	.058	10/12	7	53	0.132	.323	.014
9/29	14	97	0.144	.283	.055	10/13	9	56	0.161	.319	.018
9/30	16	99	0.162	.281	.056	10/14	5	49	0.102	.329	.008
10/1	13	97	0.134	.283	.055	10/15	8	56	0.143	.319	.018
10/4	29	102	0.284	.280	.057	10/18	9	53	0.170	.323	.014
10/5	21	104	0.202	.279	.058	10/19	9	52	0.173	.324	.013
10/6	14	101	0.139	.280	.057	10/20	10	51	0.196	.326	.011
10/7	6	55	0.109	.320	.017	10/21	9	52	0.173	.324	.013
10/8	6	48	0.125	.331	.006	10/22	10	47	0.213	.332	.005

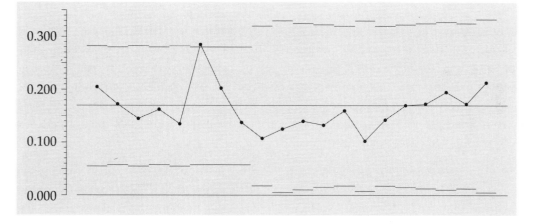

Figure 10.4: *p*-Chart for Incomplete Invoice Data

Many have suggested that if the n_i values do not vary by more than ± 20 percent from some average value, then the average Area of Opportunity, $\bar{n}$, can be used to calculate the control limits. In the preceding example, this approach would not work because the Areas of Opportunity varied from 47 to 104.

However, since most of the Areas of Opportunity are near 50 or 100, one might use two sets of approximate limits. One set could be based on $n = 50$, and the other could be based on $n = 100$. With this approach one need only calculate exact control limits for those proportions that fall "close" to the appropriate limits. The definition of "close" is subjective. Whenever a proportion is just inside or just outside the approximate limits, exact limits are in order.

A second approach to avoiding the calculation of exact control limits for each and every value of n_i is that of finding "narrow" and "wide" limits. A large Area of Opportunity yields narrow control limits. Therefore, if control limits are calculated using the largest value for n_i which is likely to occur in the normal course of events, the narrowest limits that are likely to be appropriate will be obtained. As long as the Area of Opportunity does not exceed this large value for n_i, the proportions that fall within these "narrow" control limits are certainly within their exact control limits.

Likewise, the use of the smallest value for n_i which is likely to occur in the natural course of events will yield the widest appropriate limits. Unless the Area of Opportunity is smaller than this small value for n_i, those proportions falling outside the "wide" control limits will certainly be outside their exact control limits. Such proportions can safely be interpreted as signals of a lack of control.

Proportions that fall between the "narrow" limits and the "wide" limits need to have their exact control limits calculated.

While both of these approaches help with the problem of variable control limits, the best approach is to avoid unequal Areas of Opportunity in the first place. While some types of count data seem to have inherently unequal Areas of Opportunity, such data are rarely effective on control charts anyway. Control charts for Attribute Data are most effective when the data have been specifically collected for use with the charts. In those cases, it is usually very easy to avoid unequal Areas of Opportunity. This was done with the data shown in Example 10.2—instead of using 100% of the Inspect and Pack data, samples of 60 pieces were taken twice each shift.

While the p-chart is recommended for Binomial Count Data with unequal Areas of Opportunity, it is possible to construct an np-chart for such data. This chart is seldom used, for reasons that should become obvious upon inspection of Figure 10.5. The chart in Figure 10.5 is the np-chart for the Incomplete Invoice Data.

While the charts in Figures 10.4 and 10.5 tell the same story point by point, the pictures look completely different. The variable central line in Figure 10.5 makes this chart difficult to interpret, which is the major reason that this chart is seldom used with unequal Areas of Opportunity.

Likewise, it is possible to construct a p-chart for count data which have equal Areas of Opportunity. This was done for the data on the Number of Rejected Parts per Basket, and the result is shown in Figure 10.6. A quick comparison of Figure 10.6 with the np-chart shown in Figure 10.3, will show that these two charts are exactly the same. The change from an np-chart to a p-chart is merely a matter of re-labeling the vertical scale when the Areas of Opportunity are equal for the different samples. In fact, the same scale can be labeled in percentages, or proportions, or counts. The running record and the control limits will remain unchanged.

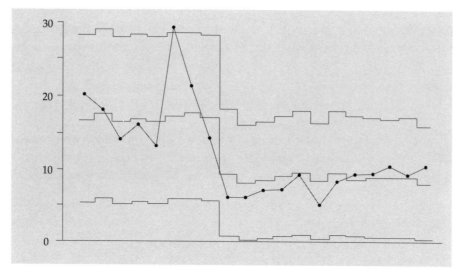

Figure 10.5: *np*-Chart for Incomplete Invoice Data

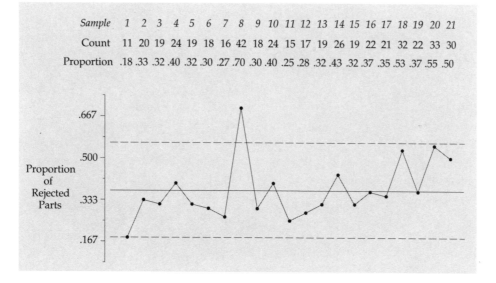

Figure 10.6: The *p*-chart for Number of Rejected Parts per Basket

How do the *p*-chart and the *np*-chart differ from the use of an *XmR* Chart? The control limits found by either method are usually quite similar. The difference lies in the way the limits are obtained. The *np*-chart and the *p*-chart are specifically targeted for Binomial Count Data. Because of this, they take advantage of the relationship between the Mean of a Binomial Distribution and the Standard Deviation of a Binomial Distribution. This relationship allows the limits for these charts to be based upon one statistic—the Average

Proportion Nonconforming. This makes the computed control limits less susceptible to sampling variation. Which is why the *np*-chart and the *p*-chart are the best charts to use whenever the Binomial Distribution provides a useful characterization of the data.

10.4 Problems With Binomial Charts

The four conditions listed earlier define when the Binomial Distribution may be used to characterize the data. Some count data, and some percentages, do not satisfy these conditions, and therefore do not belong on either *np*-charts or *p*-charts.

In particular, percentages that are based on Measurement Data, rather than Count Data, do not belong on a *p*-chart. Although the percentages may define proportions, the problem lies with the Area of Opportunity: it is no longer discrete. Such data cannot be meaningfully placed on a *p*-chart. They must be charted by using the chart for Individual Values and a Moving Range, or by an Average and Range Chart.

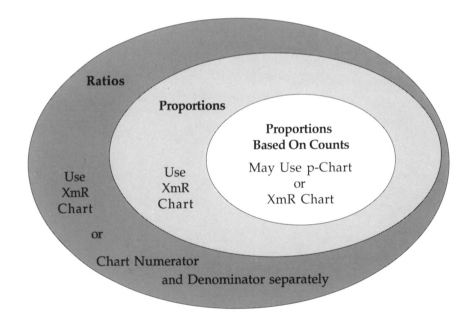

Figure 10.7: Quantities Commonly Expressed as Percentages

Likewise, ratios that are not really proportions do not belong on a *p*-chart. While all proportions are ratios, all ratios are not proportions. In order to be a proportion, a ratio must be constructed so that the denominator defines the Area of Opportunity for the value in the numerator.

Many ratios used daily in industry are not real proportions. An example of this is

Today's Rework divided by Today's Production. This ratio may be useful to someone, but it is not a proportion because Today's Production did not generate Today's Rework. The only way to chart these ratios is with the techniques for Measurement Data. Moreover, charting such ratios makes for unusual charts. A control chart for the ratio described above was bouncing out of control, from high side to low side, on adjacent days. The reason: breakdowns caused everyone to shift from production to rework. So on one day the denominator would be very small, and the ratio would be very large. The next day, with no rework to be done, the numerator would be very small and the ratio would follow suit. In general, it is better to chart individual variables rather than ratios of variables such as these.

Another situation that does not satisfy the conditions necessary for the use of the Binomial Probability Model occurs when the proportion of nonconforming product is not consistent. In particular, the p-chart and the np-chart are supposed to represent systems that have one stable proportion of nonconforming product whenever the process is in control. This assumption implies that samples known to have different values for p should not be mixed on one chart. Examples of this typically consist of samples representing different machines, different lines, or different shifts, when these different samples are *known* to have different proportions of nonconforming product. When this is the case, different charts should be kept for the different classes of samples. On the other hand, if different machines are supposed to operate identically, samples for the two machines might be tracked as separate points on the same chart. If the machines are different enough, the chart will show the difference. The guiding principle here should be to use the control charts to discover that which is not known rather than using them to discover that which is already known.

Another way in which the proportion nonconforming will not be consistent from sample to sample occurs when the Area of Opportunity becomes excessively large. When n gets to be in the thousands it is virtually impossible to obtain an np-chart or a p-chart which displays a reasonable degree of statistical control. The reasons for this are many and varied, but they usually come back to a problem of consistency in determining what to count. If one inspector is examining all of these distinct items there is the problem of fatigue—that which is nonconforming at 9 a.m. doesn't really look so bad by 3:30 p.m. Thus, even if the product stream contained a fixed percentage of nonconforming product, the chart would not see this consistency. If multiple inspectors are examining the distinct items there is the problem of inspector-to-inspector consistency in addition to fatigue. This problem is what makes the use of a p-chart questionable with 100 percent inspection data. The large Area of Opportunity will create excessively tight limits, which will in turn create false alarms, and cause people to look for Assignable Causes in the production process when the problem is in the inspection and counting procedure or in the assumption of a Binomial Probability Model. With this type of data, the XmR Chart will generally be much more satisfactory.

The p-Chart for the Premium Shipment Data:

The Premium Freight Data of Table 10.2 is reproduced in Table 10.6 along with the customary limits for placing these data on a p-chart. Because the total number of shipments varies considerably from month-to-month it was necessary to compute separate limits for each month. The p-chart is shown in Figure 10.8.

Table 10.6 Premium Freight Data

month	Y_i	n_i	p_i	LCL_p	UCL_p
1	496	7226	.0686	.0513	.0681
2	161	4440	.0363	.0490	.0704
3	232	4896	.0474	.0495	.0699
4	352	6019	.0585	.0505	.0689
5	277	4101	.0675	.0486	.0708
6	252	3775	.0668	.0481	.0713
7	229	5068	.0452	.0497	.0697
8	239	4040	.0592	.0485	.0709
9	274	4038	.0679	.0485	.0709
10	324	5275	.0614	.0499	.0695
11	268	4059	.0660	.0485	.0709
12	361	5133	.0703	.0498	.0696

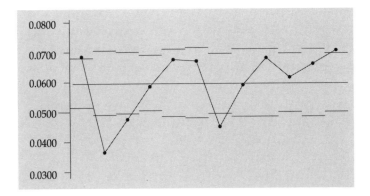

Figure 10.8: *p*-Chart for Percentage Premium Freight

The p-chart for the first 12 months of the Premium Freight Data shows two points out-of-control on the high side, and three out-of-control on the low side. The XmR Chart for these data, shown in Figure 10.1, page 258, did not show any points out of control during the first 12 months. So which chart does one believe?

The p-chart limits are constructed on the basis of a series of assumptions. If one did observe several thousand items selected from a homogeneous stream with a constant 6 percent nonconforming, then some of the percentages shown in these data would be excessively large and others would be excessively small. But is this a realistic model for *these data? All kinds of shipments are included in these data. Given the highly aggregate nature of these count data, it is unlikely that every shipment in a given month has the same likelihood of being shipped by premium freight. This lack of a constant p from shipment to shipment within any given month will undermine the use of a Binomial Model for these data. Thus, the p-chart limits shown in Figure 10.8 are inappropriate for these data.*

The XmR Chart uses the variation present in the data to construct the limits. It makes no assumptions about the nature of the data. It simply lets the data speak for themselves.

In those cases where the use of a Binomial Probability Model is questionable or uncertain, the XmR Chart will be the best choice.

Finally, situations in which nonconforming items tend to occur together should not be used for constructing attribute control charts. If blemishes or nonconforming items are known to occur in clusters, then Condition Four is not satisfied, and both the Binomial and the Poisson Probability Models will be inappropriate. When nonconformities occur in clusters, one may use 100 percent inspection to try to screen out the nonconforming items, and one may place the data from this 100 percent inspection on a running record for report card purposes, but it will be incorrect to place limits on this running record using the Binomial or Poisson Model. Example 11.5 shows two such running records. When there is clustering with 100 percent inspection data, the attribute charts will almost automatically be out of control, and this apparent "out-of-control" condition is likely to persist regardless of how good the process becomes.

10.5 Charts for Data Based on Poisson Counts

With Binomial Count Data, each distinct item is categorized as conforming or nonconforming. This becomes a problem when the items are very complex, or when the product is continuous in nature. In the first category, consider an automobile. It would hardly be worthwhile to characterize each car as conforming or nonconforming. Given the complexity of an automobile, all would be nonconforming. The real question is "How many nonconformities exist?" In the second category, consider a roll of cloth. One blemish will not, in general, make the whole roll unusable. However, an excessive number of blemishes will cause the roll to be downgraded.

In these situations, the nonconformities themselves may be counted. Such counts will still have an Area of Opportunity, but the nature of this Area of Opportunity would now be considerably different. The Areas of Opportunity for the counts of blemishes in the two preceding illustrations were, respectively, an automobile and a roll of cloth. Even though these Areas of Opportunity each consisted of one discrete unit, the count would not be limited to possible values of 0 or 1. Here, the counts could conceivably be very large indeed, and the Area of Opportunity has changed, from the "number of discrete items" to "a finite region of space, time, or product."

Another way to distinguish between Binomial Count Data and Poisson Count Data is given by the following guidelines. With Binomial Count Data one can count either the number *nonconforming*, or the number *conforming*. With Poisson Count Data one can only count the *blemishes*—it will be impossible to count the *non-blemishes*.

The prerequisites for using a Poisson Distribution to characterize a sequence of counts are:

Poisson Condition 1:   The counts are counts of discrete events.

Poisson Condition 2:   The discrete events occur within some well-defined, finite region of space or time or product. This finite region is the Area of Opportunity for the count.

Poisson Condition 3:   The events occur independently of each other.

Poisson Condition 4:   The events are rare (compared to what might be).

The first two conditions are fairly easy to verify in a particular situation. The third condition is more difficult to evaluate, and the fourth is rather subjective. The independence of the events is, in part, monitored by the control chart. If the events begin to cluster, the control chart will tend to go out of control. The rarity of the events can best be evaluated by considering what could happen if everything went wrong. If this "worst-case" situation gives counts that are at least ten times greater than those which actually occur, the events are "rare enough."

The Standard Deviation of a Poisson Distribution is equal to the square root of the Mean of that distribution. This relationship will once again allow us to dispense with the Range Chart and construct limits using a single location statistic.

Once again, in order for a set of counts to be directly comparable, each count must have the same sized Area of Opportunity. When this is the case, let the Average Count per Sample be denoted by $\bar{c}$:

$$\bar{c} = \frac{\text{total count of nonconformities in baseline samples}}{\text{number of baseline samples}}$$

The formulas for control limits for the *c*-chart are:

$$\text{UCL}_c = \bar{c} + 3\sqrt{\bar{c}}$$
$$\text{CL}_c = \bar{c}$$
$$\text{LCL}_c = \bar{c} - 3\sqrt{\bar{c}}$$

When the Poisson Distribution characterizes a sequence of counts these limits will define the natural variation present in those counts. When the four conditions listed earlier are satisfied the Poisson Distribution will generally provide a satisfactory characterization.

EXAMPLE 10.5:   *Blemishes per Sample:*

A certain process produced a sheet of vinyl 30 inches wide, composed of a colored top layer and a grey bottom layer. Blemishes primarily consisted of an area where the grey layer showed through, or an area where the grain pattern was not distinct. A two-yard sample from the end of each roll was examined for blemishes, and the results were recorded on a c-chart. The data for one color of vinyl are shown on the c-chart in Figure 10.9.

Average count per sample for these data is $\bar{c}$ = 2.725

Using the formulas above, the 3-sigma control limits are:

$$UCL_c = \bar{c} + 3\sqrt{\bar{c}} = 2.725 + 3\,(1.651) = 2.725 + 4.953 = 7.678\,(or\ 7.7)$$
$$CL_c = \bar{c} = 2.725\,(or\ 2.7)$$
$$LCL_c = \bar{c} - 3\sqrt{\bar{c}} = 2.725 - 4.953 = -2.228 \quad (so\ there\ is\ no\ LCL_c\,)$$

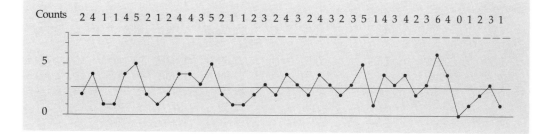

Figure 10.9: *c*-Chart for Number of Blemishes per Sample

When the product is not continuous, there is a problem that often complicates the collection of data for a *c*-chart. This is the problem of "rejection on the first nonconformity." Since most industrial inspection is geared to sorting conforming product from nonconforming product, many inspectors drop a discrete item as soon as one nonconformity is observed, and go on to the next item. The data generated by this type of inspection do not belong on a *c*-chart.

The data for a *c*-chart should consist of the counts of the total number of nonconformities (of a given type) in the region of product inspected. The inspector must, therefore, keep looking for nonconformities, even after the first one has been found (no matter how bad that first nonconformity may be). This may be a difficult adjustment for the inspectors to make, especially when the product is discrete.

Another aspect of the *c*-chart concerns the fact that the Poisson Distribution is severely skewed when the average is small. This skewness changes the chances of getting a false alarm. For average counts that are less than 1.0 per sample, there is an approximate chance of 3 to 4 percent that a point will exceed the upper 3-sigma limit. For Average Counts between 1.0 and 3.0, the chance of a false alarm is about 2 percent, and for averages between 3.0 and 7.0, the chance of a false alarm is about 1 percent. When the Average Count is between 7.0 and 12.0, the chance of a false alarm drops to about one-half percent. At the same time, the formulas for the 3-sigma limits do not produce a lower control limit until the Average Count per sample exceeds 9.0. This makes it difficult to detect improvements when the Average Count drops below about 10.

Table 10.7: 0.005 and 0.995 Probability Limits for *c*-Charts

Values for Average Count From	To	0.005 LCL	0.995 UCL	Values for Average Count From	To	0.005 LCL	0.995 UCL
0.0	0.10	no LCL	1.5	10.36	10.97	2.5	20.5
0.10	0.33	no LCL	2.5	10.97	11.08	3.5	20.5
0.33	0.67	no LCL	3.5	11.08	11.81	3.5	21.5
0.67	1.07	no LCL	4.5	11.81	12.54	3.5	22.5
1.07	1.53	no LCL	5.5	12.54	12.59	3.5	23.5
1.53	2.04	no LCL	6.5	12.59	13.28	4.5	23.5
2.04	2.57	no LCL	7.5	13.28	14.02	4.5	24.5
2.57	3.13	no LCL	8.5	14.02	14.14	4.5	25.5
3.13	3.71	no LCL	9.5	14.14	14.77	5.5	25.5
3.71	4.32	no LCL	10.5	14.77	15.53	5.5	26.5
4.32	4.94	no LCL	11.5	15.53	15.66	5.5	27.5
4.94	5.30	no LCL	12.5	15.66	16.28	6.5	27.5
5.30	5.58	0.5	12.5	16.28	17.05	6.5	28.5
5.58	6.23	0.5	13.5	17.05	17.13	6.5	29.5
6.23	6.89	0.5	14.5	17.13	17.82	7.5	29.5
6.89	7.57	0.5	15.5	17.82	18.57	7.5	30.5
7.57	8.25	0.5	16.5	18.57	18.59	8.5	30.5
8.25	8.43	0.5	17.5	18.59	19.36	8.5	31.5
8.43	8.95	1.5	17.5	19.36	20.00	8.5	32.5
8.95	9.27	1.5	18.5				
9.27	9.65	2.5	18.5				
9.65	10.36	2.5	19.5				

These problems with the usual 3-sigma limits are not overwhelming. The regular limits are sufficiently conservative to be useful in practice. However, since the assumptions justifying the use of a c-chart also justify the use of the Poisson Distribution, there is an easy way to remedy both of the shortcomings of 3-sigma limits for Poisson Counts. This may be done by using the 0.005 LCL_c and the .995 UCL_c probability limits shown in Table 10.7. Although the 0.995 UCL_c is sometimes larger and sometimes smaller than the upper 3-sigma limit, the probability of a point falling above the 0.995 UCL_c is never greater than 0.005 when the process is in control. Likewise, although the 0.005 LCL_c is always greater than the lower 3-sigma limit, the probability of a point falling below the 0.005 LCL_c is never greater than 0.005 when the process is in control. Thus, these limits provide a balance between sensitivity to process improvements and process deterioration, while minimizing the chance of a false alarm. They are a reasonable alternative to the 3-sigma limits for a c-Chart.

For Average Count values in excess of 20.0 one may use the following approximations for the 0.005 and 0.995 probability limits for a c-chart:

$$0.005 \; LCL_c \approx \bar{c} - 2.47 \sqrt{\bar{c}} \qquad\qquad 0.995 \; UCL_c \approx \bar{c} + 2.85 \sqrt{\bar{c}}$$

10.6 Charts for Nonconformities per Unit Area of Opportunity

If the Area of Opportunity changes from sample to sample, then the counts cannot be directly compared. Before these counts can be charted, they must be changed into rates. When the data satisfy the conditions for using the Poisson Probability Model, the appropriate rate is the Nonconformities Per Unit Area of Opportunity. These rates are found by dividing each count, c_i by its area of opportunity, a_i. These values are usually denoted by the symbol u_i. Once the u_i values have been obtained, they can be plotted in a running record.

A word of warning is appropriate here. If the variation of the a_i values is essentially random in nature, then the u_i values must be considered to be the ratio of two random variables, and the u-chart control limits will be inappropriate. If, on the other hand, the variation in the a_i values is deliberate, or inherent (based on physical differences in different part numbers, for example), then the following control limits will be approximately correct.

The Average Rate of Nonconformities Per Unit Area of Opportunity will be denoted by the symbol $\bar{u}$.

$$\bar{u} = \frac{\text{total count for the baseline samples}}{\text{total area of opportunity in baseline samples}}$$

Thus, $\bar{u}$ is a weighted average count per unit area of opportunity. Once the value for $\bar{u}$ has been obtained, the formulas for the 3-sigma control limits are:

$$UCL_u = \bar{u} + 3\sqrt{\frac{\bar{u}}{a_i}}$$

$$CL_u = \bar{u}$$

$$LCL_u = \bar{u} - 3\sqrt{\frac{\bar{u}}{a_i}} \qquad \text{(if positive)}$$

Just as with the p-chart, the control limits for the u-chart vary as the Area of Opportunity varies from sample to sample. An example of a u-chart is given by Example 10.6.

EXAMPLE 10.6:   *Number of Leaks per Radiator:*

W.L. Burns[1] gives the following data for the number of outlet leaks found when the two portions of an automobile radiator are assembled together for the first time.

In all, 841 radiators were inspected, and 116 leaks were detected. This gives an Average Number of Leaks Per Radiator of $\bar{u} = 116/841 = 0.138$. There are nine different Areas of Opportunity represented in the data. The 3-sigma control limits for these nine different Areas of Opportunity are shown in Table 10.9, and the u-chart is shown in Figure 10.10.

Table 10.8: Number of Outlet Leaks Per Radiator

Date	No. of Leaks c_i	No. of Radiators a_i	Rate u_i	Date	No. of Leaks c_i	No. of Radiators a_i	Rate u_i
6/3	14	39	0.36	6/14	10	50	0.20
6/4	4	45	0.09	6/17	3	32	0.09
6/5	5	46	0.11	6/18	11	50	0.22
6/6	13	48	0.27	6/19	1	33	0.03
6/7	6	40	0.15	6/20	3	50	0.06
6/10	2	58	0.03	6/24	6	50	0.12
6/11	4	50	0.08	6/25	8	50	0.16
6/12	11	50	0.22	6/26	5	50	0.10
6/13	8	50	0.16	6/27	2	50	0.04

---

[1] *Industrial Quality Control*, Volume 4, pp.12-17, 1948.

Table 10.9: Control Limits for Radiator Leak Rates

Area of Opportunity	LCL_u	UCL_u
32	none	0.335
33	none	0.332
39	none	0.316
40	none	0.314
45	none	0.304
46	none	0.302
48	none	0.299
50	none	0.296
58	none	0.284

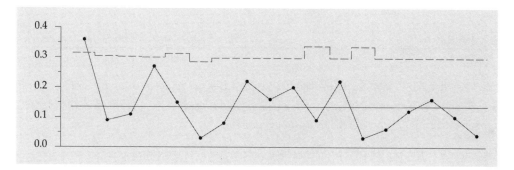

Figure 10.10: u-Chart for Radiator Leak Rates

Since the control limits for the u-chart vary as the Area of Opportunity varies from sample to sample it is impossible to know in advance the control limits which apply to a particular sample. This creates added complexity for the user of the chart. Just as with the p-chart, there are two ways of finding approximate limits that simplify this aspect of the u-chart.

If the Areas of Opportunity do not vary more than ± 20 percent from some average value, then approximate control limits may be obtained by using the average value for the Areas of Opportunity. Any points that are close to these approximate limits will need to have exact limits calculated.

Alternatively, narrow and wide limits for the u-chart could be calculated. The largest value of a_i likely to occur in practice will give the narrow limits, and the smallest likely value for a_i will give the wide limits. Points outside the wide limits are definitely out of control, and points within the narrow limits are definitely within the limits. Exact limits need to be considered only for those points that fall between the narrow limits and the wide limits, or for those samples with exceptional Areas of Opportunity.

However, the best solution is to avoid unequal Areas of Opportunity. This may not be possible with data coming from an ongoing inspection operation, but data of this type rarely yield effective Attribute Charts. Such data are usually too aggregated and too late to be of much use in improving the production process. Data that are sufficiently detailed and timely will usually have to be collected specifically for the charts. When this happens, there is little excuse for allowing the Areas of Opportunity to vary. More will be said about this in the next chapter.

Finally, one could obtain probability control limits for the *u*-chart. The limits will still vary as the Area of Opportunity varies, but the central line will still be the same as with the regular 3-sigma limits. These computations are illustrated in the next example.

EXAMPLE 10.7:   *Probability Control Limits for the u-Chart:*

Assume that 0.005 and 0.995 probability control limits are desired for the data of Example 10.6. The Average Number of Leaks Per Radiator is $\bar{u} = 0.138$, and the Areas of Opportunity range from 32 to 58 units per sample.

The steps for finding the Wide Probability Limits for Poisson Rates are:

(a)   *First one must convert the Average Rate, $\bar{u}$,*
         into a Minimum Average Count. This is done by multiplying the
         Average Rate by the Minimum Area for the data:
$$\bar{u}\ a_i = (0.138)(32) = 4.416.$$

(b)   *Use this Minimum Average Count to find probability limits from Table 10.7:*
$$A\ Count\ of\ 4.4\ gives$$
$$0.005\ LCL_c = none$$
$$0.995\ UCL_c = 11.5$$

(c)   *Now one must convert these Probability Limits for Counts into Wide*
         Probability Limits for Rates. This is done by dividing each of these probability
         limits by the Minimum Area for the data.
$$0.005\ LCL_u = none$$
$$0.995\ UCL_u = 11.5/32 = 0.3594$$

Narrow Probability Limits for Poisson Rates are found as follows:

(d)   First one must convert the Average Rate, $\bar{u}$,
      into a Maximum Average Count. This is done by multiplying the Average Rate by the Maximum Area for the data:
      $$\bar{u}\ a_i = (0.138)(58) = 8.004.$$

(e)   Use this Maximum Average Count to find probability limits from Table 10.7:
      A Count of 8.004 gives
      $$0.005\ LCL_c = 0.5$$
      $$0.995\ UCL_c = 16.5$$

(f)   Now one must convert these Probability Limits for Counts into Narrow Probability Limits for Rates. This is done by dividing each of these probability limits by the Maximum Area for the data.
      $$0.005\ LCL_u = 0.5/58\ 0.0086$$
      $$0.995\ UCL_u = 16.5/58 = 0.2845$$

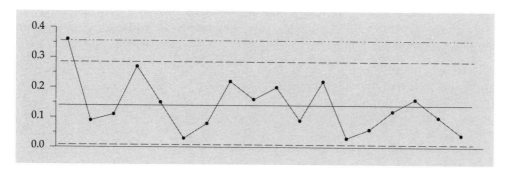

Figure 10.11: Narrow and Wide Probability Limits for Radiator Leak Rates

10.7 Summary

Table 10.1 listed the various charts which could be used with Count Data. Having laid out the options, the first question in practice will always be "Which chart to use?" To help in answering this question the flowchart of Figure 10.12 was constructed.

Attribute Data are data based upon counts. Data which are not based upon counts will have to be tracked using either an Average and Range Chart, or an *XmR* Chart, or a Moving Average Chart. When the four conditions for the use of the Binomial Model are satisfied one may use either the *np*-chart or the *p*-chart to track Attribute Data. When the four conditions for the use of the Poisson Model are satisfied one may use either the *c*-chart or the *u*-chart to track Attribute Data. If one is not sure if the conditions for either the Binomial Model or the Poisson Model are satisfied, then one may always use an *XmR* Chart to track Attribute Data. If the Areas of Opportunity vary from sample to sample, then one will have to convert the counts into rates prior to charting the Attribute Data.

The conditions for the Binomial Model and the Poisson Model are the basis for the computation of the limits for the *np*-, *p*-, *c*-, and *u*-Charts. All four of these charts assume that the variation is a function of the average, and construct limits accordingly. If these conditions are not satisfied, then the assumption is incorrect, and the use of the *np*-, *p*-, *c*-, or *u*-chart will be inappropriate. The user is responsible for actively verifying that the conditions are satisfied in each application of these charts.

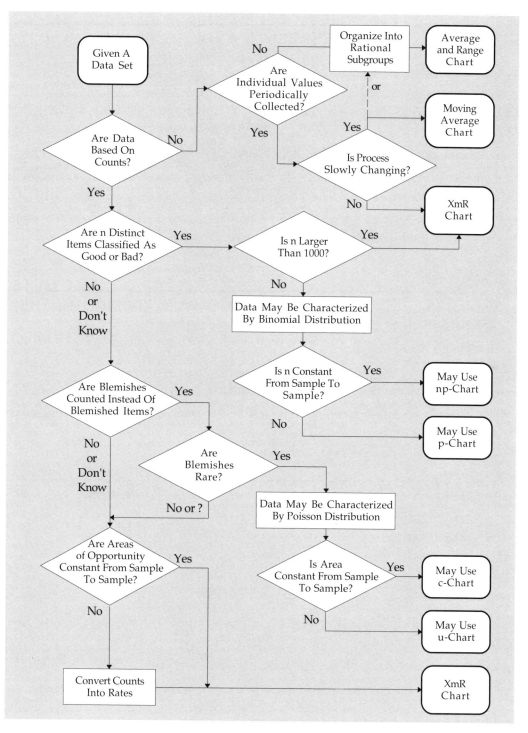

Figure 10.12: Choosing A Control Chart

Exercise 10.1:

The Number of Rejected Parts Per Basket from Example 10.2 are given below:

11 20 19 24 19 18 16 42 18 24 15 17 19 26 19 22 21 32 22 33 30

(a) Find the Moving Ranges for these data, and compute limits for a Moving Range Chart.

(b) Delete the out-of-control Moving Ranges and revise the Average Moving Range.

(c) Compute Natural Process Limits for the Number of Rejected Parts Per Basket and place these data on an *XmR* Chart.

(d) Compare this *XmR* Chart with the *np*-Chart in Figure 10.3. Are the same signals detected by the two charts?

Exercise 10.2:

The data in Exercise 10.1 were collected in November. The following April the Number of Rejected Parts Per Basket for the same part were:

18 9 14 15 10 16 12 13 25 9 9 10 10 6 4 1 2 3 5 7 13

(a) There were 60 parts in each sample. Place these data on an *np*-Chart.

(b) Has there been any appreciable change in this process between November and April?

Exercise 10.3:

The 20 proportions from Table 10.4 are shown below in four columns.

.204	.284	.140	.170
.173	.202	.132	.173
.144	.139	.161	.196
.162	.109	.102	.173
.134	.125	.143	.213

(a) Find the Moving Ranges for these data, and compute limits for a Moving Range Chart.

(b) Delete the out-of-control Moving Range and revise the Average Moving Range.

(c) Compute Natural Process Limits for the Daily Proportion of Incomplete Invoices and place these data on an *XmR* Chart.

(d) Compare this *XmR* Chart with the *p*-Chart shown in Figure 10.4. Are the same signals detected by the two charts?

Exercise 10.4:

A plant producing western boots and work shoes had the following quality assurance program.

The boots and shoes were 100% inspected as they were loaded onto racks to be sent to boxing. Each rack held 12 pairs of boots or shoes. Pairs found to have either major or minor defects were set aside and not placed on the racks.

Following this 100% inspect and sort procedure a quality audit inspector drew a daily sample of 225 pairs of boots and shoes from the material on the racks. These 225 pairs were then inspected by the auditor for the presence of major and minor defects. These 225 pairs were obtained by the quality audit inspector selecting 5 pairs "at random" from each rack until 45 racks had been sampled.

The data below are the result of this quality audit procedure. They are the proportions of pairs with major defects out of the 225 pairs inspected each day for a 36 day period.

1/2	.084	1/15	.080	1/28	.084	2/22	.098
1/3	.098	1/16	.084	1/29	.080	2/23	.102
1/4	.089	1/17	.089	1/30	.093	2/26	.093
1/7	.080	1/18	.087	1/31	.080	2/27	.089
1/8	.107	1/21	.089	2/1	.084	2/28	.107
1/9	.093	1/22	.084	2/4	.089	2/29	.089
1/10	.089	1/23	.093	2/5	.084	3/3	.084
1/11	.098	1/24	.080	2/6	.087	3/4	.098
1/14	.089	1/25	.093	2/21	.093	3/5	.080

(a) What is the Area of Opportunity for each daily sample?

(b) There are two inconsistent values in these data. They may be spotted by plotting these values in a histogram. Obtain the histogram and identify the two inconsistent values.

(c) Except for these two inconsistent values, do these 36 proportions satisfy the four conditions required for the use of the Binomial Model?

(d) Place these data on a p-Chart.

(e) What is unusual about this p-Chart? What could cause this condition?

Exercise 10.5:

Pinholes in a coated surface are blemishes. Once each hour a 300 square inch area is inspected for pinholes and the number of pinholes with an area in excess of 0.0001 square inch is recorded.

0 0 2 3 2 0 1 0 1 1 2 1 4 3 2 0 1 4 2 0 1

(a) What is the Area of Opportunity for each sample?

(b) Do these data satisfy the conditions required for the use of the Poisson Model?

(c) Plot these data on a *c*-Chart.

(d) Plot these data on an *XmR* Chart.

(e) Do the different charts tell the same story regarding these data?

Exercise 10.6:

A painting line paints parts for lawn tractors. The various parts are different sizes, and different areas. Periodically the operator will take a painted part off the line and inspect the paint for blemishes. The data for 14 samples obtained during one shift are given below. The "area" listed is the number of square inches of painted surface.

Count	2	1	3	4	1	6	4	2	2	0	3	2	1	7
Area	38	13	13	25	13	25	38	25	13	13	38	13	13	38
Rate	.053	.077	.231	.160	.077	.240	.105	.080	.154	.000	.079	.154	.077	.184

(a) Do these data satisfy the conditions required for the use of the Poisson Model?

(b) Plot these data on a *u*-Chart.

(c) What does this chart reveal about the painting process?

Exercise 10.7:

Using the distinctions made in Figure 10.7, page 268, characterize the *Premium Percentages of Total Cost* shown in Example 10.1, page 257.

(a) Are these percentages mere ratios, proportions based on measurements, or proportions based on counts?

(b) What kind of control chart could be used for these percentages?

Chapter Eleven

Using Attribute Data Effectively

The preceding chapter outlines three different ways to place Count Data on a control chart. Regardless of which approach is appropriate for a particular set of data, the ultimate effectiveness of any control chart for Count Data depends upon the structure of the data.

11.1 Three Characteristics of Attribute Data

Three characteristics are common to all types of Count Data. Understanding these characteristics is the first step toward using Attribute Data effectively.

First, the inherent frustration in Attribute Data must be recognized. The better the process, the greater the Area of Opportunity must be in order to have sensitive control charts. If the Average Count per sample is not at least 1, the charts will be insensitive. This is illustrated by the 0.995 control limits for the c-Chart. When the Average Count is 2.0, the upper limit is 6.5, which is slightly over three times as large as the Average Count. When the Average Count is 1.1, the upper limit is 5.5, which is five times larger than the Average Count, and when the Average Count is 0.50, the upper limit is 3.5, which is seven times larger than the Average Count. This insensitivity for small Average

Counts means that large Areas of Opportunity are necessary for processes that produce few nonconformities.

Secondly, Attribute Data are no substitute for Measurement Data. Even though go-no-go gauges may be used for efficient 100 percent inspection, they do *not* yield satisfactory data for use with control charts. Moreover, any time that a go-no-go gauge can be used, a measurement is possible. Measurements of a few items are much more revealing than the proportion nonconforming in a large sample. The reason for this can be seen in Figure 11.1. While the three distributions shown are considerably different, they would all show a total of 16% nonconforming on a *p*-chart.

The third common characteristic of Attribute Data is that variation coming from separate sources is difficult to identify. This characteristic is due to the inherent structure of the data. There are several ways that this

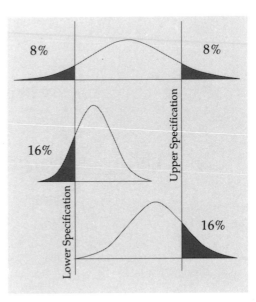

Figure 11.1: Three Distributions With 16 Percent Nonconforming

problem manifests itself. The first of these is in an ambiguity between the effects of the data collection process and the behavior of the production process.

EXAMPLE 11.1:   *Two Sets of np-Charts:*

Consider the four np-charts shown in Figure 11.2. All parts were inspected by an inspect and pack operator. Twice each shift, a data clerk monitored the disposition of 40 consecutive parts. The charts on the left of Figure 11.2 show the results of these samples from the inspect and pack station. The counts on these charts reflect the initial fraction nonconforming in this process.

Due to customer complaints, the particular part represented in these charts was also subjected to an additional 100% re-inspection. Since the parts were packaged in baskets of 40 pieces, the Area of Opportunity is the same for both sets of np-Charts. The np-Charts for the 100% re-inspection are shown on the right side of Figure 11.2. These counts reflect the number nonconforming found after the inspect and pack operator had supposedly removed all nonconforming product!

What is the explanation of the difference between the 100% re-inspections? Was there a difference between the two follow-up inspectors? Or was there a difference in the thoroughness of the inspect and pack operators? Or was there a difference in the way the process was operated from shift to shift? Did the follow-up inspection reveal a problem with the regular production and inspection operation, or was it the follow-up inspection itself that was out-of-control? These charts do not provide the answer. They merely raise important questions that would never be considered in the normal course of events.

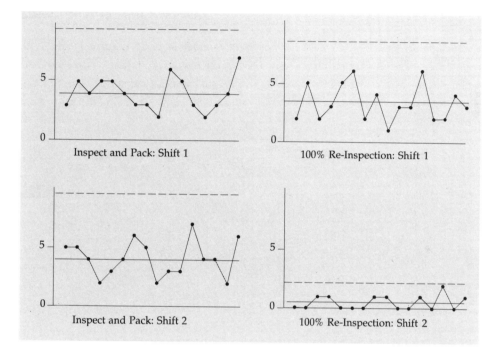

Figure 11.2: Four *np*-Charts for Number Nonconforming for One Product

This confusion between variation due to the way the data were collected and variation due to the production process is part of the difficulty in using Attribute Data effectively. This is especially true when dealing with data from 100 percent inspection at the end of the line. As soon as the results of 100 percent inspection are charted, problems similar to those in the preceding example arise. With several inspectors, how can consistency be guaranteed? With only one inspector, on the other hand, how can the contributing factor of fatigue be ruled out?

For these reasons, the results of 100 percent inspection are rarely the best data for an Attribute Chart. The purpose of the 100 percent inspection is to sort the "good" product from the "bad" product. The control chart, on the other hand, is intended to be used to improve the process to the point where there is no need to do 100 percent inspection. Simply putting the result of the inspection operation on the charts is better than nothing, but it is not the best way to use the charts. In general, a smaller amount of data, collected consistently, is much more useful than a greater amount of data collected in an inconsistent manner.

The combination of different types of nonconformity on one chart is another way that variation from separate sources gets confused on attribute charts. This is illustrated by the following example.

EXAMPLE 11.2:   *Number of Rejected Parts per Basket:*

The data in Example 10.2 consisted of the total number of parts rejected for any reason out of sixty consecutive parts arriving at the inspect and pack station. There were seven specific categories of nonconformity, in addition to a catch-all category. The breakdown of these total counts is shown in Table 11.1, and the np-chart for the total count is reproduced in Figure 11.3.

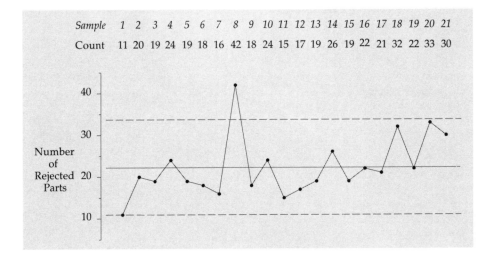

Sample	1	2	3	4	5	6	7	8	9	10	11	12	13	14	15	16	17	18	19	20	21
Count	11	20	19	24	19	18	16	42	18	24	15	17	19	26	19	22	21	32	22	33	30

Figure 11.3: *np*-Chart for Number of Rejected Parts per Basket

Table 11.1: Breakdown of Number of Rejected Parts per Basket

Sample	1	2	3	4	5	6	7	8	9	10	11	12	13	14	15	16	17	18	19	20	21
Total Count	**11**	**20**	**19**	**24**	**19**	**18**	**16**	**42**	**18**	**24**	**15**	**17**	**19**	**26**	**19**	**22**	**21**	**32**	**22**	**33**	**30**
Foreign Material	3	5	4	4	4	3	3	30	4	11	2	3	3	5	3	7	4	5	5	15	2
Damaged Edge		2	4	5	3	5	1	3	3	4	2	3	7	3	3	3	1	10	6	2	14
Sinks	1		1		1	1	1											2	1		
Damaged Mount			1	14	2					1	5	2	7	6	5	1	2				1
Stress Marks		1	5	1	7	1	1	2		1	9	3	1	11	1		2	4	3		
Bubbles		3			1	2	6	3	2				1		2	1	2	1		7	2
Bad Trim	5	1	1		1				4	6	6	1			5	1	1	3	2	2	2
Other	2	8	3			6	4		3	2	1	7	2		2	4	4	7	3	7	11

The np-chart for each of these eight categories is shown in Figure 11.4. The control lim-

its given are the revised limits calculated after deleting samples that were found to be out of control. When the information on these eight charts is combined, fourteen out of twenty-one samples show at least one point out of control on the high side. Yet the control chart for the total counts, shown in Figure 11.3, does not look like two-thirds of the samples are out of control on the high side.

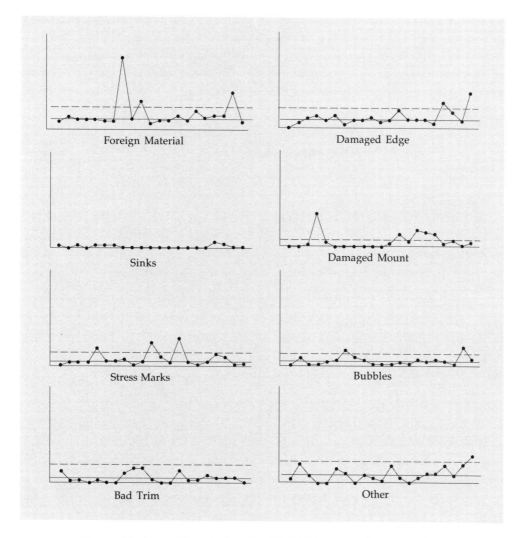

Figure 11.4: *np*-**Charts for the Eight Reasons for Rejection**

The problem with Figure 11.3 is one of charting aggregate counts. The more sources of nonconformity that are combined on one chart, the greater the likelihood that the chart will appear to be in control. Charts, such as that in Figure 11.3, may provide a useful record of what is happening, but they are not very useful in improving the process. They are simply fancy running records, good for telling how bad things have been, but of little use in identifying the Assignable Causes of excessive variation.

This is another reason that 100 percent inspection data are ineffective for use on an Attribute Chart. They rarely discriminate between the different sources of nonconformity, and the counts are generally too aggregated to be useful.

These characteristics of Attribute Data create pitfalls for the unwary. The decreasing sensitivity of the charts as the process gets better, the all-or-nothing nature of the attributes, and the possibilities for aggregating the data until they are useless, combine to make Attribute Data difficult to use effectively. However, once the nature of these problems is understood, steps can be taken to avoid them.

11.2 Using Attribute Data Effectively

The problems identified in the preceding section suggest that it may be more difficult to use Attribute Data than it is to use Measurement Data. Attribute Data have to be made useful. The user must decide between the three different approaches to charting the data, define the categories of nonconformity, and choose an Area of Opportunity that is adequate. Then, the sources of nonconformity must be dis-aggregated.

A major difficulty in defining, or dis-aggregating, the types of nonconformities is the problem of operational definitions. Since it rarely makes sense to use Attribute Data when Measurement Data can be obtained, the use of Attribute Data is generally restricted to those situations in which "blemishes" are being counted. It is the definition of a "blemish" that usually presents the greatest difficulty.

Dr. W. Edwards Deming suggests that in order to be operational, a definition must consist of three parts: (1) a criterion to be applied, (2) a way to determine whether the criterion is satisfied, and (3) a way to interpret the results of the test.[1] Until all three elements are made specific and concrete for a particular nonconformity, there will be no way to obtain consistent counts for that nonconformity. The need for operational definitions is fundamental for all types of data, but it is especially critical when the data consist of counts.

Of course, a full-blown operational definition for each type of nonconformity will take some time to develop. This evolutionary process must be based upon a real-time analysis of the control charts. For it is only by interpreting the chart as it is filled out that one can gain insights into the nature of the different sources of nonconformity. Such insights are the basis for both improved operational definitions and process improvements.

---

[1] See Chapter Nine of *Out Of The Crisis* for a more complete explanation of Operational Definitions.

EXAMPLE 11.3:   The Number of Rejected Parts per Basket (Continued):

In Example 11.2, p.288, the sources of nonconformity were divided into eight categories. Six months later, these eight categories had been subdivided into sixteen different categories. The new categories are shown in Table 11.2. With these new groupings, many categories became specific to single Assignable Causes. As such, they became effective indicators of the presence of those Assignable Causes, making identification and removal much more likely.

Table 11.2: Number of Rejected Parts Per Basket
(Six Months After Table 11.1)

Sample	1	2	3	4	5	6	7	8	9	10	11	12	13	14	15	16	17	18	19	20	21	22	23	24	25	26	27	28
Foreign Material	8		3	3	8		6	4	2	1	5	1	4	4	2		4	2			1	1	1	1	2	3		
Damaged Edge			1	2	2	1	1	1	1	4	6	1	3	5		1		5	1									
Stress Marks	2	2	2	1	3	1			1		2	1	1	2	3	1		1				1	1	1	5	10		
Flash On Edge							2											1										
Lint	1	16		2	1			2		10	5	1	1		1	1	2		1									
Flo-Line (outer)				1																								
Flo-Line (center)																												
Chatter on Edge				10	8	16																	1	3				
Sink in Center							1										1											
Sink on Edge																		1										
Bad Insert Trim	3	3					1							7	2	3	1										38	30
Bubbles	1	1	1				1	4	1		1	1					1											
Vapor Drip	1	1					1	2												1								
Flash on Center																												
Bad Trim on Edge	4						3	1	1				1			2												
Other	1	8		6	1		1	1					12	2	2	1		1	2									
Total Count	21	31	7	24	26	18	9	14	15	10	16	12	13	25	9	9	10	10	6	4	1	2	3	5	7	13	38	30

Rejects for lint were formerly counted as foreign material rejects, along with those due to vapor drip and other types of contamination. Since everyone in the department wore cotton gloves, lint seemed to be inevitable. But when lint was listed as a separate category, the data immediately challenged this commonly held notion. The rejections for lint came in clusters, as can be seen in the first 18 samples of Table 11.2. Once the data for lint were separated from other counts, it was only a short time until one worker noticed that rejections for lint correlated with the amount of rework coming to the inspect and pack station. The rework operation consisted of wiping the plastic part with an acetone-soaked cheesecloth, providing an obvious source of contamination. When further investigation confirmed this suspicion, the cheesecloth was changed to organdy at the rework *station. This change took place just before sample 19. As the data show, this simple change in the system solved the lint problem.*

By getting the categories specific to individual Assignable Causes, the counts become very effective monitors. But when the counts are aggregated, they are much less useful.

The total counts still track the overall performance, but the individual categories target the problems. Looking at the overall counts in Table 11.2, it can be seen that this process was much improved over the six month period. This improvement was primarily due to the solution of simple problems, like the one described above, and these solutions resulted from the use of the specific breakdown of the total count.

The focused nature of the breakdown of the total count is shown in the last two samples in Table 11.2. It can be seen that the sudden increase in rejections was entirely due to Bad Trim on Insert. This problem occurred whenever the trim operators were using dull trim blades. However, in an effort to control non-product inventory, the operators were only issued one blade at a time, and could not leave their station to obtain a new blade during their shift. Therefore, they remained at their station, turning out nonconforming product. This control chart opened the eyes of management to the inherent problem in this system. By simply issuing two blades to each trim operator at the start of each shift, they always had a replacement set, and thus this problem was eliminated.

This process of getting Attribute Data focused and specific is the heart of using Attribute Data effectively. The actual way to do this varies with the situation, but the principle is the same across all applications. Until Attribute Data are made specific, nothing will happen. The following example shows how to do this when the process is highly operator dependent.

EXAMPLE 11.4:   *The Looping Operation:*

A medium-sized hosiery mill, employing about 1500 workers, had the reputation of being a "quality" mill. This was based on careful 100 percent inspection operation that graded the output of the plant into four categories: Firsts, Irregulars, Seconds, and Rags.

In spite of this reputation the mill faced a real problem. Since workers were paid by the piece, each had to process a certain number of pieces per week in order to earn the minimum wage. If a worker's output did not meet the minimum wage amount the company had to make up the difference. Facing an increase in the minimum wage rate, the managers realized that it would be nearly impossible to operate with the current equipment and technology without making substantial "make-up" payments each week. Some way had to be found to increase income in spite of a soft market and stiff competition.

The obvious solution was to change the mix of Firsts, Irregulars, Seconds, and Rags. By making more Firsts, and less of the other grades, revenues could be increased without increased costs. Operators would also benefit since a penalty system for bad work was in effect (each worker was docked two good pieces for each bad piece found at final inspection).

After consultation with one of the authors, the president decided to send about 20 of his supervisors to an SPC class. Incidentally, this was the first time many of these supervisors had ever had a chance to talk with each other. After this course one of the authors sat down with the supervisors and helped to plan how to use SPC in the plant. Due to the nature of the work, and the enthusiasm of the foreman, they decided to begin in the Looping Department.

The looping operation closed the toe of a knitted stocking. It was a tedious operation, requiring the operator to thread the toe of the stocking onto a comb-like device called the looper dial. Exactly one thread, from each side of the stocking, had to go into each gap between the teeth. A missed gap would create a hole in the finished stocking, and placing two threads from the same side in one gap would create a pucker. After the stocking was threaded onto the dial, the end was trimmed. If it was trimmed too long the seam would be bulky which would result in a downgraded stocking. If it was trimmed too short, the stocking would fall off the dial and the operator would have to start all over again. Since they were paid by the piece, the loopers considered this to be "bad form." After being trimmed, the toe of the stocking was stitched by the looping machine, and the finished stocking was automatically ejected into the looper's production box.

To collect some data an inspector was brought into the looping department from the boxing department. This inspector would inspect four consecutively looped stockings, four times each day, from each operator. In this manner, sixteen pieces were obtained from each operator during the course of each day. The inspector was taught how to randomize the order in which she visited the different operators in order to prevent the operators from "loading" the output box. The inspector recorded the type and number of defects found, by operator, and records were kept on a historical basis during the months of June and July. (Since these data were considered to be personnel records, a secretary in the personnel department actually maintained these control charts.)

During that time no conscious effort was made to improve the process. The objective was merely to measure the quality of the looping work. Individual records were combined into a departmental record for each day of the two-month period. The departmental average amount of defective work was 4.8 percent for those two months. The p-chart for the department is shown in Figure 11.5. The control limits shown are based on the average Area of Opportunity.

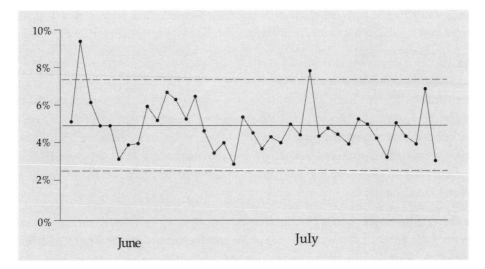

Figure 11.5: *np*-Chart for Looping Department during June and July

The chart in Figure 11.5 shows a fair degree of stability with only two points outside the limits. The first point was expected, since there had never before been an inspector located in the department. The presence of a person taking work from a machine, and inspecting it on the spot, was very upsetting to the operators. On the second day of the inspection the operators were so upset that it showed on the chart. In fact, on that day the employees were in such an uproar that it was necessary to tell the operators that the company was co-operating with a professor in gathering some "real" data for class use, and that their jobs were not threatened. This explanation seemed to reassure them and no further incidents took place.

The second out-of-limits point had a different cause. It was the custom in the hosiery industry to shut down for a week-long holiday around the 4th of July. The second point outside the control limits occurred on the Monday following this mid-summer holiday.

The chart in Figure 11.5 was explained to the Vice President for Manufacturing in the following manner. The conditions in the looping department were described as being relatively stable. Assuming that no changes were made, about 5 percent defective product would be produced weekly.

Upon hearing this the Vice President swore that the company could not continue to operate with 5 percent defective products in looping—the company would be closed within six months under these conditions!

Of course, he had not previously known what the defect level was in the looping department, nor in any other particular department. The only record ever kept had been at the final pairing and boxing operation. No one had ever known just how bad things really were in the various departments even though the company had been in operation for 65 years.

Since the Vice President was dissatisfied with 5 percent defectives in the looping operation, he was asked what a "good" level would be. After reflection, he replied that a good operation would produce "no more than 2 percent defectives." Of course, statements of this sort tend to become targets or goals, and this proved to be no exception. However, since goals do not provide the means to improve the system they can easily lead to the distortion of both the data and the system itself.[2] Fortunately, in this case, they already had an action plan for process improvement.

A meeting was called for all employees involved in the looping operation. The consensus was that the optimum method of improvement was to work individually with each operator who needed help. Accordingly, the previously-collected data were used to create an np-chart for each worker during the June-July period. The central line was placed at 0.8 units (16 times 0.048 = 0.77, and the corresponding UCL_{np} is 3.4).

These charts readily showed which operators could be classified as good, average, or poor workers. The charts were reviewed with the department supervisor, who was instructed to help each operator in a work improvement effort.

The effect of this program was almost immediate. Beginning in August, the supervisor sat down with the operators, one at a time, and showed them their own charts. (Although employees were not shown the charts of others, within 10 minutes of the review everyone seemed to know how everyone else had done. The news traveled at the speed of sound!) The operators were told that if their work was average they should have no more than three defective pieces out of sixteen. Along with this a real effort was made to study work habits and correct deficiencies. Some of the case histories follow.

---

[2] Brian Joiner lists three ways to meet a goal: Improve the system, distort the system, or distort the data.

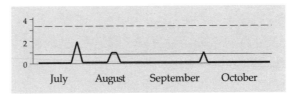

Figure 11.6: *np*-Chart for Operator 75

Operator 75 was an excellent operator. The supervisor was able to incorporate some of her techniques into a general routine that benefitted all.

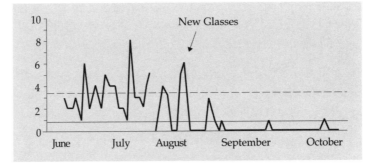

Figure 11.7: *np*-Chart for Operator 22

Operator 22 was much worse than average in July. After observing her at work, the supervisor referred her to the personnel department for a possible eye examination. Upon examination, the doctor found that she was blind in the left eye, and only had 6/20 vision in the right eye. Her right eye was correctable to 20/20, and with new glasses, her work immediately improved.

This experience caused the company to reconsider its lack of policy regarding eye exams. It finally mandated periodic vision examinations for all operators. The initial group of examinations revealed additional operators who had real difficulties in seeing well enough to do their work.

New glasses helped Operator 22 increase her hourly earnings by over 15 percent. At the same time, she increased her quality sufficiently to become a "Gold Star" looper. (The basic requirement to become a "Gold Star" looper was to produce no more than three mendable defectives per month. Being a "Gold Star" looper was a considerable honor, and those who lost this rating worked hard to regain it the next month.)

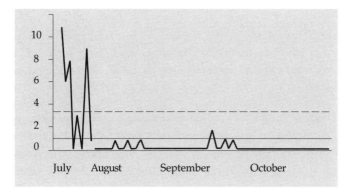

Figure 11.8: *np*-Chart for Operator 27

Operator 27 seemed to be the least capable operator during the analysis period. When the supervisor discussed her chart with her, and explained the quality improvement program, her response was: "Why, I've been here for five years, and this is the first time anybody has told me they were interested in good quality. I can do a much better job, if it makes any difference." Her record in August, and thereafter, attests to the accuracy of her statement.

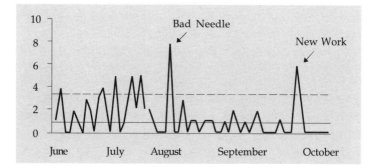

Figure 11.9: *np*-Chart for Operator 106

The record of Operator 106 deteriorated between June and July. Examination of her personnel record revealed that she had been moved from the training classes to the production line in June. Beginning in July she was pressured to improve her production in order to minimize the make-up pay. In response to this pressure she had increased production, as well as the proportion of defective stockings!

As the supervisor searched for an explanation for her poor performance, he found that her personnel record noted an impairment in her right arm. This impairment made it difficult for her to load the stockings on the looping machine, thus slowing her down.

By obtaining a "Handicapped Worker's Certificate" from the U. S. Dept. of Labor the supervisor could exempt her from the minimum wage. This removed the pressure to produce more, and allowed her to produce a higher percentage of good pieces. Following this exemption her only bad day occurred when she had to adjust to a new type of knitting.

In spite of these successes, it was the case of Operator 73 that ended resistance to SPC in the plant. Operator 73 was a lady in her early sixties who had been looping for ten years. During June and July her production had either been up or down, with nothing in between. The supervisor worked with her during August and noted some improvement. In September she decided that new glasses might help, but the chart shows no evidence of improvement.

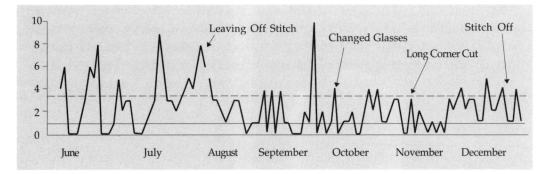

Figure 11.10: *np*-**Chart for Operator 73**

By October it was apparent that she had improved as much as possible. When compared to other operators during the same time period, her work was indeed poor. Although the supervisor did not think that she could do any other job at the plant, he was reluctant to terminate a ten-year employee. He decided to give her more time.

In November her record was no better. By that time every operator in the Looping Department knew that all employees, except Operator 73, had made vast improvements. The other loopers began to resent the effort they had made to improve when nothing seemed to be done about the poor work of Operator 73. During November she contributed 20 percent of the defectives for the whole department!

The operators began to question the supervisor about what he intended to do about Operator 73. Group pressure continued to build until the supervisor finally advised the personnel department that something had to be done. "Old 73" was disrupting progress, and requiring more and more of his time. The managers reluctantly, and with real fear of the consequences, agreed to terminate her employment at the end of December.

At the company Christmas party it turned out that "Old 73" won the first prize—an expensive electric range—in a "random" drawing. Near the end of the year, she was informed that the company could no longer use her, and that arrangements for a suitable pension had been made. When told of this action "Old 73" was neither surprised, nor dismayed. She said, in fact, that she had known for 10 years that she could not loop well, and could not learn how. She was ten years ahead of the management! She left with a good attitude, realizing that the supervisor had done everything possible to help her improve her performance.

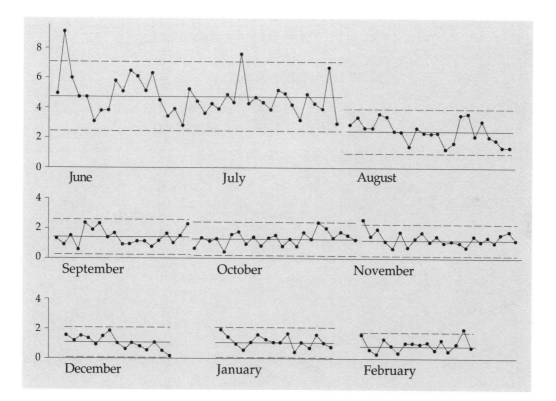

Figure 11.11: *np*-Chart for Looping Department

The overall record of the Looping Department was one of continual improvement. In the first month, the percentage of defective pieces dropped from 4.8 percent to 2.4 percent. In the following months, it rarely rose above 2 percent. By February, it was down to an average of 0.8 percent. This amounted to an 83 percent reduction in the number of defective pieces produced, and this reduction was accomplished in a period of seven months.

When the quality of the product is highly operator-dependent, Attribute Data will generally need to be made operator-specific. When operators do not have a direct influence on the product, then other factors must be used to make Attribute Data useful.

EXAMPLE 11.5:   *A Robotic Assembly Operation:*

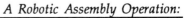

An automotive supplier was attempting to use six robots to install pal-nuts on a door trim panel. Two door trim panels would ride on a cart down a track past the robots. While the cart was stopped at each station a robot would attempt to install four pal-nuts. Each Trim panel was designed to have 12 pal-nuts in all.

Figure 11.12: A Pal-Nut

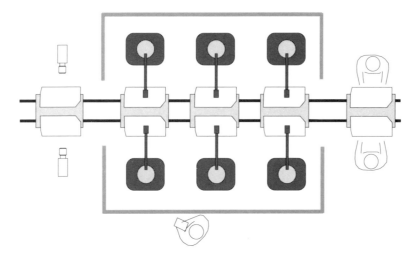

Figure 11.13: The Pal-Nut Robots

Of course these robots had a vision system to identify the parts and locate the position of the studs for the pal-nuts. With the constant attention of twelve skilled tradesmen, these six robots were consistently installing about 70 percent of the nuts. The other 30 percent simply slid down the face of the trim panel and fell off. In fact, so many nuts were falling off that these six robots had been specially modified—they had diapers! Large sheets of vinyl were attached to each robot to catch the dropped nuts and funnel them into collection boxes.

Finally, in a cramped space beside the robot station two men had the inevitable job of installing pal-nuts on mangled plastic studs. Needless to say, they were the bottleneck for this operation.

Knowing that this operation was in trouble, the engineering and production staff had spent five months collecting information about their purchased parts. The "capability studies" which they had performed filled a 2 inch binder, yet these data were all worthless. None of these capability studies had considered the production processes. None of the data had been rationally subgrouped. No one knew how many parallel sources they had for a single item, and no one knew if the production processes were in statistical control or not. In short, they had spent five months collecting data, yet they had absolutely no way to extrapolate from these data to make reasonable predictions for the future.

During this same time they had also tried to collect some data from the assembly operation. These data were collected in the following manner. Several times during the day shift one of the six robots would be randomly selected. The number of missed nuts would then be recorded, either for a certain period of time, or until a change in the part number occurred. At the end of the day, these data would be entered into a computerized data base. By the next day, the engineers would have tables of percentages to examine.

This approach was problematic in that there were nine different parts going down each assembly line, giving a total of 54 different robot-part combinations. While each "subgroup" represented only one of these combinations, successive "subgroups" did not represent the same combinations. In fact, it could be several days before the same robot-part combination reappeared in the data. This made interpretation of the data very difficult. Although the data were selected from across all combinations, the record was incoherent and fragmentary.

It was at this point that one of the authors began to work with the group. At his suggestion, the group began with a Cause and Effect diagram. Here, their broad, but unfocused, data base was useful, especially in forming a Pareto diagram of where in the process their problems occurred. Following this, they began to collect data for just one robot-part combination. The robot selected was the one which appeared to have the worst record, and the part selected was one of the high-volume parts. The intent was to observe Robot 7L continuously while Trim Panel A was being assembled in order to have a coherent record of what was happening in this process.

Two weeks later, one of the engineers excitedly gave the author a description of a problem with the stopping mechanism for the assembly-line carts. He was sure that this was the reason for the missed installations, and was trying to think of ways to measure the stop position for each cart. When asked what data confirmed that this was indeed the problem, he said that he had none. He had slipped back into the old way of problem solving: trying to leap from the statement of the problem to the solution, without any intervening steps. The author suggested that the assembly operation was a very dynamic process, and the only way to gain the necessary insight was with a dynamic monitor, such as a control chart. If the carts were suspect, then the methods of data collection should be changed in order to preserve the information about the carts. Beginning at this point a new data collection worksheet was used. In addition, a second high-volume part was *added to the data base. Now Robot 7L was observed whenever either one of these two high-volume parts was being assembled. A facsimile of the data sheet is shown in Figure 11.14.*

Robot No. __7L__
Part No. __Panel A__
Time and Date __1:15 pm 4/1__

Cart No.	Attempted	Position 1							Position 2							Position 3							Position 4							Totals
		1	2	3	4	5	6	7	1	2	3	4	5	6	7	1	2	3	4	5	6	7	1	2	3	4	5	6	7	
1	X							X																						1
2	X																													
3	X									X							X													2
4	X					X							X							X							X			4
5																														
6	X					X							X							X							X			4
7	X					X																								1
8	X																													
9	X																													
10	X																													
11																														
12																														

Figure 11.14: Data Collection Sheet for Trim Line Pal-Nut Robots

There were seven different reasons for a missed installation that could be observed from outside the robot cage. With this new data collection sheet the context for each missed installation is preserved. One can tell which robot, which trim panel, which cart, which position, and which failure mode for each and every missed installation. It would take about ten minutes for a full round of carts to pass the robots. With each round a new sheet of paper was used. Each check mark in the "attempted" column represented four attempted installations. The sum of these check marks, times four, defined the Area of Opportunity for the total number of missed installations. Thus, the data collection sheet organized the data for easy collection and the preservation of the context for each event.

With this in-depth data on specific robot-part combinations, the skilled tradesmen began

*to look over the shoulder of the data collector. They found that they could identify prob-
lems quickly and easily by looking at this data collection sheet. For example, one discovery was that the filter for the vacuum system needed to be cleaned every three days rather
than once a week. Of course, such discoveries were applied to all six robots.*

*A new data collection sheet was started each time the carts made a complete cycle of the
assembly line, or whenever the part number changed. The structure imposed by this data
collection sheet allowed many different questions to be answered from the same data. If
one location was consistently missed, then the programming would be suspect. If one
cart consistently had misses, then the cart would be suspect. Other combinations of failure mode and location would be suggestive of other problems. The running records for
the two robot-part combinations are shown in Figures 11.15 and 11.16.*

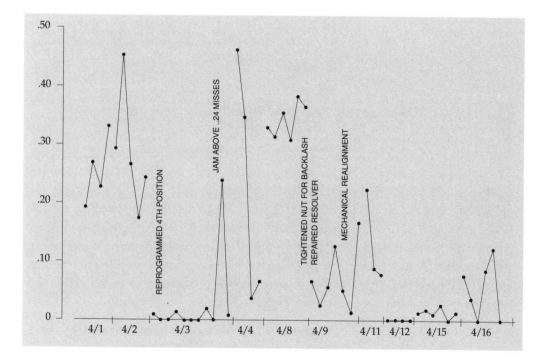

Figure 11.15: Running Record of Missed Installations for Panel A

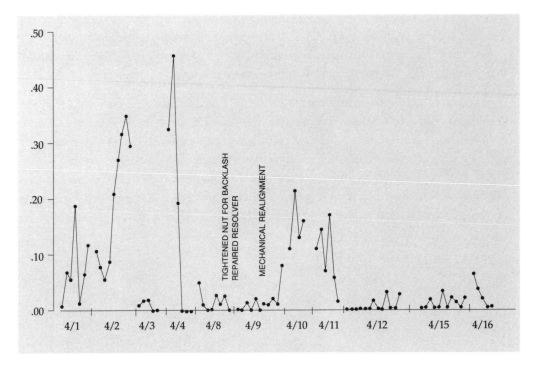

Figure 11.16: Running Record of Missed Installations for Panel B

Both of these running records show 4/3 and 4/12 to have been very good days. However, the erratic performance on other days suggested that many Assignable Causes were still present. It seemed that the equipment was capable of doing the job, but the personnel had not yet learned how to maintain it properly. In fact, on the chart for panel B, the data for 4/2 show just how fast the process could deteriorate. Each sample point represents a ten-minute interval, and most of these were sequential. From the third sample to the eighth, within a hour's time, the process went from 6 percent missed to 34 percent missed. This suggested that until the robots were maintained more consistently, they would have to be monitored almost constantly.

While many were pleased that the overall installation rate had climbed from 70 percent to 92 percent during this period when the data were used effectively, these results were nowhere near what could have been done. The robots appear to be capable of 100 percent installation, if and when they are brought into, and maintained in, a state of control.

11.3 Summary

The key feature of the data collection described in the previous example is the preservation of the ordering of each count in space and time so that this information could be used to assist in interpreting the counts. When people think of Attribute Data in terms of simple tallies, they usually fail to impose a useful structure on their data. This failure is a major cause of disappointing results in the use of Attribute Data.

This is why one must work to make the Count Data specific. With Measurement Data, this is not a major problem because the act of obtaining the measurement usually makes the values specific enough. But with Attribute Data, the act of counting allows a certain vagueness to creep in: what is being counted? Is there an operational definition for the attribute?

Moreover, once the count has been made specific, the structure of the data must be preserved by the way the counts are recorded. Measurements of different characteristics are not usually combined, but counts are routinely combined, and every time this happens, some of the structure in the data is lost. This loss of information can only be avoided by positive action on the part of the investigator.

There are two guidelines for this positive action. First, are the categories of nonconformity sufficiently focused so that there is likely to be only one Assignable Cause per category? Secondly, does the data collection system allow backtracking to identify exactly what happened, and where it happened? As long as the answer to either of these questions is minimally negative, there is room for improvement in the quality of the Attribute Data.

Good Attribute Data are not obtained by chance. They occur when management thinks about, and carefully plans, the collection of the data for the control charts. While this is important with Measurement Data, it is absolutely essential when dealing with counts.

11.4 Afterword

While dis-aggregation is the key for the use of Attribute Data, it also plays a role with Measurement Data as well—as may be seen in the following example.

EXAMPLE 11.6: _____ *The Motor Mount Story:*

A company that produced motor mounts had a continuing problem with adhesion failures. Out of each batch of mounts, a certain number were tested to failure. The value recorded for this test was the tension at which the failure occurred. Quarter by quarter, the test showed that at least 4 percent of the mounts failed at performance load levels. This poor showing was even worse in the spring and summer quarters. This high failure rate had persisted for years, in spite of many attempts by the engineers to make things better. The actual percentages of mounts that failed under performance loads are shown in Figure 11.17.

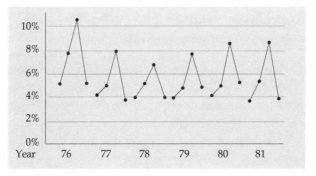

Figure 11.17: Percentage Failing Under Performance Loads 1976-1981

The motor-mount area began to implement the techniques given in this book in late winter of 1982. In the spring of that same year only 3 percent of the tested mounts failed under performance loads. In the summer quarter, this figure was down to 2.5 percent. This unparalleled improvement caught everyone's attention. When the plant manager asked what had been done to make this improvement, the engineers and supervisors could not identify any one particular thing that was different. The only identifiable difference was the use of control charts at each step of the operation. These charts showed that there had been a slight reduction in the variation for each step of the process. The lower rate of failure was due to the cumulative effect of these reductions of variation. Moreover, these improvements continued in the following quarters, as can be seen in Figure 11.18.

Making slight improvements in the consistency of each step in the production process pays off in a compound manner. As the variation is reduced at one step, subsequent steps are made easier. The material coming to each step has a lower average Taguchi loss. This makes it possible to spend less time coaxing the process to work, and more time on ways to improve the process. By continuing this cycle throughout the process, the final product can be dramatically improved.

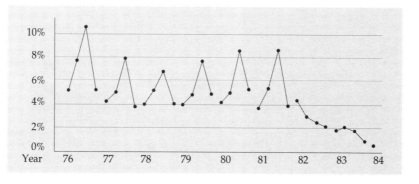

Figure 11.18: Percentage Failing Under Performance Loads 1976-1984

The charts in Figures 11.17 and 11.18 are *report card charts*. They do not actually cause the changes to take place. They do, however, record the cumulative effect of the improvements that were made by *using control charts at each of the 14 process steps.* The information in Figures 11.17 and 11.18 is far too cumulative to pin-point specific problems. Finally, note that there was no one "magic bullet" fix for this process. There was no one thing that needed to be changed in order to improve their performance. Instead, it was a matter of doing the same things they had always done, but doing them with less variation. And the key to doing this was the effective use of the control charts at each step of the process.

Chapter Twelve

Getting Started

As emphasized throughout this book, the purpose for collecting data is to have a basis for taking appropriate actions. In order to fulfill this role, the data must satisfy three conditions: (1) the data must be the right data, (2) the data must be analyzed in such a manner that the results can be easily understood, and (3) these results must be interpreted in the context of the original data.

This book has concentrated on the latter two conditions: ways of analyzing and interpreting data. This chapter enlarges upon the first condition: how to collect the right data.

Since most industrial problems arise out of the bewildering array of factors that influence a process, the first step in the use of data is that of choosing which variables to monitor. This choice is made easier by using one or more of three basic graphic techniques: Flowcharts, Cause and Effect Diagrams, or Pareto Charts.

12.1 Flowcharts

Flowcharts are tools for visualizing a process. Like all of the other tools in this book they use the power of a graph to communicate complex relationships with the greatest clarity in the least amount of time. Flowcharts are a vital first step in the process of continual improvement because they help to define the process that is to be the object of one's efforts. Whether the project involves one person or many, the proper visualization of the process is essential to having people work on the right things.

When working with administrative systems, the flowchart may be the only way to make the process visible. In fact, the construction of the flowchart may be the catalyst for getting a non-functional system fixed. This is what happened with the flowchart represented in Figure 12.1. Although the elements of Figure 12.1 are not legible, the overall complexity is immediately apparent—the simple act of ordering tools from the central tool room involved 60 steps. This flowchart not only defines the process, but it also establishes the need to refine the system. After the plant manager saw this flowchart, the system was simplified.

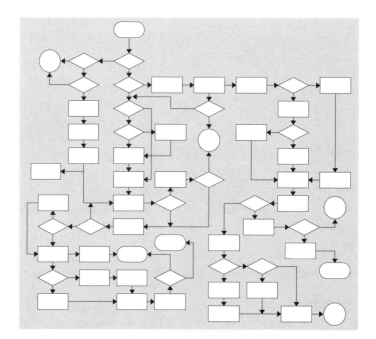

Figure 12.1: Ordering Tools From The Central Tool Room

Flowcharts are so powerful that once people get used to using them they soon find they cannot imagine working without them. Not only will they be used with the more nebulous administrative problems, but also with the more concrete production problems as well.

There are certain formal conventions for flowcharting, but one need not make this a complex or mysterious procedure. The idea of a flowchart is to show the flow of material, or paper, or communications, or information, as these pertain to the performance of a certain job or procedure. Some people like to start and end flowcharts with oval boxes. Rectangular boxes are used for steps in a process. Diamonds are commonly used for decision points, where the flow path splits into two or more branches. Circles are used to connect portions of a flowchart together. These refinements and conventions are useful, but the real power of a flowchart does not lie in the use of pretty graphics. Rather it comes from the visual connections between the various steps in the process being flowcharted. This power can only be unleashed when a flowchart is actually constructed. Just knowing how to create a flowchart doesn't count.

Finally, it is easy to draw macro-level flowcharts. Everyone may know that there is a certain sequence of steps that must be followed. Many times the power of the flowchart is not fully realized until a micro-level flowchart is created. For example, one plant was having trouble processing requests for quotations (RFQ's) in a timely manner. It was taking them an average of 71 working days to return a RFQ, and one RFQ was found to have taken 271 working days to process! The flowchart for processing RFQ's had 17 steps, or so everyone thought. When they actually sat down to flowchart the complete procedure for processing RFQ's they found that the process had over 400 steps, and that over 70% of these steps added no value to the process.

Until you have drawn your flowchart, you really do not know your process.

12.2 Cause and Effect Diagrams

Quite often a large number of factors will be involved in a problem. When this happens an organized approach is necessary in order to establish and maintain statistical control. One of the simplest tools for this organization is the Cause and Effect Diagram.

The Cause and Effect Diagram was first applied in conjunction with statistical process control in Japan. Dr. Kaoru Ishikawa found that most plant personnel were overwhelmed by the number of factors that could influence a particular product or process. Thus, in 1950, he began using a "fault tree" as a tool for organizing the attack on a particular problem. This practice proved to be so effective that it spread rapidly throughout Japan. The versatility of a Cause and Effect Diagram makes it a useful tool for organizing problem solving efforts in every area of the manufacturing and service industries.

The versatility comes from the way in which a Cause and Effect Diagram is created, while its power comes from the graphic representation of the relationship between problems and their sources. The general procedure for making a Cause and Effect Diagram follows:

1. Choose the effect to be studied, and write it at the end of a horizontal arrow.
2. List all the factors that influence the effect under consideration.
3. Arrange and stratify these factors. Choose the principal factors, operations, and subdivisions of activity. These form the major branches off the horizontal arrow.
4. Draw the sub-branches for the various sub-factors or sub-activities. This process of sub-dividing is continued until all variables are included on the diagram.
5. Check the diagram to make sure that all known causes of variation are included on the chart.

A simple Cause and Effect diagram is shown in Figure 12.2. Typical diagrams usually have more major branches than this example. Many times there will be five major branches which will be labeled as Materials, Machines, Operators, Methods, and Environment. Other organizations are also possible. The key is to make the Cause and Effect Diagram fit the problem.

Since the intent is to use the diagram to conceptualize the process, it is best if the diagram reflects the perspective of many different individuals who are closely connected with the process. Diagrams drawn by only one or two individuals are usually rather poor, because they lack this broad base of observation of the process. For this reason, Cause and Effect Diagrams are often drawn during brainstorming sessions that include the workers. Some guidelines for this type of activity are given below.

1. Everyone should be encouraged to contribute.
2. No criticism should be made of any suggestion.
3. Suggestions are not restricted to factors present in one's own work area.
4. A period of observation, between the time when the chart is started and the time when it is finished may prove helpful.
5. Concentrate on how to eliminate the trouble, rather than getting sidetracked on justifications of why the trouble has occurred.

After a Cause and Effect Diagram has been generated, it may need to be modified and realigned to show the causes in their proper relationships. There should be many sub-branches and even some sub-sub-branches. Even though this kind of chart has been called a fishbone diagram, the finished chart should *not* look like the skeleton of a fish. Such a Cause and Effect Diagram would not effectively show the relationships between the various causes and sub-causes because every factor would appear to be a primary factor, making it difficult to decide where to start.

After the Cause and Effect Diagram has been drawn, and rearranged if necessary, the group which generated the diagram should analyze all the factors, noting what is being done to control them. Questions to consider at this time are:

    a. Is there any record of this cause?

    b. Is there a control chart or running record?

    c. Is the factor regulated daily?

    d. Has the factor been standardized?

    e. Is the factor a variable or an attribute?

    f. Does the factor affect bias or precision?

    g. Does this factor interact with other factors?

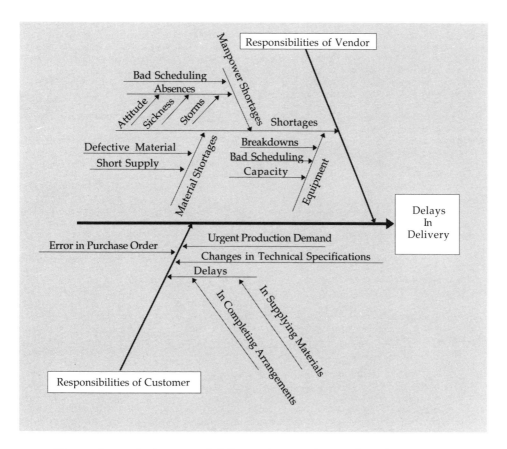

Figure 12.2: A Cause and Effect Diagram For Delays in Delivery

The advantage of having this information noted on the Cause and Effect Diagram is that it highlights areas needing immediate action. Following the initial changes resulting from the Cause and Effect Diagram, plans should be made for using it on a continuing basis.

The Cause and Effect Diagram should be used as a framework for collective efforts. If the process is in control, the diagram will help organize efforts to make the process better.

If the quality characteristic is out of control, the diagram will suggest areas that need to be brought into control in order to stabilize the product.

Secondly, the Cause and Effect Diagram is an effective way of reviewing what has already been accomplished. The diagram often prevents personnel from overlooking various aspects of the problem. Vast improvement for one principal factor may have only a slight impact on the quality characteristic, while modest improvements on several principal factors may result in dramatic improvements in product quality.

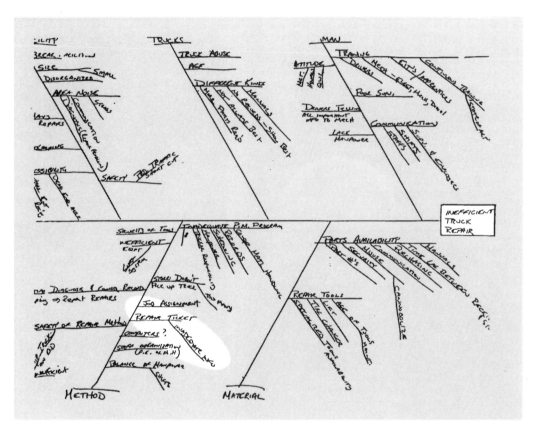

Figure 12.3: Cause and Effect Diagram for Repair of Fork Lifts

The third way that the Cause and Effect Diagram can be used on a continuing basis is to orient new personnel to the problems in a given area. Then they can be smoothly integrated into the work force, without repeating the mistakes of their predecessors.

A fourth way to use Cause and Effect Diagrams is in the integration of operations in different areas, or different departments. This can be especially important in administrative applications, since the delivery of a service is often quite hard to visualize and coordinate.

The Cause and Effect Diagram is effective in the various areas and ways listed above because the process of producing the chart is a thought-provoking and informative process. It helps all involved personnel systematize their thoughts. Yet it is so easy that virtually anyone can understand, and participate in, its construction.

Finally, the same macro/micro effect noted for Flowcharts works with Cause and Effect Diagrams as well. Figure 12.3 shows a Cause and Effect Diagram for the problems associated with the repair of fork-lifts. This Cause and Effect Diagram is rather general and comprehensive. As the team collected data, they found that problems with the repair ticket were the most frequently cited source of trouble. In Figure 12.3 the repair ticket got one sub-branch. It had a note about "inadequate info" attached and that was all. (See highlighted portion of Figure 12.3.) However, when the data focused the team on this aspect of the problem, they produced the Cause and Effect diagram in Figure 12.4 for problems with the repair ticket. Notice the increase in detail between the entry in Figure 12.3 and the diagram in Figure 12.4.

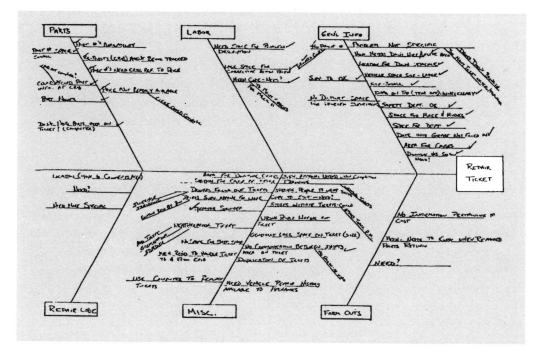

Figure 12.4: Cause and Effect Diagram for Problems With Repair Ticket

This shift from the macro-level to the micro-level is part of the effective use of Cause and Effect Diagrams. Following the Cause and Effect Diagram of Figure 12.4, the repair ticket was redesigned, the appropriate personnel were trained in how to fill out the new ticket, and then data was collected to see if this had had a positive impact upon the original problem.

12.3 Pareto Charts

A Pareto Chart is another simple tool that helps to focus efforts on the problems offering the greatest potential for improvement. This focus of effort is essential simply because of the limitations on money and manpower that are common throughout industry. By focusing everyone's attention on one or two major components of a problem, the distraction of individual agendas is avoided, and it usually becomes much easier to make progress.

The basic structure of a Pareto Chart is the same as a histogram. For each of several different problems, data are gathered to represent each accumulated cost during some period of time. These costs are then represented on a bar graph. By convention, the problems are usually arranged in order of decreasing costs, so that the chart looks something like a staircase. If costs prove too difficult to obtain, the incidence of each of the problem categories can be used.

This simple histogram for different categories can be used effectively to establish priorities for an organization. It is called a Pareto Chart because of the Pareto principle. One way of phrasing this principle is that 20 percent of the problems will cause 80 percent of the headaches. In other words, the major opportunities for improvement are usually concentrated among a minority of the problems. These few problems are the logical ones for the organization to work upon. People need to recognize this in order to coordinate their efforts.

EXAMPLE 12.1:   *A Maintenance Nightmare:*

Oscar was the general foreman of the department that was considered to be the worst one in the plant. This department had 72 machines of various ages and designs, all doing the same task. Each machine had 36 spindles, giving a total of 2592 units that could break down at any moment. Chaos was the rule, rather than the exception, in this department. The pressures and demands of the moment were all-consuming, and yesterday was ancient history.

Oscar quickly realized that he was the one who had to change this situation, and the first thing he tried was a simple Pareto chart. Down the middle of a large piece of quadrille paper he listed his 72 machines. He tallied the breakdowns of one type on one side, and those of another type on the other side of the chart. A facsimile of his chart is shown in Figure 12.5.

With this chart, Oscar could sit down at the end of a week or a month and identify which machines needed an overhaul. He could then plan for these overhauls in order of priority, and work them into the schedule. After three months of doing this, the number of breakdowns had been reduced by about 70 percent. Maintenance no longer needed to staff this department full time.

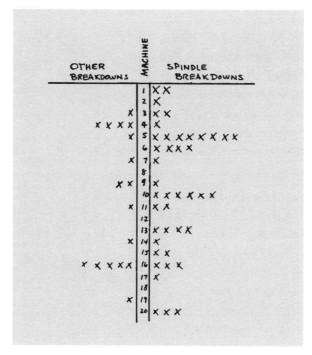

Figure 12.5   Oscar's Pareto Chart

The operators, each of whom had 144 spindles to watch, were no longer as harried as before. The Pareto chart helped to focus and clarify information that had formerly been lost in the chaos of day-to-day operations.

The ability of the Pareto chart to focus attention on the problem that is associated with the greatest cost, or the greatest incidence, is most effective when the ordering of the problems is not changing over time. So while the Pareto chart may sometimes be gainfully used with processes that are in chaos, as in the previous example, it is sometimes ineffective when the process is out of control. Note how this happens in the following example.

EXAMPLE 12.2:   *Pareto Charts for Types of Nonconformity:*

In Table 11.1, p.288, the number of rejected parts per basket is divided into eight different categories, with each different category representing a different reason for rejection. These data were used to create a Pareto chart at the end of each month. The Pareto chart would list the eight categories, arranged in order of decreasing incidence during the pre-

vious month. This Pareto Chart is shown in Figure 12.6.

For the month shown in Table 11.1 Foreign Material was the category that was identified as the major cause of rejections, followed in order by Damaged Edges, Others, Stress, Damaged Mounts, Bad Trim, Bubbles and Sinks. According to this Pareto chart, Foreign Material and Damaged Edges accounted for 45 percent of the rejections, making these two problems the natural places to start working on improvements.

Various distractions kept anything from being done during August. At the end of the month, the man from quality control prepared a Pareto chart. Imagine the chagrin when this Pareto chart showed Stress and Sinks to be the top two problems for August! In July, these had been the fourth and eighth largest reasons for rejection.

The process was out-of-control. It was not ready to be improved, but was in need of stability. The Pareto chart simply provided accident statistics for this out-of-control

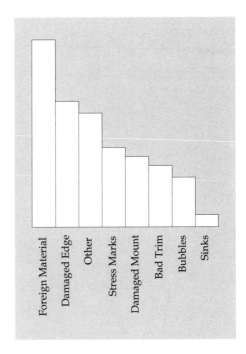

Figure 12.6: Pareto Chart for Number of Rejected Parts Per Basket

process. It showed how bad things had been, and which things were changing from month to month, but it could never help to identify and remove the assignable causes of uncontrolled variation because it would always be too late.

The two previous examples show applications of the Pareto chart to out-of-control processes. In the first, the application was successful because it was tracking deterioration, and deterioration is a one-way process. Its effects will persist until a repair is made. The second application was unsuccessful because it was tracking assignable causes of uncontrolled variation, and these causes can come and go. The only reliable way to identify these assignable causes is by an up-to-date control chart maintained as close to the operation as possible.

Consider how a Pareto Chart for annual data from the process represented by Table 11.1 would appear. As the different reasons for rejection jockeyed about from month to month, they would tend to average out over the course of a year, so that a Pareto Chart summarizing the previous year would almost certainly be very flat. No one category would stand out from the crowd. All would show about the same level of incidence.

Such a Pareto Chart could not be used to focus on one problem. But then, focusing on one problem would be a mistake. The fact that the process is out of control means that the starting point is the identification and removal of the Assignable Causes of uncontrolled variation. Rushing in to work on problems in isolation, instead of working on the process as a whole, achieves nothing. As one "problem" is fixed, another simply takes its place, and no improvement is lasting.

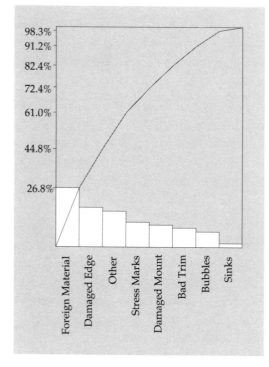

Figure 12.7: Complete Pareto Chart for Data of Table 11.1

One way that the problem with the Pareto Chart in Figure 12.6 could be seen is by completing the cumulative percentage curve portion of the Pareto Chart. This curve provides a check on whether the Pareto Principle is at work or not. The Pareto Principle may be stated as: "80 percent of your trouble comes from 20 percent of your problems." The cumulative proportion explained is found by totaling up the categories to a given point and dividing by the total for all categories. In the previous example, there were a total of 467 parts rejected (see Table 11.1). 125 of these were for Foreign Material, so Foreign Material accounts for 125/467 = 0.268 of the trouble. 209 were due to Foreign Material and Damaged Edge, so these two categories account for 209/467 = 0.448 of the trouble. The complete Pareto Chart for these data is shown in Figure 12.7. It takes *five* of the eight categories to account for 80 percent of the trouble here! This should provide a warning that the Pareto Principle is not at work here. All of the problems need to be addressed, not just the top two. This is the correct diagnosis for this process.

This brings us back to a basic principle: "A process that is out-of-control does not exist as a well-defined entity." Such processes are not operating up to their potential. Their *performance* is less than their *capability*. This is why efforts at modification of such a process are wasted. One can actually improve the consistency of the product stream by simply getting such a process into a reasonable degree of statistical control. This is why the first goal of operations should be to get a production process into statistical control. Then, if the process is not capable of meeting the specifications, one may begin to work on process modifications with some hope of success.

12.4 Summary

Seven basic tools have been presented in this book. These seven tools, when used in concert, have proven to be very effective in problem identification, problem detection, problem solving and problem prevention.

The three tools covered in this chapter are primarily organizational tools for problem solving. Flowcharts, Pareto Diagrams and Cause and Effect Diagrams are effective because of the graphic presentation of relationships. Therefore, they are useful in promoting a unified perspective within an organization.

The simple statistical tools of Histograms and Running Records provide both individuals and groups with easy, but powerful, ways to summarize data. These graphic techniques effectively communicate the content of a data set because of the way they turn digital information into a picture. People will always understand pictures and graphs more quickly and easily than they comprehend columns of numbers. Therefore, these two tools are basic to any attempt to communicate numerical information.

Finally, in addition to these simple tools, there are the more sophisticated tools of Control Charts and Setting The Process Aim. The Control Charts enable one to pursue the difficult problems with in-depth studies. The use of Control Charts, along with the procedure for Setting the Process Aim, enables the operating personnel to maintain those improvements made in the past, while they seek to identify and remove Assignable Causes of variation that occur from time to time. Thus, these techniques are effective in problem detection and problem prevention. They are a source of information for decision making in all areas of operation. Their combination of simplicity and versatility makes them, by far, the most useful statistical techniques for industrial applications that have ever been invented.

Chapter Thirteen

Further Topics

Here are collected several topics which will be of use to the more advanced student. The reader is advised to sample these sections as the need arises.

Section One discusses the interpretation of "skewness and kurtosis." The formulas for both the statistics and the parameters are given, and three examples are used to illustrate just what these parameters measure.

Section Two makes the distinction between Enumerative and Analytic Studies. This brief overview shows the different aims of these two types of studies, and outlines the way in which Shewhart's control charts differ from the techniques of statistical inference.

Section Three expands on Section Two by discussing the characterization of product relative to specifications. The concept of Probable Error is introduced to help with the characterization of measured items. The extrapolation required for the characterization of non-measured product is discussed, and the nature of the assumptions for this extrapolation are given.

Section Four discusses Modified Control Limits. Section Five explains the fallacy of Acceptance Sampling. Section Six returns to the problem of estimating the Fraction of Nonconforming Product, while Section Seven discusses the transformation of data prior to analysis.

Section Eight illustrates the effects of variation upon a "balanced" production line. A simulation study is used to explain why piles of in-process inventory will inevitably build up in any balanced system. The futility of pressing down on the in-process inventory is shown, and the right way of reducing the in-process inventory is revealed.

13.1 Interpreting Skewness and Kurtosis

With the use of statistical software many individuals are being exposed to more than just measures of location and dispersion. In addition to the Average and Standard Deviation of a set of data, they also find some strange numbers labeled as "Skewness" and "Kurtosis." Since these numbers appear automatically, one naturally might wonder how to use them in practice. The purpose of this section is to provide some insight into just what Skewness and Kurtosis mean.

First of all one will need to distinguish between the *statistics* and the *parameters*. The statistics for Skewness and Kurtosis are simply functions of the data. They are computed according to some specific formula, and characterize certain aspects of the data. The parameters are constants which describe certain characteristics of a probability distribution function.

The skewness and kurtosis statistics are often computed according to the formulas:

$$a_3 = \frac{\Sigma (X_i - \bar{X})^3}{n \; s_n^{\,3}}$$

$$a_4 = \frac{\Sigma (X_i - \bar{X})^4}{n \; s_n^{\,4}}$$

Since these two formulas use the third and fourth powers of the deviations from the average, it should be apparent that both statistics will emphasize the extreme values in any data set.

Given a probability distribution characterized by $f(x)$, the Skewness parameter for this distribution is defined to be:

$$\alpha_3 = \int\limits_{all \; x} \frac{(x - \mu)^3}{\sigma^3} \; f(x) \; dx$$

while the Kurtosis parameter is defined as:

$$\alpha_4 = \int\limits_{all \; x} \frac{(x - \mu)^4}{\sigma^4} \; f(x) \; dx$$

In these equations, μ is the Mean of the probability distribution and σ is the Standard Deviation of the probability distribution.

The Skewness and Kurtosis parameters are commonly called the *shape parameters* for a distribution. The following example will illustrate the nature of these two parameters.

EXAMPLE 13.1:   *Skewness and Kurtosis for the Right Triangular Distribution:*

Consider a probability distribution characterized by the density function f(x) where:

$$f(x) = \frac{\sqrt{8} - x}{9} \qquad \text{whenever} \quad -\sqrt{2} \le x \le 2\sqrt{2}$$

and $f(x) = 0$ *otherwise.*

This probability distribution is known as the Standardized Right Triangular Distribution. It has a Mean of 0.0, and a Standard Deviation of 1.0. It is shown in Figure 13.1.

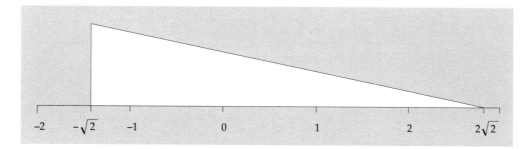

Figure 13.1: The Standardized Right Triangular Distribution

For this distribution the formulas for the Skewness and Kurtosis Parameters reduce to the following:

$$\alpha_3 = \int\limits_{all\ x} x^3\ f(x)\ dx = \int\limits_{-\sqrt{2}}^{2\sqrt{2}} x^3 \left(\frac{\sqrt{8} - x}{9} \right)\ dx$$

$$\alpha_4 = \int\limits_{all\ x} x^4\ f(x)\ dx = \int\limits_{-\sqrt{2}}^{2\sqrt{2}} x^4 \left(\frac{\sqrt{8} - x}{9} \right)\ dx$$

The first of these integrals is the "area under the curve" defined by multiplying the density function f(x) by the cubic curve x^3. The second integral is the area under the curve defined by multiplying the density function f(x) by the quartic curve x^4. This density function is shown plotted with the cubic and quartic curves in Figure 13.2.

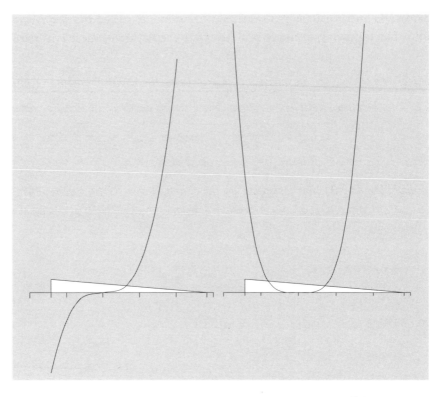

Figure 13.2: Cubic and Quartic Curves with f(x)

The products of the curves in Figure 13.2 are shown in Figures 13.3 and 13.4. The Skewness Parameter for this distribution is the area on the right side of the vertical axis minus the area on the left side in Figure 13.3.

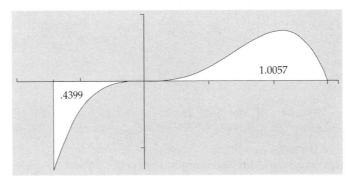

Figure 13.3: The Integrand for the Skewness Parameter

$$\alpha_3 = 1.005663 - 0.439978 = 0.565685$$

The Kurtosis Parameter for this distribution is the area under the curve in Figure 13.4.

$$\alpha_4 = 0.503704 + 1.896296 = 2.400000$$

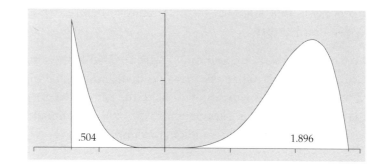

.504   1.896

Figure 13.4: The Integrand for the Kurtosis Parameter

The fact that all four regions in Figures 13.3 and 13.4 pinch down near the average suggests that the central region of the distribution contributes very little to either of these two parameters. Since the distribution in this example is already in its standardized form, the units on the horizontal axis in Figures 13.3 and 13.4 represent the standardized distance from the Mean of the distribution. Thus, the contribution of the central portion of the distribution can be seen by considering how much of the total area under the curves corresponds to X values which fall between –1.0 and +1.0. While 63 percent of the Standardized Right Triangular Distribution falls between –1.0 and +1.0, only 11 percent of the total area in Figure 13.3 and only 5 percent of the total area in Figure 13.4 correspond to this interval. Therefore, both Skewness and Kurtosis are primarily concerned with characteristics of the tails of the distribution.

The Skewness Parameter measures the relative sizes of the two tails. Distributions that are symmetric will have a Skewness Parameter of zero. If the right-hand tail is more massive, then the Skewness parameter will be positive. If the left-hand tail is more massive, the Skewness Parameter will be negative. Moreover, the greater the difference between the two tails, the greater the magnitude of the Skewness Parameter.

The Kurtosis Parameter is a measure of the combined weight of the tails relative to the rest of the distribution. As the tails of a distribution become heavier the Kurtosis will increase. As the tails become lighter the Kurtosis will decrease. Kurtosis was originally thought to measure the "peakedness" of a distribution. However, since the central portion of the distribution is virtually ignored by this parameter, Kurtosis cannot be said to measure peakedness directly. There is a correlation between peakedness and Kurtosis, but the relationship is an indirect and imperfect one at best.

Finally, the dependence of these two parameters upon the tails of the distribution suggests that a lot of data are needed to get reliable values for the statistics. Recall that the central portion of most distributions will contain from 60 percent to 75 percent of the values. This means that Skewness and Kurtosis statistics will generally be based upon the extreme 25 percent to 40 percent of the data. Thus, hundreds of data will need to be collected while the process is in a state of statistical control before one can obtain reliable statistics for Skewness and Kurtosis.

There are two fallacies that are commonly associated with the shape parameters of skewness and kurtosis. The first fallacy is that two distributions having the same Mean, Standard Deviation, Skewness and Kurtosis will have the same shape. The second fallacy is that a distribution with a Skewness parameter of zero will be symmetric. That these are indeed fallacies will be illustrated by the following examples.

EXAMPLE 13.2:   *A Simple Symmetric Distribution:*

The following equations define a probability density function:

$$f(x) = 0.6391 + 1.0337\,x \quad \text{when } -0.0091 < x < 0.5387$$
$$= 1.7527 - 1.0337\,x \quad \text{when } 0.5387 < x < 1.0864$$
$$= 0 \quad \text{otherwise}$$

This probability distribution has the following parameter values:

$$\text{Mean} = \mu = 0.5387$$
$$\text{Standard Deviation} = \sigma = 0.2907$$
$$\text{Skewness} = \alpha_3 = 0.0000$$
$$\text{Kurtosis} = \alpha_4 = 2.0000$$

The graph of this probability distribution function is shown in Figure 13.5.

Figure 13.5: A Simple Symmetric Probability Density Function

The simple symmetric distribution on the previous page has a Skewness parameter of zero, as one would expect. The Kurtosis parameter of 2.0 is fairly small, thus this distribution would be said to be a "light-tailed distribution." (The Normal Distribution has a Kurtosis parameter of 3.0. This value is considered to be the dividing line between light-tails and heavy-tails.)

The Mean, Standard Deviation, Skewness, and Kurtosis for the symmetric, light-tailed distribution on the preceding page should be compared with those of the distribution in the following example.

EXAMPLE 13.3:   *A Nonsymmetric Probability Distribution:*

A family of probability density functions is described by the following equation:

$$f(x) = ck \ x^{-(c+1)} [\ 1 + x^{-c} \ ]^{-(k+1)} \quad\quad \text{when } x > 0.0$$
$$= 0 \quad\quad\quad\quad\quad\quad\quad\quad\quad\quad\quad\quad\quad\quad \text{otherwise}$$

When the constants c and k are set to values of c = 18.1484, and k = 0.0629, the density function above has parameters of:

$$\begin{aligned}
Mean &= \mu = 0.5387 \\
Standard\ Deviation &= \sigma = 0.2907 \\
Skewness &= \alpha_3 = 0.0000 \\
Kurtosis &= \alpha_4 = 2.0000
\end{aligned}$$

This particular probability density function is shown in Figure 13.6. It is definitely not symmetric, even though it has a Skewness parameter of zero. In fact, with a couple of additions this distribution can be made into a cartoon of an elephant.

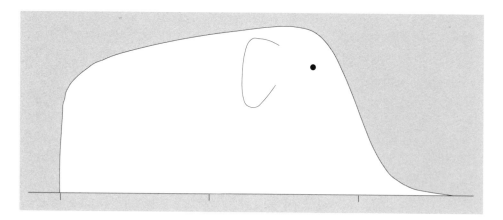

Figure 13.6: A Nonsymmetric Probability Density Function

Comparing the distributions in Figures 13.5 and 13.6 one finds that they have the same Mean, the same Standard Deviation, the same Skewness and the same Kurtosis, yet they do not look alike. Thus, one may properly conclude that the "shape parameters" of Skewness and Kurtosis cannot even discriminate between an elephant and a house!

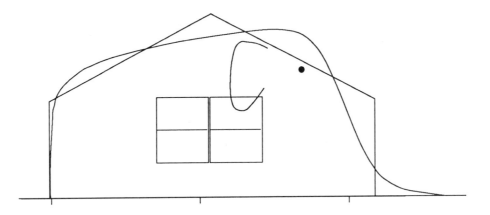

Figure 13.7: The Usefulness of Skewness and Kurtosis

If the *parameters* for Skewness and Kurtosis do this poorly, how can one ever hope to use *statistics* for skewness and kurtosis? The answer is that one cannot.

In *Economic Control of Quality of Manufactured Product* Shewhart considered constructing control charts for skewness and kurtosis. (He called Kurtosis "flatness.") After a careful evaluation of the information provided by these statistics he rejected their use. In doing this Shewhart observed that the location and dispersion statistics provide virtually all the useful information which can be obtained from *numerical summaries* of the data. The use of additional statistics such as skewness and kurtosis is superfluous. [1]

---

[1] *Economic Control of Quality of Manufactured Product,* pp.97–98.

13.2 Enumerative Studies versus Analytical Studies

The distinction between Enumerative and Analytic Studies, first made by Dr. Deming many years ago,[2] is basic to any use of data in the real world. Without making this distinction, one will inevitably be caught up and confused by the arguments of probability theory and statistical inference to the extent that one will both misapply the techniques and make incorrect decisions. In short, no one can ever fully understand any theory until he knows where it will not work. While this book has been completely dedicated to the use of statistical thinking as it applies to Analytic problems, the distinction between these problems and the problems of an Enumerative study is made here because an understanding of this difference is vital to all who wish to use data properly.

An Enumerative Study proceeds by investigation of the material in a Frame. A Frame is a list of physical units of some kind, identifiable by serial number, any or all of which may be selected and investigated.

An Enumerative Study is one in which action will be taken on the material in the Frame studied. The action to be taken on the Frame depends purely upon estimates or complete counts of one or more specific portions of the Frame. The aim of a statistical study in an Enumerative problem is descriptive—how many or how much? The aim is not to find out why there are so many, or why there is so much, but merely to quantify the material in the Frame.

An Analytical Study is one in which action will be taken on the process or cause-system that produced the Frame studied, with the intent being to improve practice in the future. Here interest centers in future product, not in the material studied.

There is a simple way to distinguish between Enumerative and Analytic Studies. A 100 percent sample of the Frame will provide an answer to the question posed for an Enumerative problem (subject, of course, to errors, to non-response, and to the limitations of the methods used to obtain and measure the items in the Frame). In contrast, a 100 percent sample of the material in a Frame will be inconclusive in an Analytic problem.

In Enumerative Studies the use of tables of random numbers to select items from the Frame will mimic the assumption of a random sample which is part of the basis for use of the theory of probability. Given a random sample, the sampling distribution of a statistic can be estimated, and probabilistic statements about the values for the statistic can be made. Thus, probability theory may be used as a guide to the uncertainties introduced by sampling in an Enumerative Study. (It still will not describe the non-sampling errors.)

In an Analytic Study there is no way to define a random sample of the future. All

---

[2] See, for example, "On Probability as a Basis for Action," *The American Statistician, v.29*, pp.146-152, 1975.

data, and all analyses of data, are historical. However, in an Analytic Study the inference of interest involves prediction, an extrapolation into the future. Probability theory offers no help here. All samples become judgment samples, and there is no way to attach a probability to a specific future outcome.

Yet we can and must use data for prediction in every type of human activity. How can we successfully extrapolate from the past to the future? This is the essence of an Analytic Study, and the control chart is the premier technique for use in this situation. The control chart will allow a reasonable (inductive) inference about how a given process has performed in the past. If a process has failed to display a reasonable degree of statistical control in the past, then we dare not assume that it will spontaneously display statistical control in the future. In such a case prediction can only be based upon knowledge of the subject matter. However, if a process has displayed a reasonable degree of statistical control in the past, it is reasonable to assume that it may continue to do so in the near future. In such a case, the prediction of the future based upon past data is reasonable, and there is some hope that the prediction will be realized. Nonetheless, there is still no such thing as a "confidence level" for such a prediction. There can be none.

This is why it is incorrect to attempt to use a probability model to convert a capability ratio or capability index into a percentage of nonconforming product. This is why the theoretical power curves for control charts do not apply in practice. This is why the whole structure of deductive probabilistic arguments, which we call statistical inference, cannot be directly applied to the inductive inferences required in the real world. At best probability and statistics can only provide a guide for practice. The ultimate proof that any given procedure will be useful in the real world will have to come from empirical evidence that it works, rather than a theoretical (probabilistic) argument.

Many techniques have been (and will be) invented to detect small changes in the mean. Among these techniques Shewhart's control chart stands out as the only one that actually examines the data for the internal consistency which is a prerequisite for any extrapolation into the future. Thus, unlike all of the various "tests" and "intervals" of statistical inference, Shewhart's control charts are tools for Analytic Studies. Rather than mathematical modeling, or estimation, Shewhart's charts are concerned with taking appropriate actions in the future, based upon an analysis of the data from the past. Out of all the statistical procedures available today, they alone were designed for the inductive inferences of the real world.

13.3 The Characterization of Product

The computation of a capability ratio is an attempt to characterize a *process* relative to specifications. As such it involves prediction, and this makes it into what Dr. Deming has called an "Analytic" use of data. The use of measurements to characterize *product* relative to specifications is a slightly different issue. Rather than trying to quantify the future quality of a product stream, one is instead trying to decide what to do with a given item, or a given batch, or a given lot, or a given shipment. Dr. Deming calls such characterizations "Enumerative" uses of data.

When measurements are used to characterize *the measured item* relative to specifications, the major source of uncertainty in the decision is the measurement process itself. When measurements are used to characterize *the batch of product* from which the measured item or items were selected, the extrapolation from the measured product to that product which was not measured will introduce an extra element of uncertainty in the decision. In the first of these cases a simple and straightforward way of accommodating the uncertainty is described in this section. In the second case it is rare that one can actually quantify the uncertainty associated with the decision. The reasons for this will also be described below.

Characterizing the Measured Item

First consider the situation where one is attempting to characterize the measured item relative to the specifications. If the measurement falls well within the specification limits, then the item is judged to be conforming. If the measurement falls well outside the specification limits, then the item is judged to be nonconforming. But when the measurement falls close to either specification limit there is some uncertainty regarding the item. One way to both quantify both the word "close" and the uncertainty regarding the item is provided by the notion of Probable Error.

The Probable Error characterizes the variation which can be attributed to the measurement process alone. In order to obtain this quantity one will have to have some data which isolates the measurement error from other sources of variation. One simple way to do this is to repeatedly measure the same thing, using the same measurement technique, the same instrument, and the same operator. (In the case of destructive testing of samples which cannot be homogenized beforehand, one will need to prepare pairs of samples which are as much alike as possible, test the pairs, and evaluate the differences between the paired measurements.)

Now consider the results of measuring the same thing a large number of times. The measurements will inevitably vary (if they are not rounded off too much). Given a particular measurement method, define the Average of the repeated measurements of the same thing to be the "best value" for the characteristic being measured. (Different methods will likely yield different "best values.") A measure of dispersion for the repeated measurements will describe the variation in the particular measurement method. For lack of a better symbol, denote this measure of variation in the measurement process by $\hat{\sigma}_e$. Figure 13.8 shows a hypothetical histogram of repeated measurements of the same thing.

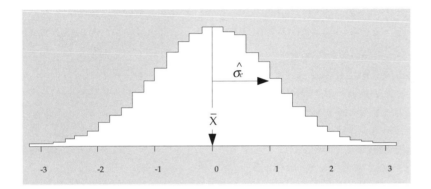

Figure 13.8: Histogram of Repeated Measurements of the Same Thing

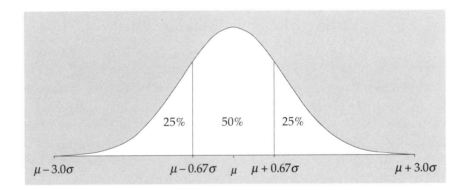

Figure 13.9: Some Areas Under a Normal Curve

If a normal distribution is used to approximate the histogram of repeated measurements, then areas under the normal curve may be used to approximate the behavior of the repeated measurements. In this case, we are interested in the middle 50 percent of the normal distribution. As shown in Figure 13.9, the middle 50 percent of the area under a normal curve, having mean μ and standard deviation σ, falls in the interval defined by

$$\mu \pm 0.6745 \, \sigma.$$

This use of the normal distribution as a model for measurement error goes back to Gauss (1809) and LaPlace (1810). It has been found to generally provide a very satisfactory approximation to the histogram in Figure 13.8. Therefore, based on the normal model, one would expect about half of the repeated measurements of the same thing to fall within the interval:

$$\bar{X} \pm 0.67\ \hat{\sigma}_e.$$

Conversely, one should also expect about half of the repeated measurements of the same thing to fall outside the interval above.

If the difference between a single measurement and the average of a large number of repeated measurements is defined to be the "error" of a measurement, then these errors will exceed the quantity $0.67\ \hat{\sigma}_e$ about half of the time, and they will fail to exceed this value about half of the time. Therefore, the quantity $0.67\ \hat{\sigma}_e$ approximates the Median "error" of a single measurement. This quantity has historically been called the Probable Error.

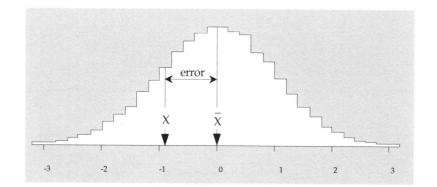

Figure 13.10: The Error of a Single Measurement

The Probable Error essentially places a lower bound on the resolution of a single measurement. If a measurement will differ from the "best value" by an amount equal to the Probable Error at least half of the time, then there will not be much point in attempting to interpret the number more precisely. The Probable Error defines the essential uncertainty in the measurement. As long as the Probable Error is larger than the unit of measurement, it will therefore define the effective resolution of a single value. Thus, the Probable Error defines the effective discreteness of a measurement, and serves as a guide on how closely one should interpret a single value.

A way to use this value in characterizing measured product relative to specifications will be described after the following example.

EXAMPLE 13.4:   *Probable Error of Viscosity Measurements:*

Product 42LF is made in small batches. The small batch size, along with the vigorous stirring which is part of the process, makes it reasonable to consider each batch as effectively homogenized. A single test sample is drawn from the batch while it is being stirred. This test sample is split in half and the viscosity is measured in duplicate. The test values, in centistokes, for seven batches are shown below:

Batch	78	79	80	81	82	83	84
Viscosities	2480	2870	2350	2990	3070	3020	2510
	2530	2730	2390	2930	3050	3000	2610
Ranges	50	140	40	60	20	20	100

The duplicate measurements provide a simple and effective way of assessing the measurement error. The ranges shown above represent test-retest error of the same product, and therefore may be used to compute a value for $\hat{\sigma}_e$:

$$\hat{\sigma}_e = \frac{\bar{R}}{d_2} = \frac{61.4}{1.128} = 54 \text{ centistokes.}$$

Therefore, the computed value for the Probable Error of these measurements will be:

$$PE = 0.67 \, (54 \text{ cs.}) = 36 \text{ centistokes.}$$

The individual measurements of viscosity are recorded to the nearest 10 cs., but they are good to the nearest 36 cs. The average of two viscosity measurements is good to the nearest:

$$\frac{36 \text{ cs.}}{\sqrt{2}} = 25 \text{ centistokes} = PE \text{ for average of two measurements.}$$

Since the Probable Error defines the effective resolution of a measurement, it will also define the effective increment to use in fuzzing up the specification limits. When the distance between a measurement and a specification limit is less than one Probable Error, it is uncertain just where the value belongs.

When a measurement is more than one Probable Error away from a specification limit the chances are at least fairly strong that the product belongs on the same side of the specification as the measurement. That is: a measurement more than one PE unit outside a specification is likely to indicate a product that is nonconforming, and a measurement that is more than one PE unit inside a specification is likely to indicate a product that is conforming.

It is impossible to calculate exact odds, but it is possible to provide some rough guidelines for just what is meant by the words "likely" in the preceding paragraph. To do this one begins with the assumption of ignorance: the product is equally likely to be either conforming or nonconforming. Then, assuming that a normal distribution will provide a satisfactory approximation for the distribution of measurement errors, one may use Bayes'

Theorem to compute some *a posteriori* probabilities of conforming product given a particular measurement. While these probabilities will not be exact, they may be used to roughly characterize the likelihood of conforming product given a particular measurement value.[3]

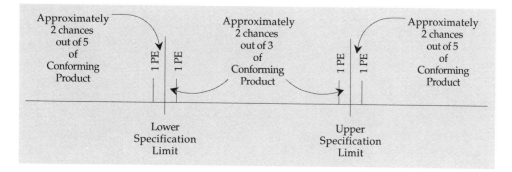

Figure 13.11: Measurements Within One Probable Error of Specification Limits

For example, consider fuzzing the specifications by ± 1 PE. If a measurement falls outside the spec, but less than one PE unit away from the spec, then there are about 2 chances out of 5 that the measurement came from a conforming item. If a measurement falls inside, but within one PE unit of the specs, then there are about 2 chances out of 3 that the measurement came from a conforming item. Clearly, measurements within one PE unit of a specification limit are rather ambiguous. In contrast to this, consider the odds that are found when the measurements fall further from the specification limits.

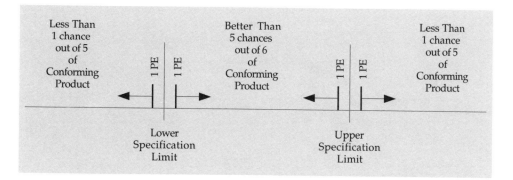

Figure 13.12: Specifications Fuzzed By One Probable Error

---

[3] Define a conforming item to be one for which the "best value" is inside the specification limits.

Measurements more than one PE unit outside the specs will have less than 1 chance out of 5 that they came from an item which conformed to the specifications. Measurements which fall more than one PE unit inside the specs will have at least 5 chances out of 6 that they came from an item which was conforming.

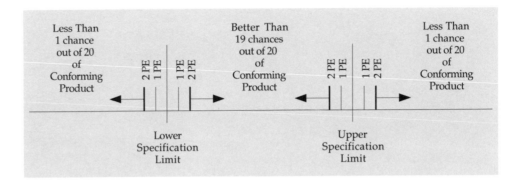

Figure 13.13: Specifications Fuzzed By Two Probable Errors

Next consider fuzzing the specifications by ± 2 PE. Measurements more than two PE units outside the specs will have less than 1 chance out of 20 that they came from an item which conformed to the specifications. Measurements which fall more than two PE units inside the specs will have at least 19 chances out of 20 that they came from an item which was conforming.

Now consider fuzzing the specifications by ± 3 PE. Measurements more than three PE units outside the specs will have less than 1 chance out of 100 that they came from an item which conformed to the specifications.

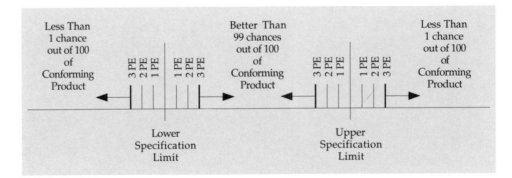

Figure 13.14: Specifications Fuzzed By Three Probable Errors

Measurements which fall more than three PE units inside the specs will have at least 99 chances out of 100 that they came from an item which was conforming.

None of these odds are given as exact probabilities. They are merely guidelines for helping the user to develop an intuitive understanding of just what specific values might mean in practice.

EXAMPLE 13.5:   *Interpreting Measurements Relative to Specs:*

The specifications for Product 42LF are 2500 to 3000 centistokes. The average of the duplicate readings are used to characterize each batch. The Probable Error for the average of two measurements was found to be 25 cs. Fuzzed specification limits are therefore:

```
2425                   |                        |                3075
   2450                |                        |          3050
      2475             |                        |       3025
         2500          |                        |    3000
            |   2525   |                        | 2975
            |      2550|                   2950 |
  |    |    |    |    |    |   2575    2925  |    |    |    |    |
```

Batch	80	82	83	78	81	84	79
Viscosities	2350	3070	3020	2480	2990	2510	2870
	2390	3050	3000	2530	2930	2610	2730
Averages	**2370**	**3060**	**3010**	**2505**	**2960**	**2560**	**2800**
	out	*out(?)*	*?*	*?*	*ok?*	*ok(?)*	*ok*

Batch 80: Value of 2370 is well outside the 3 PE widened specs: less than 0.01 odds of conforming product.

Batch 82: Value of 3060 is between 2 and 3 PE outside specs: approximately 0.05 odds of conforming product.

Batch 83: Value of 3010 is less than 1 PE outside the Upper Spec: approximately 0.39 odds of conforming product.

Batch 78: Value of 2505 is less than 1 PE inside the Lower Spec: approximately 0.64 odds of conforming product.

Batch 81: Value of 2960 is within 2 PE of Upper Spec: approximately 0.84 odds of conforming product.

Batch 84: Value of 2560 is within 3 PE of Lower Spec: approximately 0.95 odds of conforming product.

Batch 79: Value of 2800 is well within the 3 PE tightened specs: better than 0.99 odds of conforming product.

A proper understanding of the effective resolution of a measurement is crucial to a proper use of measurements. Without such an understanding, one will be misled by the apparent objectivity of the measurements and, in consequence, may make incorrect decisions.

The methodology outlined above will apply whenever one is characterizing *the measured item itself* relative to specifications. Examples of this use of measurements would be the non-destructive measurement of discrete items and tanks of homogeneous liquids where the batch identity is preserved at least up to the point of disposition of the product. These techniques will not be adequate for dealing with the characterization of that product which has not been measured.

The Characterization of Product Which Has Not Been Measured

The use of measurements to characterize *product which has not been measured* is a common feature of many operations. This is routinely done every time destructive tests are employed, and is often done even when testing is nondestructive. Whenever measurements are used to characterize lots, shipments, or potentially nonhomogeneous batches of product there is an extrapolation involved—a statement is made about product which has not been measured based upon product which has been measured. In some cases the uncertainty of this extrapolation can be quantified. In other cases one can only cross one's fingers and hope that the uncertainty of extrapolation will not lead to the wrong decision.

Just what does it take to quantify the uncertainty of extrapolation when characterizing product with one or more measurements? This question is the basic question of sampling theory. First there must be a certain rationality to the extrapolation: the measured item or items must come from the batch of product which is being characterized. Next, there must be some basis for thinking that the sample (the measured product) is representative of the batch (the unmeasured product). This is usually justified on the basis of the sampling procedure. One common feature of sampling procedures is the existence of a Frame. The Frame is simply the collection of material (product) from which the sample is to be obtained. One should note that the Frame may differ (slightly) from the batch of product being characterized. As long as the Frame approximates the batch of product, the rationality of the extrapolation is preserved. If the difference between the Frame and the batch of product becomes very great, the rationality of the extrapolation will be destroyed. Finally, in addition to the Frame, the sampling procedure must specify how items are to be selected from the Frame in such a way that every item in the Frame has an equal chance of being chosen (Dr. Deming's "equal and complete coverage"). When these conditions are satisfied, the measurements may be used to extrapolate from the product measured to that product which has not been measured, and the techniques of Enumerative statistics may be used to quantify the uncertainty of the extrapolation.

The specification of the Frame, and the specification of the selection procedure are both complex and time-consuming tasks. With expensive one-time studies, the success of the study will frequently depend upon the careful definition of Frame and sampling procedure. However, in routine industrial applications it is uncommon to find a well-defined Frame. In some of the better situations one occasionally finds a standard sampling procedure for a given product. But in most industrial situations, there is neither a Frame nor a sampling plan that gives equal and complete coverage. Therefore, given the lack of these prerequisites in industrial applications, **it will almost always be impossible to quantify the uncertainties associated with the extrapolation from the measured sample to the batch of product**. When this happens, there will be no basis for using statistical inference, and there will be no way to know how reasonable the extrapolation from measured sample to batch of product may be. At best, the samples can be characterized as convenience samples, or haphazard samples, with the explicit connotation that all extrapolation based on these samples is hazardous.

The problem with haphazard or convenience samples is the possibility of subjective bias in the selection of the sample. Any subjectivity in sample selection will undermine the hoped for "representativeness" of the sample, and destroy the rationality of the extrapolation.

Given that most industrial samples are convenience samples, how can one ever hope to use the measurements to characterize the product in a batch, or to characterize the product stream? The honest answer is that, unless the production process displays a reasonable degree of statistical control, one cannot. The existence of a state of statistical control will provide a basis for using the sample measurements to characterize the product stream. When a process displays statistical control, it is predictable and consistent. The predictability will justify the extrapolation from the sample to the product not measured, and the consistency justifies the assumption that the sample is "representative" of the product stream.

At the same time, the existence of a state of statistical control removes the rationale for characterizing each batch of product separately. As long as the process displays a reasonable degree of statistical control, the product stream should be considered to be homogeneous. When a process displays a reasonable degree of statistical control there will be no indications that the product stream is changing over time, and the classification of some portions of that product stream as "conforming batches" and other portions as "nonconforming batches" is both arbitrary and capricious.

Therefore, when each "lot" or "batch" in a product stream is characterized by the measurements obtained from a sample drawn from that lot or batch, one should plot the sequence of measurements on a control chart. If this control chart displays a reasonable degree of statistical control, then one is reassured that the product stream is consistent from "batch" to "batch," and all the "batches" should be treated alike. That is, either the product stream contains some nonconforming items, and every single item must be measured and judged relative to specifications, or else the product stream should be considered to consist of 100% conforming product, and individual items only need to be checked for the purposes of maintaining the control chart.

When the control chart of sample measurements does not display statistical control, one may attempt to subdivide the product stream into "conforming batches" and "nonconforming batches." However, the very unpredictability of an out-of-control process will usually make this subdivision imperfect. If the process is changing quickly relative to the sample frequency, there is little hope that any single measurement is "representative" of the product produced shortly before or shortly after the sampled product, and the subdivision of the product stream will be arbitrary and ineffective. On the other hand, if the process is one which changes slowly relative to the sample, frequency, then this slow change reassures the user that a sample measurement will characterize the product produced shortly before and shortly after the sampled product. Such a product stream might be rationally subdivided into "conforming batches" and "nonconforming batches." However, when this latter situation exists, the process will usually be "out-of-control."

13.4 The Problem of Modified Control Limits

Given the problem of using measurements to characterize non-measured product relative to the specifications, some have attempted to use Modified Control Limits to "fuzz" the specification limits. (These fuzzed limits are sometimes called Reject Control Limits.)

Say one is using the Average of several measurements. Then the Modified Control Limits would be:

$$Upper\ Specification \quad - \quad 3\ Sigma(X) \quad + \quad 3\ Sigma(\overline{X})$$
$$Lower\ Specification \quad + \quad 3\ Sigma(X) \quad - \quad 3\ Sigma(\overline{X})$$

The rationale for this inversion of the control chart is the thought that as long as the Subgroup Average is within these limits the process will be producing conforming product. Even though a case can be made for using such limits *in conjunction with ordinary control limits*, it is much more likely that such limits will be used by themselves. The consequences of such use are outlined below.

Two types of problems may occur with Modified Control Limits. In one case the Subgroup Averages may be bouncing around inside the Modified Control Limits yet be out-of-control with respect to a proper control chart. Here the lack of control will undermine the very extrapolation that is required to characterize the non-measured product. Since the use of this procedure is specifically aimed at the characterization of the non-measured product, this is a serious problem.

In the other case, the Subgroup Averages may all fall within the limits of a proper control chart while some of them fall on the wrong side of the Modified Control Limits. The existence of a reasonable degree of statistical control indicates a homogeneous product stream, yet the use of the Modified Control Limits will chop this product stream into segments which are then treated differently. With the Subgroup Averages falling within the control limits, these decisions regarding the product will be the equivalent of tampering.

To operate a process with a reasonable degree of statistical control is to achieve only that which the process is capable of achieving. The use of Modified Control Limits does not attempt to achieve this potential. Instead, while requiring the same amount of work as a regular control chart, it aims at *less* than that which the process is capable of achieving.

Thus, the use of Modified Control Limits is contrary to continual improvement. It does nothing to encourage constancy of purpose, consistency of operation, or the stabilization of the process since it is focused solely upon the conformance to specifications. It will only encourage alternating periods of benign neglect and intense panic. Assignable causes can come and go without being detected, and these opportunities for discovering how to improve the process will be lost. Finally, since the extrapolation from the measured items to the non-measured product depends upon a reasonable degree of process stability, Modified Control Limits will never allow one to be sure if this extrapolation is safe and appropriate.

13.5 The Fallacy of Acceptance Sampling

All Acceptance Sampling is built upon the notion that one can accept some batches (or lots), and reject others, based upon the value for a sample drawn from each batch. The use of such a procedure is equivalent to playing roulette with the product.

The implicit assumption of Acceptance Sampling is the assumption that the lot quality is highly variable from batch to batch. If this were not so, why would one need to accept some batches and reject others? However, if the lot quality is varying widely from batch to batch, then how can one be assured regarding the homogeneity of the product within each batch? The acceptance or rejection of each batch will depend upon the extrapolation from the product measured to that product which has not been measured, and the assumption of homogeneity within each batch will be essential for this extrapolation to make sense. So using acceptance sampling is rather like wanting to eat your cake and have it too; one must assume that the product quality is highly variable from batch to batch, but that, at the same time, it is very uniform within each batch.

If the product quality is highly variable between batches and within batches, then the extrapolation from the sample to a statement about the lot quality will be very uncertain. If the product quality is very uniform within the batches and between the batches, then the acceptance of some batches and the rejection of others will be arbitrary and capricious.

Finally, if it is known that the lot quality is highly variable from batch to batch, yet each batch is very uniform, then the known homogeneity of the batches assures that the product not measured is essentially the same as the measured product. In this case one can use the specification limits fuzzed by Probable Error to characterize each batch.

EXAMPLE 13.6:   *The Quality in the Warehouse:*

A company making hardwood flooring used the following procedure as their quality assurance plan. Six-by-six parquet tiles were fabricated, glued together into 12-by-12 squares, and boxed. As each pallet of boxes was ready to move to the warehouse the quality auditor would select a specified number of boxes for inspection based upon a Dodge-Romig 5% Average Outgoing Quality Limit plan. If the number of defective "squares" found in the selected boxes exceeded the rejection number, the pallet would be rejected and subjected to 100% inspection, with bad squares being replaced by good squares. If the number of defective squares was less than the rejection number, the pallet would be accepted, the defectives found in the sample would be replaced with good squares, the boxes would be closed up, and the pallet would be moved to the warehouse.

Thus, the warehouse was filled with pallets of parquet floor tiles. Some pallets would contain material that had been subjected to 100% screening inspection. Other pallets would contain material just as it came from the production line. One day the quality control manager called the author and asked if he could assure the president of the company that there was at least 95% good product in the warehouse. Although the answer to his question is yes, the question is the wrong question because the customers don't buy the warehouse—they buy this product one pallet at a time.

A distributor gets a pallet of floor tiles, and sells a few boxes at a time to his customers, the jobbers. When the distributor gets a screened pallet, the jobbers find the material to be satisfactory, and everyone builds up certain expectations regarding this product. When the distributor gets an unscreened pallet, the jobbers find more defective squares than they had expected. As a result, they may not have enough material to finish their job. They have to get more material. In the meantime the final customer is unhappy about the delay. Thus, the customer is unhappy, the jobber is unhappy, and the distributor is unhappy about all the complaints and the returned material he has to handle. Yet the president and the quality control director are sleeping soundly each night, comforted by the knowledge that there is at least 95% good stuff in the warehouse.

When it is a matter of rectifying defects, the only economic levels of inspection are all or nothing. Hit-or-miss inspection based upon Acceptance Sampling will not minimize the cost of any operation. In fact, it can actually make things worse!

13.6 Estimating the Fraction Nonconforming

Chapter Six described the fallacy of converting capability numbers into fractions non-conforming. There it was stated that the best estimate of the fraction nonconforming is the simple ratio of the number of items found to be nonconforming to the total number of items examined. This ratio is known as the Binomial Point Estimate.

Many books attach "confidence intervals" to the Binomial Point Estimate. Such intervals are attempts to quantify the uncertainty of this estimate. As such, the problems outlined earlier in this section will apply. In short, the conditions required for these confidence intervals to apply will almost never be satisfied in industrial situations. That means that these intervals cannot be used to describe how good an estimate may be. In practice one cannot verify if the necessary conditions exist. However, one may use these confidence intervals to define how *bad* a particular Binomial Point Estimate may be.

Confidence intervals only attempt to quantify the uncertainty due to sampling errors. Earlier in this section it was argued that the non-sampling errors of estimation are usually greater than the sampling errors. Thus, the uncertainty for a particular Binomial Point Estimate of the fraction of nonconforming product will usually be greater than it would appear to be based upon a confidence interval. The confidence interval can only place a lower bound on the uncertainty. Thus, while a narrow confidence interval cannot guarantee a good estimate, a wide confidence interval can define a useless estimate.

EXAMPLE 13.7:   *Fraction Nonconforming and Acceptance Sampling:*

Shipments consisting of 1000 items each are subjected to the following incoming sampling scheme: 10 pieces are to be selected and inspected, the number nonconforming will be recorded as Y, and the Binomial Point Estimate of the lot fraction nonconforming will be computed as:

$$p = \frac{Y}{10} .$$

As usual, no mention is made of how the sample is to be selected, and no Frame is defined—just draw the sample and get on with it!

As long as the number inspected, n, is not larger than 10% of the lot size, the following formula may be used for an approximate 95% confidence interval for the Binomial Point Estimate:

$$p \pm 2 \sqrt{\frac{p(1-p)}{n}}$$

The problem is that this interval is a BEST CASE scenario. Non-sampling errors will always degrade the quality of the estimate so that it is not this good. So if this interval is too wide to instill confidence in the user, he will know that he will need additional data before making a decision.

Say 1 of the 10 items is found to be nonconforming. The Binomial Point Estimate for the lot fraction nonconforming is $p = 0.1$. The approximate 95% confidence interval is 0 to .29. Sampling errors alone introduce this amount of uncertainty into the computations. Nonsampling errors will introduce even more uncertainty. AT BEST, you do not have enough information to narrow the lot fraction nonconforming down more precisely than "less than 30 percent nonconforming." And things could be worse.

Are you willing to make a decision about rejecting or accepting this shipment based on these results?

So while the Binomial Point Estimate may be the best general estimate for the fraction nonconforming, the uncertainty of this estimate will usually be impossible to completely quantify. A "confidence interval" will quantify how *poor* a given estimate may be in the best of circumstances, but it will not tell you how *good* the estimate may be.

13.7 The Transformation of Data

When using data in a business setting one should take care to present the data in a form that is easy to interpret. This will generally mean that one should avoid nonlinear transformations of the data such as logarithms, square roots, trigonometric functions, and probabilistic transformations. The following paraphrase of an argument by H.C. Tippett bears on this point.

Let x be an observable variable, and let y be a (non-linear) transformation of x, where y has convenient statistical properties (such as variance independent of mean). Then, if y can be meaningfully substituted for x in the technical interpretation and application of the results, one should have no hesitation about using the transformed variable in the analysis. However, if y cannot be meaningfully substituted for x in the technical interpretation of the results, then the use of y in the analysis makes the interpretation obscure. For example, suppose that one is measuring the Warp Breakage Rate and that there is an interaction between the treatments and the looms. This interaction may well disappear when one analyzes the logarithm of the Warp Breakage Rate. So how would one interpret these results? Does the loom make a difference when interpreting the treatment effects? Clear thinking, both in terms of the mathematics and in terms of the process, is required in order to correctly interpret the analysis of logarithm Warp Breakage Rate. Moreover, the situation becomes even more obscure when one remembers that a verdict of "no detectable interaction" is not equivalent to "no interaction."

If one has to interpret the results of an experiment in terms of the observable variable x, and the analysis is performed using a transformed variable y, then all of the Subgroup Averages and Treatment Effects must be transformed back. This inverse transformation will present difficulties of interpretation that will overwhelm many. The waters become deep, and "readers are advised not to make transformations *on statistical grounds alone* unless they are good swimmers and have experience of the currents."[4]

Since nonlinear transformations are rarely used in business, their use in the analysis of business data is to be discouraged. Robust yet simple methods, such as the control chart, will be much better than less robust, more complex, analyses which depend upon transformations of the data.

---

[4] *The Methods of Statistics, 4th Ed*, 1952, pp.344-345. Emphasis in the original.

13.8 The Effect of Variation on Balanced Systems

Ever since the dawn of the industrial revolution engineers have worked to "balance" manufacturing operations. The objective of a "balanced system" is to match the capacities of the various steps, so that there will be no excess capacity anywhere in the system. Unfortunately, things never seem to work out quite the way they are planned. Because there will always be some variation in the rate at which production systems work, no stated capacity is exact and unchanging. Regardless of whether the stated capacity is a maximum value, or an average value, there will always be some variation in the capacity because things do not work perfectly. Set-ups take longer than planned, materials are not available, parts take extra effort to assemble, etc. This inevitable variation causes havoc in a "balanced system."

The following example presents the results of a simulation of a multi-step process, consisting of balanced steps, each having the same average production rate and the same amount of variation in that rate. If the demand is equal to the average production rate, then each step is a bottleneck, and the results described below are inevitable.

EXAMPLE 13.8:   *A Balanced System:*

Consider a process with five sequential operations. Assume that each of these five operations can produce an average of ten units per hour. In the normal course of events, each step will sometimes produce more than ten units in an hour, and at other times they will produce less than ten units in an hour. In order to characterize this variation, assume that the standard deviation of the hourly capacity for each step is 1.6 units. Since these five steps have the same average capacity, and the same variation in capacity, they should be perfectly balanced. This would seem an ideal situation for using the just-in-time concept. But consider what actually happens.

    Cycle One:

        Step A produces 11 units in the first hour;

        Step B has capacity for 14 units, but only gets 11 units from A;

        Step C has capacity for 8 units, so 3 get left behind;

        Step D has capacity for 12 units, but only gets 8 from C;

        Step E has capacity for 7 units, so 1 unit gets left behind.

            In all, 7 units are produced, 3 units are stuck between

            Steps B and C, and 1 unit is stuck between Steps D and E.

    Cycle Two:

        Step A makes 9 units in the second hour;

        Step B has capacity for 13 units, but only 9 are available;

        Step C has capacity for 13 units, 3 are available from the backlog,

> *and 9 more are passed along,*
> > *giving an output of 12 units from Step C;*
> *Step D has capacity for 9 units, so 3 are left behind;*
> *Step E has capacity for 10 units, which exactly matches the*
> > *backlog plus the current throughput. In all, 10 units are*
> > *produced and 3 are left in process between Steps C and D*

> *Cycle Three:*
> > *Step A produces 12 units in the third hour;*
> > *Step B has capacity for 8 units, leaving 4 stranded;*
> > *Step C has capacity for 10 units, but only 8 are available;*
> > *Step D has capacity for 10 units so 2 are drawn from the backlog to go*
> > > *with the 8, and 1 unit is left in process;*
> > *Step E has capacity for 8 units, so 2 are left stranded.*
> > > *In all, 8 units are produced, and 7 are left in process*
> > > *Four of these are in front of Step B,*
> > > *1 is in front of Step D,*
> > > *and 2 are in front of Step E.*

So in three cycles, only 25 units have been produced, even though materials for 32 units have been released into the system. The difference between these two figures represents the growth of the in-process inventory.

Notice that for any one cycle, the number of units produced is equal to the minimum capacity of the five steps during that cycle. This relationship will always be present whenever the bottlenecks are dependent. Since the minimum will almost always be less than the average, there is no way that a sequence of dependent bottlenecks can ever produce at a rate equal to the average capacity of the individual steps.

In this example, each step has a capacity that varies above and below 10 units per hour. In any one cycle, one of the steps will almost surely have a capacity that is less than 10 units, so that the effective capacity of the system will always be something less than 10 units as long as the steps are dependent.

After 24 cycles, the simulation begun above had produced 216 units, and had 21 units in-process, for an average yield of 9 units per cycle, rather than the expected 10. For the second 24 cycles, the output increased to 9.875 units per cycle, and the inventory in-process averaged 20.5 units. Thus, the process can eventually get to the point where it averages 10 units per hourly cycle, but this comes only after the in-process inventory reaches a certain level. This leveling off of the in-process inventory is shown in Figure 13.15.

As long as the steps are locked together and dependent on one another, a certain amount of the materials released at the front end of the process will inevitably go into building the stockpiles of in-process inventory. As these backlogs of in-process product accumulate, they will tend to uncouple the process steps, so that they can operate independently of each other. At this point, two things will occur. The occasional idle time that was inevitable when the steps were dependent on one another will disappear, and the output of the process will increase to the stated average capacity of the balanced steps.

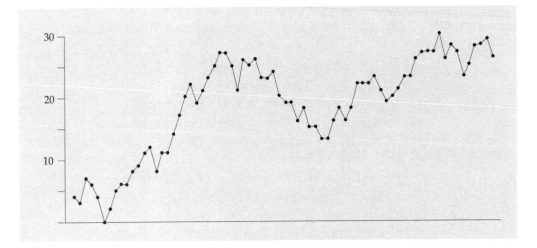

Figure 13.15: In-Process Inventory for 72 Cycles

This cycle of waiting on the previous step, with the result of occasional idle time and the accumulation of in-process inventory, is inevitable with any "balanced system" of bottlenecks. Until the stockpiles of in-process inventory increase to the level that unlocks the dependent steps, the output of the system will always be less than the average capacity of the individual steps. Moreover, this cycle is repeated with every product change that occurs in the system. If there are enough product changes, then the steady-state condition is never reached, and the yield will never be as large as the average capacity of the individual steps. When this happens and the demand happens to be equal to the average capacity, the plant will fall further and further behind its production schedules. For this reason, the modern manufacturing environment, with short production runs for each product, effectively prohibits a "balanced system" from ever operating to capacity.

Variation in the rate of production is the cause of these problems, and by reducing this variation, the magnitude of these problems can be reduced. Since much of the variation in the production rate is due to things not working right, this variation will naturally decrease as the product is produced with increasing consistency. The Taguchi Quadratic Loss is simply an abstract way of describing this phenomenon. A second factor that will reduce this variation is increased consistency in the way the equipment is operated and maintained. In each case, the techniques of statistical process control will be the key to achieving these increased consistencies. The examples given in Section 7.3 illustrate the effect that the reduction of variation can have on the capacity of a production operation.

Until these increased consistencies are realized, the only way to avoid the accumulation of in-process inventories is to operate the "balanced system" as a sequence of non-bottlenecks. This means that the demand must be less than the average capacity of each of the steps. How much less? Enough so that the material does not accumulate between the steps. In the example above, a demand of 8 units per cycle would be low enough to avoid the problems noted.

A second approach is to increase the average capacity of some of the steps, so that only one step is a bottleneck. This will tend to eliminate the piles of in-process inventory if the flow of material is managed in accord with the bottleneck. If the demand is equal to the average production rate for the one bottleneck, then the system can meet schedule.

Unfortunately, both of these adjustments in the system involve increased capacities for the production operation. (One should note that they do have the beneficial effect of reducing the in-process inventory.) The only way to reduce these excess capacities is first to reduce the variation in the production rate by increasing the consistency of materials, machines, and operations. These increases only come from a program of continual improvement that is vigorously promoted throughout the whole organization and implemented with the tools of statistical process control.

Efforts to trim capacity, balance the work, and improve the efficiency factors, will not yield the desired results unless they also seek to achieve process stability and to reduce process variation. They will simply shift investment in capacity into investment in inventory.

Appendices

Glossary of Terms

See page number indicated for contextual definition of the following terms

Acceptance Sampling	341	Median Range	47
Assignable Cause	4	Minimum Variance	146
Attribute Data	255	Moving Average	219
Autocorrelation	80	Moving Range	48
Average	22	Natural Process Limits	46, 119
Average Chart	41	Normally Distributed	77
Average Loss	145	On-Target	146
Average Range	44	Pareto Diagram	316
Average Run Length	97	Periodically Collected Data	217
Between Subgroup	100	Poisson Counts	271
Binomial Counts	261	Process Aim	193
Brink of Chaos	14	Process Average	193
Capability Ratio	126	Process Capability Index	126
Capable Process	118	Process Performance Ratio	134
Cause and Effect Diagram	311	Proportions	268
Centered Capability Ratio	127	Quadratic Loss	144
Centered Performance Ratio	134	Range	24
Central Limit Theorem	78	Range Chart	56
Chance Cause	4	Ratios	268
Control Limit	40	Root Mean Square Deviation	24
Controlled Variation	4	Running Record	32
Count Data	255	Runs	90
Detection Rules	96	Sampling from a Frame	329
Distance to Nearest Spec	124	Skewness	322
Empirical Rule	61	Specified Tolerance	121
Flowchart	310	Stable Process	118
Fraction Nonconforming	129	Standard Deviation	26
Grand Average	44	Standard Deviation Chart	57
Histogram	27	State of Chaos	14
Hypothetical Process Limits	136	Stem and Leaf Plot	31
Hypothetical Process Spread	135	Subgroup Average	40
Ideal State	12	Subgroup Range	40
Individual Values	46	Taguchi Loss Function	161
Kurtosis	322	Target	193
Loss Function	143	Three-Way Charts	221
Mean Square Deviation	147	Threshold State	13
Measurement Data	255	Uncontrolled Variation	4
Median	22	Within Subgroup	100

Glossary of Symbols

a_i	Area of Opportunity for the Poisson Count from the ith sample, p. 275
a_3	skewness statistic for a set of data, p. 322
a_4	kurtosis statistic for a set of data, p. 322
α_3	skewness parameter for a theoretical probability distribution, p. 322
α_4	kurtosis parameter for a theoretical probability distribution, p. 322
A_1, A_2, A_3	Control Chart constants: Tables A.2 to A.5, p. 394–397
A_4, A_6, A_9	Control Chart constants: Tables A.3 to A.7, p. 395–399
B_3, B_4	Control Chart constants: Tables A.4 to A.5, p. 396–397
c_i	the Poisson count for the ith sample, p. 275
$\bar{c}$	average count per sample for Poisson Count Data, p. 272
c_2	a bias correction factor for converting s_n into $Sigma(X)$, p. 393
c_4	a bias correction factor for converting s into $Sigma(X)$, p. 393
CL	the Central Line of a control chart, p. 45
C_p	a capability ratio, p. 126
C_{pk}	a centered capability ratio, p. 127
C_{scrap}	the cost of scrapping a single item, p. 147
D	the critical distance for setting Process Aim, p. 200
D_3, D_4, D_5, D_6	Control Chart constants: Tables A.2 to A.3, p. 394–395
d_2	a bias correction factor for converting ranges into $Sigma(X)$, p. 46, 393
d_3	a bias correction factor for converting ranges into $Sigma(R)$, p. 244, 393
DNS	Distance to Nearest Specification, p. 124
$E[\mathcal{L}(x)]$	the Expected Value of $\mathcal{L}(x)$, p. 146
$f(x)$	a probability density function for a theoretical distribution, p. 322.
k	the number of subgroups in a set of data, p. 44
K	the conversion factor for Average Loss per Unit of Production, p. 144
LCL	Lower Control Limit for a control chart, p. 44
LNPL	Lower Natural Process Limit, p. 46
LSL	Lower Specification Limit, p. 142
$\mathcal{L}(x)$	the loss function associated with variation from target, p. 143

Glossary of Symbols

MEAN(X) or μ the mean of a theoretical probability distribution, p. 146, 332

$\overline{mR}$ the Average Moving Range, p. 48

$m\overline{X}$ the Moving Average, p. 219

$MSD(\tau)$ Mean Square Deviation About Target for a stable process, p. 146

n the number of items in a subgroup, p. 26

n or **n$_i$**   the Area of Opportunity for a Binomial Count, p. 261

p   a parameter for the Binomial Probability Model, p. 261

$\overline{p}$ Average Proportion Nonconforming statistic for Binomial Data, p. 261

p_i the sample proportion nonconforming for Binomial Count Data, p. 263

PCI a process capability index, p. 126

P_p a process performance ratio, p. 134

P_{pk} a centered performance ratio, p. 134

R the range of a set of data, p. 24

$\overline{R}$ the Average Range, p. 44

$\tilde{R}$ the Median Range, p. 47, 228

s the Standard Deviation for a set of data, p. 26

$\overline{s}$ the Average Standard Deviation, p. 57

s_n the Root Mean Square Deviation of a set of data, p. 24

$s_{\overline{x}}$ the Standard Deviation of the Subgroup Averages, p. 59

SD(X) or σ the standard deviation parameter for a theoretical distribution, p. 322

σ^2 the variance parameter of a theoretical probability distribution, p. 146

σ_θ a generic dispersion parameter used by Shewhart, p. 60

$Sigma(X)$ a measure of dispersion for Individual Values, pp. 111, 244, 393

$Sigma(\overline{X})$ a measure of dispersion for Subgroup Averages, pp. 93, 244, 393

$Sigma(R)$ a measure of dispersion for Subgroup Ranges, pp. 93, 244, 393

t Shewhart's multiplier for control chart limits, p. 60

τ the Target value for a product quality characteristic, p. 143

Glossary of Symbols

$\bar{\theta}$	a generic location parameter used by Shewhart, p. 60
u_i	the Poisson Rate for the ith sample, p. 275
$\bar{u}$	the average rate of nonconformities per unit area of opportunity, p. 275
UCL	Upper Control Limit for a control chart, p. 44
UNPL	Upper Natural Process Limit, p. 46
USL	Upper Specification Limit, p.142
$\bar{X}$	the average of a set of data, p. 22
$\bar{\bar{X}}$	the Grand Average, the average of the Subgroup Averages, p. 44
$\bar{\tilde{X}}$	the average of a collection of subgroup medians, p. 232
X or X_i	a single measurement, p. 26
$\tilde{X}$	a median for a set of data, p. 22
x_{scrap}	the product dimension at which an item is scrapped, p. 147
XmR	symbol for Individual and Moving Range chart, p. 49
Y_i	a Binomial Count, p. 260
Z_L	the standardized distance between the Grand Average and the Lower Specification Limit, p. 123
Z_U	the standardized distance between the Grand Average and the Upper Specification Limit, p. 123

List of Examples

Examples (continued)

List of Figures

Figures (continued)

Figures (continued)

Figures (continued)

Figures (continued)

Figures (continued)

Bibliography

Burr, Irving W., *Elementary Statistical Quality Control*, Marcel Dekker Inc., New York, 1979.

Burr, Irving W., *Statistical Quality Control Methods*, Marcel Dekker Inc., New York, 1976.

Deming, W. Edwards, *Elementary Principles of the Statistical Control of Quality*, Nippon Kagaku Gijutsu Renmei, Tokyo, 1952.

Deming, W. Edwards, *Out of the Crisis*, Massachusetts Institute of Technology, Center for Advanced Engineering Study, Cambridge, 1986.

Deming, W. Edwards, *Quality, Productivity, and Competitive Position*, Massachusetts Institute of Technology, Center for Advanced Engineering Study, Cambridge, 1982.

Duncan, A.J., *Quality Control and Industrial Statistics*, Richard D. Irwin Inc., Homewood, Illinois, 1982.

Gitlow, Howard S. and Shelly J. Gitlow, *The Deming Guide to Quality and Competitive Position*, Prentice Hall, Inc., Englewood Cliffs, New Jersey, 1987.

Gitlow, Howard S. & Process Management International Inc., *Planning for Quality, Productivity, & Competitive Position*, Dow Jones-Irwin, Homewood, Illinois, 1990.

Gitlow, Howard S., *Tools and Methods for the Improvement of Quality*, Richard D. Irwin Inc., Homewood, Illinois, 1989.

Grant, E.L., and R.S. Leavenworth, *Statistical Quality Control*, McGraw Hill, New York, 1980.

Ishikawa, Kaoru, *Guide to Quality Control*, Asian Productivity Organization, Tokyo, 1976.

Ishikawa, Kaoru, and D.J. Lu, *What is Total Quality Control? The Japanese Way*, Prentice-Hall, Inc., Englewood Cliffs, New Jersey, 1986.

Kane, Victor E., *Defect Prevention, Use of Simple Statistical Tools*, Marcel Dekker, Inc., New York, 1989.

Kilian, Cecelia S., *The World of W. Edwards Deming*, 2nd ed., SPC Press, Inc., Knoxville, Tennessee, 1992.

Mann, Nancy R., *The Keys to Excellence*, Prestwick Books, Los Angeles, 1985.

Neave, Henry R., *The Deming Dimension*, SPC Press, Inc., Knoxville, Tennessee, 1990.

Bibliography

Scherkenbach, William W., *The Deming Route to Quality and Productivity*, CEEPress, Washington, D.C., 1987.

Scherkenbach, William W., *Deming's Road to Continual Improvement*, SPC Press, Inc., Knoxville, Tennessee, 1991.

Scholtes, Peter R., *The Team Handbook*, Joiner Associates, Madison, Wisconsin, 1988.

Shewhart, Walter A., *Economic Control of Quality of Manufactured Product*, American Society for Quality Control, Milwaukee, Wisconsin, 1980.

Shewhart, Walter A., *Statistical Method from the Viewpoint of Quality Control*, Dover Publications, New York, 1986.

Tukey, John W., *Exploratory Data Analysis*, Addison-Wesley Publishing Company, Reading, Massachusetts, 1977.

Walton, Mary, *Deming Management at Work*, G. P. Putnum's Sons, New York, 1990.

Walton, Mary, *The Deming Management Method*, Dodd, Mead & Co., New York, 1986.

Western Electric, *Statistical Quality Control Handbook*, AT&T, Indianapolis, 1985.

Wheeler, Donald J., "Comparing Control Charts for Individual Values and Control Charts for Moving Averages," 32nd Annual ASQC/ASA Fall Technical Conference, East Rutherford, N.J., October 20-21, 1988. Manuscript No. 35, Statistical Process Controls, Inc. Reprint Series, 1988.

Wheeler, Donald J., "Correlated Data and Control Charts," The Fifth Annual Forum of the British Deming Association, Birmingham, England, April 28–30, 1992, Manuscript No. 37, Statistical Process Controls, Inc. Reprint Series, 1989.

Wheeler, Donald J., *Short Run SPC*, SPC Press, Inc., Knoxville, Tennessee, 1991.

Wheeler, Donald J., *Understanding Industrial Experimentation*, 2nd ed., SPC Press, Inc., Knoxville, Tennessee, 1990.

Wheeler, Donald J., and Richard W. Lyday, *Evaluating the Measurement Process*, 2nd ed. SPC Press, Inc., Knoxville, Tennessee, 1989.

Answers to Exercises

Exercise 2.3:

(a)   The histogram of the 100 weights is:

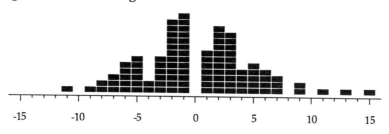

(b)   The absence of zero values is unusual. The person was told to record the deviations from nominal weight, and he did it with a vengeance—every part deviated from the nominal.

(c)   The running record for these data is:

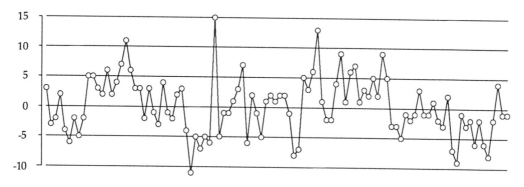

Exercise 2.4:

(a)   The Stem-and-Leaf Plot for these 99 values is:

The shape of the histogram will not be influenced by the order in which one reads through the data, but the order of the values in each column of the Stem-and-Leaf plot will depend on whether the data are read in rows or columns. The Stem-and-Leaf plot shown here was obtained by reading the data in rows.

(b)   The running record for these 99 values is:

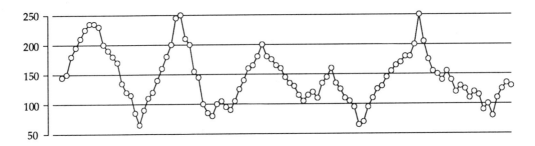

(c)   The running record reveals a cyclical pattern which is not revealed by the Stem-and-Leaf Plot.

Exercise 2.5:

(a)   A histogram for these transit times is:

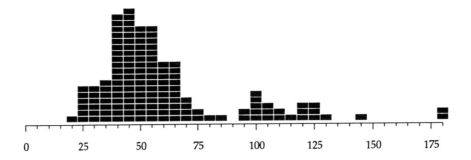

(b)   Between the values of 20 and 85 this histogram shows a mound shape which is commonly found in many different types of data. However, above a value of 85 the tail is greatly elongated and contains several clusters of values. Thus, the upper tail values do not appear to belong to the same system as the data in the mound. Or, in the words of the steel furnace superintendent: "there are two things going on here!" He was right, there were. The long transit times occurred when the locomotive crew unhooked from the hot metal and performed another job before delivering the hot metal to the furnace.

Exercise 3.1:

(c)   The Grand Average for these data is 0.22.
      The Average Range is 8.85.
      The Upper Control Limit for Averages is 5.33.
      The Lower Control Limit for Averages is − 4.89.
      The Upper Control Limit for Ranges is 18.7.

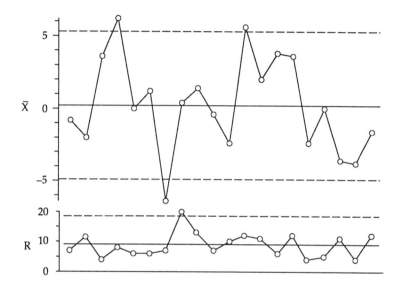

(d)   The Running Record of the 100 Individual Values is superimposed on the Average
      Chart below. While both running records show the same basic trends, the Subgroup
      Averages do it without the clutter of the Individuals. On the other hand, the Indi-
      viduals show details which are lost on the Average Charts. For some data the Indi-
      viduals Chart will reveal the interesting detail better than the Average Chart. For
      other data this situation will be reversed.

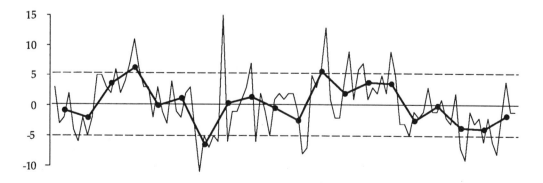

Exercise 3.2:

(a) The running records for the Subgroup Averages and Subgroup Ranges are:

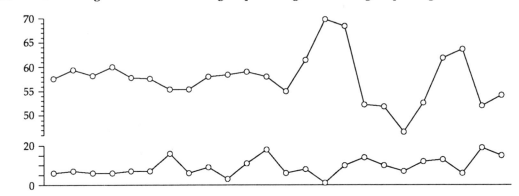

(b) The engineer used the first 12 subgroups to calculate the control limits because he was afraid that the use of all 24 subgroups would contaminate the control limits. For the first 12 subgroups, the Grand Average is 57.883, and the Average Range is 8.5. This gives an Upper Control Limit for Averages of 62.79, a Lower Control Limit for Averages of 52.98, and an Upper Control Limit for Ranges of 17.97.

(c) Using all 24 subgroups the Grand Average is 57.242, and the Average Range is 9.29. This gives an Upper Control Limit for Averages of 62.60, a Lower Control Limit for Averages of 51.88, and an Upper Control Limit for Ranges of 19.64. The two sets of limits are shown on the following chart.

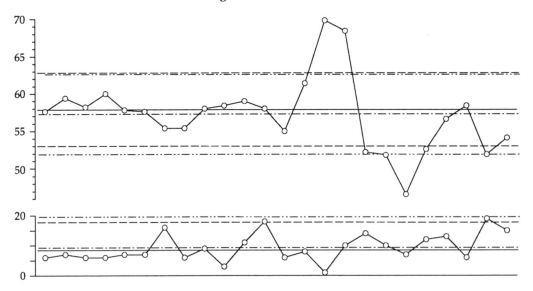

(d) Based on the first set of limits, 7 of the last 12 Subgroup Averages were out-of-control. Using all 24 Subgroup Averages the Grand Average dropped from 57.883 to 57.242. Thus, the out-of-control Averages had a minimal impact upon the limits computed in part (c).

(e) Based on the first set of limits, two of the 24 ranges were out-of-control. Using all 24 Subgroup Ranges the Average Range increased from 8.5 to 9.29. This increase in the Average Range did widen the limits slightly. Although none of the ranges appear to be out-of-control with the second set of limits, there are still five Subgroup Averages outside the limits computed in part (c). Whichever set of limits one may use, the message is the same: the cooling water pressures are out of control from day-to-day.

Exercise 3.3:

The Upper Control Limit for the Subgroup Averages is $936.08 + 1.88 (27.84) = 988.42$.
The Lower Control Limit for the Subgroup Averages is $936.08 - 1.88 (27.84) = 883.74$.
The Upper Control Limit for the Subgroup Ranges is $3.268 (27.84) = 90.98$.
The chart for these data is shown in Figure 9.6, page 220.

Exercise 3.4:

(a) The Moving Ranges are:

$$4, 1, 4, 5, 0, 2, 2, 0, 3, 1, 0, 1, 4, 6$$

The Average is 38.333.
The Average Moving Range is 2.357.
The Upper Natural Process Limit is 44.6.
The Lower Natural Process Limit is 32.06.
The Upper Control Limit for the Ranges is 7.7.

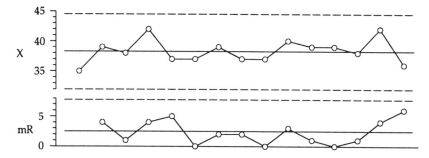

(b) A test value of 34 pounds for Batch 16 is consistent with the values shown on the Individuals Chart above.

(c) A test value of 44 pounds for Batch 17 would also be consistent with the previous values. However, the Moving Range from Batch 16 to Batch 17 would be out-of-control, suggesting a shift in the process. Although the Individual Values are consistent with those which have gone before, the change from 34 to 44 signals some sort of upset in the process and should be investigated.

Exercise 3.5:

(a) The Grand Average is 48.20.
The Average Range is 5.15.
The Upper Control Limit for Averages is 51.17.
The Lower Control Limit for Averages is 45.23.
The Upper Control Limit for Ranges is 10.9

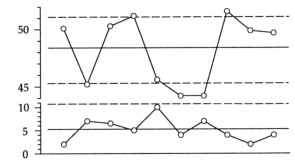

(b) No, this process is not operating consistently. These data show the process to be operating at two different levels.

Exercise 4.1:

(a) Some INCORRECT control limits for Subgroup Averages are:

$$48.20 \pm \frac{3\,(3.54)}{\sqrt{5}}$$
$$= 43.45 \text{ to } 52.95$$

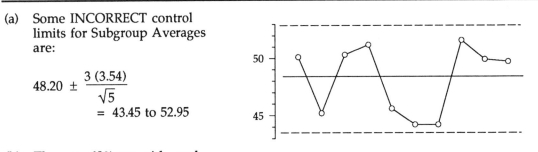

(b) They are 60% too wide, and none of the Subgroup Averages fall outside these inflated limits, even though 5 of the 10 Subgroup Averages were outside the correct limits in Exercise 3.5.

(c) $s_{\bar{x}} = 3.0089$, so another set of INCORRECT limits for Averages is:

$$48.20 \pm 3\,(3.01)$$
$$= 39.17 \text{ to } 57.23.$$

These limits are 204% too wide.

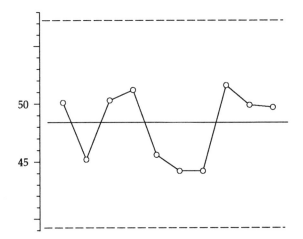

Exercise 4.2:

(a) The Upper Control Limit for Ranges is 2.282 (658.6) = 1502.9.

(b) Yes, the ranges for Subgroups 4 and 15 exceed this Upper Control Limit.

(c) The Upper Control Limit for Averages is 4498.18 + 0.729 (658.6) = 4978.3.
The Lower Control Limit for Averages is 4498.18 − 0.729 (658.6) = 4018.1.
These limits are consistent with the picture drawn by Dr. Shewhart.
TEN of the Subgroup Averages are outside these limits. (See page 81.)

(d) The INCORRECT control limits for the Subgroup Averages are 3798.6 to 5197.8.
These limits are 46% too wide. Only two of the Subgroup Averages fall outside these incorrect limits.

(e) These INCORRECT control limits for the Subgroup Averages are 3441.3 to 5555.1.
These limits are 120% too wide. None of the Subgroup Averages fall outside these incorrect limits.

(f) The correct limits are the most sensitive to the lack of control.

Exercise 5.1:

(a) Grand Average is 144.525. Average Range is 30.697. Subgroup Size is $n = 3$.
Upper Control Limit for Averages = 144.525 + 1.023 (30.697) = 175.928.
Lower Control Limit for Averages = 144.525 − 1.023 (30.697) = 113.122.
Upper Control Limit for Ranges = 2.574 (30.697) = 79.01.
17 of the 33 Subgroup Averages are outside these limits.

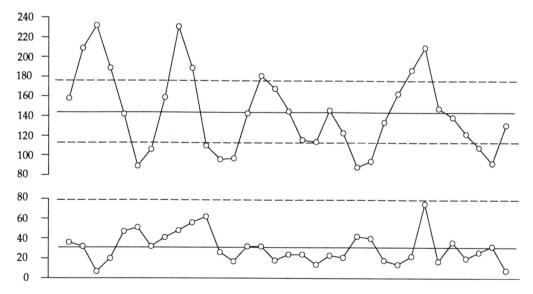

(b) The variation within-a-day is seen on the Range Chart.

(c) The day-to-day variation is seen on the Average Chart.

(d) 113 to 176 are the limits on the daily averages that one might expect to see if and when this process is brought into a reasonable degree of statistical control.

Exercise 5.2:

(a)   Any chart that separates the data for positions 1, 2, and 3 into different subgroups from those containing data for positions 6, 7, and 8 will make the desired comparison. The following chart uses the hinge-end data from each of the 10 pieces for the first 10 subgroups, and the clamp-end data from each piece for the last 10 subgroups.

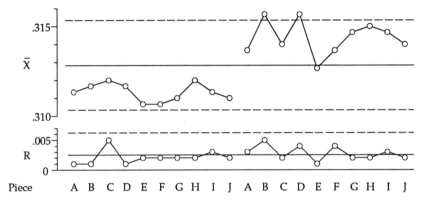

(b)   Yes, there is a detectable difference between the average end thicknesses.

(c)   Eight subgroups of size $n = 10$ would allow one to compare the average thicknesses at each of the 8 positions. This would give information about the cavity used for baking these ten pieces. The Average and Range Chart for these 8 subgroups would be:

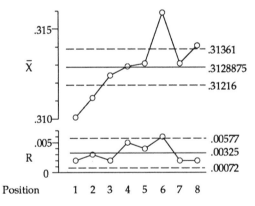

Once again, there are detectable differences. This chart shows detectable differences between the eight positions. Positions 1 and 2 are detectably lower than the Grand Average, and positions 6 and 8 are detectably thicker than the Grand Average.

Exercise 6.1:

(a) $Sigma(X) = \dfrac{\bar{R}}{d_2} = \dfrac{4.05}{2.059} = 1.967$

(b) Natural Process Limits are: $4.763 \pm 3\,(1.967) = -1.14$ to 10.66

(c) Specified Tolerance $= 20$ units $= \dfrac{20 \text{ units}}{1.967 \text{ units/sigma}} = 10.17$ sigma

so $C_p = \dfrac{10.17}{6} = 1.69$

(d) $Z_U = \dfrac{15 - 4.763}{1.967} = 5.20$ $Z_L = \dfrac{4.763 - (-5)}{1.967} = 4.96$
and so

$DNS = $ Minimum $\{\,5.20, 4.96\,\} = 4.96$ and

$C_{pk} = \dfrac{DNS}{3} = 1.65.$

(e) $MSD(5) = \{\,(1.967)^2 + (4.763 - 5)^2\,\} = 3.93$ units^2

(f) With a K value of 0.05 cents/unit^2, this $MSD(5)$ value yields an average cost per unit of production of $3.93\,(0.05) = 0.1965$ cents. With a daily production of 50,000 pieces, this results in a cost of variation of \$98.25 per day. Since they are in control and reasonably well on target, this amounts to only 4% of the total cost of production. Poor targeting, or large variation can inflate this dramatically.

Exercise 6.2:

(a) $Sigma(X) = \dfrac{2.36}{1.128} = 2.092$ units/sigma

(b) $Z_L = \dfrac{38.33 - 25 \text{ units}}{2.092 \text{ units/sigma}} = 6.37$ sigma $= DNS$ so $C_{pk} = \dfrac{6.37}{3} = 2.12$

(c) If $C_{pk} = 1.33$, then target would be $25 + 4\,(2.092) = 33.37$ units.

(d) $MSD(\infty) = \dfrac{1}{15}\left\{ \dfrac{1}{35^2} + \dfrac{1}{39^2} + \dfrac{1}{38^2} + \dfrac{1}{42^2} + \dfrac{1}{37^2} + \dfrac{1}{37^2} + \dfrac{1}{39^2} + \dfrac{1}{37^2} + \dfrac{1}{37^2} + \dfrac{1}{40^2} + \dfrac{1}{39^2} + \dfrac{1}{39^2} + \dfrac{1}{38^2} + \dfrac{1}{42^2} + \dfrac{1}{36^2} \right\}$
$= 0.0006856$

Exercise 6.3:

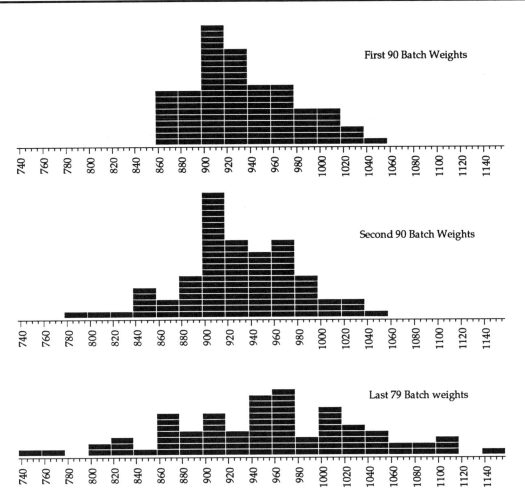

First 90 Batch Weights

Second 90 Batch Weights

Last 79 Batch weights

(d) Because every batch was weighed these three histograms do summarize the performance during the past week, but they also show, in a graphic form, the inconsistency and unpredictability of this process.

Exercise 6.4:

(a) The C_p values for all six distribution in figure 6.5 are 1.00. The C_{pk} values for the bottom three distributions in Figure 6.5 are 0.667, 0.500, and 0.333 respectively.

(b) The proportions falling within specifications for these three distributions are 0.9986, 0.9978, and 0.9975 respectively.

(c) There is no inherent and fixed relationship between C_{pk} and the proportion of conforming or nonconforming product.

Exercise 7.1:

(a) $Sigma(X) = \dfrac{0.0304 \text{ mm}}{2.059 \text{ sigma units}} = 0.0148 \text{ mm/sigma}$

(b) Natural Process Limits are 15.899 mm ± 3 (0.0148 mm) = 15.855 mm to 15.943 mm.

(c) The Specified Tolerance is 0.200 mm or 13.5 sigma units, so $C_p = 2.25$.

(d) $Z_U = 6.82$ sigma, while $Z_L = 6.69$ sigma, so $DNS = 6.69$ sigma and $C_{pk} = 2.23$.

(e) $MSD(15.90) = (0.0148)^2 + (15.899 - 15.900)^2 = 0.000220 \text{ mm}^2$

(f) If the cost of scrap is 20 Yen per piece and a part is scrapped if it has a dimension equal to the specification limit, then we can write an equation of the following form:

$$L(x) = L(16.0) = ¥20 = K(x - \tau)^2 = K(16.0 \text{ mm} - 15.90 \text{ mm})^2 = K(0.01 \text{ mm}^2)$$

thus: $\qquad\qquad\qquad\qquad K = ¥2000 \text{ per mm}^2$

(g) Thus, in September 1980, the average loss per piece due to variation is estimated as:
$$K\{MSD(\tau)\} = 2000 (0.000220) = ¥0.44$$

Exercise 7.2:

(a) $Sigma(X) = \dfrac{0.0207 \text{ mm}}{2.059 \text{ sigma units}} = 0.0101 \text{ mm/sigma}$

(b) Natural Process Limits are 15.906 mm ± 3 (0.0101 mm) = 15.876 mm to 15.936 mm.

(c) The Specified Tolerance is 0.200 mm or 19.8 sigma units, so $C_p = 3.30$.

(d) $Z_U = 9.34$ sigma, while $Z_L = 10.47$ sigma, so $DNS = 9.34$ sigma and $C_{pk} = 3.11$.

(e) $MSD(15.90) = (0.0101)^2 + (15.9057 - 15.900)^2 = 0.000135 \text{ mm}^2$

(f) C_p increased 47%, C_{pk} increased 39 %, and $MSD(15.90)$ dropped 39%.

(g) Thus, in March 1981, the average loss per piece due to variation is estimated as:
$$K\{MSD(\tau)\} = 2000 (0.000135) = ¥0.27$$

Exercise 7.3:

(a) $Sigma(X) = \dfrac{0.0225 \text{ mm}}{2.059 \text{ sigma units}} = 0.0109 \text{ mm/sigma}$

(b) Natural Process Limits are 15.886 mm ± 3 (0.0109 mm) = 15.853 mm to 15.919 mm.

(c) The Specified Tolerance is 0.300 mm or 27.5 sigma units, so $C_p = 4.59$.

(d) $Z_U = 15.01$ sigma, while $Z_L = 12.51$ sigma,
so $DNS = 12.51$ sigma and $C_{pk} = 4.17$.

(e) $MSD(15.88) = (0.0109)^2 + (15.8864 - 15.880)^2 = 0.000160 \text{ mm}^2$

(f) The change in the specifications caused C_p to increase 39%, and C_{pk} to increase 34%. While the $MSD(15.88)$ value did increase by 18%, this increase was not related to the relaxation of the specifications.

(g) Thus, in January 1982, the average loss per piece due to variation may be estimated as:

$$K\{MSD(\tau)\} = 2000 \,(0.000160) = ¥\,0.32$$

(If they changed the "scrap point" from 15.8 and 16.0 mm to coincide with the new specifications of 15.75 and 16.05 mm, the K value would drop to ¥1183.4 per mm^2 and the average loss would be ¥ 0.19.)

Exercise 8.1:

(a) A process which displays statistical control will produce at least 90% to 98% within two sigma units of the average (both sides). Thus, one can expect from 1% to 5% beyond the two sigma line on one side of the histogram. If the Target is set two sigma units above the net weight of 16 oz., and the Process Average is close to the Target, then one would expect to get at least 95% of the containers to exceed the net weight. Therefore, with $Sigma(X) = 0.36$ oz. the Target would be 16.72 oz.

(b) Target $\pm\, 0.50\, Sigma(X) = 16.72 \pm 0.18 = 16.54$ oz. to 16.90 oz. is the Do Not Adjust Interval for use with the average of $n = 10$ fill weights.

(c) For the X Chart:

UNPL	17.80 oz.
+2 sigma line	17.44 oz.
+1 sigma line	17.08 oz.
Central Line = Target	16.72 oz.
–1 sigma line	16.36 oz.
–2 sigma line	16.00 oz.
LNPL	15.64 oz.

(d) That the past measurements are appropriate for characterizing the current process.

(e) Out-of-control values or runs on either the Average Chart or an Individuals Chart will signal if the average fill weight changes.

(f) Out-of-control values or runs on the Range Chart will signal any changes which may occur in the variation of the fill weights.

(g) The only way to reduce the "give-away" while meeting the legal requirement is to reduce the variation of the process. This will allow the Target to be moved closer to the net weight value.

Exercise 9.1:

(a) Three possible values are found within the limits of this range chart. This indicates that the round-off of the measurements has intruded upon the calculation of these limits.

(b) No, the tightened limits are a consequence of the Inadequate Measurement Units, not a sign of process improvement. The Tokai Rika chart operates on the border of Inadequate Measurement Units throughout this 20 month history. In this one instance they compute control limits with only a few subgroups, and the multiplicity of zero ranges in the baseline period is adequate to tug them over the brink.

Exercise 9.2:

(a) Deleting the three out-of-control ranges shown in Figure 9.7 the Average Range becomes 0.50. With this value the Upper Control Limit for Ranges becomes 1.057.

Subgroup 22 has a range of 1.5. Deleting this value the Average Range becomes 0.04524. With this value the Upper Control Limit for Ranges becomes 0.956.

Now the ranges for Subgroups 7, 11, and 14 are out-of-control. Deleting these values the Average Range becomes 0.3611, and the Upper Control Limit is 0.763.

(b) With an Upper Control Limit of 0.763, there are only two possible values for the range within the control limits: 0 and 0.5. This means that the revised Range Chart displays inadequate measurement discrimination, while the initial Range Chart had limits that were almost certainly inflated by the out-of-control ranges.

(c) The inadequate discrimination will obscure the Within-Batch Variation. The only way to solve this problem would be to measure the tensile strengths more precisely. Measuring the the nearest 500 pounds is not sufficient to detect the variation within the batches.

(d) The Median Range is 0.5. Using this, the Upper Control Limit for Ranges is 1.089.

(e) The inflated limit based on the average of all of the ranges was used in Figures 9.8 and 9.9.

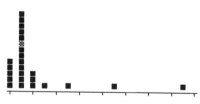

(f) The out-of-control ranges in Figure 9.9 exceed this inflated upper limit, and so they definitely represent batches which have excessive variation in tensile strengths. These heats of steel are not as homogeneous as the others.

(g) The out-of-control averages in Figure 9.9 represent heats of steel that are detectably lower in tensile strength than the other heats.

(h) The anomaly in these data is the reading of 49.6 in Subgroup 12. How can one get a tensile strength of 49,600 pounds when measuring to the nearest 500 pounds?

Exercise 9.3:

(a) The 23 moving ranges are, respectively, .06, .02, .08, .03, .01, .04, .04, .07, .04, .03, .03, .02, .01, .05, .04, .02, .02, .02, .04, .03, .07, .06, and .10. The Average of the first 24 values is 0.1567. The Average Moving Range is 0.0404. The Natural Process Limits are 0.049 to 0.264, and the Upper Control Limit for the ranges is 0.132. There is no indication of a lack of control in these first 24 values.

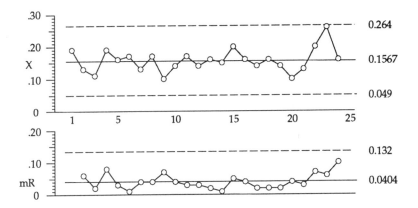

(b) The continuation of this *XmR* Chart is:

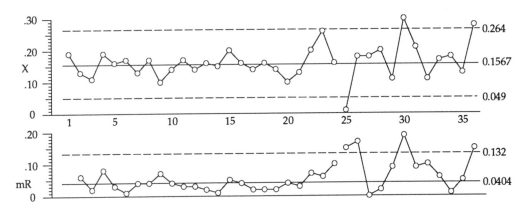

(c) This process is out-of-control. The out-of-control condition consists of isolated points outside the limits of the X chart. Thus, this process can change suddenly.

Exercise 9.4:

(a) The 23 Two Period Moving Averages are: 0.16, 0.12, 0.15, 0.175, 0.165, 0.15, 0.15, 0.135, 0.12, 0.155, 0.155, 0.15, 0.155, 0.175, 0.18, 0.15, 0.15, 0.15, 0.12, 0.115, 0.165, 0.23, and 0.21. The Two-Period Moving Average Chart is shown below. The average of the 23 Moving Averages is 0.1559, and the Average Moving Range is 0.0404. The limits for the Moving Average Chart are 0.0799 to 0.2318.
The Upper Limit for the Range Chart is 0.132.
None of the first 23 Moving Averages or Moving Ranges fall outside these limits.

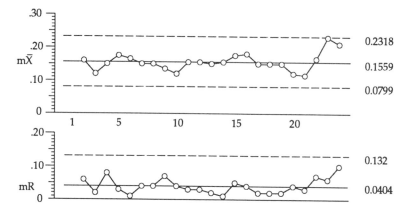

(b) The next 12 Moving Averages are: 0.085, 0.095, 0.18, 0.19, 0.155, 0.205, 0.255, 0.16, 0.14, 0.175, 0.155, and 0.205. The continuation of this Moving Average Chart is:

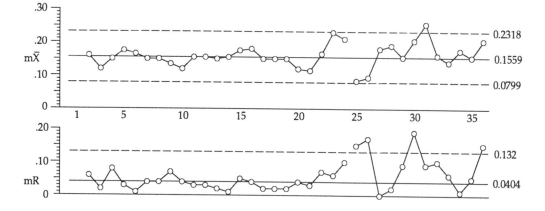

(c) One Moving Average (hour 31) falls outside the limits of this Moving Average Chart. Thus, while this is an indication of a lack of control, there is not as much evidence here as there was on the Individuals Chart in Exercise 9.3.

(d) Only the Moving Range Chart shows that something happened at hour 25 and hour 36.

(e)   The *XmR* Chart is a far better chart for these data than is the Moving Average Chart.

Exercise 9.5:

(a)   The 12 Subgroup Averages are: 0.16, 0.15, 0.165, 0.15, 0.12, 0.155, 0.155, 0.18, 0.15, 0.12, 0.165, and 0.21. The Average and Range Chart is shown below. The Grand Average for the first 12 subgroups is 0.1567, and the Average Range is 0.0450. The limits for the Average Chart are 0.0721 to 0.2413.
The upper limit for the Range Chart is 0.147.
None of the first 12 Subgroup Averages or Subgroup Ranges fall outside these limits.

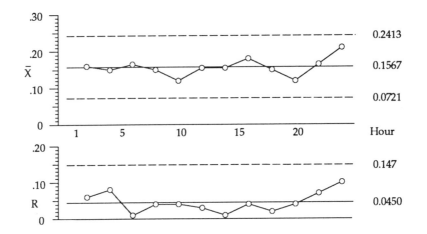

(b)   The next 6 Subgroup Averages are: 0.095, 0.19, 0.205, 0.16, 0.175, and 0.205. The continuation of this Average and Range Chart is:

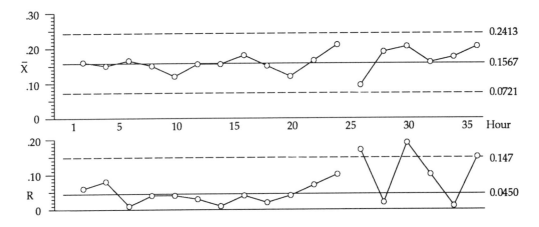

(c)   The signals in these data show up on the Range Chart, but not on the Average Chart.

(d)   Thus, the *XmR* Chart is the most revealing control chart for these data.

(e)   The Average Chart and the Moving Average Chart both average across potential signals. The principle is to "average across noise, not across signals."

Exercise 9.6:

(a)   The average of these ten transformed values is 47.65

(b)   The 9 Moving Ranges are: 1, 0.5, 1.5, 1, 7, 1, 3, 2, and 2.
       The Average Moving Range is 2.111.

(c)   This Average and Average Moving Range yield Natural Process Limits of:

$$47.65 \pm 3 \frac{2.111}{1.128} = 42.03 \text{ to } 53.26$$

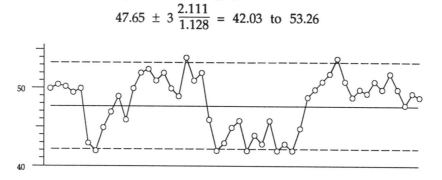

(d)   Yes, the five observations with values of 42 and the two observations with values of
       54 are outside these limits. This is sufficient evidence to say that the fabrication pro-
       cess is out-of-control.

(e)   Yes, the upper control limit for the Moving Ranges is 6.9, so the Moving Range of
       7.0 is out-of-control. This did not prevent the limits computed in part (c) from detect-
       ing the out-of-control condition of these data.

(f)   Deleting the value of 7.0 the Average Moving Range drops to 1.50. Using this value,
       the Natural Process Limits become 43.66 to 51.64. A total of 17 Individual Values fall
       outside these revised limits.

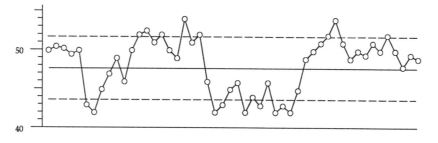

Exercise 9.7:

The average of the first 20 weights is 1.75 grams.

The Average Moving Range is 3.368.

The computed Natural Process Limits are: 1.75 ± 2.66 (3.368) = –7.21 to 10.71.

The Upper Control Limit for the Range Chart is 11.007.

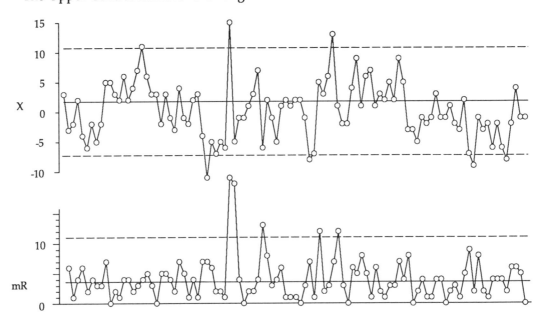

In addition to the process drift seen on the Individuals Chart, the out-of-control Moving Ranges identify five abrupt changes in the process.

Exercise 9.8:

The first 5 subgroups in the first column of Table 9.7, p.236, have a Grand Average of 10.28, and an Average Range of 4.60. These values yield control limits for the Average Chart of 7.63 to 12.93, and a limit for the Range Chart of 9.72. All of the remaining 90 Subgroup Averages and the 90 Subgroup Ranges fall within these limits. When a limited amount of data is available one may still compute control limits. As more data become available these trial control limits may be revised. However, useful control limits may be computed using small amounts of data.

Exercise 9.9:

(a) The within Zone Ranges would not reflect the possible variation between Zones. Since the Zone controllers operate independently, they should be thought of as parallel operations and therefore are best charted separately.

(b) The Zone Averages could be placed on three separate XmR charts. The average for a given zone being the individual value for the purposes of this chart, and a moving range constructed from roll-to-roll. Such charts would track the roll-to-roll consistency of the average tensile strengths for each zone separately.

(c) The Zone Ranges could be placed on three separate Range Charts. Values for a given zone would be placed on a chart as each roll was tested. The control limits for these Range Charts would be obtained by the usual formulas for subgroups of size three since each Zone Range is the range of three tensile values. Such charts would track the roll-to-roll homogeneity of the tensile values for each zone separately.

(d) Placing all nine tensile values in a single subgroup for each roll ignores the potential differences between zones. This would average across potential signals, and thus would violate a principle of subgrouping. Furthermore, the ranges *across* the film are the wrong yardstick for setting limits from roll-to-roll. The proposed subgroups would have roll-to-roll differences between subgroups, but the range chart would only allow for variation across the film, not roll to roll.

(e) The range of the Zone Averages would track the consistency between the three zones for a given roll. It would signal when the zone-to-zone differences became excessively large. This characteristic would be specific to each roll, and is not tracked on any of the charts described above.

(f) If the master roll is split into three slave rolls, the range chart above would still tell when the difference between the slave rolls was exceptionally large.

Exercise 9.10:

(a) Deleting the two out-of control ranges, the Average Range drops to 612.1, giving an upper control limit for Subgroup Ranges of 1369.9. Subgroups 11 and 16 show ranges that exceed this limit. Deleting these two values the Average Range drops to 577.2, giving an upper control limit for ranges of 1317.2. Subgroups 45 and 50 have ranges which exceed this limit. Deleting these two Subgroup Ranges, the Average Range drops to 541.8, giving an upper control limit for ranges of 1236.5. No further Subgroup Ranges exceed this limit.

(b) Using the Average Range value of 541.8, control limits for Subgroup Averages are 4103.2 to 4893.2, while $Sigma(X)$ is 263.1.

(c) The Histogram for the 51 Subgroup Ranges is shown on the right. The Median Range is 570. Based on this value, the limits for Subgroup Averages are 4066.1 to 4930.2, while $Sigma(X)$ is 288.2.

```
 0
 1
 2    00 05 30 45 45 50 55 65 65 80
 3    00 00 35 35 40 90 90
 4    00 45 90
 5    00 00 05 20 40 70
 6    05 35 50 55 65 75 80
 7    00 25 30 45 85
 8    00 15
 9    10
10    00 70
11    15 25
12
13    60 85
14    10 55
15
16    95
17
18
19    00
```

Exercise 10.1:

(a) The 20 Moving Ranges are: 9, 1, 5, 5, 1, 2, 26, 24, 6, 9, 2, 2, 7, 7, 3, 1, 11, 10, 11, and 3. The Average Moving Range is 7.25.
The Upper Control Limit for these Moving Ranges is 23.69.

(b) Deleting the two out-of-control Moving Ranges yields an Average Moving Range of 5.278, with an Upper Control Limit for Ranges of 17.25.

(c) With an Average of 22.24, the Natural Process Limits for the Number of Rejected Parts per Basket are 22.2 ± 2.66 (5.278) = 8.20 to 36.28.

(d) The Natural Process Limits are slightly wider than the limits found on the *np*-chart. While both charts show Sample 8 to be out-of-control, only the *np*-chart shows Sample 1 to be out-of-control.

Exercise 10.2:

(a) n = 60, $\bar{p} = \frac{211}{1260} = 0.1675$ and the *np*-chart is:

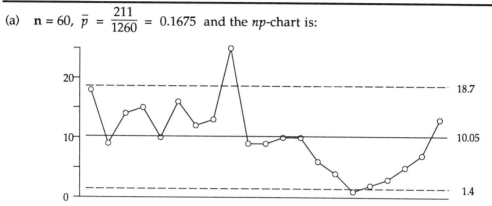

(b) Yes, there has been a substantial change. The Upper Limit in April is smaller than the central line in November. Moreover, this *np*-chart shows two levels of operation—the first 9 samples are not centered on the central line, while the next 11 values are all below the central line.

Exercise 10.3:

(a) The 19 Moving Ranges are: .031, .029, .018, .028, .150, .082, .063, .030, .016, .015, .008, .029, .059, .041, .027, .003, .023, .023, and .040. The Average Moving Range is 0.03763, which gives an Upper Control Limit for Ranges of 0.12298.

(b) The value of 0.150 is out-of-control. Deleting this value, the revised Average Moving Range is 0.03139, giving an Upper Limit for ranges of 0.1026.

(c) With an Average of 0.16395, the Natural Process Limits for the Daily Proportion of Incomplete Invoices are 0.16395 ± 2.66 (0.03139) = 0.0804 to 0.2474.

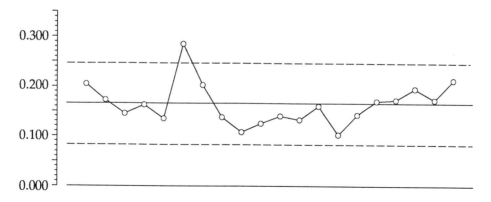

(d) This *XmR* chart shows the same indications of a lack of control that were found on the *p*-chart in Figure 10.4, page 265.

Exercise 10.4:

(a) The Area of Opportunity for each quality audit sample is the 225 pairs selected daily.

(b) The histogram for these data shows the data to have a definite discreteness. In particular, each proportion should be an integer divided by 225. The two values of 0.087 do not fit into this pattern, and they do not correspond to an integer divided by 225. Thus, these two values must be incorrect.

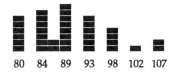

Histogram of Proportions

(c) Yes, these proportions satisfy the four conditions for the use of the Binomial Model.

(d) Rounding the 0.087 values off to 0.089, the p-chart for these data is:

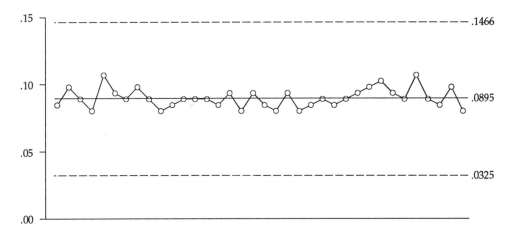

(e) The limits on this p-chart are very wide relative to the running record. Since the running record has a long run below the central line (15 of 18 values) there is already evidence that the data are not in-control, yet if the limits are correct the data are too good to be true. In this case, the quality audit inspector was making up the data. He was afraid that if he didn't find at least 8 percent defectives he would loose his job. On the other hand, if the percentage defective ever exceeded 11 percent, he was convinced that the company vice-president would shut down the whole plant! Thus, motivated by fear, he made sure that each day's data fell between 8 percent and 11 percent, with not too many days near 11 percent.

Exercise 10.5:

(a)   The Area of Opportunity for each of these counts is 300 square inches of coated surface.

(b)   Yes, these data satisfy the four conditions for the use of the Poisson Model.

(c)   The average count is 1.428, and the upper limit is 5.01. The c-chart for these data is:

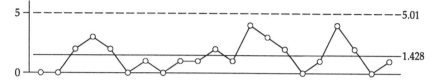

(d)   The Average is 1.428, the Average Moving Range is 1.35, so the upper limit is 5.02 and the upper limit for ranges is 4.4. The *XmR* Chart for these data is:

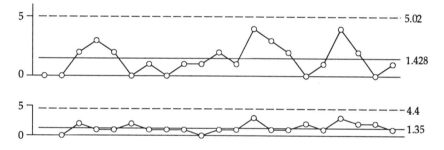

(e)   The c-Chart and the XmR Chart tell the same story for these data.

Exercise 10.6:

(a) Yes, these data do satisfy the conditions for the use of the Poisson Model.

(b) The average rate is 0.1195. When the Area of Opportunity is 13 the upper limit is 0.407. When the Area is 25 the upper limit is 0.327, and when the Area is 38 the upper limit is 0.288. There are no lower limits. The *u*-chart is:

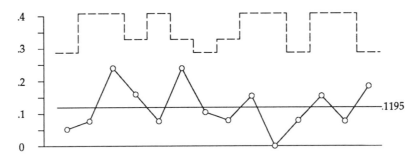

(c) This *u*-chart shows the painting process to be in control.

Exercise 10.7:

(a) Since the numerator of the *Premium Percentages of Total Costs* is bounded by the denominator, these ratios are percentages. At the same time, they are not the ratio of counts, therefore, these data must be classified as "proportions based on measurements."

(b) Such data cannot be placed upon a p-chart, therefore, one may only use an *XmR* chart with these proportions.

Table A.1: Bias Correction Factors [1]

n	d_2	c_2	c_4	d_3	d_4	n	d_2	c_2	c_4	d_3	d_4
2	1.128	0.5642	.7979	0.8525	0.954	21	3.778	0.9638	.9876	0.7272	3.730
3	1.693	0.7236	.8862	0.8884	1.588	22	3.819	0.9655	.9882	0.7199	3.771
4	2.059	0.7979	.9213	0.8798	1.978	23	3.858	0.9670	.9887	0.7159	3.811
5	2.326	0.8407	.9400	0.8641	2.257	24	3.895	0.9684	.9892	0.7121	3.847
6	2.534	0.8686	.9515	0.8480	2.472	25	3.931	0.9695	.9896	0.7084	3.883
7	2.704	0.8882	.9594	0.8332	2.645	30	4.086	0.9748	.9915	0.6927	4.037
8	2.847	0.9027	.9650	0.8198	2.791	35	4.213	0.9784	.9927	0.6799	4.166
9	2.970	0.9139	.9693	0.8078	2.915	40	4.322	0.9811	.9936	0.6692	4.274
10	3.078	0.9227	.9727	0.7971	3.024	45	4.415	0.9832	.9943	0.6601	4.372
11	3.173	0.9300	.9754	0.7873	3.121	50	4.498	0.9849	.9949	0.6521	4.450
12	3.258	0.9359	.9776	0.7785	3.207	60	4.639	0.9874	.9957	0.6389	4.591
13	3.336	0.9410	.9794	0.7704	3.285	70	4.755	0.9892	.9963	0.6283	4.707
14	3.407	0.9453	.9810	0.7630	3.356	80	4.854	0.9906	.9968	0.6194	4.806
15	3.472	0.9490	.9823	0.7562	3.422	90	4.939	0.9916	.9972	0.6118	4.892
16	3.532	0.9523	.9835	0.7499	3.482	100	5.015	0.9925	.9975	0.6052	4.968
17	3.588	0.9551	.9845	0.7441	3.538						
18	3.640	0.9576	.9854	0.7386	3.591						
19	3.689	0.9599	.9862	0.7335	3.640						
20	3.735	0.9619	.9869	0.7287	3.686						

Given k subgroups of size n, the *Adjusted Average Dispersion Statistics*:

$$\frac{\overline{s}_n}{c_2} \quad \text{or} \quad \frac{\overline{s}}{c_4} \quad \text{or} \quad \frac{\overline{R}}{d_2} \quad \text{or} \quad \frac{\widetilde{R}}{d_4} \quad \text{will be denoted by the generic symbol } Sigma(X).$$

Likewise denote the following ratios:

$$\frac{\overline{s}_n}{c_2 \sqrt{n}} \quad \text{or} \quad \frac{\overline{s}}{c_4 \sqrt{n}} \quad \text{or} \quad \frac{\overline{R}}{d_2 \sqrt{n}} \quad \text{or} \quad \frac{\widetilde{R}}{d_4 \sqrt{n}} \quad \text{by the generic symbol } Sigma(\overline{X}),$$

$$\text{and let } Sigma(R) \text{ denote either } \frac{d_3 \overline{R}}{d_2} \quad \text{or} \quad \frac{d_3 \widetilde{R}}{d_4}$$

---

[1] Values for d_2, d_3, and d_4 from H.L. Harter, "Tables of Range and Studentized Range," *Annals of Mathematical Statistics*, v.31, p.1122-1147, 1960. Values for c_2 and c_4 were computed from the formulas:

$$c_2 = \sqrt{\frac{2}{n}} \; \frac{\Gamma(\frac{n}{2})}{\Gamma(\frac{n-1}{2})} \qquad\qquad c_4 = c_2 \sqrt{\frac{n}{n-1}}$$

Table A.2: Factors for Using the Average Range, $\bar{R}$ to Find Control Limits for Subgroup Averages and Subgroup Ranges

n	A_2	D_3	D_4
2	1.880	–	3.268
3	1.023	–	2.574
4	0.729	–	2.282
5	0.577	–	2.114
6	0.483	–	2.004
7	0.419	0.076	1.924
8	0.373	0.136	1.864
9	0.337	0.184	1.816
10	0.308	0.223	1.777
11	0.285	0.256	1.744
12	0.266	0.283	1.717
13	0.249	0.307	1.693
14	0.235	0.328	1.672
15	0.223	0.347	1.653

Given k subgroups each with n observations with Grand Average, $\bar{\bar{X}}$ and Average Range, $\bar{R}$ use these constants with the formulas below

$$UCL_{\bar{X}} = \bar{\bar{X}} + A_2 \bar{R} = \text{Grand Average} + A_2 \text{ times the Average Range}$$

$$CL_{\bar{X}} = \bar{\bar{X}} \qquad\qquad = \text{the Grand Average}$$

$$LCL_{\bar{X}} = \bar{\bar{X}} - A_2 \bar{R} = \text{Grand Average} - A_2 \text{ times the Average Range}$$

$$UCL_R = D_4 \bar{R} \qquad\quad = D_4 \text{ times the Average Range}$$

$$CL_R = \bar{R} \qquad\qquad\quad = \text{the Average Range}$$

$$LCL_R = D_3 \bar{R} \qquad\quad = D_3 \text{ times the Average Range}$$

And for $n > 15$ the control chart constants may be computed using the following formulas and the basic bias correction factors shown in Table A.1:

$$A_2 = \frac{3}{d_2\sqrt{n}} \qquad\qquad D_3 = \left[1 - \frac{3\,d_3}{d_2} \right] \qquad\qquad D_4 = \left[1 + \frac{3\,d_3}{d_2} \right]$$

Table A.3: Factors for Using the Median Range, $\tilde{R}$
to Find Control Limits for
Subgroup Averages and Subgroup Ranges

n	A_4	D_5	D_6
2	2.224	–	3.865
3	1.091	–	2.745
4	0.758	–	2.375
5	0.594	–	2.179
6	0.495	–	2.055
7	0.429	0.078	1.967
8	0.380	0.139	1.901
9	0.343	0.187	1.850
10	0.314	0.227	1.809
11	0.290	0.260	1.773
12	0.270	0.288	1.744
13	0.253	0.312	1.719
14	0.239	0.333	1.697
15	0.226	0.352	1.678

Given k subgroups

each with n observations

with Grand Average, $\bar{\bar{X}}$

and Median Range, $\tilde{R}$

use these constants

with the formulas below

$$UCL_{\bar{X}} = \bar{\bar{X}} + A_4 \tilde{R} = Grand\ Average + A_4\ times\ the\ Median\ Range$$

$$CL_{\bar{X}} = \bar{\bar{X}} \qquad\qquad = the\ Grand\ Average$$

$$LCL_{\bar{X}} = \bar{\bar{X}} - A_4 \tilde{R} = Grand\ Average - A_4\ times\ the\ Median\ Range$$

$$UCL_R = D_6 \tilde{R} \qquad = D_6\ times\ the\ Median\ Range$$

$$CL_R = \tilde{R} \qquad\qquad = the\ Median\ Range$$

$$LCL_R = D_5 \tilde{R} \qquad = D_5\ times\ the\ Median\ Range$$

And for $n > 15$ the control chart constants may be computed using the following formulas using the basic bias correction factors shown in Table A.1.

$$A_4 = \frac{3}{d_4 \sqrt{n}} \qquad\qquad D_5 = \frac{d_2 - 3\,d_3}{d_4} \qquad\qquad D_6 = \frac{d_2 + 3\,d_3}{d_4}$$

Table A.4: Factors for Using the Average RMS Deviation, $\bar{s}_n$
to Find Control Limits for
Subgroup Averages and Subgroup RMS Deviations

n	A_1	B_3	B_4
2	3.760	–	3.267
3	2.393	–	2.568
4	1.880	–	2.266
5	1.595	–	2.089
6	1.410	0.030	1.970
7	1.277	0.118	1.882
8	1.175	0.185	1.815
9	1.095	0.239	1.761
10	1.028	0.284	1.716
11	0.973	0.322	1.678
12	0.925	0.354	1.646
13	0.884	0.382	1.619
14	0.848	0.407	1.593
15	0.816	0.428	1.572

Given k subgroups
each with n observations
with Grand Average, $\bar{\bar{X}}$, and
Average RMS Deviation, $\bar{s}_n$
use these constants
with the formulas below

$$UCL_{\bar{X}} = \bar{\bar{X}} + A_1\,\bar{s}_n = \text{Grand Average} + A_1 \text{ times the Average RMS Deviation}$$

$$CL_{\bar{X}} = \bar{\bar{X}} = \text{the Grand Average}$$

$$LCL_{\bar{X}} = \bar{\bar{X}} - A_1\,\bar{s}_n = \text{Grand Average} + A_1 \text{ times the Average RMS Deviation}$$

$$UCL_{s_n} = B_4\,\bar{s}_n = B_4 \text{ times the Average RMS Deviation}$$

$$CL_{s_n} = \bar{s}_n = \text{the Average RMS Deviation}$$

$$LCL_{s_n} = B_3\,\bar{s}_n = B_3 \text{ times the Average RMS Deviation}$$

And for $n > 15$:

$$A_1 = \frac{3}{c_2\sqrt{n}} \qquad B_3 = 1 - \frac{3}{c_2}\sqrt{\frac{(n-1)}{n} - (c_2)^2} \qquad B_4 = 1 + \frac{3}{c_2}\sqrt{\frac{(n-1)}{n} - (c_2)^2}$$

or approximately: $B_3 \approx 1 - \dfrac{3}{\sqrt{2(n-1)}} \qquad\qquad B_4 \approx 1 + \dfrac{3}{\sqrt{2(n-1)}}$

Table A.5: Factors for Using the Average Standard Deviation, $\bar{s}$ to Find Control Limits for Subgroup Averages and Subgroup Standard Deviations

n	A_3	B_3	B_4
2	2.659	–	3.267
3	1.954	–	2.568
4	1.628	–	2.266
5	1.427	–	2.089
6	1.287	0.030	1.970
7	1.182	0.118	1.882
8	1.099	0.185	1.815
9	1.032	0.239	1.761
10	0.975	0.284	1.716
11	0.927	0.322	1.678
12	0.886	0.354	1.646
13	0.850	0.382	1.619
14	0.817	0.407	1.593
15	0.789	0.428	1.572

Given k subgroups

each with n observations

with Grand Average, $\bar{\bar{X}}$, and

Average Standard Deviation, $\bar{s}$

use these constants

with the formulas below

$UCL_{\bar{X}} = \bar{\bar{X}} + A_3\,\bar{s}$ = Grand Average + A_3 times the Average Standard Deviation

$CL_{\bar{X}} = \bar{\bar{X}}$ = the Grand Average

$LCL_{\bar{X}} = \bar{\bar{X}} - A_3\,\bar{s}$ = Grand Average + A_3 times the Average Standard Deviation

$UCL_S = B_4\,\bar{s}$ = B_4 times the Average Standard Deviation

$CL_S = \bar{s}$ = the Average Standard Deviation

$LCL_S = B_3\,\bar{s}$ = B_3 times the Average Standard Deviation

And[2] for $n > 15$:

$$A_3 = \frac{3}{c_4\sqrt{n}} \qquad B_3 = 1 - \frac{3}{c_4}\sqrt{1-(c_4)^2} \qquad B_4 = 1 + \frac{3}{c_4}\sqrt{1-(c_4)^2}$$

or approximately: $B_3 \approx 1 - \dfrac{3}{\sqrt{2(n-1)}}$ $B_4 \approx 1 + \dfrac{3}{\sqrt{2(n-1)}}$

---

[2] While these formulas for B_3 and B_4 differ from those on the preceding page, they are the same constants. The difference is the relationship between the constants c_2 and c_4.

Table A.6: Factors for Using the Average Range, $\bar{R}$
to Find Control Limits for
Subgroup Medians and Subgroup Ranges

n	A_6	D_3	D_4	
3	1.187	–	2.574	Given k subgroups
5	0.691	–	2.114	each with n observations with Average Median, $\bar{\bar{X}}$
7	0.509	0.076	1.924	and Average Range, $\bar{R}$
9	0.412	0.184	1.816	use these constants
11	0.350	0.256	1.744	with the formulas below

$UCL_{\tilde{X}} = \bar{\bar{X}} + A_6 \bar{R} = $ *Average Median* $+ A_6$ *times the Average Range*

$CL_{\tilde{X}} = \bar{\bar{X}} \qquad\quad = $ *the Average Median*

$LCL_{\tilde{X}} = \bar{\bar{X}} - A_6 \bar{R} = $ *Average Median* $- A_6$ *times the Average Range*

$UCL_R = D_4 \bar{R} \qquad = D_4$ *times the Average Range*

$CL_R = \bar{R} \qquad\quad = $ *the Average Range*

$LCL_R = D_3 \bar{R} \qquad = D_3$ *times the Average Range*

Table A.7: Factors for Using the Median Range, $\tilde{R}$
to Find Control Limits for
Subgroup Medians and Subgroup Ranges

n	A_9	D_5	D_6
3	1.265	–	2.745
5	0.712	–	2.179
7	0.520	0.078	1.967
9	0.419	0.187	1.850

Given k subgroups
each with n observations
with Average Median, $\bar{\bar{X}}$
and Median Range, $\tilde{R}$
use these constants
with the formulas below

$$UCL_{\tilde{X}} = \bar{\bar{X}} + A_9\,\tilde{R} = Average\ Median\ +\ A_9\ times\ the\ Median\ Range$$

$$CL_{\tilde{X}} = \bar{\bar{X}} \qquad\qquad = the\ Average\ Median$$

$$LCL_{\tilde{X}} = \bar{\bar{X}} - A_9\,\tilde{R} = Average\ Median\ -\ A_9\ times\ the\ Median\ Range$$

$$UCL_R = D_6\,\tilde{R} \qquad = D_6\ times\ the\ Median\ Range$$

$$CL_R = \tilde{R} \qquad\qquad = the\ Median\ Range$$

$$LCL_R = D_5\,\tilde{R} \qquad = D_5\ times\ the\ Median\ Range$$

Index

Table A.1: Bias Correction Factors

n	d_2	c_2	c_4	d_3	d_4	n	d_2	c_2	c_4	d_3	d_4
2	1.128	0.5642	.7979	0.8525	0.954	21	3.778	0.9638	.9876	0.7272	3.730
3	1.693	0.7236	.8862	0.8884	1.588	22	3.819	0.9655	.9882	0.7199	3.771
4	2.059	0.7979	.9213	0.8798	1.978	23	3.858	0.9670	.9887	0.7159	3.811
5	2.326	0.8407	.9400	0.8641	2.257	24	3.895	0.9684	.9892	0.7121	3.847
6	2.534	0.8686	.9515	0.8480	2.472	25	3.931	0.9695	.9896	0.7084	3.883
7	2.704	0.8882	.9594	0.8332	2.645	30	4.086	0.9748	.9915	0.6927	4.037
8	2.847	0.9027	.9650	0.8198	2.791	35	4.213	0.9784	.9927	0.6799	4.166
9	2.970	0.9139	.9693	0.8078	2.915	40	4.322	0.9811	.9936	0.6692	4.274
10	3.078	0.9227	.9727	0.7971	3.024	45	4.415	0.9832	.9943	0.6601	4.372
11	3.173	0.9300	.9754	0.7873	3.121	50	4.498	0.9849	.9949	0.6521	4.450
12	3.258	0.9359	.9776	0.7785	3.207	60	4.639	0.9874	.9957	0.6389	4.591
13	3.336	0.9410	.9794	0.7704	3.285	70	4.755	0.9892	.9963	0.6283	4.707
14	3.407	0.9453	.9810	0.7630	3.356	80	4.854	0.9906	.9968	0.6194	4.806
15	3.472	0.9490	.9823	0.7562	3.422	90	4.939	0.9916	.9972	0.6118	4.892
16	3.532	0.9523	.9835	0.7499	3.482	100	5.015	0.9925	.9975	0.6052	4.968
17	3.588	0.9551	.9845	0.7441	3.538						
18	3.640	0.9576	.9854	0.7386	3.591						
19	3.689	0.9599	.9862	0.7335	3.640						
20	3.735	0.9619	.9869	0.7287	3.686						

Given k subgroups of size n, the *Adjusted Average Dispersion Statistics*:

$$\frac{\bar{s_n}}{c_2} \quad \text{or} \quad \frac{\bar{s}}{c_4} \quad \text{or} \quad \frac{\bar{R}}{d_2} \quad \text{or} \quad \frac{\tilde{R}}{d_4} \quad \text{will be denoted by the generic symbol } Sigma(X).$$

Likewise denote the following ratios:

$$\frac{\bar{s_n}}{c_2 \sqrt{n}} \quad \text{or} \quad \frac{\bar{s}}{c_4 \sqrt{n}} \quad \text{or} \quad \frac{\bar{R}}{d_2 \sqrt{n}} \quad \text{or} \quad \frac{\tilde{R}}{d_4 \sqrt{n}} \text{ by the generic symbol } Sigma(\bar{X}),$$

and let $Sigma(R)$ denote either $\dfrac{d_3 \bar{R}}{d_2}$ or $\dfrac{d_3 \tilde{R}}{d_4}$